ISLAM AND ENGLIS

Former Archbishop of Canterbury Rowan Williams triggered a storm of protest when he suggested that some accommodation between British law and Islam's *shariʿa* law was 'inevitable'. His foundational lecture introduced a series of public discussions on Islam and English Law at the Royal Courts of Justice and the Temple Church in London. This volume combines developed versions of these discussions with new contributions. Theologians, lawyers and sociologists look back on developments since the Archbishop spoke, and forwards along trajectories opened by the historic lecture. The contributors provide and advocate a forward-looking dialogue, asking how the rights of all citizens are to be honoured and their responsibilities met. Twenty-one specialists explore the evolution of English law; the implications of Islam, *shariʿa* and *jihad*; and the principles of the European Convention on Human Rights, family law and freedom of speech. This book is for anyone interested in the interaction between religion and secular society.

ROBIN GRIFFITH-JONES is Master of the Temple at the Temple Church and Senior Lecturer in Theology, King's College, London. He is author of *The Four Witnesses* (2000), *The Gospel according to Paul* (2004) and *Mary Magdalene* (2008). He initiated and managed the series of public discussions at the Temple Church, Islam and English Law, that was launched with the Archbishop of Canterbury's historic lecture on *shariʿa* law.

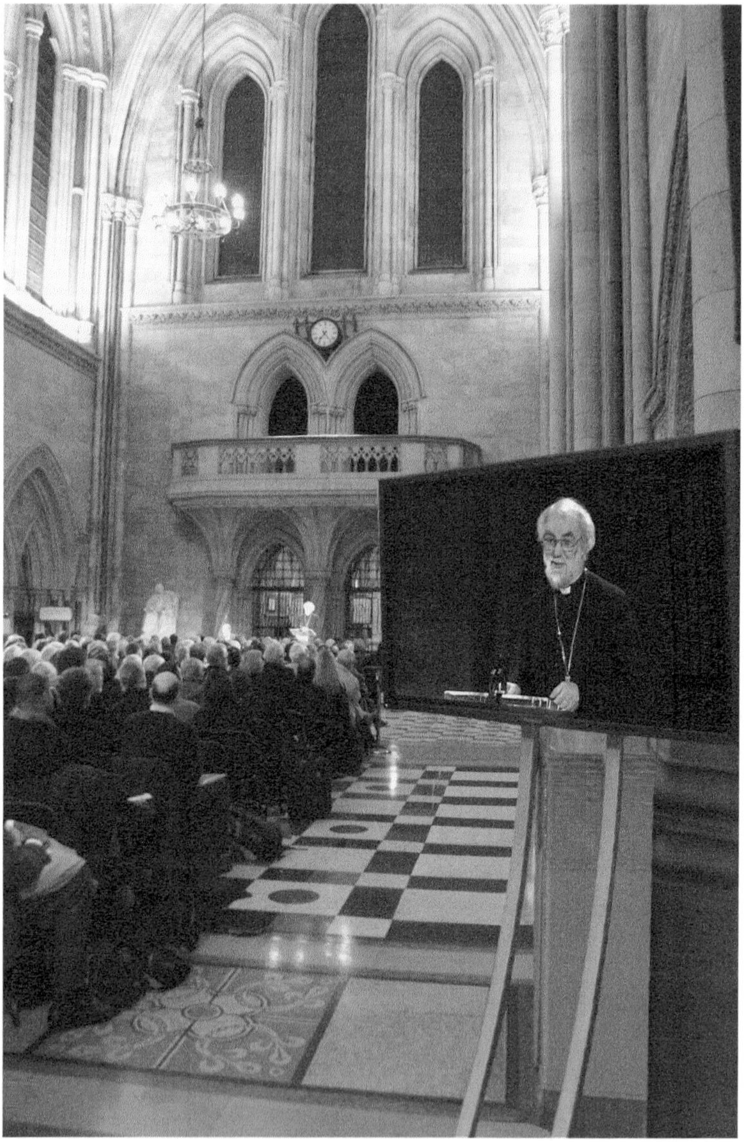

ISLAM AND ENGLISH LAW

Rights, Responsibilities and the Place of Shariʿa

EDITED BY
ROBIN GRIFFITH-JONES

CAMBRIDGE
UNIVERSITY PRESS

CAMBRIDGE UNIVERSITY PRESS
Cambridge, New York, Melbourne, Madrid, Cape Town,
Singapore, São Paulo, Delhi, Mexico City

Cambridge University Press
The Edinburgh Building, Cambridge CB2 8RU, UK

Published in the United States of America by Cambridge University Press, New York

www.cambridge.org
Information on this title: www.cambridge.org/9781107021648

© Cambridge University Press 2013

This publication is in copyright. Subject to statutory exception
and to the provisions of relevant collective licensing agreements,
no reproduction of any part may take place without the written
permission of Cambridge University Press.

First published 2013

Printed and bound in the United Kingdom by the MPG Books Group

A catalogue record for this publication is available from the British Library

Library of Congress Cataloguing in Publication data
Islam and English law : rights, responsibilities, and the place of Shari'a / [edited by]
Robin Griffith-Jones.
p. cm.
ISBN 978-1-107-02164-8 (hardback)
1. Religion and law – Great Britain. 2. Islamic law – Great Britain. 3. Conflict of laws – Great Britain. 4. Conflict of laws (Islamic law) – Great Britain. 5. Islamic law – Europe. 6. Religion and law – Europe. 7. Conflict of laws – Europe. I. Griffith-Jones, Robin.
KBP69.G7185 2013
340.90942–dc23
2012024125

ISBN 978-1-107-02164-8 Hardback
ISBN 978-1-107-63987-4 Paperback

Cambridge University Press has no responsibility for the persistence or
accuracy of URLs for external or third-party internet websites referred to
in this publication, and does not guarantee that any content on such
websites is, or will remain, accurate or appropriate.

Contents

List of contributors   *page* viii
List of abbreviations   x

    Preface
    Robin Griffith-Jones   xiii

    Introduction
    Stephen Hockman   1

PART I   THE ARCHBISHOP OF CANTERBURY AND *SHARI'A* LAW   7

1   The 'unavoidable' adoption of *shari'a* law – the generation of a media storm
    Robin Griffith-Jones   9

2   Civil and religious law in England: a religious perspective
    Rowan Williams   20

PART II   THE ARCHBISHOP'S PROPOSAL FOR 'TRANSFORMATIVE ACCOMMODATION'   35

Shari'a and secular democracy: is Islamic law compatible with the European Convention on Human Rights?   37

3   The *Refah* case at the European Court of Human Rights
    Nicolas Bratza   38

4   The compatibility of an Islamic/*shari'a* law system or *shari'a* rules with the European Convention on Human Rights
    Dominic McGoldrick   42

5 An analysis of the relationship between *shari'a* and secular democracy and the compatibility of Islamic law with the European Convention on Human Rights
Mashood A Baderin — 72

6 Dignity and religion
Christopher McCrudden — 94

Legal pluralism: should English law give greater recognition to Islamic law? — 107

7 Family law: current conflicts and their resolution
Elizabeth Butler-Sloss and Mark Hill — 108

8 Islamic finance, alternative dispute resolution and family law: developments towards legal pluralism?
Ian Edge — 116

9 Judging Muslims
Prakash Shah — 144

10 From Muslim migrants to Muslim citizens
Shaheen Sardar Ali — 157

11 Ontario's '*shari'a* court': law and politics intertwined
Marion Boyd — 176

Accommodation or conflict: trajectories in the United Kingdom — 187

12 Religious rights and the public interest
Robin Griffith-Jones — 188

PART III RESPONSIBILITIES AND RIGHTS — 205

Freedom of speech, incitement to religious hatred: beyond the divide? — 207

13 Where to draw the line, and how to draw it
Sydney Kentridge — 208

A note: *The Satanic Verses* and the Danish cartoons
Robin Griffith-Jones — 211

		Contents	vii
14	Censor or censure: maintaining civility *Tariq Modood*		216
15	In praise of 'fuzzy law' *Albie Sachs*		225

Religion, the state and the meaning of *'jihad'* 237

16	Towards an Islamic society, not an Islamic state *Abdullahi An-Na'im*		238
17	Following *shari'a* in the West *Tariq Ramadan*		245
18	Violence, personal commitment and democracy *Khaled Abou El Fadl*		256

PART IV PROSPECT: EQUALITY BEFORE GOD AND BEFORE
THE LAW 273

19	Equal before God *David F Ford*		275
20	Equal before the law *Nicholas Phillips*		286

Select bibliography 294
Index of cases 306
Index 311

Contributors

KHALED ABOU EL FADL is the Omar and Azmeralda Alfi Distinguished Professor in Islamic Law at the UCLA School of Law and Chair of the Islamic Studies Program at UCLA (US).

ABDULLAHI AN-NA'IM is Charles Howard Candler Professor of Law at Emory Law School (US).

MASHOOD A BADERIN is Professor of Law and Head of the School of Law at the School of Oriental and African Studies, London University (UK).

THE HON MARION BOYD has served in the Ontario Cabinet as Minister of Education, Minister of Community and Social Services, Minister Responsible for Women's Issues and Attorney General; in 2004 she wrote 'The Boyd Report', 'Dispute Resolution in Family Law: Protecting Choice, Promoting Inclusion' (Canada).

THE HON SIR NICOLAS BRATZA sat in the European Court of Human Rights, 1998–2012. He was the Court's President, 2011–2012.

BARONESS ELIZABETH BUTLER-SLOSS was President of the Family Division, 1999–2005 (UK).

IAN EDGE is the Director of the Centre for Islamic and Middle East Studies at the School of Oriental and African Studies, London University, and is in practice at 3 Paper Buildings, London (UK).

DAVID F FORD is Regius Professor of Divinity at Cambridge University (UK) and Director of the Cambridge Inter-faith Programme.

THE REV ROBIN GRIFFITH-JONES is Master of the Temple at the Temple Church and Senior Lecturer in Theology, King's College, London (UK).

MARK HILL QC is Professor of Law at Cardiff University and in practice at Francis Taylor Building, London (UK).

STEPHEN HOCKMAN QC is in practice at Six Pump Court, London (UK).

List of contributors

SIR SYDNEY KENTRIDGE QC is in practice at Brick Court Chambers, London (UK).

CHRISTOPHER MCCRUDDEN is Professor of Human Rights and Equality Law at Queen's University Belfast (Northern Ireland) and is in practice at Blackstone Chambers, London (UK).

DOMINIC MCGOLDRICK is Professor of International Human Rights Law at the University of Nottingham (UK).

TARIQ MODOOD MBE is Professor of Sociology at Bristol University and founding Director of the University Research Centre for the Study of Ethnicity and Citizenship at the Bristol Institute for Public Affairs (UK).

LORD PHILLIPS OF WORTH MATRAVERS was the President of the Supreme Court, 2009–12 (UK).

TARIQ RAMADAN is President of the European Muslim Network in Brussels (Belgium) and Professor of Islamic Studies at the University of Oxford (UK).

JUSTICE ALBIE SACHS sat in the Constitutional Court of South Africa, 1994–2009; he is Founding Director of the South Africa Constitution Studies Centre and holds chairs at the Universities of West Cape and of Cape Town (South Africa).

SHAHEEN SARDAR ALI is Professor of Law at Warwick University (UK) and has been Professor of Law at the University of Peshawar (Pakistan) and the Minister for Health, Population Welfare and Women's Development in the Government of the North West Frontier Province (Pakistan).

PRAKASH SHAH is Senior Lecturer in Law at Queen Mary, University of London (UK).

THE MOST REV AND RT HON ROWAN WILLIAMS was Archbishop of Canterbury 2002–2012 and is Master of Magdalene College, Cambridge (UK).

Abbreviations

AJCL	*American Journal of Criminal Law*
AJIL	*American Journal of International Law*
APSA	*American Political Science Review*
CLJ	*Cambridge Law Journal*
CLR	*Cardozo Law Review*
Comp Lab L & Pol'y J	*Comparative Labor Law & Policy Journal*
CST	*Critical Studies in Terrorism*
ECMI	*European Yearbook (Centre of Minority Issues)*
EHRLR	*European Human Rights Law Review*
EJIL	*European Journal of International Law*
EJIR	*European Journal of International Relations*
Ecc LJ	*Ecclesiastical Law Journal*
Fam Law	*Family Law*
FLR	*Family Law Review*
Harv Int'l LJ	*Harvard International Law Journal*
HIR	*Harvard International Review*
HRLR	*Human Rights Law Review*
HRQ	*Human Rights Quarterly*
ICLQ	*International and Comparative Law Quarterly*
IJCL	*International Journal of Constitutional Law*
IJMES	*International Journal of Middle East Studies*
ILJ	*Industrial Law Journal*
Int J Law Pol Fam	*International Journal of Law, Policy and Family*
Int Migr	*International Migration*

JCL	*Journal of Comparative Law*
JCSL	*Journal of Conflict and Security Law*
JEMS	*Journal of Ethnic and Migration Studies*
JIMMA	*Journal of [the Institute of] Muslim Minority Affairs*
JLP	*Journal of Legal Pluralism*
JLR	*Journal of Law and Religion*
JLS	*Journal of Law and Society*
JMP	*Journal of Moral Philosophy*
JRAI	*Journal of the Royal Anthropological Institute*
L&J	*Law & Justice*
Loy LA Int'l & Comp L Rev	*Loyola of Los Angeles International and Comparative Law Journal*
McGill LJ	*McGill Law Journal*
Med LR	*Medical Law Review*
MEJ	*Middle East Journal*
MEQ	*Middle East Quarterly*
Mich LJ	*Michigan Law Journal*
Mich L Rev	*Michigan Law Review*
MJECL	*Maastricht Journal of European and Comparative Law*
MJIL	*Melbourne Journal of International Law*
MLJ	*Malaysian Law Journal*
MLLWR	*The Military Law and Law of War Review*
MLR	*Modern Law Review*
MWJHR	*Muslim World Journal of Human Rights*
New York ULR	*New York University Law Review*
OJLS	*Oxford Journal of Legal Studies*
SAR	*South Asia Research*
SLR	*Sydney Law Review*
STP	*Social Theory and Practice*
USTLJ	*University of St Thomas Law Journal*
YLJ	*Yale Law Journal*

Preface

An editor gladly and gratefully incurs many debts. Many of the chapters in this book have grown (almost beyond recognition) from public discussions held in the Temple Church. The discussions were organised jointly by Ian Edge, Barrister and Director of the Centre for Islamic and Middle East Law at the School of Oriental and African Studies, University of London, and by myself. The series was part of the Festival mounted by Inner and Middle Temple to celebrate the four hundredth anniversary of the Letters Patent from James I which entrusted the Temple Church to the Inns' care. It is above all the Inns themselves, their setting and their sustained encouragement that have made possible this whole project from its inception, the lecture by the Archbishop of Canterbury shown in the frontispiece.[1]

The series was generously supported by CIM Investment Management, The JC Baker Trust, The Yves Guihannec Foundation, The Worshipful Company of Mercers and The Golden Bottle Trust.

Further chapters for this book were commissioned from academic and practising lawyers whose work has added greatly to the breadth, depth and value of the whole.[2]

Several colleagues have been loyal friends to the book and to myself in its gestation: in particular, John Bowen, Christopher McCrudden, Mark Hill, Stephen Hockman, Aina Khan and Robin Knowles. Laura Morris and Finola O'Sullivan at Cambridge University Press have been warmly supportive throughout. Here at the Temple Church, Liz Clarke, Catherine de Satgé, Henrietta Amodio and Frank Wright have given patient and valuable help. Kim Elcoate May has, by her assiduous accuracy, saved colleagues and myself much time.

The discussions themselves engendered a further series of round-table conversations on English and Muslim family law, chaired by Stephen

---

[1] Photo, edited: © RNA (Rod Natkiel Associates Ltd.)
[2] In the transliteration of Arabic we have in general adhered to the orthography preferred by each author.

Hockman, that have led steadily to the participants' closer co-operation and deeper understanding of each others' priorities, concerns and hopes. These conversations have been models (not of seeming agreement but) of honesty; it is our hope that what we have gained from the public discussions, from the round-table conversations and from all our contributors we can, in this present volume, offer to our readers.

ROBIN GRIFFITH-JONES

Introduction

Stephen Hockman

The Temple Church in London was built by the Knights Templar during the Crusades, a time of bitter division between Christian and Muslim cultures. Such a gulf may appear to be deepening again in our own time. It was therefore highly appropriate that the Church should have been the venue for a series of discussions on Islam and English law, set up to articulate, understand and, if possible, to begin to bridge, at one crucial point, the apparent chasm between the two cultures. Most of the chapters in this volume have their origin in those discussions; they have been transformed since by the authors themselves – to all of whom we have good reason to be grateful for the care and passion with which they have written. The book, although naturally focused on the UK, is offered as part of an ongoing conversation on topics of international concern; our contributors work in Canada, France, South Africa, the UK and USA.

The twentieth-century resurgence of Islam in some parts of the world is graphically described by Ali Allawi as follows:

Islam burst out of its confinement as an elemental, even inchoate force, flying in every direction and trying to seek its balance … Islam's reappearance as a guiding principle in state and society obliged Muslims to confront a whole multitude of fundamental issues, which were covered up when the reins of power were in the hands of others.[1]

At the same time, these fundamental issues have had to be confronted in other societies, particularly in Western Europe, which have a growing Muslim population. Britain now has more than two million people of Muslim origin. A society which had become predominantly secular, in which, in the words of the Indian writer Milinda Banerjee, modernity itself had become a religion, has had to face the need to accommodate those

---

[1] A A Allawi, *The Crisis of Islamic Civilisation* (New Haven, 2009), p 83.

whose religious adherence today is as proud and profound as at any time in history.[2]

English law, renowned for its flexibility and adaptability, has already evolved in response to these developments. The initial lecture by Rowan Williams, then Archbishop of Canterbury, and the subsequent discussions, consider in detail, and sometimes with personal intensity, the implications of these developments, and whether further adjustments to our law, and indeed to moral and social practices, ought to be considered. The discussions reach no firm conclusions; that was not their purpose. But few of those who were able to attend and participate will have disputed the pressing need for such debate and analysis to continue.

The Archbishop delivered his lecture to an invited audience of nearly a thousand people in the Great Hall of the Royal Courts of Justice, London, in February 2008. Robin Griffith-Jones charts, in Chapter 1, the political and religious context of the time and the memorable furore that the lecture stirred in the popular press. The Archbishop, quite wrongly believed to have recommended the introduction of oppressive legal practices to the UK, was (in cruelly personal attacks) condemned for a culpable naivety. Over the months and years that have followed, however – and remote from the bubbling cauldron of public opinion – his lecture has come to be recognised as a foundational statement of the concerns and questions confronting political, social and religious thinkers of all casts. Rowan Williams set an agenda which, as this book bears witness, continues to inform discussions in many parts of the world.

The discussions in the Temple Church itself were largely conducted by and for academic and practising lawyers. The tone of this volume's chapters is, in the way of lawyers, practical. The authors have ever in mind conventions and laws and their application. The authors ask: What is to be *done*? In listening to their answers, we are hearing a conversation, with a welcome variety of viewpoints, proposals and styles of argument.

The European Convention on Human Rights is incorporated into English law. In 2001 the European Court of Human Rights famously held, in relation to the Convention, that:

it is difficult to declare one's respect for democracy and human rights while at the same time supporting a regime based on *shariʿa* which clearly diverges from Convention values, particularly with regard to its criminal law and criminal

---

[2] M Banerjee, 'Eternity and the Abyss', review of G Beckerlegge (ed), *Colonialism, Modernity, and Religious Identities: religious reform movements in South Asia* (New Delhi, 2008), *The Sunday Statesman* (India), 12 April 2009, p 16.

procedure, its rules on the legal status of women and the way it intervenes in all spheres of private and public life in accordance with religious precepts.[3]

This was a dramatic claim, heavy with implications. Nicolas Bratza, the UK's judge in the Court at the time, sets the scene for its exploration. Dominic McGoldrick and Mashood Baderin then offer (strikingly divergent) responses to the Court's claim. Christopher McCrudden looks forward: he points out how little attention has so far been given, in discussion of human rights, to the potentially central category of human dignity.

The most impassioned debate and the deepest misunderstandings have been stirred, since the Archbishop's lecture, in relation to family law and the fuller accommodation there of Islamic law. Elizabeth Butler-Sloss and Mark Hill sketch the present rules governing the settlement of family disputes. Ian Edge engages in detail with arbitration law on the one hand and on the other with the quite different world – so often and so seriously confused with arbitration law – of marriage and divorce law. Prakash Shah asks whether the English courts and their procedures are still (unwittingly) prejudiced against Islam and Muslims. Shaheen Sardar Ali writes a movingly personal account of the questions confronting Muslims in a Muslim-minority culture.

It is too easy to confine our gaze to the UK. Marion Boyd tells and reflects on the dramatic story of Ontario's struggle over Islamic law, a story in which she herself – the author of the seminal 'Boyd Report' – played a leading role. Griffith-Jones then returns, to look back on the years since the Archbishop's lecture and on the quiet, low-key developments that the lecture itself helped to engender in understanding and co-operation between English lawyers and Muslim leaders.

So our consideration of the Archbishop's own themes comes to an end. But there are other concerns, widespread in the UK and the USA, which it would be evasive to ignore. Two are prominent: non-Muslims can be angered – not least, because they can be frightened – by the sometimes violent reaction of Muslims against others' use of free speech to speak ill of Muslims, the Prophet or Islam; and more generally, non-Muslims can be angered by the violence espoused by extreme and political Islamists. To address the first of these topics, we brought together Tariq Modood and Albie Sachs for an evening's discussion; their conversation about the character and limits of civility was itself a model of civility. We hope that the

---

[3] Majority Judgment, *Refah Partisi (Welfare Party) and Others v Turkey* (No 1) (2002) 35 EHRR 3, para 72.

more formal version of their conversation that we publish here still exudes something of their generosity and willingness to learn from each other.

As to the second topic, namely the violence espoused by extremists, this requires discussion of the concept of *jihad*. Khaled Abou El Fadl starts his chapter with a proposition which will be striking to many readers: 'to engage in *jihad* means to strive or exert oneself in a struggle to achieve a morally laudable or just aim'. But by what means is such an aim to be achieved? To illumine *jihad* and some *jihadis*' war for an Islamic state, we have a total of three chapters from three leading Muslim scholars who, working in the West, are well placed to interpret the history and character – and, as these scholars point out, the abandonment – of Islamic principles in violent extremism.

The book began with the Archbishop's reflections on law and religion together. It ends with a reunion of these two themes: David Ford, Regius Professor of Divinity at Cambridge, and Nicholas Phillips, until recently President of the UK's Supreme Court, look backwards in gratitude to Dr Williams' prophetic lecture and forwards to the work that he foresaw and that is yet to be done. In December 2012, nearly five years after Dr Williams delivered his lecture, he retired from being Archbishop. We have prepared this book for publication early in 2013, a good moment at which both to acknowledge our debt to Dr Williams and to sketch out some possible routes towards that more just and cohesive society to whose creation Dr Williams devoted so much of his primacy.[4]

We owe as well a great debt of gratitude to Robin Griffith-Jones: his vision and energy engendered the public discussions in the Temple Church and have now brought this book into being. Every page that follows is informed by his editorial care, many by his own research; and his eye has throughout been on the book's part in the long-term socio-legal project launched with the Archbishop's lecture. That lecture and the following public discussions have themselves prompted an ongoing debate far more gracious and fruitful than the newspapers in February 2008 would have led anyone to credit. Now we hope that the present volume will lead to further conversations and perhaps even to consideration of practical changes,

---

[4] The law, in an area of acute concern, can evolve rapidly. As we conclude this book in autumn 2012, judgment is pending on four cases discussed in it which have been brought before the European Court of Human Rights: *Ladele and McFarlane v United Kingdom* (App nos 51671/10, 36516/10) and *Eweida and Chaplin v United Kingdom* (App nos 48420/10, 59842/10). The Arbitration and Mediation Services (Equality) Bill [HL], also discussed in the following chapters, had its second reading in the House of Lords, 19 October 2012 (Hansard HL, vol 739, cols 1682–1716; <http://www.theyworkforyou.com/lords/?id=2012-10-19a.1682.4>).

however modest, in law and social practice which would further the development of harmonious relations between Islam and English law. Many may think that this would not only be beneficial from the point of view of social harmony and self-confidence within the United Kingdom, but that it could show a possible path to greater reconciliation in those troubled areas of the world in which the resurgence of Islam, and the reactions to it by others, are a source of so much current anxiety.

PART I

The Archbishop of Canterbury and shariʻa *law*

It might be possible to think in terms of what [the legal theorist Ayelet Shachar] calls 'transformative accommodation': a scheme in which individuals retain the liberty to choose the jurisdiction under which they will seek to resolve certain carefully specified matters, so that 'power-holders are forced to compete for the loyalty of their shared constituents.' ... It is uncomfortably true that this introduces into our thinking about law what some would see as a 'market' element, a competition for loyalty as Shachar admits. But if what we want socially is a pattern of relations in which a plurality of diverse and overlapping affiliations work for a common good, and in which groups of serious and profound conviction are not systematically faced with the stark alternatives of cultural loyalty or state loyalty, it seems unavoidable.
– From the Archbishop of Canterbury's Lecture, 'Civil and religious law in England', in the Royal Courts of Justice, 7 February 2008.

Question to the Archbishop: Must we accommodate Islam or not, as Christians?

Archbishop: Must we accommodate Islam or not as Christians? Must I love my Muslim neighbour? Yes, without qualification or hesitation. Must I pretend to my Muslim neighbour that I do not believe my own faith? No, without hesitation or qualification. Must I as a citizen in a plural society work for ways of living constructively, rather than tensely or suspiciously with my Muslim neighbour? Yes, without qualification or hesitation.
– From the Questions and Answers following the Archbishop's Lecture, 'Civil and religious law in England', 7 February 2008.

CHAPTER I

The 'unavoidable' adoption of shari'a law – the generation of a media storm

Robin Griffith-Jones

Rowan Williams, then Archbishop of Canterbury, gave his lecture on 'Civil and Religious Law in England' on 7 February 2008 in the Great Hall of the Royal Courts of Justice. He had recently given two speeches touching on the themes that he would explore more deeply there: the first at the Building Bridges Seminar in Singapore on 6 December 2007;[1] and the second, 'Religious Hatred and Religious Offence', as the James Callaghan Memorial Lecture in the House of Lords on 29 January 2008 (when the planned abolition of the common law offence of blasphemous libel was the subject of heated debate).[2] 'Civil and Religious Law in England' might then be seen as the completion of a series of three lectures.

In the lecture at the House of Lords the Archbishop had suggested:

> It is commonly said that since a religious believer chooses to adopt a certain set of beliefs, he or she is responsible for the consequences, which may, as every believer well knows, include strong disagreement or even repugnance from others. But this assimilation of belief to a plain matter of conscious individual choice does not square with the way in which many believers understand or experience their commitments. For some – and this is especially true for believers from outside the European or North Atlantic setting – religious belief and practice is a marker of shared identity, accepted not as a matter of individual choice but as a given to which allegiance is due in virtue of the intrinsic claims of the sacred. We may disagree; but I do not think we have the moral right to assume that this perspective can be simply disregarded.
>
> It is one thing to deny a sacred point of reference for one's own moral or social policies; it is another to refuse to entertain – or imagine – what it might be like for someone else to experience the world differently ... The uncomfortable truth is that a desacralised world is not, as some fondly believe, a world without violence, but a world in which there can be no ultimate agreement about the worth of human or other beings.

---

[1] Accessible at <http://www.archbishopofcanterbury.org/1329>.
[2] Accessible at <http://www.archbishopofcanterbury.org/1561>. The House of Lords on 5 March 2008 finally voted by 148 to 87 to add to the Criminal Justice and Immigration Bill a clause which abolished the common law crime of blasphemous libel.

The Archbishop resisted 'a lack of imagination about the experience and self-perception of others, especially those from diverse ethnic and cultural contexts, the arrogant assumption of the absolute "naturalness" of one's own position'. For 'none of this makes for an intelligent public discourse or for anything like actual debate, as opposed to plain assertion'.[3]

The Archbishop was speaking about *all* faith-communities, not just Islam. His concern was with the Churches' members too, and with the role that their outlook, convictions and conscience are allowed to play in our public life. The Archbishop mentioned, in 'Civil and Religious Law', two groups who, in the recent past, had found themselves challenged to comply with legislation that ran counter to their own convictions: the medical professionals who were granted an opt-out from the requirements to undertake abortions;[4] and the Roman Catholic adoption agencies who were not granted any opt-out from working on children's placements with gay couples.[5]

The Archbishop referred back to 'Civil and Religious Law' four days after the lecture, in his Opening Address to the Church of England's General Synod. Speaking of religious believers, he remarked that:

while there is no dispute about our common allegiance to the law of the land, that law still recognises that religious communities form the consciences of believers and has not pressed for universal compliance with aspects of civil law where conscientious matters are in question. However, there are signs that this cannot be taken for granted as the assumptions of our society become more secular.[6]

Such secular assumptions have become more vividly apparent since the lecture's delivery.[7] The Churches may seem to be fighting a permanent

---

[3] For a definition of religion with a striking emphasis on the individual and free choice, see Iacobucci J in *Syndicat Northcrest v Amselem* in the Supreme Court of Canada [2004] 2 SCR 551; [2004] SCC 47, para 22: 'In essence, religion is about freely and deeply held personal convictions or beliefs connected to an individual's spiritual faith and integrally linked to one's self-definition and spiritual fulfilment, the practices of which allow individuals to foster a connection with the divine or with the subject or object of that spiritual faith.'

[4] No person shall be under a duty to 'participate in any treatment' authorised by the Abortion Act 1967 to which they have a conscientious objection; see D McGoldrick, 'The compatibility of an Islamic/*shari'a* law system or *shari'a* rules with the European Convention on Human Rights', infra p 55.

[5] For details (including the progress of the appeal mounted by the Roman Catholic diocese of Leeds for exemption from the regulations), see McGoldrick, 'The compatibility of an Islamic/*shari'a* law system or *shari'a* rules with the European Convention on Human Rights', supra n 4.

[6] Accessible at <www.archbishopofcanterbury.org/1583>.

[7] The Churches secured generous provision under the UK Human Rights Act 1998, s 13(1): 'If a court's determination of any question under this Act might affect the exercise by a religious organisation (itself or its members collectively) of the Convention right to freedom of thought, conscience and religion it must have particular regard to the importance of that right.' The tide, however, is not now running in the Churches' favour. 'For the last 150 years English law has proceeded on the assumption that religion generally is an unqualified human good ... Standard modern accounts of the relationship between

battle, with limited success, to maintain their ground. We might follow just some events in a particularly active few weeks. The Pope spoke on 1 February 2010 to the Roman Catholic Bishops of England and Wales about some of the legislation designed to achieve equality for all members of society. Its effect 'has been to impose unjust limitations on the freedom of religious communities to act in accordance with their beliefs. In some respects it actually violates the natural law upon which the equality of all human beings is grounded'.[8] Five days later, the Pope addressed the Bishops of Scotland, with particular reference to euthanasia and some advances in embryology: the Bishops were 'to grapple firmly with the challenges presented by the increasing tide of secularism in your country'.[9] Within a week, the Archbishop of Canterbury reminded the General Synod of the freedom sought by the Churches – in amendments to the Equality Bill 2010 – to continue to employ in certain positions only people who complied with the Churches' public teaching on sexual life. The Court of Appeal then rejected an appeal from an employee of British Airways who claimed discrimination on having been forbidden to wear a cross visibly at work.[10] Before the month's end there was a noisy and mixed response to an amendment entered at a late stage into the Children, Schools and Families Bill 2009–10, allowing faith-schools some liberty in the form (but not in the content) of their sex education.[11] And then, on 2 March, Lord Alli moved an amendment to the Equality Bill, to put in

---

law, religion and gender do not share this confidence in the value of religion. Instead, they tell a different story: in the course of the twentieth century, and increasingly in recent decades, western societies have come to abandon a millennium-long tradition of more or less oppressive heterosexist patriarchy to adopt an ethic of gender equality.' J Rivers, 'Law, religion and gender equality', (2007) 9 Ecc LJ 24, 33. On the expanding legal and educational agenda intrinsic to a totalising liberalism, see RJ Ahdar, 'Religious group autonomy, gay ordination and human rights law' in R O'Dair and A Lewis (eds), *Law and Religion* (fourth edition, Oxford, 2001), pp 275–7.

[8] Pope Benedict XVI, 'Address to the Bishops of the Episcopal Conference of England and Wales', 1 February 2010, accessible at <http://www.vatican.va/holy_father/benedict_xvi/speeches/2010/february/documents/hf_ben-xvi_spe_20100201_bishops-england-wales_en.html>.

[9] Pope Benedict XVI, 'Address to the Bishops of the Episcopal Conference of Scotland', 5 February 2010, accessible at <http://www.vatican.va/holy-father/benedict_xvi/speeches/2010/february/documents/hf_ben-xvi_spe_20100205_bishops-scotland_en.html>.

[10] *Eweida v British Airways Plc* [2010] EWCA Civ 80. *Eweida* has perhaps been liable to misunderstanding. Sedley LJ, para 8, quoted the tribunal (33.4) which had heard evidence from a number of practising Christians in addition to the claimant. 'None, including the claimant, gave evidence that they considered visible display of the cross to be a requirement of the Christian faith.' Ms Eweida, having been refused leave to appeal to the Supreme Court, took her case to the European Court of Human Rights (App no 48420/10, [2011] ECHR 738). See infra p 64.

[11] Amendment 70, at Clause 11. Among the responses to the amendment was an interview on BBC Radio 4's *Today*, 24 February 2010, with David Laws, the Liberal Democrat's spokesman on schools: this amendment, he said, 'completely undermines the objectives of this part of the bill'. 'The issue is, in the twenty-first century, are we going to have a school system which is going to be tolerant of

the necessary regulations to allow religious buildings to be used to host civil partnerships.[12]

The Archbishop kindly agreed to launch the series *Islam in English Law* with a lecture in February 2008 that would explore these themes. It was expected that the lecture would be hosted in the Temple Church itself. It became clear by the middle of January that far more people hoped to hear the lecture than could fit in the Church; the then Lord Chief Justice, who was also due to chair the lecture, made it possible to hold the lecture to the Great Hall of the Royal Courts of Justice, where nearly a thousand people would gather to hear the Archbishop.

BEFORE THE LECTURE: DR WILLIAMS ON BBC RADIO

On the morning of 7 February, a few hours before the lecture, the Archbishop was interviewed by Christopher Landau for a broadcast on that day's *World at One* on BBC Radio 4. Landau, having read the Archbishop's text in advance, could see what in the lecture was likely to be most contentious. According to the Archbishop's text,

> it might be possible to think in terms of what [the legal theorist Ayelet Shachar] calls 'transformative accommodation': a scheme in which individuals retain the liberty to choose the jurisdiction under which they will seek to resolve certain carefully specified matters, so that 'power-holders are forced to compete for the loyalty of their shared constituents'.
> ... It is uncomfortably true that this introduces into our thinking about law what some would see as a 'market' element, a competition for loyalty as Shachar admits. But if what we want socially is a pattern of relations in which a plurality of diverse and overlapping affiliations work for a common good, and in which groups of serious and profound conviction are not systematically faced with the stark alternatives of cultural loyalty or state loyalty, it seems unavoidable.[13]

In his interview with the Archbishop, Landau drew on this last sentence for his opening remarks and question. In the broadcast itself these were replaced by an introduction from Martha Kearney. It may be helpful to note the changes in tone and detail.

intolerance in the name of religious freedom? Or should we say in the twenty-first century that it is right that all state-funded schools should be teaching tolerance and respect for diversity?' The Bill's most contentious clauses were withdrawn in the 'wash-up' prior to the 2010 General Election.

[12] Lord Alli insisted: 'The amendment does not – I repeat, does not – place an obligation on any religious organisations to host civil partnerships in their buildings.' In December 2011 the House of Lords Statutory Instruments Merits Committee considered the Marriages and Civil Partnerships (Approved Premises) (Amendment) Regulations. It was not clear that the conscience clause as drafted did give the promised protection. There was a motion to annul the Instrument.

[13] 'Civil and Religious Law in England', lecture in the Royal Courts of Justice, 7 February 2008, infra pp 20–33.

The interview[14]	The broadcast[15]
Christopher Landau, speaking to the Archbishop on the morning of 7 February 2008:	*Martha Kearney, introducing the interview on The World at One on 7 February 2008:*
To begin with you've given this vision of, – if as a nation Britain wants to achieve social cohesion, that challenge is how to accommodate those of religious faith in relation to the law; and your words are, that the application of *shari'a* in certain circumstances – if we want to achieve this cohesion and take seriously peoples' religion – seems unavoidable?	The lecture may have been intended as a scholarly contribution to the relationship between English law and Islam but the Archbishop of Canterbury's statement that *shari'a* law 'seems unavoidable' in parts of Britain is highly controversial ... His lecture comes just a month after an Anglican bishop warned that there were no-go areas in parts of Britain.[16]
	The Archbishop of Canterbury this morning gave an exclusive interview to our reporter Christopher Landau. He asked him whether the adoption of *shari'a* law really was necessary for community cohesion.
Archbishop of Canterbury	*Archbishop of Canterbury*
It seems unavoidable and indeed as a matter of fact certain provisions of *shari'a* are already recognised in our society and under our law.	It seems unavoidable and indeed as a matter of fact certain provisions of *shari'a* are already recognised in our society and under our law.

The Archbishop had not mentioned *shari'a* 'in parts of Britain'; Landau had not asked if 'the adoption of *shari'a* law really was necessary'. The Archbishop was going to suggest in his lecture that supplementary jurisdiction and the consequent competition for loyalty seem unavoidable. In the interview Landau paraphrased the Archbishop's suggestion, a paraphrase picked up by the Archbishop; Landau's lead-in was, in editing, rewritten for the broadcast. The Archbishop was now heard answering a question that he had not been asked.

The media leapt upon the interview. By the time the Archbishop began his lecture at 6.00 that evening, he could remark wryly that many in his audience were no doubt confident that they already knew what he was going to say.

---

[14] Accessible at <http://www.archbishopofcanterbury.org/1573>.
[15] M Kearney, interview with Dr Williams on the BBC website, <http://news.bbc.co.uk/1/hi/uk/7232661.stm>; the introduction had by 4 March 2010 been excised.
[16] M Nazir-Ali, The Bishop of Rochester, 'Extremism flourished as UK lost Christianity', *The Sunday Telegraph*, 6 January 2008.

This whole volume testifies to the importance of the Archbishop's lecture. The media, however, stirred up an angry public response.[17] 'What a Burkha!', cried *The Sun*'s headline on 8 February. (In UK slang, a 'berk' is a fool.) Most of this anger was directed at the Archbishop, we might think, only in displacement: what can no longer be said publicly about Muslims can be said about an Archbishop (representing an apparently delusional élite in favour of multiculturalism) who seems to speak up for Muslims. 'The prevailing attitude', remarked the Archbishop to General Synod the next week, quoting Ronald Knox,[18] 'was one of heavy disagreement with a number of things which the [speaker] had not said.'

Many of us in Britain are ignorant of Islam, and so frightened of it, and so angered by it. In a population that largely looks back (perhaps with a naive belief in its own ancestral Britishness) on generations of life in the UK, this poisonous boil of anger is covered by the thin skin of a welcoming courtesy extended to newer arrivals. The Archbishop surely knew that the first people to scratch through the skin would suffer from the release of that scarcely hidden venom; and he responded with all his characteristic courtesy to the furore that followed his lecture. And after that outpouring of anger in February 2008, the rest of our series was frank, robust and courteous; the discussions were the object of no further attacks. The Archbishop had been the lightning conductor for a storm that could then pass.

The Archbishop has written much about the character of Christ. 'There is no sense in which Jesus uses counter-violence of a verbal or any other variety. "When he suffered, he did not threaten," (1 Peter 2.23) ... So far from being passive, it is the pure victim alone who is capable of creative action, the transformation of the human world, the release from the pendulum swing of attack and revenge.'[19] So the Archbishop in turn was willing to draw upon himself the fears and anger with which uncertainties and powerlessness infect us, and to absorb them without engaging the pendulum of attack and revenge. We would not want to overstate the importance of a single, small incident; but it is in the accumulation – a rising tide – of such incidents (I suggest) that Dr Williams sees hope for the transformation of the human world.

---

[17] The media's response is well detailed in R Shortt, *Rowan's Rule* (London, 2008), pp 390–402. For a range of (thoughtful) responses to the lecture, see <http://www.opendemocracy.net/forums/thread.jspa>. It was ironic that a liberal press, standing up for liberalism against what they believed the Archbishop to have said, unleashed such a stridently illiberal response.

[18] On the discussion at a student society in the 1930s. A clarifying summary of the Archbishop's argument was posted on his website, 8 February 2008, <http://www.archbishopofcanterbury.org/1647?q=shari?a+february+2008>.

[19] R Williams, *Resurrection* (London, 2002), pp 7–9.

THE MANIFESTATION OF RELIGION

It may be helpful to clarify in advance some of the terms and norms that will dominate the book. For a summary of law's role in Islam, I quote from Hashim Kamali's classic *Principles of Islamic Jurisprudence*:[20]

Sovereignty in Islam is the prerogative of Almighty God alone. He is the absolute arbiter of values and it is His will that determines good and evil, right and wrong. It is neither the will of the ruler nor of any assembly of men, nor even the community as a whole, that determines the values and the laws which uphold those values. In its capacity as the vicegerent of God, the Muslim community is entrusted with the authority to implement the *Sharī'ah*, to administer justice and to take all necessary measures in the interest of good government. The sovereignty of the people, if the use of the word 'sovereignty' is appropriate at all, is a delegated, or executive, sovereignty only. And lastly, unlike its Western counterpart, Islamic jurisprudence is not confined to commands and prohibitions, and far less to commands which originate in a court of law. Its scope is much wider, as it is not only concerned with what a man must do or must not do, but also with what he ought to do or ought not to do, and the much larger area of permissibilities where his decision to do or to avoid doing something is his own prerogative. *Usul al-fiqh*[21] provides guidance in all these areas, most of which remain outside the scope of Western jurisprudence.

In this way Islamic jurisprudence sees both law and religion informing all areas of life. The European Convention on Human Rights (ECHR) and its jurisprudence have tended to define religion far more narrowly. Article 9(1) ECHR protects the freedom of religion:

Everyone has the right to freedom of thought, conscience and religion; this right includes freedom to change his religion or belief, and freedom, either alone or in community with others and in public or private, to manifest his religion or belief, in worship, teaching, practice and observance.[22]

The question naturally arises, what shall count as a 'manifestation' of religion. 'Article 9 primarily protects the sphere of personal beliefs and religious creeds, ie the area which is sometimes called the *forum internum*. In addition, it protects acts which are intimately linked to those attitudes, such as acts of worship and devotion which are aspects of a religion or a belief in a generally

---

[20] MH Kamali, *Principles of Islamic Jurisprudence* (Cambridge, 2003), pp 7–8.
[21] That is, the body of principles and methods in conformity to which the rules of the law are derived from the Qur'an and Sunna (the words, actions and practices of Muhammad).
[22] In French, 'les pratiques et l'accomplissement des rites' more clearly suggests liturgy. Article 9(2) qualifies the right of manifestation.

recognised form.'[23] Acts that manifest religion must be distinguished from those that are (merely) motivated by it.[24]

A rich jurisprudence has grown up, case by case, on the forms and limits of manifestation protected by the Article. In *Williamson*, Rix LJ argued against too narrow a definition. He emphasised the importance of law in Judaism as well as Islam.[25]

> The practice of Judaism, for instance, may be said to depend in large part not merely on faith but on a law based or developed obligation to obey God's commands. Thus I do not think that circumcision, or the dietary laws, could be correctly (or other than metaphorically) referred to as an 'article of faith' of Judaism or Islam, although they are regarded as divine commandments. It is hard to conceive, however, that Jews or Muslims could be prevented from manifesting their religion or belief in such respects without an engagement of Convention rights . . .

Rix LJ asked in response, about the Christian schools whose practice of corporal punishment was at issue in *Williamson*:

> How *can* they exercise their freedom to manifest that belief (other than merely theoretically, in word rather than in deed) save by having a school system of corporal punishment? The deed does not have to express the belief in the form of proclaiming it. A Muslim or Jew who adheres to his religion's dietary laws does not proclaim it (unless perchance there is any need for request or explanation); he does it. To all outward appearances he is like any other person eating a meal: but he is manifesting his religious belief and duty.[26]

Far more than just formally stipulated laws inform such a life. We may be inclined, particularly when a community wishes to isolate some abhorrent practice from the religious sanction claimed for it by its practitioners, to distinguish between religion and 'mere' culture. At other times, analysts of religion more realistically acknowledge the compound formed by religion and culture in the lives of devout believers. A religion, after all, is itself a culture, and seeks to inform every part of its adherents' lives. Moving

---

[23] *X v United Kingdom* [1984] 6 EHRR 558.
[24] *Arrowsmith v UK* [1978] 3 EHRR 218, paras 70–1, confirmed in *Kalac v Turkey* [1997] 27 EHRR 522, para 27, and subjected to important analysis by Arden LJ in R *(Williamson and Others) v The Secretary of State for Education and Employment* [2002] EWCA Civ 1926, paras 268–70. (As a test of a religion's requirements as interpreted by Arden LJ, the *Arrowsmith* test may seem to set the bar too high. Mother Teresa herself would not claim that it was a requirement of Christian belief to live as she did; was her life then only 'influenced or motivated' by her beliefs, rather than being their manifestation?)
[25] *Williamson*, supra n 24 paras 123, 164. At one point in *Williamson* (para 173) Rix LJ invoked Maimonides's exposition of Leviticus 19.14.
[26] Ritual slaughter for the satisfaction of dietary laws had already been accepted as a manifestation 'in observance', *Jewish Liturgical Association Cha'are Shalom Ve Tsedek v France* [2000] 9 BHRC 27, paras 73–4.

testimony to this was given by Lord Sacks, Chief Rabbi, in a passage quoted in the House of Lords in the *Jewish Free School* case. Conversion to Judaism, said Lord Sacks, is 'irreducibly religious'.

Converting to Judaism is a serious undertaking, because Judaism is not a mere creed. It involves a distinctive, detailed way of life. When people ask me why conversion to Judaism takes so long, I ask them to consider other cases of changed identity. How long does it take for a Briton to become an Italian, not just legally but linguistically, culturally, behaviourally? It takes time . . . It is from Ruth's reply to her mother-in-law Naomi that the basic principles of conversion are derived. She said: 'Where you go, I will go. Where you stay, I will stay. Your people will be my people, and your God my God.' That last sentence – a mere four words in Hebrew – defines the dual nature of conversion to this day. The first element is an identification with the Jewish people and its fate ('Your people will be my people'). The second is the embrace of a religious destiny, the covenant between Israel and God and its commands ('Your God will be my God').[27]

We may have been inclined to think that the purposeful observance of divine law informs the lives of Muslims in the West more widely and deeply than the lives of any other citizens. I have cited an example from Judaism to remind us that Islam is only one of the three Abrahamic faiths represented in the UK. And the diffusion of a diluted and secularised 'Christian' culture (invoking little more than the example and teaching of Christ and the roots of England's polity in historically Christian soil) may disguise the similar rigour and vigour of many church congregations at all points on the ecclesiological spectrum. An appeal to divine law for the close daily management of communal, family and individual life is not symptomatic of some newly arrived otherness, alien to Western life and norms.

We will in the following chapters be reading much about the different roles, rights and capacities in English law of the English courts on the one hand and of Islamic councils or tribunals on the other. These religious councils have given rise to some public anxiety: a fear that, through the neglect or even the connivance of England's political establishment, such councils are now available to impose the application of *shariʿa* principles upon Muslims at times of family breakdown; and that these principles inescapably favour the man over the woman, his interests over hers. We hope, in the following chapters, to disentangle some confusions over such tribunals and their authority. It may be helpful at the outset to introduce and so to humanise some of these generally anonymous bodies. Here is a

---

[27] *R (On the Application of E) v Governing Body of JFS and the Admissions Appeal Panel of JFS and Others* [2009] UKSC 15, paras 4, 39.

sketch of three major councils. They have emerged from different parts of Britain's Muslim community to meet different needs and so on different trajectories.

The Islamic Shari'a Council (ISC) in Leyton, East London, grew out of a 'national conference' in Birmingham in 1982, at which it was hoped to generate a single, conservative umbrella-body whose members could with good grounds claim to represent as a whole the five schools of Sunni jurisprudence. The judges, from diverse national and religious backgrounds, are all men; they do not disguise their particular (and sometimes uncompromising) characters and views.[28] In relation to a major theme in the following chapters, ISC will facilitate an Islamic divorce only if the couple has already begun the process that will lead to an English, civil divorce.[29]

The Birmingham Shari'a Council grew out of a women's crisis centre run by Dr Wageha Syeda, a Muslim woman and community paediatrician. Many of the women who came to her were seeking divorce; in 2005 she asked the Birmingham Central Mosque to sponsor a council that could oversee Islamic divorces. Dr Syeda advises the Council on the cases that come before it; the Council's clerk is a woman; and of the three judges one, Amra Bone, is a woman who on occasion chairs and leads the sessions. The Council will facilitate an Islamic divorce only if an English, civil divorce has already been completed.

The Muslim Arbitration Tribunal (MAT), established in 2007, is part of a Sufi network in the UK inspired by the late *pir* or Sufi saint, Shaykh Shaykh Allama Muhammad Abdul Wahab Siddiqi (died 1994), whose mausoleum is in the grounds of Hijaz College at Nuneaton. MAT was founded by Siddiqi's son, the present principal of the College, Shaykh Faizul Siddiqi. The Tribunal's original emphasis was on commercial disputes (which in English law can be subjected by the parties themselves to binding arbitration); more recently it has come to advise couples on Islamic divorces (which cannot). MAT, approached by many couples seeking protection or rescue from forced marriage, is arguing for the criminalisation of forced marriages.[30]

Faizul Siddiqi is himself an English barrister, and MAT offers accredited training for the English Bar and for trainee solicitors. Siddiqi travels the

---

[28] Dr Suhaib Hasan (Secretary) on the role of women, *The Daily Mail*, 4 July 2009, accessible at <http://www.dailymail.co.uk/news/article-1197478/Sharia-law-UK–How-Islam-dispensing-justice-side-British-courts.html>; Shaykh Abu Sayeed (President) on rape within marriage, *The Independent*, 14 October 2010, accessible at <http://www.independent.co.uk/news/uk/home-news/rape-impossible-in-marriage-says-muslim-cleric-2106161.html>.
[29] See further, infra pp 134, 151–5.   [30] See further, infra pp 198–200.

country; reports that eighty or more *shariʿa* courts are active in the UK count his sessions in different cities as the sittings of different courts.[31]

It was Dr Williams' discussion of Islam that attracted attention in his lecture. Bernard Jackson identified, however, a broader agenda. He asked where was the Archbishop's primary interest; 'the answer appears to be that Dr Williams is seeking to build a religious coalition, led by the Church of England (as the "established" Church), in favour of exemptions from secular law on grounds of religious conscience.'[32] Dr Williams continued throughout his primacy to argue for the legal accommodation of conscience. He did not need to spell out the likelihood that religious consciences of all faiths – and in particular, perhaps, conservative and counter-cultural consciences – would be among the beneficiaries. 'Good, "legitimate" government', he said in 2012, 'involves both direct election and mechanisms for representing . . . minority interests that can be silenced by large electoral majorities, . . . [and] groups with conscientious reservations about aspects of public policy'. Law

includes as a basic principle the protection of conscience – and also the protection of minority interest of whatever kind . . . Justice is always going to be a matter of seeking what is most fair to the specific needs and identity of any group or person in society rather than trying to make comprehensive prescriptions in advance which secure every conceivable claim.[33]

We do well to recognise in the Archbishop's lecture an analysis of the place of all religions in our public life. It was a privilege to hear Dr Williams, from his unparalleled viewpoint, adumbrate a future for England's civil and religious law which forms chapter 2 of this volume.

---

[31] I am grateful to Professor John Bowen for his guidance on these summaries. See further J Bowen, *Blaming Islam* (Cambridge, 2012), pp 71–94.
[32] B Jackson, '"Transformative accommodation" and religious law', (2009) 11 Ecc LJ 131, 150.
[33] 'Sovereignty, democracy, justice', The Magna Carta Lecture, Royal Holloway College, 15 June 2012, accessible at <http://www.archbishopofcanterbury.org/articles.php/2527/soverignty-democracy-justice-archbishops-magna-carta-lecture>.

CHAPTER 2

Civil and religious law in England: a religious perspective

Rowan Williams

The title of this series of lectures, 'Islam in English Law', signals the existence of what is very widely felt to be a growing challenge in our society – that is, the presence of communities which, while no less 'law-abiding' than the rest of the population, relate to something other than the British legal system alone. But, as I hope to suggest, the issues that arise around what level of public or legal recognition, if any, might be allowed to the legal provisions of a religious group, are not peculiar to Islam: we might recall that, while the law of the Church of England is the law of the land, its daily operation is in the hands of authorities to whom considerable independence is granted. And beyond the specific issues that arise in relation to the practicalities of recognition or delegation, there are large questions in the background about what we understand by and expect from the law, questions that are more sharply focused than ever in a largely secular social environment. I shall therefore be concentrating on certain issues around Islamic law to begin with, in order to open up some of these wider matters.

Among the manifold anxieties that haunt the discussion of the place of Muslims in British society, one of the strongest, reinforced from time to time by the sensational reporting of opinion polls, is that Muslim communities in this country seek the freedom to live under *shariʻa* law. And what most people think they know of *shariʻa* is that it is repressive towards women and wedded to archaic and brutal physical punishments; just a few days ago, it was reported that a 'forced marriage' involving a young woman with learning difficulties had been 'sanctioned under *shariʻa* law' – the kind of story that, in its assumption that we all 'really' know what is involved in the practice of *shariʻa*, powerfully reinforces the image of – at best – a pre-modern system in which human rights have no role. The problem is freely admitted by Muslim scholars. 'In the West', writes Tariq Ramadan in his groundbreaking *Western Muslims and the Future of Islam*, 'the idea of *shariʻa* calls up all the darkest images of Islam ... It has reached the extent that many Muslim intellectuals

20

do not dare even to refer to the concept for fear of frightening people or arousing suspicion of all their work by the mere mention of the word.'[1] Even when some of the more dramatic fears are set aside, there remains a great deal of uncertainty about what degree of accommodation the law of the land can and should give to minority communities with their own strongly entrenched legal and moral codes. As such, this is not only an issue about Islam but about other faith groups, including Orthodox Judaism; and indeed it spills over into some of the questions which have surfaced sharply in the last twelve months about the right of religious believers in general to opt out of certain legal provisions – as in the problems around Roman Catholic adoption agencies which emerged in relation to the Sexual Orientation Regulations last spring.

This lecture will not attempt a detailed discussion of the nature of *shari'a*, which would be far beyond my competence; my aim is only, as I have said, to tease out some of the broader issues around the rights of religious groups within a secular state, with a few thoughts about what might be entailed in crafting a just and constructive relationship between Islamic law and the statutory law of the United Kingdom. But it is important to begin by dispelling one or two myths about *shari'a*; so far from being a monolithic system of detailed enactments, *shari'a* designates primarily – to quote Ramadan again – 'the expression of the universal principles of Islam [and] the framework and the thinking that makes for their actualisation in human history.'[2] *Universal* principles: as any Muslim commentator will insist, what is in view is the eternal and absolute will of God for the universe and for its human inhabitants in particular; but also something that has to be 'actualised', not a ready-made system. If *shar'* designates the essence of the revealed law, *shari'a* is the *practice* of actualising and applying it; while certain elements of the *shari'a* are specified fairly exactly in the Qur'an and Sunna and in the *hadith* recognised as authoritative in this respect, there is no single code that can be identified as 'the' *shari'a*. And when certain states impose what they refer to as *shari'a* or when certain Muslim activists demand its recognition alongside secular jurisdictions, they are usually referring not to a universal and fixed code established once for all but to some particular concretisation of it at the hands of a tradition of jurists. In the hands of contemporary legal traditionalists, this means simply that the application of *shari'a* must be governed by the judgements of representatives of the classical schools of legal interpretation. But there are a good many voices arguing for an extension of the liberty of *ijtihad* – basically

---

[1] T Ramadan, *Western Muslims and the Future of Islam* (Oxford, 2004), p 31. [2] Ibid, p 32.

reasoning from first principles rather than simply the collation of traditional judgements.[3]

Thus, in contrast to what is sometimes assumed, we do not *simply* have a standoff between two rival legal systems when we discuss Islamic and British law. On the one hand, *shari'a* depends for its legitimacy not on any human decision, not on votes or preferences, but on the conviction that it represents the mind of God; on the other, it is to some extent unfinished business so far as codified and precise provisions are concerned. To recognise *shari'a* is to recognise a *method* of jurisprudence governed by revealed texts rather than a single system. In a discussion based on a paper from Mona Siddiqui at a conference in 2007 at Al Akhawayn University in Morocco, the point was made by one or two Muslim scholars that an excessively narrow understanding *shari'a* as simply codified rules can have the effect of actually undermining the universal claims of the Qur'an.[4]

But while such universal claims are not open for renegotiation, they also assume the voluntary consent or submission of the believer, the free decision to be and to continue a member of the *umma*. *Shari'a* is not, in that sense, intrinsically to do with any demand for Muslim dominance over non-Muslims. Both historically and in the contemporary context, Muslim states have acknowledged that membership of the *umma* is not coterminous with membership in a particular political society: in modern times, the clearest articulation of this was in the foundation of the Pakistani state under Jinnah; but other examples (Morocco, Jordan) could be cited of societies where there is a concept of *citizenship* that is not identical with belonging to the *umma*. Such societies, while not compromising or weakening the possibility of unqualified belief in the authority and universality of *shari'a*, or even the privileged status of Islam in a nation, recognise that there can be no guarantee that the state is religiously homogeneous and that the relationships in which the individual stands and which define him or her are not exclusively with other Muslims. There has therefore to be some concept of common good that is not prescribed solely in terms of revealed Law, however provisional or imperfect such a situation is thought to be. And this implies in turn that the Muslim, even in a predominantly Muslim state, has something of a dual identity, as citizen and as believer within the community of the faithful.

---

[3] See, eg, L Gardet, 'Un préalable aux questions soulevées par les droits de l'homme: l'actualisation de la Loi religieuse musulmane aujourd'hui', (1983) 9 *Islamochristiana* 1–12 and A Saeed, 'Trends in contemporary Islam: a preliminary attempt at a classification', (2007) 97(3) MWJHR 395, 401–2.

[4] M Siddiqui, at the conference 'Towards a Muslim Theology of World Religions', May 2007, Ifrane, Morocco.

It is true that this account would be hotly contested by some committed Islamic primitivists, by followers of Sayyid Qutb and similar polemicists; but it is fair to say that the great body of serious jurists in the Islamic world would recognise this degree of political plurality as consistent with Muslim integrity. In this sense, while (as I have said) we are not talking about two rival systems on the same level, there is some community of understanding between Islamic social thinking and the categories we might turn to in the non-Muslim world for the understanding of law in the most general context. There is a recognition that *our social identities are not constituted by one exclusive set of relations or mode of belonging* – even if one of those sets is regarded as relating to the most fundamental and non-negotiable level of reality, as established by a 'covenant' between the divine and the human (as in Jewish and Christian thinking; once again, we are not talking about an exclusively Muslim problem). The danger arises not only when there is an assumption on the religious side that membership of the community (belonging to the *umma* or the Church or whatever) is the only significant category, so that participation in other kinds of socio-political arrangement is a kind of betrayal. It also occurs when secular government assumes a monopoly in terms of defining public and political identity. There is a position – not at all unfamiliar in contemporary discussion – which says that to be a citizen is essentially and simply to be under the rule of the uniform law of a sovereign state, in such a way that any other relations, commitments or protocols of behaviour belong exclusively to the realm of the private and of individual choice.

As I have maintained in several other contexts, this is a very unsatisfactory account of political reality in modern societies; but it is also a problematic basis for thinking of the legal category of citizenship and the nature of human interdependence. Maleiha Malik, following Alasdair MacIntyre, argues in an essay on 'Faith and the state of jurisprudence' that there is a risk of assuming that 'mainstream' jurisprudence should routinely and unquestioningly bypass the variety of ways in which actions are as a matter of fact understood by agents in the light of the diverse sorts of communal belonging they are involved in. If that is the assumption, 'the appropriate temporal unit for analysis tends to be the basic action. Instead of concentrating on the history of the individual or the origins of the social practice which provides the context within which the act is performed, conduct tends to be studied as an isolated and one-off act.'[5] And another essay in the same collection, Anthony Bradney's 'Faced by faith' offers some examples of legal rulings which have

---

[5] M Malik, 'Faith and the state of jurisprudence' in P Oliver, S Douglas Scott and V Tadros (eds), *Faith in Law: essays in legal theory* (Oxford, 2000), pp 139–40.

disregarded the account offered by religious believers of the motives for their own decisions, on the grounds that the court alone is competent to assess the coherence or even sincerity of their claims. And when courts attempt to do this on the grounds of what is 'generally acceptable' behaviour in a society, they are open, Bradney claims, to the accusation of undermining the principle of liberal pluralism by denying someone the right to speak in their own voice.[6] The distinguished ecclesiastical lawyer, Chancellor Mark Hill, has also underlined in a number of papers the degree of confusion that has bedevilled recent essays in adjudicating disputes with a religious element, stressing the need for better definition of the kind of protection for religious conscience that the law intends.[7]

I have argued recently in a discussion of the moral background to legislation about incitement to religious hatred that any crime involving religious offence has to be thought about in terms of its tendency to create or reinforce a position in which a religious person or group could be gravely disadvantaged in regard to access to speaking in public in their own right: offence needs to be connected to issues of power and status, so that a powerful individual or group making derogatory or defamatory statements about a disadvantaged minority might be thought to be increasing that disadvantage.[8] The point I am making here is similar. If the law of the land takes no account of what might be for certain agents a proper rationale for behaviour – for protest against certain unforeseen professional requirements, for instance, which would compromise religious discipline or belief – it fails in a significant way to *communicate* with someone involved in the legal process (or indeed to receive their communication), and so, on at least one kind of legal theory (expounded recently, for example, by RA Duff), fails in one of its purposes.

The implications are twofold. There is a plain procedural question – and neither Bradney nor Malik goes much beyond this – about how existing courts function and what weight is properly give to the issues we have been discussing. But there is a larger theoretical and practical issue about what it is to live under more than one jurisdiction, which takes us back to the question we began with – the role of *shariʿa* (or indeed Orthodox Jewish practice) in relation to the routine jurisdiction of the British courts. In general, when there is a robust affirmation that the law of the land should protect individuals on

---

[6] A Bradney, 'Faced by faith', in Oliver, Douglas Scott and Tadros (eds), *Faith in Law*, supra n 5, pp 102–3.
[7] See particularly his essay with R Sandberg, 'Is nothing sacred? Clashing symbols in a secular world', (2007) 3 *Public Law* 488, 488–506.
[8] R Williams, 'The James Callaghan Memorial Lecture' in the House of Lords, 29 January 2008, accessible at <http://www.archbishopofcanterbury.org/1561>.

the grounds of their corporate religious identity and secure their freedom to fulfil religious duties, a number of queries are regularly raised. I want to look at three such difficulties briefly. They relate both to the question of whether there should be a higher level of attention to religious identity and communal rights in the practice of the law, and to the larger issue I mentioned of something like a delegation of certain legal functions to the religious courts of a community; and this latter question, it should be remembered, is relevant not only to Islamic law but also to areas of Orthodox Jewish practice.

The first objection to a higher level of public legal regard being paid to communal identity is that it leaves legal process (including ordinary disciplinary process within organisations) at the mercy of what might be called vexatious appeals to religious scruple. A recent example might be the reported refusal of a Muslim woman employed by Marks and Spencer to handle a book of Bible stories.[9] Or we might think of the rather more serious cluster of questions around forced marriages, where again it is crucial to distinguish between cultural and strictly religious dimensions. While Bradney rightly cautions against the simple dismissal of alleged scruple by judicial authorities who have made no attempt to understand its workings in the construction of people's social identities, it should be clear also that any recognition of the need for such sensitivity must also have a recognised means of deciding the relative seriousness of conscience-related claims, a way of distinguishing purely cultural habits from seriously-rooted matters of faith and discipline, and distinguishing uninformed prejudice from religious prescription. There needs to be access to recognised authority acting for a religious group: there is already, of course, an Islamic Shari'a Council, much in demand for rulings on marital questions in the UK; and if we were to see more latitude given in law to rights and scruples rooted in religious identity, we should need a much enhanced and quite sophisticated version of such a body, with increased resources and a high degree of community recognition, so that 'vexatious' claims could be summarily dealt with. The secular lawyer needs to know where the potential conflict is real, legally and religiously serious, and where it is grounded in either nuisance or ignorance. There can be no blank cheques given to unexamined scruples.

The second issue, a very serious one, is that recognition of 'supplementary jurisdiction' in some areas, especially family law, could have the effect of reinforcing in minority communities some of the most repressive or retrograde elements in them, with particularly serious consequences for the role and

---

[9] January 2008. Reported, for example, by N Britten, 'Muslim M&S worker "refused to touch Bible"', *The Daily Telegraph*, 15 January 2008.

liberties of women. The 'forced marriage' question is the one most often referred to here, and it is at the moment undoubtedly a very serious and scandalous one; but precisely because it has to do with custom and culture rather than directly binding enactments by religious authority, I shall refer to another issue. It is argued that the provision for the inheritance of widows under a strict application of *shari'a* has the effect of disadvantaging them in what the majority community might regard as unacceptable ways. A legal (in fact Qur'anic) provision which in its time served very clearly to secure a widow's position at a time when this was practically unknown in the culture becomes, if taken absolutely literally, a generator of relative *insecurity* in a new context.[10] The problem here is that recognising the authority of a communal religious court to decide finally and authoritatively about such a question would in effect not merely allow an additional layer of legal routes for resolving conflicts and ordering behaviour, but would actually *deprive* members of the minority community of rights and liberties that they were entitled to enjoy as citizens; and while a legal system might properly admit structures or protocols that embody the diversity of moral reasoning in a plural society by allowing scope for a minority group to administer its affairs according to its own convictions, it can hardly admit or 'license' protocols that effectively take away the rights it acknowledges as generally valid.

To put the question like that is already to see where an answer might lie, though it is not an answer that will remove the possibility of some conflict. If any kind of plural jurisdiction is recognised, it would presumably have to be under the rubric that no 'supplementary' jurisdiction could have the power to deny access to the rights granted to other citizens or to punish its members for claiming those rights. This is in effect to mirror what a minority might themselves be requesting – that the situation should not arise where membership of one group restricted the freedom to live also as a member of an overlapping group, that (in this case) citizenship in a secular society should not necessitate the abandoning of religious discipline, any more than religious discipline should deprive one of access to liberties secured by the law of the land, to the common benefits of secular citizenship – or, better, to recognise that citizenship itself is a complex phenomenon not bound up with any one level of communal belonging but involving them all.

But this does not guarantee an absence of conflict. In the particular case we have mentioned, the inheritance rights of widows, it is already true that some Islamic societies have themselves proved flexible (Malaysia is a case in point). But let us take a more neuralgic matter still: what about the historic

---

[10] See, eg, AE Mayer, *Islam and Human Rights: tradition and politics* (Boulder, 1999), p 111.

Islamic prohibition against apostasy, and the draconian penalties entailed? In a society where freedom of religion is secured by law, it is obviously impossible for any group to claim that conversion to another faith is simply disallowed or to claim the right to inflict punishment on a convert. We touch here on one of the most sensitive areas not only in thinking about legal practice but also in interfaith relations. A significant number of contemporary Islamic jurists and scholars would say that the Qur'anic pronouncements on apostasy which have been regarded as the ground for extreme penalties reflect a situation in which abandoning Islam was equivalent to adopting an active stance of violent hostility to the community, so that extreme penalties could be compared to provisions in other jurisdictions for punishing spies or traitors in wartime; but that this cannot be regarded as bearing on the conditions now existing in the world.

Of course such a reading is wholly unacceptable to 'primitivists' in Islam, for whom this would be an example of a rationalising strategy, a style of interpretation (*ijtihad*) uncontrolled by proper traditional norms. But, to use again the terminology suggested a moment ago, as soon as it is granted that – even in a dominantly Islamic society – citizens have more than one set of defining relationships under the law of the state, it becomes hard to justify enactments that take it for granted that the only mode of contact between these sets of relationships is open enmity; in which case, the appropriateness of extreme penalties for conversion is not obvious even within a fairly strict Muslim frame of reference. Conversely, where the dominant legal culture is non-Islamic, but there is a level of serious recognition of the corporate reality and rights of the *umma*, there can be no assumption that outside the *umma* the goal of any other jurisdiction is its destruction. Once again, there has to be a recognition that difference of conviction is not automatically a lethal threat.

As I have said, this is a delicate and complex matter involving what is mostly a fairly muted but nonetheless real debate among Muslim scholars in various contexts. I mention it partly because of its gravity as an issue in interfaith relations and in discussions of human rights and the treatment of minorities, partly to illustrate how the recognition of what I have been calling membership in different but overlapping sets of social relationship (what others have called 'multiple affiliations') can provide a framework for thinking about these neuralgic questions of the status of women and converts. Recognising a supplementary jurisdiction cannot mean recognising a liberty to exert a sort of local monopoly in some areas. The Jewish legal theorist Ayelet Shachar, in a highly original and significant monograph on *Multicultural Jurisdictions: Cultural Differences and Women's Rights*, explores the risks of any model that ends up 'franchising' a non-state jurisdiction so as to reinforce its most problematic features and further disadvantage its weakest members: 'we must be alert,' she writes, 'to the potentially injurious effects of well-meaning external protections upon different categories of group members here – effects which may unwittingly exacerbate preexisting internal power hierarchies'. She argues that if we are serious in trying to move away from a model that treats one jurisdiction as having a monopoly of socially defining roles and relations, we do not solve any problems by a purely uncritical endorsement of a communal legal structure which can only be avoided by deciding to leave the community altogether. We need, according to Shachar, to 'work to overcome the ultimatum of "either your culture or your rights."'.[11]

So the second objection to an increased legal recognition of communal religious identities can be met if we are prepared to think about the basic ground rules that might organise the relationship between jurisdictions, making sure that we do not collude with unexamined systems that have oppressive effect or allow shared public liberties to be decisively taken away by a supplementary jurisdiction. Once again, there are no blank cheques. I shall return to some of the details of Shachar's positive proposal; but I want to move on to the third objection, which grows precisely out of the complexities of clarifying the relations between jurisdictions. Is it not both theoretically and practically mistaken to qualify our commitment to legal monopoly? So much of our thinking in the modern world, dominated by European assumptions about universal rights, rests, surely, on the basis that the law is the law; that everyone stands before the public tribunal on exactly equal terms, so that recognition of corporate identities or, more seriously, of supplementary jurisdictions is simply incoherent if we want to preserve the great political and social advances of Western legality.

There is a bit of a risk here in the way we sometimes talk about the universal vision of post-Enlightenment politics. The great protest of the Enlightenment was against authority that appealed only to tradition and refused to justify itself by other criteria – by open reasoned argument or by standards of successful provision of goods and liberties for the greatest number. Its claim to override traditional forms of governance and custom by looking towards a universal tribunal was entirely intelligible against the background of despotism and uncritical inherited privilege which prevailed in so much of early modern Europe. The most positive aspect of this moment in our cultural history was its focus on equal levels of accountability for all and equal levels

---

[11] A Shachar, *Multicultural Jurisdictions: cultural differences and women's rights* (Cambridge, 2001), pp 113–14.

of access for all to legal process. In this respect, it was in fact largely the foregrounding and confirming of what was already encoded in longstanding legal tradition, Roman and mediaeval, which had consistently affirmed the universality and primacy of law (even over the person of the monarch). But this set of considerations alone is not adequate to deal with the realities of complex societies: it is not enough to say that citizenship as an abstract form of equal access and equal accountability is either the basis or the entirety of social identity and personal motivation. Where this has been enforced, it has proved a weak vehicle for the life of a society and has often brought violent injustice in its wake (think of the various attempts to reduce citizenship to rational equality in the France of the 1790s or the China of the 1970s). Societies that are in fact ethnically, culturally and religiously diverse are societies in which identity is formed, as we have noted, by different modes and contexts of belonging, 'multiple affiliation'. The danger is in acting as if the authority that managed the abstract level of equal citizenship represented a sovereign order which then *allowed* other levels to exist. But if the reality of society is plural – as many political theorists have pointed out – this is a damagingly inadequate account of common life, in which certain kinds of affiliation are marginalised or privatised to the extent that what is produced is a ghettoised pattern of social life, in which particular sorts of interest and of reasoning are tolerated as private matters but never granted legitimacy in public as part of a continuing debate about shared goods and priorities.

But this means that we have to think a little harder about the role and rule of law in a plural society of overlapping identities. Perhaps it helps to see the universalist vision of law as guaranteeing equal accountability and access primarily in a negative rather than a positive sense – that is, to see it as a mechanism whereby any human participant in a society is protected against the loss of certain elementary liberties of self-determination and guaranteed the freedom to demand reasons for any actions on the part of others for actions and policies that infringe self-determination. This is a slightly more gentle or tactful way of expressing what some legal theorists will describe as the 'monopoly of legitimate violence' by the law of a state, the absolute restriction of powers of forcible restraint to those who administer statutory law. This is not to reduce society itself primarily to an uneasy alliance of self-determining individuals arguing about the degree to which their freedom is limited by one another and needing forcible restraint in a war of all against all – though that is increasingly the model which a narrowly rights-based culture fosters, producing a manically litigious atmosphere and a conviction of the inadequacy of customary ethical restraints and traditions of what was once called 'civility'. The picture will not be unfamiliar, and there is a modern legal culture which loves to have it so. But the point of defining legal universalism as a negative thing is that it allows us to assume, as I think we should, that the important springs of moral vision in a society will be in those areas which a systematic abstract universalism regards as 'private' – in religion above all, but also in custom and habit. The role of 'secular' law is not the dissolution of these things in the name of universalism but the monitoring of such affiliations to prevent the creation of mutually isolated communities in which human liberties are seen in incompatible ways and individual persons are subjected to restraints or injustices for which there is no public redress.

The rule of law is thus not the enshrining of priority for the universal/abstract dimension of social existence but the establishing of a space accessible to everyone in which it is possible to affirm and defend a commitment to human dignity *as such*, independent of membership in any specific human community or tradition, so that, when specific communities or traditions are in danger of claiming finality for their own boundaries of practice and understanding, they are reminded that they have to come to terms with the actuality of human diversity – and that the only way of doing this is to acknowledge the category of 'human dignity as such', a non-negotiable assumption that each agent (with his or her historical and social affiliations) could be expected to have a voice in the shaping of some common project for the well-being and order of a human group. It is not to claim that specific community understandings are 'superseded' by this universal principle, rather to claim that they all need to be undergirded by it. The rule of law is – and this may sound rather counterintuitive – a way of honouring what in the human constitution is not captured by any one form of corporate belonging or any particular history, even though the human constitution never exists without those other determinations. Our need, as Raymond Plant has well expressed it, is for the construction of 'a moral framework which could expand outside the boundaries of particular narratives while, at the same time, respecting the narratives as the cultural contexts in which the language [of common dignity and mutually intelligible commitments to work for certain common moral priorities] is learned and taught'.[12]

I would add in passing that this is arguably a place where more reflection is needed about the theology of law; if my analysis is right, the sort of foundation I have sketched for a universal principle of legal right requires both a certain valuation of the human as such and a conviction that the human subject is always endowed with some degree of freedom over against

---

[12] R Plant, *Politics, Theology and History* (Cambridge, 2001), pp 357–8.

any and every actual system of human social life; both of these things are historically rooted in Christian theology, even when they have acquired a life of their own in isolation from that theology. It never does any harm to be reminded that without certain themes consistently and strongly emphasised by the 'Abrahamic' faiths, themes to do with the unconditional possibility for every human subject to live in conscious relation with God and in free and constructive collaboration with others, there is no guarantee that a 'universalist' account of human dignity would ever have seemed plausible or even emerged with clarity. Slave societies and assumptions about innate racial superiority are as widespread a feature as any in human history (and they have persistently infected even Abrahamic communities, which is perhaps why the Enlightenment was a necessary wake-up call to religion . . .).

But to return to our main theme: I have been arguing that a defence of an unqualified secular legal monopoly in terms of the need for a universalist doctrine of human right or dignity is to misunderstand the circumstances in which that doctrine emerged, and that the essential liberating (and religiously informed) vision it represents is not imperilled by a loosening of the monopolistic framework. At the moment, as I mentioned at the beginning of this lecture, one of the most frequently noted problems in the law in this area is the reluctance of a dominant rights-based philosophy to acknowledge the liberty of conscientious opting-out from collaboration in procedures or practices that are in tension with the demands of particular religious groups: the assumption, in rather misleading shorthand, that if a right or liberty is granted there is a corresponding duty upon every individual to 'activate' this whenever called upon. Earlier on, I proposed that the criterion for recognising and collaborating with communal religious discipline should be connected with whether a communal jurisdiction actively interfered with liberties guaranteed by the wider society in such a way as definitively to block access to the exercise of those liberties; clearly the refusal of a religious believer to act upon the legal recognition of a right is not, given the plural character of society, a denial to anyone inside or outside the community of access to that right. The point has been granted in respect of medical professionals who may be asked to perform or co-operate in performing abortions – a perfectly reasonable example of the law doing what I earlier defined as its job, securing space for those aspects of human motivation and behaviour that cannot be finally determined by any corporate or social system. It is difficult to see quite why the principle cannot be extended in other areas. But it is undeniable that there is pressure from some quarters to insist that conscientious disagreement should always be overruled by a monopolistic understanding of jurisdiction.

I labour the point because what at first seems to be a somewhat narrow point about how Islamic law and Islamic identity should or might be regarded in our legal system in fact opens up a very wide range of current issues, and requires some general thinking about the character of law. It would be a pity if the immense advances in the recognition of human rights led, because of a misconception about legal universality, to a situation where a person was defined primarily as the possessor of a set of abstract liberties and the law's function was accordingly seen as nothing but the securing of those liberties irrespective of the custom and conscience of those groups which concretely compose a plural modern society. Certainly, no one is likely to suppose that a scheme allowing for supplementary jurisdiction will be simple, and the history of experiments in this direction amply illustrates the problems. But if one approaches it along the lines sketched by Shachar in the monograph quoted earlier, it might be possible to think in terms of what she calls 'transformative accommodation': a scheme in which individuals retain the liberty to choose the jurisdiction under which they will seek to resolve certain carefully specified matters, so that 'power-holders are forced to compete for the loyalty of their shared constituents'.[13] This may include aspects of marital law, the regulation of financial transactions and authorised structures of mediation and conflict resolution – the main areas that have been in question where supplementary jurisdictions have been tried, with native American communities in Canada as well as with religious groups like Islamic minority communities in certain contexts. In such schemes, both jurisdictional stakeholders may need to examine the way they operate: a communal/religious *nomos*, to borrow Shachar's vocabulary, has to think through the risks of alienating its people by inflexible or over-restrictive applications of traditional law, and a universalist Enlightenment system has to weigh the possible consequences of ghettoising and effectively disenfranchising a minority, at real cost to overall social cohesion and creativity. Hence '*transformative* accommodation': both jurisdictional parties may be changed by their encounter over time, and we avoid the sterility of mutually exclusive monopolies.

It is uncomfortably true that this introduces into our thinking about law what some would see as a 'market' element, a competition for loyalty as Shachar admits. But if what we want socially is a pattern of relations in which a plurality of diverse and overlapping affiliations work for a common good, and in which groups of serious and profound conviction are not systematically faced with the stark alternatives of cultural loyalty or state loyalty, it seems

[13] Shachar, *Multicultural Jurisdictions*, supra n 11, p 122.

unavoidable. In other settings, I have spoken about the idea of 'interactive pluralism' as a political desideratum; this seems to be one manifestation of such an ideal, comparable to the arrangements that allow for shared responsibility in education: the best argument for faith schools from the point of view of any aspiration towards social harmony and understanding is that they bring communal loyalties into direct relation with the wider society and inevitably lead to mutual questioning and sometimes mutual influence towards change, without compromising the distinctiveness of the essential elements of those communal loyalties.

In conclusion, it seems that if we are to think intelligently about the relations between Islam and British law, we need a fair amount of 'deconstruction' of crude oppositions and mythologies, whether of the nature of *shariʿa* or the nature of the Enlightenment. But as I have hinted, I do not believe this can be done without some thinking also about the very nature of law. It is always easy to take refuge in some form of positivism; and what I have called legal universalism, when divorced from a serious theoretical (and, I would argue, religious) underpinning, can turn into a positivism as sterile as any other variety. If the paradoxical idea which I have sketched is true – that universal law and universal right are a way of recognising what is least fathomable and controllable in the human subject – theology still waits for us around the corner of these debates, however hard our culture may try to keep it out. And, as you can imagine, I am not going to complain about that.

PART II

The Archbishop's proposal for 'transformative accommodation'

Shariʿa 'clearly diverges from Convention values, particularly with regard to its criminal law and criminal procedure, its rules on the legal status of women and the way it intervenes in all spheres of private and public life in accordance with religious precepts.'
  – Majority Judgment, *Refah Partisi Welfare Party and Others v Turkey* (No 1), (2002) 35 EHRR 3, para 72.

Shariʿa law has no jurisdiction in England and Wales and there is no intention to change this position . . . . Any order in a family case is made or approved by a family judge applying English family law.
  – Bridget Prentice, MP, Parliamentary Under Secretary in the Ministry of Justice, Written Parliamentary Answer, 23 October 2008.

Shari'a and secular democracy: is Islamic law compatible with the European Convention on Human Rights?

CHAPTER 3

The Refah *case at the European Court of Human Rights*

Nicolas Bratza

The Refah or Welfare Party was founded in Turkey in 1983. In the general election of December 1995, the party obtained 22 per cent of the votes cast and in the local elections of November 1996, it obtained 35 per cent of the votes cast. The results of the 1995 election made Refah the largest political party in Turkey with a total of 158 seats in the Grand National Assembly.

In June 1996, Refah came to power by forming a coalition with the Centre-Right True Path Party led by Mrs Tansu Ciller. According to opinion polls carried out in January 1997, the Refah Party would have obtained 38 per cent of the votes if a general election had taken place at that time; and, according to later polls, 67 per cent of the vote if it had taken place four years later. But that was not to be, for in May 1997 the public prosecutor brought proceedings in the Turkish Constitutional Court for the compulsory dissolution of the party on the grounds that it had become a centre of activities contrary to the principles of secularism. In January 1998, the Constitutional Court dissolved the Refah Party. It was the fifteenth political party to have been compulsorily dissolved in Turkey in recent times. But it was by far the most important party in terms of its public support. It was also different in two other ways. First, the other parties had been dissolved because of their alleged separatist policies and not their alleged anti-secularist activities. Second, unlike the other parties where the objections were founded on the programme of the party, there was nothing in Refah's programme or statutes to suggest that the party was anti-secularist or that it advocated a theocratic state or that it pursued policies which would undermine the secular nature of the state. The decision to dissolve was founded instead exclusively on the activities and statements of the chairman

---

Sir Nicolas Bratza was one of the three judges who dissented in *Refah Partisi (Welfare Party) and Others v Turkey* (No 1) (2002) 35 EHRR 3 before the Chamber. The subsequent Grand Chamber judgment is at *Refah Partisi (Welfare Party) and Others v Turkey* (No 2) (2003) 37 EHRR 1 (GC).

of the party, Mr Erbakan, its two vice-chairmen and four members of the party, of whom three were elected members of the Assembly and one was a city mayor. It was held by the Constitutional Court that these actions and statements, which for the most part dated back some years before Refah came to power, showed that whatever its programme might say, the Refah Party intended to set up a plurality of legal systems leading to discrimination based on religious beliefs; that it intended to apply *shariʿa*, which was said to be the antithesis of democracy; and that several of the statements made reference to the possibility of recourse to force as a political method.

The Refah Party then complained to the European Court of Human Rights (ECtHR) that its rights under the European Convention on Human Rights (ECHR) had been violated. By four votes to three a Chamber of the Court found that the dissolution of the Refah Party had not violated the applicant's right to freedom of association in Article 11 of the ECHR.[1] I should make clear that in dissenting from this opinion, the three judges in the minority did not dispute that the intemperate statements, advocating the introduction of *shariʿa*, had been made.

It was the minority view, however, that nothing had been done to suggest that the party itself had taken any steps to realise political aims incompatible with ECHR norms or to undermine secular society or to engage in or encourage acts of violence or otherwise to threaten the legal and democratic order. It was our view that although steps could have been taken against the individuals concerned for making anti-secularist statements, the compulsory dissolution of the party as a whole was a disproportionate interference with its right to freedom of association.

We were told that we were wrong by the Grand Chamber of the ECtHR. The Grand Chamber held in summary that the acts and statements of the party leaders and members were justifiably imputable to the party as a whole; that the party's aim of introducing a plurality of legal systems was incompatible with the Convention because it would involve discrimination on the basis of religion; that the aim of introducing *shariʿa* was also incompatible with the Convention because it had no place for principles

---

[1] Article 11 ECHR: Freedom of assembly and association. (1) Everyone has the right to freedom of peaceful assembly and to freedom of association with others, including the right to form and to join trade unions for the protection of his interests. (2) No restrictions shall be placed on the exercise of these rights other than such as are prescribed by law and are necessary in a democratic society in the interests of national security or public safety, for the prevention of disorder or crime, for the protection of health or morals or for the protection of the rights and freedoms of others. This article shall not prevent the imposition of lawful restrictions on the exercise of these rights by members of the armed forces, of the police or of the administration of the State.

such as political pluralism; and that there had been ambiguity in the statements made concerning the use of violence to attain or keep power. The Constitutional Court was held to have been entitled to act when it did to prevent Refah from implementing a programme which would be dangerous for rights and freedoms.

It is the view of the Grand Chamber of the Court on *shari'a* and its compatibility with the ECHR which is perhaps most relevant to this volume's discussion. The Grand Chamber concurred with the Chamber's view that *shari'a* was incompatible with the fundamental principles of democracy as set forth in the ECHR. This view was encapsulated in Paragraph 72 of the Chamber's judgment which bears reading in full. The Chamber said this:

Like the constitutional court, the court considers that *Shari'a* which faithfully reflects the dogmas and divine rules laid down by religion is stable and invariable. Principles such as pluralism in the political sphere, or the constant evolution of public freedoms, have no place in it. The court notes that when read together the offending statements which contain explicit references to the introduction of *Shari'a*, are difficult to reconcile with the fundamental principles of democracy as conceived in the Convention taken as a whole. It is difficult to declare one's respect for democracy and human rights while at the same time supporting a regime based on *Shari'a* which clearly diverges from Convention values, particularly with regard to its criminal law and criminal procedure, its rules on the legal status of women and the way it intervenes in all spheres of private and public life in accordance with religious precepts. In the Court's view, a political party whose actions seem to be aimed at introducing *Shari'a* in a state party to the Convention can hardly be regarded as an association complying with the democratic ideal that underlies the whole of the Convention.

The Grand Chamber added for good measure that Refah's policy was to apply some of *shari'a*'s private law rules to a large part of the population of Turkey within a framework of a plurality of legal systems. It was the Court's view that Turkey might legitimately prevent the application within its jurisdiction of private law rules of religious inspiration prejudicial to public order and the values of democracy for ECHR purposes. The Court cited those rules which permitted discrimination based on the gender of the parties concerned, as in polygamy, and privileges for the male sex in matters of divorce and succession.

The Strasbourg Court's decision raises a number of questions. What is meant by *shari'a* law? Is *shari'a* law to be regarded, as the Court says, as stable and invariable? Do principles of pluralism have no place in it? Is *shari'a* inconsistent with fundamental principles of democracy or with

ECHR values in the particular respects found by the Court or more generally? And should the Court's statements be seen as general or be confined to the specific context of Turkey and the particular emphasis in that country on secularism? It is to these questions that the following chapters turn.[2]

---

[2] I have considered some more recent cases in N Bratza, 'The "precious asset": freedom of religion under the European Convention of Human Rights' in M Hill (ed), *Religion and Discrimination Law in the European Union* (Trier, 2012), pp 9–26.

CHAPTER 4

*The compatibility of an Islamic/*shariʿa *law system or* shariʿa *rules with the European Convention on Human Rights*

Dominic McGoldrick

INTRODUCTION

One day there was a student at one of our famous universities who was sitting in front of an examination paper. Unfortunately he couldn't answer any of the questions. So he began his essay: 'I'm terribly sorry, I don't know the answer to any of these questions; but here are some questions I do know the answers to,'– and then he proceeded to write the answers. For this chapter, the question posed was 'whether an Islamic/*shariʿa* law system would be compatible with the European Convention on Human Rights (ECHR)?' I am in a more fortunate position than the student, because I think I know the answer. The answer is 'No'. Or, if one is being really diplomatic, at least generally 'No'.

THE CHALLENGE

The challenge that lies behind the question is clear to all. The numbers, visibility and demands of Muslims are growing as Europe is 'once again becoming a land of Islam'.[1] What should be the place of Islam in the many European states that now contain significant and permanent Muslim minorities?[2] Calls for a greater degree of recognition for *shariʿa* law can be seen as a reaffirmation of Islamic identity.[3] Are Muslims to be considered different or unique as compared to other minorities,

---

[1] N AlSayyad and M Castells, 'Introduction: Islam and the changing identity of Europe' in N AlSayyad and M Castells (eds), *Muslim Europe or Euro-Islam* (Lanham, MD, 2002), p 1.

[2] See MLP Loenen and JE Goldschmidt (eds), *Religious Pluralism and Human Rights in Europe: where to draw the line?* (Antwerp, 2007); HA Hellyer, *Muslims of Europe: the 'other' Europeans* (Edinburgh, 2009).

[3] See WB Hallaq, *The Origins and Evolution of Islamic Law* (Cambridge, 2005), p 1. On the various ways in which *shariʿa* law is already given some degree of recognition through issues of fact, state law, arbitration and private international law, see R Sandberg, 'Islam and English law', (2010) 164 L&J 27; and *The Official Solicitor to the Senior Courts v Yemoh and Others* [2010] EWHC 3727 (Ch) (on the application of the intestacy rules in relation to polygamous marriages).

religious or otherwise? How should Muslims be positively accommodated and integrated within European states?[4] Should it be by the general adoption of a *shari'a* system or just of particular substantive or procedural rules? Alternatively, should there be more opt-outs from generally applicable laws for religions generally or for Muslims in particular, and, if so, on what principled basis?[5] What implications would more opt-outs have for the accommodation of other religions and non-religious beliefs?[6] Are these questions more comprehensible than the general question of compatibility and, therefore, ones that might attract better answers?

IS THE COMPATIBILITY QUESTION UNANSWERABLE?

There is an easy way out: to say that the question is unanswerable because we do not know what *shari'a* law is and no one can beyond controversion define it. There is a range of conceptions of *shari'a* law. It can be understood as an abstract philosophical concept or overarching meta-norm approximating to the rule of law. Alternatively, it can be understood as more of a moral conception, for '*shari'a*, properly understood, is not just a set of legal rules. To believing Muslims, it is something deeper and higher, infused with moral and metaphysical purpose. At its core, *shari'a* represents the idea that all human beings and all human governments are subject to justice under the law'.[7] It can be more narrowly conceived as embodying Islamically derived rules and norms.[8] Finally, it can also be understood as a flexible general system of law (like common law or civil law). In systemic terms there are established sources for making legal decisions – Qur'an, *Sunna*, consensus, analogy

---

[4] See S Ferrari and R Cristofori (eds), *Law and Religion in the 21st Century* (Farnham, 2010), pp 333–67; M Rohe, '*Shari'a* in Europe: perspectives of segregation, assimilation or integration for European Muslims?', accessible at <http://cmes.hmdc.harvard.edu/files/Mathias.Rohe_.lecture.pdf>; E Bleich, 'Muslims and the state in the post-9/11 West', (2009) 35 JEMS 353; S Motha, 'Veiled women and the *affect* of religion in democracy', (2007) 34 JLS 139; G Singh and S Cowden, 'Multiculturalism's new fault lines', (2011) 31 *Crit Soc Policy* 343.
[5] See D McGoldrick, 'Accommodating Muslims in Europe: from adopting *shari'a* law to religiously based opt outs from generally applicable laws', (2009) 9 HRLR 603; U Shavit, 'Should Muslims integrate into the West?', (2007) 14 MEQ 13.
[6] On existing accommodation in UK law in a range of areas, see A Bradney, *Law and Faith in a Sceptical Age* (Abingdon, 2008).
[7] N Feldman, 'Why *shari'a*?', *The New York Times*, 16 March 2008. See also N Feldman, *The Fall and Rise of the Islamic State* (Princeton, NJ, 2009).
[8] See J Rehman, 'The *Shari'ah*, Islamic family laws and international human rights law: examining the theory and practice of polygamy and talaq', (2007) 21 *Int J Law Pol Fam* 108, 109–13. For a historical account, see Hallaq, *The Origins and Evolution of Islamic Law*, supra n 3.

and reason, – but there are differences of opinion as to their use and interrelationship. There are some recognisable methodologies of interpretation[9] that can be taught although there are differences in their use between and within different Shia and Sunni schools and traditions.[10] However, 'there is no single code that can be identified as "the" *shariʿa*'.[11] There is also no central or universal *shariʿa* authority or universal *shariʿa* institution. For example, debate on the Islamic headscarf often revolves around whether a particular practice is mandatory or discretionary, and whether it is a religious rule or a cultural rule or both.[12] In a sense we are often at the mercy of Islamic source-interpreting 'experts' or 'authorities' who may in any event take different views. This lack of certainty is important in an ECHR context because one of the central elements of jurisprudence under the ECHR is that laws regulating and interfering with rights have to be both accessible and foreseeable.[13] However, while an abstract notion of *shariʿa* law is thus problematic in this context, the practical reality may be that in modern states the *shariʿa* law is overlaid with detailed administrative and legislative secular provisions which are both accessible and foreseeable but which can also vary significantly between states and between Islamic schools of jurisprudence. Human rights law is focused on whether the rights recognised are practical and effective. As long as the rights are, then references to *shariʿa* as the ultimate source of rights may to an extent be a rhetorical device. Thus a distinction is often drawn between the classical or pre-modern *shariʿa* and *shariʿa* as it is currently reflected in modern Islamic state practices.[14]

---

[9] See J Rehman, *Islamic State Practices, International Law and the Threat from Terrorism* (Oxford, 2005), pp 10–27; AE Mayer, *Islam and Human Rights: tradition and politics* (fourth edition, Boulder, Co, 2007); O Bakircioglu, 'A socio-legal analysis of the concept of jihad', (2010) 59 ICLQ 413, pp 414–6.

[10] See T Ramadan, *Radical Reform: Islamic ethics and liberation* (New York, 2009), p 41.

[11] R. Williams, 'Civil and religious law in England: a religious perspective', supra p 20. The same is true for Jewish law, see The Centre for Social Cohesion, *Beth Din: Jewish Law in the UK* (London, 2009). See also I Yilmaz, 'The question of incorporation of Muslim personal law into the English law', (2011) 21 JIMMA 297 (on differences between Islamic traditions).

[12] See F Raday, 'Culture, religion, and gender', (2002) 4 IJCL 663; M Sunder, 'Piercing the veil', (2003) 112 YLJ 1399; D McGoldrick, *Human Rights and Religion: the Islamic headscarf debate in Europe* (Oxford, 2006); and further references, infra nn 125–7.

[13] D Harris, M O'Boyle and C Warbrick, *Law of the European Convention on Human Rights* (second edition, Oxford, 2009), pp 341–60. A good example is *Dogru v France* (2009) 49 EHRR 8, on the regulation under French law of the wearing of Islamic headscarves at schools.

[14] See JJ Nasir, *The Status of Women under Islamic Law and Modern Islamic Legislation* (third edition, Boston, MA, 2009). For a revisionist interpretation of where Islam came from and what it is, see T Holland, *In the Shadow of the Sword: the battle for global empire and the end of the ancient world* (London, 2012).

IS *SHARIʿA* LAW INCOMPATIBLE WITH THE VERY
CONCEPT OF HUMAN RIGHTS?

Another easy way out is to reframe the question in terms of whether Islamic law is necessarily incompatible with or discordant with the very concept (rather than the practice) of human rights? The answer to that question must be 'No'. There is much in the history of Islamic doctrine that is entirely consistent with the philosophy and content of human rights.[15] Many issues are unproblematic in human rights terms. Islam can be a significant factor in improving the human rights situation in predominantly Muslim states that recognise Islam as the state religion or apply Islamic law or Islamic principles as part of state law.[16] Being a 'political party animated by the moral values imposed by a religion' is also not intrinsically inimical to the fundamental principles of democracy, as set forth in the ECHR.[17] It can be accepted that *shariʿa* law is complex and dynamic and constantly evolving through processes of interpretation and reinterpretation of sources by clerics, jurists, scholars, state legislatures, courts and feminists.[18] There are also efforts to 'reinterpret' Islamic governance based on the rule of law rather than the rule of a jurist.[19] All of these efforts by individuals and communities deserve respect, recognition, encouragement, sympathy, support and admiration. However, they do not deserve pretence. They cannot be allowed to disguise the central point, namely that 'theological re-interpretations' are needed to update *shariʿa* and bring it into conformity with modern

---

[15] See MA Baderin, *International Human Rights and Islamic Law* (Oxford, 2003); AA An-Naʿim, *Islam and the Secular State: negotiating the future of Shariʿa* (Harvard, 2008); A Sachedina, *Islam and the Challenge of Human Rights* (New York, 2009).

[16] MA Baderin, 'Islam and the realization of human rights in the Muslim world: a reflection on two essential approaches and two divergent perspectives', (2007) 4 MWJHR, accessible at <http://www.bepress.com/mwjhr>.

[17] *Refah Partisi (Welfare Party) and Others v Turkey (No 1)* (2002) 35 EHRR 3, para 100, though this was not repeated in the Grand Chamber. There are a number of religiously based political parties in European states.

[18] See, eg F Mernissi, *The Veil and the Male Elite: a feminist interpretation of women's rights in Islam* (Reading, MA, 1991); Ramadan, *Radical Reform*, supra n 10 (arguing against literalist reduction and cultural projection and for greater attention to context and objectives); S Bainbridge, 'War and peace: negotiating meaning in Islam', (2008) 1 CST 263; A Sachedina, *Islam and the Challenge of Human Rights*, supra n 15; SS Haneef, 'Debate on methodology of renewing muslim law: a search for a synthetic approach' (2010) 10(1) *Global Jurist*, accessible at <http://www.bepress.com/gj/vol10/iss1/art4>; Z Sardar, *Reading the Qur'an* (London, 2011). Such 'reinterpretations' are common, eg within the different schools of the Jewish faith.

[19] B Rahimi, 'The discourse of democracy in Shiʿi Islamic jurisprudence: the two cases of Montazeri and Sistani', RSCAS Policy Paper 2008/09 (European University Institute, 2008), accessible at <http://cadmus.iue.it/dspace/bitstream/1814/8223/3/RSCAS_2008_09.pdf>.

human rights law. To the extent that *shari'a* law is evolutionary then it has a long way to evolve.[20]

THE *REFAH* CASE

'Is an Islamic/*shari'a* law system compatible with the ECHR?' The principal authority in support of answering this question in the negative is the *Refah* case concerning the dissolution of an Islamic political party in Turkey.[21] I stress the reference to *system* because for the European Court of Human Rights (ECtHR) it was certain systemic aspects that caused the majority in the Chamber (four judges) and all of the Grand Chamber (another fifteen judges) to have fundamental concerns. It is those concerns that supported a negative answer to the question and which led to the finding that the party's dissolution was consistent with the ECHR. In *Refah*, Turkey had relied in part on the concept of 'militant democracy', that is, that the measures were permissible to defend democracy from being subverted through the political process.[22] Essentially, the Court accepted Turkey's argument. For the Court the real chances that Refah would implement its programme after gaining power made that danger more tangible and more immediate. That being so, the Court considered that it could not criticise the national courts for not acting earlier, at the risk of intervening prematurely and before the danger concerned had taken shape and become real. Nor could it criticise them for not waiting, at the risk of putting the political regime and civil peace in jeopardy, for Refah to seize power and swing into action (eg by tabling bills in Parliament) in order to implement its plans.[23] It is helpful to recall that one of the historical motivations of the ECHR system was to stop small-scale violations becoming larger ones.

The Grand Chamber had three particular problems with the Refah party, two of which are of concern here. The first was a systemic problem, namely that it had proposed a plurality of legal systems. Turkish society would be divided into several religious orders requiring each individual to choose the order to which he or she would be subject. The Court considered that such a

---

[20] For a critical evaluation, see K Samuel, *The Organization of the Islamic Conference, the UN and Counter-Terrorism Law-Making: competing or complementary legal orders?* (forthcoming, Oxford, 2013).

[21] Supra n 17. See also N Bratza, 'The *Refah* Case at the European Court of Human Rights', supra pp 38–41.

[22] The concept was used to describe the activities of the National Socialist Party in Germany, which through elections became the largest party in Germany and then imposed a dictatorship. See P Macklem, 'Militant democracy, legal pluralism, and the paradox of self-determination', (2006) 4 ICL 488.

[23] *Refah*, supra n 17, para 100.

societal model could not be considered compatible with the ECHR system, for two reasons. First, it would do away with the state's role as the guarantor of individual rights and freedoms and the impartial organiser of the practice of the various beliefs and religions in a democratic society, since it would oblige individuals to obey, not rules laid down by the state in the exercise of its above-mentioned functions, but static rules of law imposed by the religion concerned. States have a positive obligation to ensure that everyone within their jurisdiction enjoys in full, and without being able to waive them, the rights and freedoms guaranteed by the ECHR.[24] Second, such a system would undeniably infringe the principle of non-discrimination between individuals as regards their enjoyment of public freedoms, which was one of the fundamental principles of democracy. A difference in treatment between individuals in all fields of public and private law according to their religion or beliefs manifestly could not be justified under the ECHR, and more particularly under its Article 14 which prohibits discrimination. Such a difference in treatment could not maintain a fair balance between, on the one hand, the claims of certain religious groups who wished to be governed by their own rules and, on the other hand, the interest of society as a whole, which must be based on peace and on tolerance between the various religions and beliefs.[25]

The second problem was both systemic and content based. It was that Refah intended to set up a regime based on *shari'a* in the sense of being a state and society organised according to religious rules. The Court's response could not have been clearer: *shari'a* was incompatible with the fundamental principles of democracy, as set forth in the ECHR.[26] It considered that *shari'a*, which faithfully reflected the dogmas and divine rules laid down by religion, was stable and invariable. Principles such as pluralism in the political sphere or the constant evolution of public freedoms had no place in it. In addition to these systemic concerns about *shari'a*, there were fundamental concerns about its content. It was difficult to declare one's respect for democracy and human rights while at the same time supporting a regime based on *shari'a*, which clearly diverged from ECHR values, particularly with regard to (i) its criminal law, (ii) its criminal procedure, (iii) its rules on the legal status of women and (iv) the way it intervened in all spheres of private and public life in accordance with religious precepts. In the Court's view, a political party whose actions

---

[24] *Refah*, supra n 17, paras 117–9.   [25] *Refah*, supra n 17, para 119.
[26] See P Cumper, 'Europe, Islam and democracy: balancing religious and secular values under the ECHR', (2003–2004) 3 ECMI 163.

seemed to be aimed at introducing *shariʿa* in a state party to the Convention could hardly be regarded as an association complying with the democratic ideal that underlay the whole of the ECHR.[27]

The Court could hardly have been more explicit. Democracy was the only political model contemplated by the ECHR and accordingly the only one compatible with it and '*Shariʿa* was incompatible with the fundamental principles of democracy as set forth in the Convention'.[28] The Grand Chamber's concerns at some of the content of *shariʿa* law were echoed by the House of Lords in *EM (Lebanon) (FC) v Secretary of State for the Home Department*.[29] Their Lordships approved a description of *shariʿa* law relating to child custody as 'arbitrary and discriminatory' if measured by the human rights standards in the ECHR.[30] There was 'no place in it for equal rights between men and women'.[31] By contrast the equality of men and women has a central place under ECHR jurisprudence.[32]

It can be argued that the Grand Chamber's statements about *shariʿa* were specific to Turkey given its strategic and political importance to Europe and its overwhelmingly Muslim population. However, on the face of it, the Court's pronouncement on *shariʿa* was unqualified. On the basis of the Grand Chamber's judgment in *Refah*, one can assert with reasonable confidence that any general adoption of a *shariʿa* law system as such as part of the constitutional system of a state party to the ECHR would raise the same central concerns of the Court relating to a plurality of legal systems, indeterminacy, the divergence from Convention values and compatibility with the fundamental principles of democracy as set forth in the ECHR.

CRITIQUING THE *REFAH* CASE

The Grand Chamber's decision in *Refah* has been subjected to various critiques.[33] First, the evidence for dissolution was arguably weaker than it

---

[27] *Refah*, supra n 17, para 123.   [28] Ibid.
[29] [2008] UKHL 64, holding that the UK could not send the mother and her son back to Lebanon because their removal would constitute a flagrant breach of the right to family life (Article 8 of the ECHR), such as would completely deny or nullify the right in the destination country.
[30] Ibid., para 6 (per Lord Hope).
[31] Ibid. A more refined analysis might be that the Islamic perspective sees women as equal but different and so should be dealt with equally but often separately. See H Bielefeld, 'Muslim voices in the human rights debate', (1995) 17 HRQ 587.
[32] See A Stuart, 'Freedom of religion and gender equality', (2010) 10 HRLR 429; cf Y Nehustan, 'Female segregation for religious justifications: the unfortunate Israeli case', (2010) *Droit et Religions* 441.
[33] K Boyle, 'Human rights, religion and democracy: the Refah Partisi case', (2004) 1 Essex Human Rights Review 1; C Moe, 'Refah revisited: Strasbourg's construction of Islam', accessible at <http://www.strasbourgconference.org/papers/Refah%20Revisited-%20Strasbourg%27s%20Construction%20of%20Islam.pdf>; Cumper, 'Europe, Islam and democracy', supra n 26, 163.

should have been and a low standard of proof was applied. There was a minority in the Constitutional Court in Turkey and in the Chamber of the ECtHR that considered that the evidence was not sufficient and therefore the dissolution was disproportionate. However, it is striking that so many of the judges in the ECtHR thought that it was consistent with the Convention to intervene at an early stage. Second, the applicants in *Refah* expressly sought to impugn the Chamber's observation that it was difficult to reconcile respect for democracy and human rights with support for a regime based on *shari'a*. This, they submitted, could lead to a distinction between 'Christian-democrats' and 'Muslim-democrats' and constituted discrimination against the 150 million Muslims in Europe. Their efforts failed as the Grand Chamber repeated the Chamber's view.[34] Christian Moe has criticised the explicit determinations that support for a regime based on *shari'a* was incompatible with respect for democracy and human rights and questioned 'the appropriateness of absolutist categorisations such as this in place of, or even in addition to, case-by-case consideration of the compatibility of a State's conduct with the rights and freedoms guaranteed by the Convention'.[35] Kevin Boyle called for expert pleadings to bring to light debates within Islam on *shari'a* and democracy and elements of *shari'a* that conflict with international human rights standards.[36] Sarah Bracke and Nadia Fadil have critiqued the Court's view of Islam as a totalising religion.[37] Given the importance of perceptions the Court could also have gone to greater lengths to explain the possible distinctions between the *Refah* case and the other cases on the dissolution of political parties that it has considered and found to violate the ECHR.[38]

A third line of critique concerns legal pluralism. On the face of it, the Court's concerns were more substantial but even here the Court did not do justice to the complexity of the issues raised.[39] The ECtHR may have less of

---

[34] Though Judge Kovler, in a separate opinion in *Refah*, supra n 17, was concerned at the negative language used by the Court, the assessment made of *shari'a* and the caricature of polygamy.
[35] Moe, 'Refah revisited', supra n 33.
[36] Boyle, 'Human rights, religion and democracy', supra n 33.
[37] S Bracke and N Fadil, 'Islam and secular modernity under Western eyes: a genealogy of a constitutive relationship', RSCAS Policy Paper 2008/05 (European University Institute, 2008), <http://cadmus.iue.it/dspace/bitstream/1814/8102/1/RSCAS_2008_05.pdf>.
[38] See *United Communist Party of Turkey and Others v Turkey* (1998) 26 EHRR 121 (GC); and *Socialist Party v Turkey* (1998) 27 EHRR 51 (GC). See also P Danchin, 'Islam in the secular *nomos* of the European Court of Human Rights', (2011) 32 Mich JIL 663 accessible at <http://papers.ssrn.com/sol3/papers.cfm?abstract_id=1670671>.
[39] See Judge Kovler, *Refah*, supra n 17. See also A Tucker, 'The Archbishop's unsatisfactory legal pluralism', (2008) *Public Law* 463.

a theory of pluralism[40] and more of a Lockean view of toleration.[41] Finally, there is the Court's approach to democracy. The Court advances in its case law what has been described as a 'particularly Western liberal model of democracy'.[42] It has stressed political plurality, non-discrimination on grounds of religion, the disavowal of recourse to violence to obtain power and that democratically elected governments remain subject to restrictions imposed by constitutional and human rights norms. One element of the Court's disposition against a regime based on *shari'a* in the *Refah* case was founded on its view that *shari'a* 'faithfully reflects the dogmas and divine rules laid down by religion, is stable and invariable' and is not conducive to 'the constant evolution of public freedoms'.[43] But, as Moe has observed, such observations have, at least from time to time, been made about most of the world's leading religions.[44] Patrick Macklem accepted that it may be difficult to reconcile *shari'a* with the ECHR's values of democracy and human rights but criticised the wholesale rejection of *shari'a* and argued for a case by case assessment.[45] The Court stresses the centrality of democracy as the only European political model. Islamic views on democracy do cover a wide spectrum.[46] Another criticism is that the Court advanced abstract notions of democracy and respect for human rights rather than analysing the actual situation in Turkey. In a sense it de-contextualised the case and then abstracted specific normative concerns. A specific focus on Turkey reveals a different frame for analysis. Court proceedings are often prompted

---

[40] See J Gadirov, 'Freedom of religion and legal pluralism', in MLP Loenen and JE Goldschmidt (eds), *Religious Pluralism and Human Rights in Europe: where to draw the line?* (Antwerp, 2007), pp 81–95; BZ Tamanaha, 'Understanding legal pluralism: past to present, local to global', (2007) 29 SLR 375 (particularly on the distinction between normative pluralism and legal pluralism and the fundamental conceptual problem of defining 'law' for the purposes of legal pluralism).

[41] See J Locke, *A Letter Concerning Toleration*, 1689, trans W Popple, accessible at <http://www.constitution.org/jl/tolerati.htm>.

[42] See A Mowbray, 'The role of the European Court of Human Rights in the promotion of democracy', (1999) *Public Law* 703; and S Wheatley, 'Minorities under the ECHR and the construction of a "democratic society"', (2007) *Public Law* 770.

[43] *Refah*, supra n 17, para 123.

[44] See Moe, 'Refah Revisited', supra n 33. Of course the critical element is whether the regime exercises governmental power. Presumably, if the rules of *shari'a* are in fact 'stable and invariable' then part of the indeterminacy concerns suggested above, pp 43–44, are partly addressed. Accessibility appears more problematic but may be addressed by specific modern legislative provisions.

[45] Macklem, 'Militant democracy', supra n 22.

[46] See JL Esposito and JO Voll, 'Islam and Democracy', (2001) 22 *Humanities*, accessible at <http://www.neh.gov/news/humanities/2001-11/islam.html>, who conclude that, 'it is clear that Islam is not inherently incompatible with democracy'. See also E Cotran and AO Sherif, *Democracy, the Rule of Law and Islam* (London, 1999); D Bukay, 'Can there be an Islamic democracy?', (2007) 14 MEQ 71; Samuel, *The Organization of the Islamic Conference, the UN and Counter-Terrorism Law-Making*, supra n 20.

by the military which sees itself as the defender of secularism. Somewhat ironically the human rights record of the government in which the Refah Party took part was arguably much better than those before it.

Given these four strands of the critiques, it may be asked why the Court made its pronouncements on *shari'a* in the way that it so strikingly did? One way of seeing the decision is that it is one of the Court's 'constitutional judgments' setting out the fundamental parameters of the ECHR. It was drawing a line in the sand to give states directions on how to achieve and maintain compatibility with the Convention. If starting from a general *shari'a* based system would always be problematic, then this necessarily strengthens the hands of those arguing for more secular based regimes. As previously noted, one of the historical motivations of the Convention system was to stop small-scale violations becoming larger systemic ones. The Court may also have taken a kind of judicial notice of what have undeniably been major issues in terms of the compatibility of the content of *shari'a* law with international human rights law.[47]

THE WRONG QUESTION: GENERAL ADOPTION OF SHARI'A LAW?

Another response is to suggest that discussing the general adoption of a *shari'a* law system is to address the wrong question because it is not at all clear who, beyond some radical Islamist groups, is asking for it. Rowan Williams, then Archbishop of Canterbury, made it clear that he was advocating no such thing in his lecture in 2008 on 'Civil and Religious Law in England'.[48] The acute sensitivities of affording any greater legal accommodation and recognition to Islamic customs and practices (*shari'a* law) within the law of the land at all were exemplified by the extremely hostile reactions to the idea that there might even have been such a suggestion by the Archbishop. At least part of the hostility was founded on the view that such a step would inevitably lead to some members of religious communities, and women in particular, having their national and international human rights restricted to a much greater extent than at present. The Archbishop himself recognised this. He subsequently sought to make clear that he had made no proposals for *shari'a* in either the lecture or in interviews, and certainly did not call for its introduction

---

[47] See the works referred to in n 15.
[48] Supra, pp 20–33; P Shah, 'Transforming to accommodate? Reflections on the shari'a debate in Britain' in R Grillo, R Ballard, A Ferrari, AJ Hoekema, M Maussen and P Shah (eds), *Legal Practice and Cultural Diversity* (Farnham, 2009), pp 73–92. For further reflections arising from the lecture see R Ahdar and N Aroney (eds), *Shari'a in the West* (Oxford, 2010).

as some kind of parallel jurisdiction to the civil law. Further controversy followed after some perceived degree of support for accommodation from Lord Phillips (subsequently President of the Supreme Court), although that speech was very cautiously expressed and strongly stressed both existing equality before the law and that any sanctions for a failure to comply with the agreed terms of mediation would be drawn from the laws of England and Wales.[49]

Some of the critical response to the Archbishop's lecture was to the implicit suggestion that British Muslims want a more general adoption of *shari'a* law when there is little evidence to suggest that they do. A report on British Muslims in 2007 entitled 'Living apart together: British Muslims and the paradox of multiculturalism' served to illustrate how complex issues of identity are and how difficult it is to frame policies around them.[50] It revealed growing religiosity in the younger generation, and a more politicised interest in religion. Fifty-nine per cent of Muslims would prefer to live under British law, compared with 28 per cent who would prefer to live under *shari'a* law. Views changed with age: 37 per cent of sixteen to twenty-four year-olds preferred *shari'a* compared with 17 per cent of those over fifty-five years old. There was considerable diversity amongst Muslims, with many adopting a more secular approach to their religion. The report argued that there was a conflict within British Islam between what it termed as a 'moderate majority' who accepted the norms of Western democracy and a growing minority who did not. Some Muslims were turning to religion as part of a search for meaning and community. Interestingly, despite widespread concerns about Islamophobia, 84 per cent of Muslims believed they had been treated fairly in UK society; and 28 per cent of Muslims believed that the authorities in Britain went over the top in trying not to offend Muslims. Comparative research has also revealed that for state policies to be more accommodating does not necessarily result in reduced religious tensions between Muslims and the state.[51]

---

[49] NA Phillips, 'Equality before the law', East London Muslim Centre, 3 July 2008, [2008] L&J 75. Lord Phillips reflects further on the theme in 'Equal before the Law', infra pp 286–93.
[50] See M Mirza, A Senthilkumaran and Z Ja'far, 'Living Apart Together: British Muslims and the paradox of multiculturalism', accessible at <http://www.policyexchange.org.uk/assets/Living_Apart_Together_text.pdf>. See also Hellyer, *Muslims of Europe*, supra n 2, pp 13–76, 143–75; D Mogahed and Z Nyriki, 'Reinventing integration', (2007) 29 HIR, accessible at <http://hir.harvard.edu/courting-africa/reinventing-integration>, (on the need for an evidence-based understanding of European Muslims); S Akbardazeh and J Roose, 'Muslims, multiculturalism and the question of the silent majority', (2011) 31 JIMMA 309.
[51] See S Fetzer and JC Soper, *Muslims and the State in Britain, France and Germany* (Cambridge, 2005); and C Joppke, 'Limits of integration policy: Britain and her Muslims', (2009) 35 JEMS 453.

ACCOMMODATION BY THE ADOPTION OF PARTICULAR RULES OF *SHARI'A* LAW

If one accepts the ECtHR's general concerns as to an Islamic system, then an alternative approach might be to argue for adoption by European states of particular rules of *shari'a* law.[52] It can be argued that the approach via particular rules is more realistic in the sense of being consonant with the lived experience of Muslims, what has been described as the hybridisation of 'lived legal cultures'.[53] Ours is not a world of binary opposites: state law or religious law, religious or secular, traditional or modern.[54] Modern identity is too complex to be captured by such stereotypes. There is also some Islamic jurisprudence that deals with the status of Muslims living in foreign lands, which in this sense are any non-Muslim states.[55] The practical and political reality would be that the debate would be focused on a softer European version or, for example, different national modified versions of *shari'a* (a kind of *shari'a*-lite).[56]

To some extent this approach returns to the issues that have been addressed above on the indeterminacy of the *shari'a* and the range of sources and schools of *shari'a* law. It is not too difficult to outline a series of major rules or practices which some Islamic religious authorities and some states consider as being consistent with *shari'a* law, but which would be inconsistent with the ECHR and its Protocols. In many of these areas there is debate over what the rules actually are and, even when they are asserted to be consistent with *shari'a* law, they may be tempered in practice or now governed by clear secular state law which imposes particular

---

[52] For historical reasons Islamic legal norms are applied in Greece to the Muslims of Turkish and Bulgarian origin in Thrace but the judicial jurisdiction is optional, see K Tsitselikis, 'The legal status of Islam in Greece', (2004) 44(3) *Die Welt des Islams (Shari'a in Europe)* 402; *Serif v Greece* (1999) 31 EHRR 561.

[53] See P Shah, *Legal Pluralism in Conflict* (London, 2005), p 4. See also AA An-Na'im, 'The compatability dialectic: mediating the legitimate co-existence of Islamic law and state law', (2010) 73 MLR 22.

[54] In survey results published in 2005, 70 per cent of British Muslim leaders came out in favour of 'legal dualism', that is, of applying religious *shari'a* rules in private law, such as marriage and divorce: J Klausen, *The Islamic Challenge* (New York, 2005), p 192.

[55] See Hellyer, *Muslims of Europe*, supra n 2, pp 59–99; and C Joppke, 'Liberalism and Muslim integration: through the Prism of Headscarf Restrictions in Europe', accessible at <http://131.130.1.78/veil/Home3/index.php?id¼36,79,0,0,1,0>.

[56] See M Rohe, 'The formation of a European *Shari'a*' in J Malik (ed), *Muslims in Europe* (Munster, 2004), p 161 who evidences a range of opinions of the European Council for Expert Opinions and Studies; JS Nielsen and L Christoffersen, *Shari'a as Discourse: legal traditions and the encounter with Europe* (Farnham, 2010); L Fulton, 'Islamic Law: Europe's *Shari'a* debate', accessible at <http://www.euro-islam.info/key-issues/islamic-law/>.

restrictions or some degree of judicial control.[57] In many instances the modifications imposed by secular law represent a gradual move towards recognition of the equality of women specifically or human rights more generally. However, to the extent that they do exist in modern *shari'a* law, the following rules or practices would clearly be problematic in ECHR terms: severe punishments for crimes, including executions or limb amputations; stoning or imprisoning women for adultery;[58] the criminalisation of sexual activities outside of marriage;[59] and for homosexual or lesbian activities;[60] non-recognition of the transgendered;[61] certain rules concerning marriage and polygamy, even with more modern legislative and administrative limitations and restrictions that make polygamy difficult;[62] honour killings or attacks;[63] *talaq*, ie unilateral divorce by men, without the consent of the wife, even with more modern legislative and administrative limitations and restrictions on it;[64] allowing women divorce with their husband's consent but only upon the basis of foregoing financial benefits;[65] child

---

[57] 'In Islamic countries, there is a trend towards permitting judicial intervention in the breakdown of marriage, and the courtroom is increasingly becoming "a negotiation area" for conjugal conflicts', A Madera, 'Juridical bonds of marriage for Jewish and Islamic women', (2009) 11 Ecc LJ 51, p 63.

[58] See *Jabari v Turkey*, App no 40035/98, [2000] ECHR 369 (real risk of the applicant being subjected to treatment contrary to Article 3 of the ECHR if she were to be returned to Iran where she might face stoning for adultery).

[59] Harris et al., *Law of the European Convention on Human Rights*, supra n 13, pp 370–1.

[60] See *HJ (Iran) (FC) v Secretary of State for the Home Department; HT (cameroon)(FC) v secretary of state for the Home Department* [2010] UKSC 31 (to compel a homosexual person to pretend that their sexuality did not exist, or that the behaviour by which it manifested itself can be suppressed, was to deny him his fundamental right to be who he was).

[61] See Harris et al., *Law of the European Convention on Human Rights*, supra n 13, pp 385–6, 552–3.

[62] Under classical *shari'a* law, a man is permitted to marry up to four wives at any one time. See Rehman, supra n 8, especially 'The shari'ah, Islamic family laws and international human rights law', 113–18. On the shadow of polygamy as a powerful bargaining tool see P Fournier, 'In the (Canadian) shadow of Islamic law: translating mahr as a bargaining endowment' in R Moon (ed), *Law and Religious Pluralism in Canada* (Vancouver, 2008). See also *Serife Yigit v Turkey*, App no 3976/05, (2010) (no violation of ECHR in the Turkish courts' refusal to award the applicant social security benefits based on the entitlements of her deceased partner, with whom she had contracted a religious but not a civil marriage). In a concurring opinion, Judge Kovler stated that it was 'wiser to refrain from making any assessment of the complexity of the rules of Islamic marriage, rather than portraying it in a reductive and highly subjective manner'.

[63] See H Carter, 'Parents of Shafilea Ahmed deny "honour killing" of daughter', *The Guardian*, 20 December 2011. The parents were convicted in August 2012, *R v Iftikhar Ahmed and Farzana Ahmed*. Admittedly, this is an issue on which the basis may be cultural, or more cultural than religious, but that is a divide which is often not clear with respect to *shari'a* rules. The issue is by no means particular to Muslims.

[64] See Rehman, 'The *Shari'ah*, Islamic family laws and international human rights law', supra n 8.

[65] For a call for judges to stop granting civil divorces to separating Muslim couples unless they had already been through a religious divorce, see M Beckford, 'Butler-Sloss urges courts to recognise *Shari'a* divorces', *The Daily Telegraph*, 27 December 2008. The wording of the Divorce (Religious Marriages) Act 2002 (UK) is arguably wide enough to cover all religious marriages; see further R Griffith-Jones, 'Religious rights and the public interest', infra p 201. See also P Fournier, 'In the

custody only for fathers when children reach the age of seven;[66] lack of succession rights for women, illegitimate children and female children;[67] penalties for apostasy;[68] and the absence of adoption.[69]

ADOPTING *SHARI'A* IN THE SENSE OF ALLOWING MORE RELIGIOUSLY BASED OPT-OUTS

Bernard Jackson, one of the world's leading experts on Jewish law, has suggested that the Archbishop's primary interest in his 2008 lecture was actually in building 'a religious coalition, led by the Church of England (as the 'established' Church), in favour of exemptions from secular law on grounds of religious conscience'.[70] The result would be more religiously based opt-outs or exemptions from generally applicable laws. An unwillingness to extend the principle to cover analogous issues of religious conscience would cast doubt on the justifiability of that exemption.

The case for exemptions

The case for religiously based exemptions can be explained in a number of ways.[71] First, they are necessary for persons of faith to participate in social, economic and political life. Otherwise such persons cannot participate on equal terms and so will be marginalised. Second, religion is a source of value for many community members. They may not comprehend the notion of a distinction between religious and secular views. In any event the latter are

---

(Canadian) shadow of Islamic law', supra n 62, on how a neoliberal vision of choice can ignore the socioeconomic and distributive background of women and minority groups; *Bruker v Marcovitz* (2007) SCC 54.

[66] Given the description of this system in *EM (Lebanon)*, supra n 29, then it would be impossible to argue for such a system in the UK itself.

[67] See Harris et al., *Law of the European Convention*, supra n 13, p 594. See also S Ishaque, 'Islamic principles on adoption', (2008) 22 Int J Law Pol Fam 39.

[68] See M Adil, 'Restrictions in freedom of religion in Malaysia: a conceptual analysis with special reference to the law of apostasy', (2007) 4 MWJHR 14. Apostasy is criminalised in more than fifteen states. Under Article 9 of the ECHR, there is an express right for an individual to 'change his religion'. Archbishop Williams, 'Civil and religious law in England: a religious perspective', supra p 27, noted that changing from the Islamic religion was originally seen as treason but that it cannot rationally be seen as such now.

[69] *Shari'a* law does not recognise adoption as such: see Ishaque, 'Islamic principles on adoption', supra n 67. The Adoption and Children Act 2002 took account of this by introducing 'special guardianship' as an alternative to adoption.

[70] B Jackson, '"Transformative accommodation" and religious law', (2009) 11 Ecc LJ 131. See also Hellyer, *Muslims of Europe*, supra n 2, p 191, on the shared values of Christianity and Islam.

[71] See R Moon, 'Introduction' in R Moon (ed), *Law and Religious Pluralism in Canada* (Vancouver, 2008), p 1; *Alberta v Hutterian Brethren of Wilson Colony* (2009) SCC 37; Y Nehushtan, 'Religious conscientious exemptions', (2011) 30 *Law and Philosophy* 143 (arguing for an anti-religious approach).

perceived as anti-religious rather than neutral. Third, not to grant exemptions is to privilege a secular worldview. Fourth, exemptions make space for, and give visibility to, different moral commitments and associations and reflect the normative authority of faith communities as alternatives or counterpoints to modern states. Fifth, religious beliefs and associations have historically and philosophically be seen as worthy of special protection. They reflect the cultural identity and membership of individuals and groups. To protect them ultimately reflects human dignity and worth, autonomy and self-determination. Sixth, in many cases the particular religions constitute a minority and the generally applicable law reflects the social, political and legal constructions of the dominant majority.

The Archbishop discussed the kind of protection needed for religious conscience against certain unforeseen professional requirements which would compromise religious discipline or belief.[72] He noted that there would be a need for access to a recognised authority acting for a religious group to decide the relative seriousness of conscience-related claims, a way of distinguishing purely cultural habits from seriously rooted matters of faith and discipline, and for distinguishing uninformed prejudice from religious prescription. He cited the increasing role played by the Islamic Shari'a Council in this context. He specifically challenged the assumption that if a right or liberty is granted there is a corresponding duty upon every individual to 'activate' this whenever called upon. For him the criterion was whether a communal jurisdiction actively interfered with liberties guaranteed by the wider society in such a way as definitively to block access to the exercise of those liberties. In many cases, given the plural character of society, there would be no denial to anyone inside or outside the community of access to that right. He cited the conscience clause in the Abortion Act 1967 (UK) as an example of a principle that could be extended in other areas. That clear legislative provision is central to any argument of principle on religiously based opt-outs from generally applicable laws. For example, when a Christian registrar was demoted after refusing to preside over a civil partnership, she asked why, if doctors can opt out of performing abortions on conscience grounds, she could not opt out of civil partnerships?[73]

---

[72] Williams, 'Civil and religious law in England', supra p 21. The argument has been put even more strongly by the former Archbishop of Canterbury, Lord Carey, 'Christians are being persecuted', *The Guardian*, 14 April 2012.

[73] Cited in U Khan, 'Christian registrar [Theresa Davies] demoted to receptionist after she refused to preside over gay "marriages"', *The Daily Telegraph*, 22 June 2009. On the scope of the exemptions from having to 'participate' in abortions, see *R (Doogan and Wood) v Greater Glasgow and Clyde Health Board* [2012] Scots CSOH 32.

The case against exemptions

In large part the case against exemptions simply constitutes a rejection of the elements of the case for it. Accommodating religious exemptions may compromise the law's public purpose and its social effectiveness. It can undermine other fundamental rights or social values and the human dignity of those affected. Those of faith are equally entitled to participate but cannot expect to dominate. Religious beliefs and associations should not be privileged. Non-religious 'beliefs' and convictions should not be entitled to lesser protection. Generally applicable laws may reflect religious origins but should now be understood to reflect modern cultural habits and modes of organisation. Exemptions may have complex and subtle distributional impacts and consequences on minorities within religious groups, for example, on women.[74] With respect to the forty-seven members of the Council of Europe, exemptions from generally applicable laws also have to be tested for compliance with the ECHR, in terms both of the right to religion and of the other substantive articles, particularly its increasingly sophisticated jurisprudence on non-discrimination.[75] Non-discrimination does not require identical treatment. Indeed the ECtHR has made it clear that discrimination may also arise where states without an objective and reasonable justification fail to treat differently persons whose situations are significantly different.[76] However, there may be conflict between the prohibition of discrimination on grounds of religion or belief and the prohibition of discrimination on other grounds. Aileen McColgan has argued that such conflict was inevitable and that it was a mistake to protect religion and/or belief in like manner to grounds such as sex, race, sexual orientation and disability. While such protection is, at present, required by EU law, she suggested that legislation along these lines is not required by the Convention and that it is not justified by any special quality of religion. McColgan argues that requiring the accommodation of practices or beliefs categorised as 'religious' tends to perpetuate practices and beliefs which are problematic on equality and other grounds.[77] Similarly, Mark Freedland and Lucy Vickers argue that there has been a transition from a state of

---

[74] See Fournier, 'In the (Canadian) shadow of Islamic law', supra n 62, p 140.
[75] See Harris et al., *Law of the European Convention on Human Rights*, supra n 13, pp 577–615; R O'Connell, 'Cinderella comes to the ball: Article 14 and the right to non-discrimination in the ECHR', (2009) 29 *Legal studies* 211; S Stavros, 'Freedom of religion and claims for exemption from generally applicable, neutral laws: lessons from across the pond?', (1997) 6 EHRLR 607.
[76] See *Thlimmenos v Greece* (2001) 31 EHRR 15 (GC), para 44. The principle is commonly attributed to Aristotle.
[77] A McColgan, 'Class wars? Religion and (in)equality in the workplace', (2009) 38 ILJ 1.

religious tolerance to one of multi-culturalism and that this will raise increasingly difficult questions as to whether there is, or should be, a hierarchy of equality rights.[78] Sensitive and intelligent employment practices may resolve many practical problems but some may require weighing of claims that have at least an appearance of equal weight.

Cases have already arisen which put the different grounds of discrimination in conflict with each other.[79] In *Ladele v Islington London Borough Council and Liberty (Intervening)*,[80] Ms Ladele was a Christian registrar responsible for conducting civil marriages and, with the recognition in UK law of same-sex civil partnerships, such partnerships. She took the view that participation in same-sex civil partnerships was inconsistent with her disapproval, as a Christian, of homosexuality. Her employers had allowed her to avoid a requirement, of general application, that all registrars officiate at civil partnerships, but did require that, in common with all other registrars, she perform administrative, as distinct from ceremonial, functions in relation to such partnerships if required to do so.[81] Ladele's refusal to comply with the attenuated job requirements exposed her to the threat of disciplinary action and she was refused promotion and subjected to a number of other detriments including disciplinary proceedings, being required to carry out civil partnership duties and being described as homophobic. Ms Ladele's employers were under threat of sexual orientation discrimination claims by members of staff who had been made aware,

---

[78] See MR Freedland and L Vickers, 'Religious expression in the workplace in the United Kingdom', (2009) 30 Comp Lab L & Pol'y J 597. C McCrudden, 'Multiculturalism, freedom of religion, equality, and the British constitution: the JFS case considered', (2011) 9 *International Journal of Constitutional Law* 200, accessible at <http://ssrn.com/abstract=1701289>, argues that UK has reached the stage of 'post-multiculturalism'. See also L Vickers, 'Promoting equality or fostering resentment: the public sector equality duty and religion and belief', (2010) 30 *Legal Studies* 135.

[79] See also *McFarlane v Relate Avon Ltd* [2010] EWCA Civ 880: M, who believed that same-sex activity was sinful and that he should do nothing to endorse it, unsuccessfully claimed religious discrimination against his employer, which provided counselling services concerning sexual issues to heterosexual and homosexual couples; the employer was committed to non-discrimination on grounds of sexual orientation). *R (Eunice Johns and Owen Johns) v Derby City Council* [2011] EWHC 375 (Admin): applicants for local authority approval as foster carers who claimed that their views on sexuality were not a legitimate fostering concern and that the local authority's approach constituted religious discrimination failed to obtain permission to apply for judicial review. *Bull and Bull v Hall and Preddy* [2012] EWCA Civ 83: refusal of hotel owners, on grounds of Christian principles, to let double rooms to unmarried individuals, was direct discrimination on grounds of sexual orientation; the restriction on the hotel owners did not violate their rights under Articles 8, 9 and 14 of the ECHR. The Supreme Court, in August 2012, granted permission to appeal in *Bull and Bull*.

[80] UKEAT/453/08, [2009] ICR 387; [2009] IRLR 154. See A Hambler, 'A no-win situation for public officials with faith convictions', (2010) 12 Ecc LJ 3. Another example is *Azmi v Kirklees MBC* [2007] ICR 1154: a school had not discriminated against a female Muslim language support teacher in a school who insisted on wearing a veil when assisting with the teaching of small children.

[81] Interestingly, a Muslim registrar in another borough had agreed to such a compromise.

by Ladele, of her views on same-sex relationships and who took the view that her refusal to be involved in civil partnerships was indicative of homophobia and breached the employer's dignity at work policy.[82] An employment tribunal accepted Ms Ladele's claim that she had been the victim of direct discrimination on grounds of her religious beliefs, but this was reversed by the Employment Appeal Tribunal (EAT) before which her claims of direct or indirect discrimination failed.[83] The Court of Appeal upheld the view of the EAT.[84] However, it went even further. It held that the impact of the Equality Act (Sexual Orientation) Regulations 2007[85] was that once Ms Ladele had been designated as a 'civil partnership registrar', Islington were not merely entitled to require her to perform civil partnerships but were obliged to do so. The prohibition of discrimination took precedence over any right which a person would otherwise have, by virtue of his or her religious belief or faith, to discriminate on the ground of sexual orientation.[86] The practical significance of this is that what an employer might have considered to be an exercise in reasonable accommodation arguably becomes unlawful.[87]

These kinds of conflicts can raise very complex issues for legislators and the individuals involved. They can sometimes be resolved by common sense, good practice and a sense of proportionality. However, sometimes a hard choice has to be made and one principle or right is given preference over another. A difficult example arose with the implementation of the EU Directive covering discrimination on grounds of sexual orientation to the provision of adoption services by the UK Catholic Adoption Society (CAS). When the UK Parliament was considering the Sexual Orientation Regulations in Parliament early in 2007, the CAS sought an exemption on the basis that their religious views conflicted with providing adoption services to homosexuals and lesbians. The then Archbishop of Westminster, Cormac Murphy O'Connor, wrote to the Prime Minister, Tony Blair, seeking a statutory exemption to permit Catholic adoption agencies to

---

[82] Islington Borough Council is in the top twenty of 'gay-friendly' employers in the UK.
[83] See Hambler, 'A no-win situation', supra n 80.   [84] [2009] EWCA Civ 1357.
[85] Statutory Instrument 2007/1263.
[86] *Ladele*, supra n 80, para 69. See L Vickers, 'Religious discrimination in the workplace: an emerging hierarchy?', (2010) 12 Ecc LJ 280, who observes that the employer was under no obligation to offer L the least disadvantageous accommodation available and questions whether it was proportionate to designate L as a 'civil partnership registrar' in the first place.
[87] See L Vickers, 'Religious discrimination in the workplace', supra n 86, 293. The matter is not clear. The Court of Appeal in *Ladele* noted that some registration authorities had decided not to designate registrars who shared L's beliefs as civil partnership registrars and stated that 'such decisions may well be lawful', para 75. That arguably leaves room for a degree of accommodation.

apply a policy of refusing to assess same sex couples as potential adopters. He submitted that 'it would be unreasonable, unnecessary and unjust discrimination against Catholics for the Government to insist that if they wish to continue to work with local authorities, Catholic adoption agencies must act against the teaching of the Church and their own consciences by being obliged in law to provide such a service'.[88] He suggested that if the exemption was not granted, the agencies might be forced to close.

The government refused the Archbishop's request. While it expressed some sympathy for their position, it ultimately took what is considered to be the position of principle that there could be 'no exemptions for faith-based adoption agencies offering publicly-funded services from regulations which prevent discrimination'.[89] However, it did grant a temporary exemption to permit the agencies to continue to apply such a policy until the end of December 2008 in order to provide time for them to decide how to adapt to the new regulatory environment. Over that period, the majority of the Catholic agencies succeeded in finding a way of accommodating the change, in some cases by transferring the adoption work to other agencies and in some cases by offering adoption services in accordance with the new regulations. Three agencies (Westminster, Leeds and Birmingham) announced their intention to continue to apply discriminatory policies. However, in 2009, the Charity Commissioners and the Charities Tribunal refused the three agencies permission to change their charitable objects in order to be able to refuse gay couples. In 2010 the Leeds diocese successfully appealed on the basis that it could, in principle, rely on an exemption in the regulations when 'the restriction of benefits to persons of that sexual orientation is imposed by reason of or on the grounds of the provisions of the charitable instrument'.[90] On reconsideration the Charity Commission maintained its view that on the facts of the case the diocese could not rely on the exemption.[91] The issue has been appealed.

---

[88] M Mackay 'Cardinal tells Blair of opposition to gay adoption', *Christian Today*, 23 January 2007, accessible at <http://www.christiantoday.com/article/cardinal.tells.blair.of.opposition.to.gay.adoption/9242.htm>.

[89] Tony Blair, 'No place for discrimination in society', PM Statement, 29 January 2007, accessible at <http://www.number10.gov.uk/Page10869>.

[90] *Catholic Care (Diocese of Leeds) v Charity Commission for England and Wales* [2010] EWHC 520 (Ch).

[91] See Charity Commission for England and Wales, *Catholic Care (Diocese of Leeds) Decision of 21 July 2010, on Application for Consent to a Change of Objects under s. 64 of the Charities Act 1993*, accessible at <http://www.charity-commission.gov.uk/Library/about_us/catholic_care.pdf>. The Diocese lost an appeal to the First-Tier Tribunal in April 2011. A subsequent appeal to the Upper Tribunal was lost in November 2012.

Existing exemptions

The case for exemptions has to be premised on the view that there is something special about religion that makes it more deserving. The basis of what makes it special can be a combination of insights drawn from philosophy, history, politics, traditions, culture, the treatment of minorities and a particular view of the contribution of religion to community or society. In any event, UK and EU law already contain a number of exemptions from generally applicable laws that are either religiously based or would cover religious reasons.[92] No person shall be under a duty to 'participate in any treatment' authorised by the Abortion Act 1967 to which they have a conscientious objection. There are exemptions for Sikh turbans on building sites and on motorcycles. A range of exemptions that were contained in a variety of legislative instruments – including the Sex Discrimination Act 1975, Employment Equality (Religion or Belief) Regulations 2003, Employment Equality (Sexual Orientation) Regulations 2003 and 2007, and the Equality Act 2006 – have been consolidated in the Equality Act 2010.[93] They relate to aspects of charities (section 193), civil partnerships on religious premises (section 202: no obligation on religious organisations to host civil partnerships if they do not wish to do so; the Government is consulting on the appropriate regulations), schools (schedule 3, part 2 and schedule 11),[94] immigration (schedule 3, part 4 and schedule 18), marriage of persons reasonably believed to have acquired gender under the Gender Recognition Act 2004 (schedule 3, part 4), services related to religion (schedule 3, part 7), occupational requirements (schedule 9), institutions with a religious ethos (schedule 12, part 2), specified educational appointments (schedule 22), organisations relating to religion or belief (schedule 23). Such exemptions raise complex legal and religious questions relating to their justification and scope.[95] Some of the

---

[92] See L Vickers, *Religious Freedom, Religious Discrimination and the Workplace* (Oxford, 2007); R Sandberg and N Doe, 'Religious exemptions in discrimination law', (2007) 66 CLJ 302; L Woodhead, *'Religion or Belief: identifying issues and priorities'*, Equality and Human Rights Commission Report no 48, 2009, accessible at <http://www.equalityhumanrights.com/uploaded_files/research/research_report_48__religion_or_belief.pdf>.

[93] 2010 c 15. The main provisions came into force on 1 October 2010. See <http://www.equalities.gov.uk/equality_act_2010.aspx>.

[94] Faith schools have no exemption from race discrimination even if the relevant rules are grounded in religious doctrine: see *R (On the Application of E) v Governing Body of JFS and the Admissions Appeal Panel of JFS and Others* [2009] UKSC 15. See C McCrudden, 'Multiculturalism', supra n 78; N Harris, *Education, Law, Diversity* (Oxford, 2007).

[95] See MP Ferretti and L Strnadová (eds), 'Rules and exemptions: the politics and difference within liberalism', (2009) 15 Res Publica 213; M Beckford, 'Equality Bill "dangerously" trying to force

most controversial provisions of what became the Equality Act 2010 concerned the scope of exemptions from equality/non-discrimination laws on the basis of religion or belief. The EU is considering a proposed Directive on implementing the principle of equal treatment between persons irrespective of religion or belief, disability, age or sexual orientation. The objective of the legislation would be to extend the scope of existing equal treatment rights to protect against discrimination based on religion or belief, disability, age or sexual orientation in certain non-work situations.[96]

In terms of 'transformative accommodation', Archbishop Williams referred in his lecture to 'aspects of marital law, the regulation of financial transactions and authorised structures of mediation and conflict resolution'. Lord Phillips subsequently agreed that it was not very radical to advocate embracing *shari'a* law in the context of family disputes and noted that our system already went a long way towards accommodating the Archbishop's suggestion.[97] It was possible for persons entering into a contract to agree that it shall be governed by a law other than English law. As for the 'the regulation of financial transactions', existing regulations accommodate financial institutions or products that comply with *shari'a* principles. As a conventional mortgage offends *shari'a* law, UK banks have devised alternative system of financing house purchases and investments conformable to *shari'a* principles.[98]

OPT-OUTS OR EXEMPTIONS FOR MUSLIMS?

Many of the opt-outs or exemptions considered in the previous section are available to Muslims as much as to any other religious believer. What other exemptions or opt-outs might Muslims desire and what criteria should govern their acceptability? What if Muslim doctors were unwilling to treat women or to give them advice on abortion or contraception, or to

---

religious belief behind closed doors, Bishops warn', *The Daily Telegraph*, 15 January 2010. On the narrow interpretation of such exemptions, see *R (On the Application of Amicus MSF and Others) v Secretary of State for Trade and Industry and Others* [2004] EWHC 860 (Admin).

[96] See Commission of the European Communities, 'Proposal for a Council Directive on implementing the principle of equal treatment between persons irrespective of religion or belief, disability, age or sexual orientation', COM/2008/0426 final, accessible at <http://eur-lex.europa.eu/LexUriServ/LexUriServ.do?uri=COM:2008:0426:FIN:EN:PDF>. There is no current prospect of achieving unanimity, see Council of the European Union, 'Progress Report of the Presidency', Doc 8724/12, 10 May 2012, accessible at <http://register.consilium.europa.eu/pdf/en/12/st08/st08724.en.12.pdf>.

[97] Phillips, 'Equality before the law', supra n 49.

[98] See Finance Act 2003, ss 72–3. See generally JG Ercanbrack, 'The regulation of Islamic finance in the United Kingdom', (2011) 13 Ecc LJ 69, and I Edge, 'Islamic finance, alternative dispute resolution and family law: developments towards legal pluralism?', infra pp 119–21.

treat persons with alcohol or drug addictions or sexually transmitted diseases? Or even to be taught about such problems at medical school?[99] Unless there were a legislative exemption, in this and similar cases there would be issues with the professional regulatory authorities. The General Medical Council in the UK has made it clear that doctors cannot opt out of any part of their training for religious reasons.[100] Prejudicing patients' treatment on account of their gender or their responsibility for their condition ran counter to the basic principles of ethical medical practice. Interestingly, medical students who objected to such training did not receive support from the Islamic Medical Association which stressed the difference between learning about medicine and practising it.[101] In the UK it is understood that Sainsburys and Boots (both major retailers) allow their pharmacists to refuse to sell the morning-after contraceptive pill to customers if they have 'ethical' concerns. It is difficult to defend that practice if the result was to deny customer access to the morning-after pill, for example, because only one pharmacist is on duty or there were no other reasonably accessible local pharmacies. That would, in the language of the Archbishop, have blocked access. In October 2006, Lloyds Chemist was forced to apologise to a mother after a Muslim pharmacist refused her a morning-after pill on religious grounds.[102] Could safe substitutes for illegal drugs or tobacco similarly be refused on the basis of religious objections? How should the reported issue of blind passengers being ordered off buses or refused taxi rides because Muslim drivers or passengers object to their 'unclean' guide dogs be dealt with?[103] It presents an issue of religious belief clashing with disability discrimination.

What if there is a Muslim employee who does not want to work on a Friday afternoon? In ECHR jurisprudence there is a very strong non-interference

---

[99] The example is drawn from D Martin, 'Muslim medical students refuse to learn about alcohol or sexual diseases', *The Daily Mail*, 7 October 2007. There have been reports of students, including Muslim students of medicine, refusing to attend lectures on evolution. See A Gayathri, 'Creationist Muslim medical students say no to evolution lectures' *International Business Times*, 29 November 2011.

[100] See also *McClintock v Department of Constitutional Affairs* [2008] IRLR 29 (EAT) (judge resigned because he might have been required to place children for adoption with gay and lesbian couples). The EAT held that magistrates must apply the law of the land as their oath required, and could not opt out of cases on the grounds that they may have to apply or give effect to laws to which they have a moral or other principled objection.

[101] In *Pichon and Sajous v France*, App. no 49853/99 (2 October 2001), the European Court of Human Rights held that the conviction of pharmacists for refusing, for religious reasons, to supply contraceptives lawfully prescribed by doctors did not raise an issue under Article 9 of the ECHR. The UK has relied heavily on this case in the four religious discrimination cases heard by the ECtHR in 2012, infra n. 112.

[102] Reported in Martin, 'Muslim medical students', supra n 99.

[103] See A Dolan, 'Muslim bus drivers refuse to let guide dogs on board', *The Daily Mail Online*, 19 July 2010, accessible at <http://www.dailymail.co.uk/news/article-1295749/Muslim-bus-drivers-refuse-let-guide-dogs-board.html>.

principle: that is, in many cases it is not accepted that there has actually been an interference with the individual's right to religion in such a case.[104] It has been appreciated that the ECHR's 'non-interference' principle can be harsh in its application.[105] The ECHR institutions have readily accepted constraints imposed upon religious individuals in their engagement with the wider world, even where those constraints have prevented them from reconciling their religious convictions with their occupational or educational ambitions.[106] However, under the Employment Equality (Religion or Belief) Regulations 2003,[107] a refusal to allow time and facilities for religious or belief observance could be indirectly discriminatory. Employers who refuse would have to demonstrate a legitimate aim and proportionality and how such requests (which could be on different equality grounds) are prioritised. They would need to consider whether reasonable adjustments could be made.[108] The Guidance from the Arbitration and Conciliation Service (ACAS) on 'Religion and belief in the workplace' gave some practical examples.[109]

How should employers deal with Muslim shop assistants who do not want to sell alcohol or bibles or tobacco or to handle pork?[110] Should employers have a duty of reasonable accommodation in such cases?[111] A number of religious cases concerning the UK have recently been referred to the European Court of Human Rights. These include *Ladele* and

---

[104] See *Kalac v Turkey* (1997) 27 EHRR 522.
[105] See the majority view in *Copsey v WWB Devon Clays Ltd* [2005] EWCA Civ 932; and the views of Lords Scott, Hoffmann and Bingham in *R (On the Application of Begum (By Her Litigation Friend, Rahman)) v Headteacher and Governors of Denbigh High School* [2006] UKHL 15.
[106] See *Ahmad v UK* (1982) 4 EHRR 126; *Stedman v UK* (1997) 23 EHRR CD 168.
[107] SI 2003/1660, accessible at <http://www.opsi.gov.uk/si/si2003/20031660.htm#29>. Now replaced by the Equality Act 2010, supra n 93.
[108] See Arbitration and Conciliation Council (ACAS), *A Guide for Employers and Employees: religion and belief in the workplace*, at para 4.9 and p 34, accessible at <http://www.acas.org.uk/CHttpHandler. ashx?id¼107&p¼40>. For an excellent example see *Cherfi v G4S Securities Services Ltd* [2011] EqLR 825 (EAT) (a refusal to let C, a Muslim, leave a security site on a Friday to attend a mosque in Finsbury Park was held to be a proportionate means of achieving a legitimate aim; C had refused alternative arrangements to work over the weekend).
[109] ACAS, *A guide for employers and employee* supra n 108, p 19.
[110] The examples are drawn from M Brown, 'Outcry as Muslim M&S worker refuses to sell "unclean" Bible book', *The Daily Express*, 15 January 2008, accessible at <http://www.express.co.uk/posts/view/31491/Outcry-as-Muslim-M-S-worker-refuse>.
[111] McColgan, 'Class wars?', supra n 77, 23–4, supports such a duty. See also Vickers, *Religious Freedom*, supra n 92, pp 19–23; and A Lawson, *Disability and Equality Law in Britain: the role of reasonable adjustment* (Oxford, 2008). In Canada the duty of reasonable accommodation has been developed to become more stringent and will not be met unless due hardship can be proved. The duty is based in the concept of human dignity, see Moon, *Law and Religious Pluralism in Canada*, supra n 71, and C McCrudden, 'Dignity and religion', infra pp 94–106.

McFarlane, noted above, and *Eweida* and *Chaplin*, concerning employees wishing to wear a Christian cross and crucifix respectively at work.[112] In each case the applicants complained, *inter alia*, that domestic law failed adequately to protect their right to manifest their religion, contrary to Article 9 of the ECHR, taken alone or in conjunction with Article 14. The UK submitted to the ECtHR that none of the four cases (including wearing a cross (*Eweida*) or a crucifix (*Chaplin*)) concerned a manifestation of their religion or belief, and in any event that there were no interferences with their Article 9 ECHR rights. In terms of the balance in *Ladele* and *McFarlane* between individuals' rights not to be discriminated against because of their sexual orientation and the right to manifest religious beliefs, the UK government acknowledged that there was a difficult balance which had to be struck. In its view, determining the circumstances in which individual religious beliefs should give way to wider public interests, especially on the question of discrimination because of sexual orientation, was a matter in which individual states should be accorded a wide margin of appreciation, in particular where a decision had been taken by a democratically elected legislature as to how the competing interests should be balanced. It is notable that the UK Equality and Human Rights Commission has intervened in the cases (along with a number of other intervenors). The Commission submitted that in the cases of *Eweida* and *Chaplin* the Courts may not have given sufficient weight to Article 9(2) of the ECHR; and in the cases of *Ladele* and *McFarlane* that the domestic courts came to the correct conclusions. It argued (i) that the way existing human rights and equality law had been interpreted by judges was insufficient to protect freedom of religion or belief; (ii) that judges had interpreted the law too narrowly in religion or belief discrimination claims; (iii) that the courts had set the bar too high for someone to prove that they had been discriminated against because of their religion or belief; and (iv) that it was possible to accommodate expression of religion alongside the rights of people who were not religious and the needs of businesses.[113] In sum this equates to some form of a doctrine of reasonable accommodation.[114] It would be more

---

[112] *Nadia Eweida and Shirley Chaplin v United Kingdom*, App no 48420/10 [2011] ECHR 738. *Ladele and McFarlane v United Kingdom* (App nos 51671/10, 36516/10) and *Eweida and Chaplin v United Kingdom* (App nos 48420/10, 59842/10, [2011] ECHR 738). The webcast of this hearing, 4 September 2012, can be viewed on the website of the ECtHR.

[113] See Equality and Human Rights Commission, 'Commission proposes "reasonable accommodation" for religion or belief is needed', 11 July 2011, accessible at <http://www.equalityhumanrights.com/news/2011/july/commission-proposes-reasonable-accommodation-for-religion-or-belief-is-needed/>. See also Carey, 'Christians are being persecuted', supra n 72.

[114] There is extensive comparative jurisprudence on reasonable accommodation in Canada and the US. See G Moon, 'From equal treatment to appropriate treatment: what lessons can Canadian equality

difficult for employers, for example, to meet this test than the current proportionality test applied under discrimination law or as part of Article 9 of the ECHR. Some employers have positively sought to accommodate such objections. It has been reported that Islamic checkout staff at Sainsburys who refuse to sell alcohol are allowed to opt out of handling bottles and cans of drink by calling other staff to take their place.[115] Staff who had refused to work stacking shelves with wine, beer and spirits had been found alternative, and seemingly equivalent, roles in the company. Should it be more problematic and open to challenge if they had been demoted or denied promotion opportunities?

Opt-outs are not a free for all. Claims for religiously grounded exemptions have to be judged on their individual merits against their societal impact. Schools are a site of particular importance for religious teaching. There are over 160 Muslim schools in the UK. A Muslim Council of Great Britain Report in 2007 entitled 'Towards greater understanding: meeting the needs of Muslim pupils in state schools'[116] called for special considerations for Muslims in almost every aspect of school life: collective worship, PE, dance, swimming, exams, school meals, sex education and parents' evenings. While non-Muslim children should learn about Islam, students from Muslim families should have the right to withdraw from any lessons dealing with Christianity or other faiths. The Muslim Council of Britain submitted that special treatment was necessary to avoid Muslim children from feeling left out of school lessons and activities. However, separating children in these various ways at such a young age would mean that they would grow up with less and less understanding and knowledge of each other. Trevor Phillips, the then Chair of the Commission for Equality and Human Rights, has warned against sleepwalking into segregation.[117] Given concerns at the existing elements of segregation within the general education system, for example, by the operation of selective and faith schools, this would be walking into further segregation with one's eyes wide open.

---

law on dignity and on reasonable accommodation teach the United Kingdom?', (2006) 6 EHRLR 695; CF Stychin, 'Faith in the future: sexuality, religion and the public sphere', (2009) 29 OJLS 729; D Schiek, L Waddington and M Bell (eds), *Cases, Materials and Texts on National, Supranational and International Non-discrimination Law* (Oxford, 2007), pp 629–756. For an excellent analysis of the concept of reasonable accommodation in a number of jurisdictions, see E Bribosia, J Ringelheim and I Rorive, 'Reasonable accommodation for religious minorities: a promising concept for European antidiscrimination law?', (2010) 17 MJECL 137.

[115] Brown, 'Outcry', supra n 110.
[116] Accessible at <http://www.mcb.org.uk/downloads/Schoolinfoguidance.pdf>.
[117] T Phillips, 'After 7/7: sleepwalking to segregation', 22 September 2005, accessible at <http://83.137.212.42/sitearchive/cre/Default.aspx.LocID-ohgnew07s.RefLocID-ohg00900c002.Lang-EN.htm>.

ISLAMIC MEDIATION AND ARBITRATION

The idea of Islamically directed mediation obviously sounds much more acceptable because it accords with a conception of it being voluntaristic and consensual. However, a study by Samia Bano of the operation of mediation in a divorce context by *shari'a* councils in the UK stressed that it was framed in opposition to state law mediation practices. Moreover, it is 'conceptualised in terms of a duty upon all Muslims to abide by the requirements of the *shari'a* and the stipulations of the *shari'a* councils'.[118] The study also examined the experience of Muslim women in using *shari'a* councils in the UK. It found that 'participation takes place in a space that is preoccupied with reconciling the parties, is male dominated and is often imbued with conservative interpretations regarding the position of women in Islam (as mothers, wives and daughters)'; 'under this model of reconciliation, husbands were given greater room for negotiation, which led to better outcomes for them' and 'women reported that they had existing injunctions issued against their husbands on the grounds of violence and yet they were urged to sit only a few feet away from these violent men during the reconciliation sessions'.[119] The study concluded that, '*shari'a* councils construct boundaries for group membership that rely upon traditional interpretations of the role of women in Islam, primarily as wives, mothers and daughters. Under such conditions, the multicultural accommodation of Muslim family law in Britain can lead to the violations of human rights for Muslim women'.[120] Women used the *shari'a* councils because of a need to obtain a religious divorce but they also used state law to deal with issues of access, custody and financial settlements. Bano concluded that 'Muslim women remained extremely cautious of initiatives to accommodate *shari'a* into English law'.[121]

As for arbitration, in September 2008 it was reported that both formal *shari'a* courts and informal *shari'a* tribunals had been working in the UK

---

[118] S Bano, 'In pursuit of religious and legal diversity: a response to the Archbishop of Canterbury and the "*shari'a* debate" in Britain', (2008) 10 Ecc LJ 282.
[119] For similar criticisms of negotiations in a Jewish law context, see Madera, 'Juridical bonds of marriage', supra n 57.
[120] Bano, 'In pursuit of religious and legal diversity', supra n 118, 306–7.
[121] Ibid., 309. The Arbitration and Mediation Services (Equality) Bill [HL] 2012–13 was introduced into the House of Lords by Baroness Caroline Cox (independent) in 2011; see Hansard HL, vol 739, cols 1682–1716 (19 October 2012) (second reading; Bill committed to a Committee of the whole House). Its intention is to tackle the discrimination suffered by Muslim women within the *shari'a* court system. See also G Douglas, N Doe, S Gilliat-Ray, R Sandberg and A Khan, *Social Cohesion and Civil Law: marriage, divorce and religious courts* (Cardiff, 2011) on the work of the Beth Din, Shari'a Council and Catholic Tribunal, accessible at <http://www.law.cf.ac.uk/clr/Social%20Cohesion%20and%20Civil%20Law%20Full%20Report.pdf>.

and, since 2007, had resolved over a hundred cases ranging from Muslim divorce and inheritance to nuisance neighbours.[122] Under the provisions of the Arbitration Act 1996, the *shariʿa* courts are classified as arbitration tribunals for arbitrable matters. As such the rulings are binding in law, provided that both parties in the dispute agree to give such a court the power to rule on their case. Bano has submitted that different socio-legal orders are being created all the time and *shariʿa* councils already operate 'as a complementary system of dispute resolution'.[123] In Ontario, a proposal for *shariʿa*-based arbitration under the Arbitration Act 1991, enforced by the courts of law, proved very controversial and attracted almost universal opposition. It ended with a legislative prohibition for all faith-based arbitration for family matters under the Act.[124] Concerns at the proposal were both procedural and (in relation to the rights enshrined in the Canadian Charter of Rights, many of which parallel the rights in the ECHR) substantive.

THE WAY FORWARD FOR MUSLIMS IN EUROPE

If the ECtHR was right in *Refah* and a general *shariʿa* system is incompatible with the ECHR, and many of the general areas of *shariʿa* law are problematic under the ECHR, then the better question might be: 'What's the value of the ECHR for Muslims who live in Europe?' The ECHR is itself an expression of modern European liberal democracy. It imposes positive obligations on states but also obligations of restraint or non-interference. For example, states that want to impose restrictions on religions have to satisfy a series of justificatory tests: the restrictions must be prescribed by law, have a legitimate aim, meet pressing social need

---

[122] See A Tamer, 'Revealed: UK's first official *shariʿa* courts', *The Sunday Times*, 14 September 2008; and F Hamilton, 'Non-Muslims turning to *shariʿa* courts to resolve civil disputes', *The Times*, 21 July 2009. See also the website of the Muslim Arbitration Tribunal (MAT), established in 2007, accessible at <http://www.matribunal.com/>. The parties to a commercial arbitration agreement can stipulate that the tribunal be drawn from members of a particular religious group as this does not contravene the Employment Equality (Religion and Belief) Regulations 2003, *Jivraj v Hashwani* [2011] UKSC 40; see also Edge, 'Islamic finance, alternative dispute resolution and family law', infra pp 121–5.

[123] S Bano, 'In pursuit of religious and legal diversity', supra n 118. For a more recent review, see D Talwar, 'Growing use of *shariʿa* by UK Muslims', BBC News, 16 January 2012, accessible at <http://www.bbc.co.news/uk-16522447>.

[124] See LE Weinrib, 'Ontario's *shariʿa* law debate: law and politics under the Charter's shadow', in Moon, *Law and Religious Pluralism in Canada*, supra n 71, p 239; and M Boyd, 'Ontario's "Shariʿa Court": law and politics intertwined', infra pp 176–86. More recently there have been amendments to the law of the State of Oklahoma in the US in an effort to ban the use of religious law when deciding cases. See also M Helfand, 'Religious arbitration and the new multiculturalism: negotiating conflicting legal orders', (2011) 86 New York ULR 1232.

and finally be subjected to a proportionality analysis. If it can be convincingly demonstrated that the ECHR, along with EU law and national laws, offers substantial protection for a wide spectrum of Muslims, this might encourage Muslims to support the ECHR as an accommodation strategy.[125] A more explicit adoption of an approach based on a duty of reasonable accommodation might also assuage the concerns of many Muslims (and adherents to other religions and beliefs). However, it must be acknowledged that Muslims may have a more negative perception of the ECHR's protection of religion. Article 9 of the ECHR 'does not require that one should be allowed to manifest one's religion at any time and place of one's own choosing'.[126] It does not protect each act motivated or influenced by religion or belief, although the Court has accepted that the Islamic headscarf is a manifestation of religion.[127] There are critiques of the Court's jurisprudence on the wearing of the Islamic headscarf allowing states a wide margin of appreciation to regulate and even ban headscarves in certain places.[128] Some judges in the Court have detected a negative attitude to Islam in the jurisprudence.[129] However, the reality – of which we can lose sight – is that most Muslim women in most places in Europe can wear headscarves most of the time. A rights based discourse has been used by Muslims to argue for the right to wear headscarves via a redefinition or reinterpretation of secularism.[130] Moreover, often the disputes on headscarves have not simply set Muslims against non-Muslims. Rather they have often

---

[125] See McGoldrick, 'Accommodating Muslims in Europe', supra n 5. Of course other religious adherents would benefit from such an approach, see B Almond, 'The right to disagree: challenging the new orthodoxy about the family', accessible at <http://thomasmoreinstitute.wordpress.com>.

[126] Lord Hoffman in *Begum*, supra n 105, para 50. See also N Bratza, 'The "precious asset": freedom of religion under the ECHR', (2012) Ecc LJ 256.

[127] See D McGoldrick, 'Muslim veiling controversies in Europe', (2009) 1 *Yearbook of Muslims in Europe* 427; and C Joppke, *Veil: mirror of identity* (London, 2009). In *R (Imran Bashir) v The Independent Adjudicator and Anor* [2011] EWHC 1108 (Admin) the High Court adopted a broader approach to what is a manifestation of a religion. Following *Jakobski v Poland* (2010) 30 BHRC 417, App no 18429/06 (2010), it held that a prisoner's decision to fast before a court appearance was motivated by his Islamic faith and disciplinary sanctions taken against him for failure to give a urinary sample had to be justified.

[128] P Cumper and T Lewis, '"Taking religion seriously"? Human rights and *hijab* in Europe: some problems of adjudication', (2009) 24 JLR 101; S Leader, 'Freedom of futures: personal priorities, institutional demands and freedom of religion', (2007) 70 MLR 713; A Vakulenko, '"Islamic headscarves"' and the European Convention on Human Rights: an intersectional perspective', (2007) 16 *Social and Legal Studies* 183; C Evans. 'The "Islamic scarf" in the European Court of Human Rights', (2006) 7 MJIL 52.

[129] In particular see the opinions of Judge Kovler in *Refah*, supra n 17 and in *Serife Yigit*, supra n 62.

[130] See A Barras, 'A rights-based discourse to contest the boundaries of state secularism? The case of the headscarf bans in France and Turkey', (2009) 16(6) *Democratization* 1237.

reflected complex intra-Muslim controversies. Both the *Begum*[131] and *Azmi v Kirklees MBC*[132] cases were of this kind. Both individuals attracted significant criticism from other Muslims, including religious and political leaders. While prohibitions on the headscarf can always be seen as insignificant and trivial, they do represent a line in the sand against, and a rejection of, an Islamic perspective that does not regard or treat women as equals. The argument is that, if the line is not drawn at the headscarf, more extensive veiling will follow, and then a more general claim for the application of *shari'a* law. The headscarf debates are only one element of growing Islamicisation in Europe, but because of their increasing visibility they have been one of its most public and controversial elements. The banning of the *burka* and the *niqab* in public places by Belgium[133] and France[134] are likely to be the next battleground.[135]

This chapter has advocated Muslim engagement with the ECHR rather than claims for the incorporation of *shari'a* law into the law of European states. It encourages European Muslims to become actively engaged as citizens and political actors in governance and other participatory activities. It suggests that Muslims in Europe can conceive of themselves as having an identity which is both European and Islamic.[136] The national and European debates and public dialogues on these

---

[131] See supra n 105. See also *R (On the Application of X (By Her Father and Litigation Friend)) v The Headteachers of Y School, The Governors of Y School* (2007) EWHC 298 (Admin) (school could refuse to admit a schoolgirl who wanted to wear a *niqab*).

[132] *Amzi*, supra n 80.

[133] See I Trayner, 'Belgium moves towards public ban on *burka* and *niqab*', *The Guardian*, 31 March 2010.

[134] See Loi No. 2010–1192 of 11 October 2010 'interdisant la dissimulation du visage dans l'espace public', published in *Journal Officiel* of 12 October 2010, accessible at <http://www.legifrance.gouv.fr>. The French Law makes it illegal to wear the Islamic *burqa* or other full face veils in public ('une tenue destinée à dissimuler son visage'). Women who wear the veil can be required by police to show their face, and, if they refuse, they can be forced to attend citizenship classes or be fined Euro 150. The legislation also makes it a crime to force a woman to cover her face, with a penalty of one year in prison and a fine of Euro 30,000. The law will inevitably be challenged before the ECtHR. See S Mullally, 'Civic integration, migrant women and the veil: at the limits of rights?', (2011) 74 MLR 27.

[135] See Resolution 1743 (2010) pr 16 of the Parliamentary Assembly of the Council of Europe (legal restrictions to this freedom may be justified where necessary in a democratic society, in particular for security purposes or where public or professional functions of individuals require their religious neutrality or that their face can be seen. However, a general prohibition of wearing the *burqa* and the *niqab* would deny women who freely desire to do so their right to cover their face). In March 2010, the Canadian province of Quebec introduced parliamentary measures to proscribe facial covering in public service employment, apparently with strong public support.

[136] See T Ramadan, *Western Muslims and the Future of Islam* (New York, 2004); S Amghar, A Boubekeur and M Emerson, *European Islam: challenges for public policy and society* (Brussels, 2007), p 6 (arguing that 'European Islam is already a reality for Muslims'); AlSayyad and Castells, 'Introduction', supra n 1, p 1.

questions provide a crucial forum or theatre for articulating matters that will ultimately determine the shape and character of the complex construct that is Europe.[137] If Muslims want recognition and respect in the public space, both conceptual and architectural,[138] they, along with other religions and religious believers, will have to argue their case in the arena of public reason.[139] In modern, secular-based[140] European states they will face a difficult battle.[141]

---

[137] See Hellyer, *Muslims of Europe*, supra n 2, pp 177–94, particularly at p 186 on the idea of 'integralisation': that Muslim citizens 'feel essential to their societies, and are recognized as such by their societies'.

[138] A number of applications concerning the 2009 decision by Swiss voters to prohibit the building of minarets have been submitted to the Court. See *Hafid Ouardiri v Switzerland*, App no 65840/09, 28 June (2011) and *Ligue des Musulmans de Suisse and Others v Switzerland*, App no 66274/09 (2011) (declared inadmissible on the ground that the particular applicants could not claim to be the 'victims' of a violation of the ECHR). See A Peters, 'The Swiss referendum on the prohibition of minarets', accessible at <http://www.ejiltalk.org/?s=minarets>.

[139] See J Rawls, *The Law of Peoples: with 'the idea of public reason' revisited* (Cambridge, MA, 1999), pp 129–80; P Smith, 'Engaging with the state for the common good: some reflections on the role of the Church', (2009) 11 Ecc LJ 169; An-Na'im, 'The compatibility dialectic: mediating the legitimate coexistence of Islamic law and state law', (2010) 73 MLR 1; C McCrudden, 'Religion, human rights, equality and the public sphere', (2011) 13 Ecc LJ 26; D McGoldrick, 'Religion in the European public square and in European public life: crucifixes in the classroom?', (2011) 11 HRLR 451; J Finnis, *Religion and Public Reasons* (Oxford, 2011); FI Michelman, 'Constitutional theocracy', (2012) *Public Law* 173. In a submission to the ECtHR, Lord Carey argued that there was a drive to remove Judeo-Christian values from the public square. His intervention was reported by *The Guardian*, 14 April 2012.

[140] For helpful discussion see J Rivers, *The Law of Organized Religions: between establishment and secularism* (Oxford, 2010), particularly at pp 289–347; L Vickers, 'Twin approaches to secularism: organized religion and society', (2012) 19 OJLS 197. Vickers argues that protection of religious rights based on proportionality, rather than on separation, offers the best chance of developing a culture of 'respectful pluralism' in the modern world, in which religious interests can be viewed in equilibrium with equality, autonomy and dignity.

[141] See, for example, the trenchant comments of Laws LJ in *McFarlane*, supra n 79, cited with approval in *Bull and Bull v Hall and Preddy*, supra n 79, para 49. See also *R (Eunice Johns and Owen Johns)*, supra 79 ('the laws and usages of the realm do not include Christianity, in whatever form', para 39); R Sandberg, 'Laws and religion: unravelling McFarlane v Relate Avon Limited' (2010) 12 Ecc LJ 361; J Chaplin, 'Law, religion and public reasoning', (2012) 1 *Oxford Journal of Law and Religion* 1. In his final Easter sermon before retirement Archbishop Williams observed that a 'tide may be turning in how serious and liberal-minded commentators think about faith: no longer seen as a brainless and oppressive enemy, it is recognized as a potential ally in challenging a model of human activity and social existence that increasingly feels insane, a model in which unlimited material growth and individual acquisition still seem to trump every other argument about social coherence, international justice and realism in the face of limited resources', Easter Sermon, Canterbury Cathedral, accessible at <http://www.archbishopofcanterbury.org/articles.php/2440>. See also R Williams, *Faith in the Public Square* (London, 2012).

CHAPTER 5

An analysis of the relationship between shariʿa and secular democracy and the compatibility of Islamic law with the European Convention on Human Rights

Mashood A Baderin

INTRODUCTION

The relationship between *shariʿa* and secular democracy, with the question whether Islamic law is compatible with the European Convention on Human Rights (ECHR),[1] is far more complex than sensational media reports would suggest. In the present context we are asking whether formal recognition of (aspects of) *shariʿa*/Islamic law as part of the laws of the UK, in any form, would be repugnant to the country's 'secular' democratic system or would create problems in respect of its international obligations under the ECHR. We must ask as well, more generally, whether or not *shariʿa*/Islamic law and democracy/human rights are or can be compatible or can coexist at all. The pragmatic answer to both questions has to be, 'Yes' and 'No'.

BEYOND THE QUESTION OF COMPATIBILITY

In such discussions in the West, it is the *shariʿa* or Islamic law that is usually put on the defensive and characterised narrowly as an archaic, imprecise and unchanging legal system that is stuck in the past and consisting only of women's oppression and of such punishments as flogging, amputation and stoning. However, it is doubtful whether Muslims in Europe are actually asking for the application of traditional Islamic criminal law (which is not currently applied even in most Muslim majority states that recognise *shariʿa* or Islamic law as part of their legal systems). The argument is rather for a

---

[1] European Convention for the Protection of Human Rights and Fundamental Freedoms, adopted 4 November 1950, entered into force 3 September 1953 (CETS No. 005).

formal recognition of the *shariʿa* relating to Islamic personal law in 'aspects of marital law, the regulation of financial transactions and authorised structures of mediation and conflict resolution' as indicated by Rowan Williams, then Archbishop of Canterbury, in his lecture.[2]

The challenge goes beyond the apparent problem of compatibility. Rather, it puts in question the scope of the right to religious liberty and of the restrictions – and the limits to those restrictions – that can legitimately be placed, under the ECHR, on the right to manifest one's religion 'in public and private'. Within the tenets of both Islam and Christianity, the right to practise or manifest one's religion should be broad enough to 'embrace a huge variety of activity if one takes the view – as many religions do – that all life is inspired by or generated by faith and belief'.[3] From an Islamic perspective, this broad view of religious liberty is often expressed in the assertion that 'Islam is a complete way of life' by reference to Qur'an 6.162: 'Say: Truly, my prayer, my service of sacrifice, my life and my death are all for God, the Lord of the worlds.'

While religious liberty under Article 9(1) of the ECHR includes, broadly, 'freedom, either alone or in community with others and in public or private, to manifest [one's] religion or belief, in worship, teaching, practice and observance', Article 9(2) allows such restrictions on the manifestation of one's religion, 'as are prescribed by law and are necessary in a democratic society in the interests of public safety, for the protection of public order, health or morals, or the protection of the rights and freedoms of others'. Some commentators have argued, on the basis of European Court of Human Rights (ECtHR) jurisprudence, that current interpretation of the restrictions permissible under Article 9(2) does not offer the protection to Islamic religious liberty due under the ECHR.[4] Malcolm Evans has observed that in recent cases:

'the Strasbourg organs have themselves blurred the freedom of religion into a mélange of mutual respect not only between religions but between the freedom of religion and other human rights . . . [which] suggests that while international law might provide a degree of protection for religious liberty, it may not go as far as

---

[2] Supra p 32.   [3] R Ahdar and I Leigh, *Religious Freedom in the Liberal State* (Oxford, 2005), p 155.
[4] See, eg, R Hopkins and CV Yeginsu, 'Religious liberty in British courts: a critique and some guidance' (2008) 49 Harv Int'l L J 28, p 39; P Danchin, 'Islam in the secular *nomos* of the European Court of Human Rights', (2011) 32 Mich JIL 663, accessible at <http://papers.ssrn.com/sol3/papers.cfm?abstract_id=1670671&>; T Lewis, 'What not to wear: religious rights, the European Court, and the margin of appreciation', (2007) 56 ICLQ 395; A Vakulenko, 'Islamic dress in human rights jurisprudence: a critique of current trends', (2007) 7 HRLR 717; M Hill and R Sandberg, 'Is nothing sacred? Clashing symbols in a secular world' (2007) *Public Law* 488.

some religious believers consider necessary and this opens up the question of whether, and how, they might choose to go beyond the limits set by the international legal order.'[5]

Asking for formal domestic accommodation of aspects of the *shari'a* relating to Islamic personal law is one of the legitimate ways for Muslims to seek the protection of their religious liberty due under the ECHR; and such accommodation would give them an opportunity to express and manifest their faith, in a 'democratic society' of which they form a part.

This becomes a more general issue. Peter Danchin has observed that 'what is most interesting about these controversies involving Islam and the place of Islamic norms in European nation states (and the international legal sphere more broadly) is how such encounters are unsettling existing normative legal categories and catalyzing rethinking of both the historical and theoretical premises of modern liberal political orders'. He has identified the two critical questions that this raises for ECHR jurisprudence: 'what is the nature and scope of the right to freedom of religion and belief?' and 'what is the relationship between religion and morality in the "secular" public sphere?'[6] As the Archbishop was making clear, these questions are as relevant to Christianity as to Islam.

In this chapter, I challenge some of the typical misrepresentations and assumptions associated with these complex questions. I provide a relative and functional understanding of the *shari'a* and Islamic law, analyse the contrasting theoretical perspectives that take the discussion in radically divergent directions and argue that an appropriate and realistic perspective reveals the *shari'a* and Islamic law not to be inherently inimical to secular democracy and to the ECHR respectively. I close by challenging a further assumption that has dogged recent discussion: that religion is properly a purely private matter for believers, and should have no role in the public spheres informed by democratic or human rights principles.

RELATIVE AND FUNCTIONAL UNDERSTANDING OF THE *SHARI'A* AND ISLAMIC LAW

We need from the outset a properly relative and functional understanding of the nature and scope of the '*shari'a*' and of 'Islamic law'. The two concepts are often perceived and used as synonyms, as was apparent in the decision of the ECtHR in the *Refah* case to which we return below. Such

---

[5] MD Evans, *Religious Liberty and International Law in Europe* (Cambridge, 2008), p 365.
[6] Danchin, 'Islam in the secular *nomos*', supra n 4, pp 4–5.

conflation of the two concepts can be misleading. '*Shari'a*' and 'Islamic law' are not synonymous. The *shari'a*, strictly speaking, refers to the fundamental sources of Islam, namely, the Qur'an and the *Sunna*, both of which Muslims consider as being divine and immutable, and from which Islamic religious, moral, social, economic, political and legal norms are derived. Thus, the *shari'a* covers more than just law; it is 'law-plus'. On the other hand, Islamic law refers to the rulings or law *(ahkām)* that are derived from the *shari'a* by Muslim jurists and applied by Muslim judges. Muslim jurists therefore often talk of applied law as *ahkām al-shari'a*, '*shari'a* rulings' or '*shari'a* law' – ie rulings derived from the *shari'a* – when they are referring to Islamic law. Islamic law emerges through a human process called *fiqh*, literally 'understanding', that is, human juristic understanding of the divine sources using different well-defined classical and post-classical jurisprudential principles formulated by Muslim jurists over time. These derived rules, unlike the *shari'a* itself, are neither divine nor immutable.

Islamic law, as rulings derived from the *shari'a* by jurists, can be construed and applied either in historical or in evolutionary terms. Perceived in historical terms, Islamic law is often restricted to the traditional rulings of the classical jurists as if those rulings were immutable, like the *shari'a* itself. This creates a reductionist approach to Islamic law that hinges on the disputed theory of the 'closing of the gate of legal reasoning *(ijtihad)*' in Islamic legal theory around the thirteenth century. According to this theory, Islamic law must be restricted to the legal rulings of the classical jurists as recorded in the legal treatises of the different established schools of Islamic jurisprudence which date back to the tenth century; this in essence represents and applies Islamic law historically as a legal system stuck in the past.[7] It is this historical emphasis which leads critics to describe *shari'a*/Islamic law as an archaic system of law that cannot be harmonised with modern concepts such as democracy and human rights. By contrast, an evolutionary perception and application of Islamic law does indeed see in the traditional legal rulings of the classical jurists a rich source of jurisprudence; but these do not preclude the continual development of Islamic law based on modern jurisprudence *(fiqh)* through the continued process of legal reasoning *(ijtihad)*. In essence, the evolutionary outlook represents and applies Islamic law as a system that evolves in necessary response to the dynamic

---

[7] This theory of the 'closing of the gate of legal reasoning' under Islamic legal theory has been effectively challenged by many modern scholars of Islamic law. See W Hallaq, 'Was the gate of *ijtihad* closed?', (1984) 16 IJMES 3.

nature of human life and that can therefore respond effectively to the modern concepts of democracy and human rights.

The evolutionary nature of Islamic law is currently reflected in the practices of some Muslim majority states (such as Morocco and Malaysia) and in Muslim communities in different parts of the modern world, as well as in the views of different contemporary Muslim jurists and scholars globally. Hashim Kamali has illustrated the development of this evolutionary approach to Islamic law as follows:

> In modern times, legal interpretation or reasoning [in Islamic law] has occurred in the following three ways: statutory legislation, judicial decision and learned opinion (*fatwa*), and scholarly writings. Instances of legislative interpretation, which Noel Coulson referred to as 'neo-*ijtihad*', can be found in the modern reforms of family law in many Muslim countries, particularly with reference to polygyny and divorce, both of which have been made contingent upon a court order, and therefore are no longer the unilateral privilege of the husband. Current reformist legislation on these subjects derives some support from the jurists' doctrines of the *Maliki* and *Hanafi* schools, but these reforms are essentially based on novel interpretations of the Quran's relevant portions. Numerous instances of independent reasoning are also found in the views of the *ulama* [religious scholars], such as the collections of published opinions of Muhammad Rashid Rida in the 1920s and those of the late *shaykh* of Azhar, Mahmud Shaltut, in the 1950s. In the 1967 case of *Khursid Bibi* vs. *Muhammad Amin*, the supreme court of Pakistan's decision to validate a form of divorce, known as *khula*, that can take place at the wife's initiative, even without the consent of the husband, can be cited as an example of judicial *ijtihad*. Another example of ongoing reinterpretation is the scholarly contribution of the Egyptian scholar Yusuf al-Qaradawi, who validated air travel by women unaccompanied by male relatives. According to the rules of *fiqh* that were formulated in premodern times, women were not permitted to travel alone. Al-Qaradawi based his conclusion on the analysis that the initial ruling was intended to ensure women's physical and moral safety, and that modern air travel fulfills this requirement. He further supported this view with an analysis of the relevant *hadiths* on the subject and arrived at a ruling better suited to contemporary conditions.[8]

Once we understand this distinction between *shariʿa* as the source of Islamic precepts generally, and Islamic law as the law derived from that source, we are nearly ready for the principal discussion of this chapter. I will relate the fundamental *shariʿa* to democracy as a political doctrine whose supreme virtue is fundamental to Western thought, and Islamic law to the ECHR as a legal instrument. But we need one last preliminary: we must refine the presuppositions with which we approach the topic.

---

[8] MH Kamali, 'Law and society: the interplay of revelation and reason in the Shariʿah' in JL Esposito (ed), *The Oxford History of Islam* (Oxford, 1999), p 118.

RELEVANT THEORETICAL PERSPECTIVES TO THE DEBATE

Much of this debate is shaped by traditional dichotomies and presumptions. Anyone's decision will be affected by the theoretical perspective adopted from the start. I have observed in earlier articles that the views within both human rights and Islamist discourse on these issues could be categorised into two main theoretical perspectives: the 'adversarial' or 'separationist' perspective on the one hand, and the 'harmonistic' or 'accommodationist' perspective on the other.[9] These two perspectives have been reflected in different academic and judicial views on the subject.

The adversarial or separationist perspective reflects the view that *shari'a* and democracy – and then in turn, Islamic law and human rights – cannot be compatible with each other nor accommodate one another. With reference to the ECHR, this appears to be the general perspective adopted by the ECtHR as reflected in its highly critiqued decision in *Refah*,[10] first in a majority Chamber decision of 2001 and further confirmed by a unanimous Grand Chamber decision of 2003. In that case, the Court made a generic observation in respect of the *shari'a* and Islamic law in relation to democracy and human rights as follows:

> The Court considers that the *shari'a*, which faithfully reflects the dogmas and divine rules laid down by religion, is stable and invariable. Principles such as pluralism in the political sphere or the constant evolution of public freedoms have no place in it. ... It is difficult to declare one's respect for democracy and human rights while at the same time supporting a regime based on *shari'a*, which clearly diverges from Convention values.[11]

This adversarial view has been criticised, not only by Muslim scholars or advocates of *shari'a*/Islamic law, but also by different human rights scholars and commentators. For example, Kevin Boyle observed, *inter alia*, that '[s]uch broad and seemingly hostile formulation ... will not promote understanding or contribute to the essential distinction that needs to be drawn between the extreme networks promoting terrorism in the name of Islam, such as Al Qaeda, and the millions of Islamic moderate believers who are also Europeans, European Muslims in fact'.[12] Christian Moe has also noted

---

[9] See, eg, MA Baderin, 'Human rights and Islamic law: the myth of discord', (2005) 2 EHRLR 165 and MA Baderin, 'Islam and the realization of human rights in the Muslim world: a reflection on two essential approaches and two divergent perspectives', (2007) 4(1) MWJHR, Article 5.
[10] (2002) 35 EHRR 3. Judgment upheld by the Grand Chamber (2003) 37 EHRR 1.
[11] Ibid., at para 72 of the Chamber's judgment of 2001.
[12] K Boyle, 'Human rights, religion and democracy: the Refah party case', (2004) 1 EHHR 1, 13–14; cf M Evans and P Petkoff, 'Secularism, religious rights and international law in the ECtHR jurisprudence',

that the Court ignored the diverse interpretation of such key concepts as *shari'a* and *jihad* by Muslims themselves.[13] Moussa Abou Ramadan makes a similar observation that '[t]here is an implicit assumption in the Court's view that it is impossible to find a concept in Islamic law that is immutable and respects human rights'[14] and noted that the Court refused guidance from the Muslims pleading before it.[15] Boyle had also suggested in his critique that the Court should 'have sought expert pleadings, for example by means of an amicus curiae brief, which at the very least would have brought to the Court's attention the considerable ongoing debate within Islam on *shari'a* and democracy and those aspects of Islamic law that are in conflict with international human rights standards'.[16]

An endorsement of this adversarial perspective would apparently suggest that a large number of Muslims in Europe may not hope to be able to enjoy some significant aspect of their religious rights while living within the democratic society envisaged under Article 9(2) of the ECHR. This, I submit, would be inimical to the very spirit of the ECHR.

That adversarial character of the discussion becomes all the more intense if we view the ECHR as a general human rights treaty that contains and guarantees a unified package of different specific rights. If the scope of the specific rights guaranteed under the ECHR were examined individually and right by right, there would be areas of convergence and areas of divergence between Islamic law and the different rights. There are, certainly, areas of legitimate concern with regard to historical traditional interpretations of some *shari'a* provisions, in relation (for example) to women's rights, minority rights and criminal punishments; but these do not necessarily create a generic or fundamental discord between the two systems. Such areas of concern are resolvable through an evolutionary approach to Islamic law and, my next point, through a *harmonistic* perspective on its relationship with human rights.

Contrary to the adversarial perspective, the harmonistic or accommodationist perspective *presupposes the possibility* that the elements of those two pairs – *shari'a* and democracy, Islamic law and human rights – are not essentially discordant but can accommodate each other, and that the underlying principles of the two systems could be positively harmonised. Essentially, this is a

---

p15, accessible at <http://www.ku.dk/satsning/religion/sekularism_and_beyond/pdf/Paper_Petkoff.pdf>.

[13] C Moe, 'Refah revisited: Strasbourg's construction of Islam' (2005), p 1, accessible at <http://folk.uio.no/chrismoe/research/hr-isl/refah.en.htm>.

[14] MA Ramadan, 'Notes on the *shari'a*: human rights, democracy, and the European Court of Human Rights', (2007) 40(1) *Israel Law Review* 156, p 158.

[15] Ibid.   [16] Boyle, 'Human rights, religion and democracy', supra n 12, p 13.

receptive outlook that seeks to develop positive ways in which the right to religious freedom could be fully enjoyed in synergy with other human rights within a liberal democratic state. This harmonistic perspective encourages an open-minded and constructive engagement and dialogue between *shari'a*/Islamic Law and democracy/human rights. It emphasises and explores the possibilities offered by alternative, moderate and legitimate juristic views of Islamic law in relation to democracy and human rights. The harmonistic perspective, then, promotes dialogue and understanding. Areas of differences and conflict are not downplayed or avoided; but they are addressed with the aim of finding constructive resolutions.

From this harmonistic perspective we can take either an idealist's or a realist's view. An idealist would argue that every aspect of *shari'a*/Islamic law is compatible with democracy/the ECHR, and would answer the questions we raised at the beginning with an emphatic 'Yes'. But such emphatic and unambiguous 'Yes' would be no more credible than the emphatic 'No' derivable from the adversarial perspective. The ECHR lays down different specific rights; and there are some features of *shari'a*/Islamic law which, if applied in their traditional and historic ways, are indeed inconsistent with particular ECHR provisions. A realist, on the other hand, would adopt what I have elsewhere referred to as the 'double-edged' theory,[17] and would argue that while some aspects of *shari'a*/Islamic law are compatible with democracy/the ECHR, there are other historical/traditional aspects that, adopted without modification, are not. Such a realist within our harmonistic or accomodationist perspective, asked whether *shari'a*/Islamic law and democracy/human rights were compatible, would answer 'Yes and No'; for the answer depends on the specific ECHR right and the specific aspect of the *shari'a*/Islamic law under consideration.

The realist's application of the harmonistic theory provides us with a pragmatic tool of analysis for a critical evaluation of the relationship between *shari'a*/Islamic law and democracy/the ECHR.

SHARI'A AND SECULAR DEMOCRACY

In the words of David Held, '[d]emocracy seems to have scored an historic victory over alternative forms of governance'[18] in today's world, despite its

---

[17] MA Baderin, 'Religion and international law: friends or foes?', (2009) 5 EHRLR 637, p 649.
[18] D Held, *Democracy and the Global Order* (Cambridge, 1996), p 3; F Fukuyama, *The End of History and the Last Man* (London, 1993), where he argues that liberal capitalist democracy is the best and final form of governance to which humanity can aspire.

different models[19] and disagreements about its exact nature.[20] Its appeal as a process of governance lies in the fact that it is seen to offer 'the most compelling principle of legitimacy – "the consent of the people" – as the basis of political order',[21] and is thus the form of polity best suited to the promotion of fundamental freedoms and human rights. Democracy and democratic governance are an important political safeguard for protecting the rights which the ECHR guarantees. This is first reflected in the preamble of the ECHR itself, which states that the fundamental freedoms guaranteed under the Convention 'are best maintained on the one hand by an *effective political democracy* and on the other by a common understanding and observance of the human rights upon which they depend'.[22] The concept of a 'democratic society', in which the rights guaranteed under the ECHR are expected to hold, is also mentioned in some substantive articles of the Convention. In Articles 6, 8, 9, 10 and 11 the right to public trials, the right to respect for private and family life, freedom to manifest one's religion, freedom of expression and freedom of assembly and association are subject to such limitations as are, *inter alia*, 'in the interest of ... national security in *a democratic society*' (Article 6), or 'in accordance with the law / prescribed by law and necessary in *a democratic society*' (Articles 8, 9, 10, 11). The ECtHR itself has emphasised that 'the only type of necessity capable of justifying an interference with any of those rights [in 8, 9, 10, 11] is ... one which may claim to spring from a "democratic society"'.[23] In relation to the *shari'a* and Islamic law, interpretation of the restriction of the freedom to manifest one's religion in the context of what is 'necessary in a democratic society' under Article 9(2) has been particularly controversial.

Jurisprudentially, the ECtHR has elaborated on various occasions that democracy is a fundamental feature of the European public order and 'appears to be the only political model contemplated by the Convention, and accordingly, the only one compatible with it',[24] but has also acknowledged that 'some compromise between the requirements for defending democratic society and individual rights is inherent in the system of the Convention'.[25] Although neither the ECHR itself nor the Court provides a

---

[19] See, eg, D Held, *Models of Democracy* (third edition, Cambridge, 2006).
[20] See, eg, PC Schmitter and TL Karl, 'What democracy is ... and is not', (1991) 2(3) *Journal of Democracy* 75.
[21] Held, *Models of Democracy*, supra n 19, p ix.
[22] Fourth Preambular Paragraph, ECHR (emphasis added).
[23] *United Communist Party of Turkey and Others v Turkey* (1998) 26 EHRR 121 (GC), para 45.
[24] Ibid.   [25] *Klass and Others v Federal Republic of Germany* (1979–80) 2 EHRR 214, para 59.

specific definition of democracy, the implied reference to *effective political democracy* under the Convention is generally to secular liberal democracy constituted by popular elections, rule of law, pluralism in the political sphere and respect for public freedoms and human rights. For example, in its Resolution 800 (1983)[26] the Parliamentary Assembly of the Council of Europe elaborated the legal standards of democracy as follows:

  i. Democracy is the government of the people by the people. Its basic principles are the rule of law and the separation of powers ...
 ii. It is the responsibility of the democratic system to strike a proper balance between effective action on the part of government and administration, and the protection of citizens' rights and freedoms. In particular, the system must be capable of maintaining such a balance between the requirements of the general interest of the community and those of the protection of every individual's fundamental rights as set forth in the European Convention on Human Rights. This entails the respect of minority rights by the majority ...
iii. In a crisis or state of emergency, all means available under ordinary law should be exhausted before exceptional measures are taken. Should this extreme solution prove necessary, it should be used only to the extent strictly required by the situation. On no account should the 'hard core' of human rights be affected ...[27]

In the Chamber decision of the *Refah* case, the ECtHR stated *inter alia*, that:

Democracy requires that the people should be given a role. Only institutions created by and for the people may be vested with the powers and authority of the State; statute law must be interpreted and applied by an independent judicial power. There can be no democracy where the people of a State, even by a majority decision, waive their legislative and judicial powers in favour of an entity which is not responsible to the people it governs, whether it is secular or religious.[28]

The Court then expressed its belief that these liberal democratic principles cannot be guaranteed under a political system based on the *shariʿa*.[29] But is that conclusion correct? The Court's view is based on its assumption that a political system based on the *shariʿa* must be a strict theocracy as opposed to democracy and cannot therefore accommodate 'pluralism in the political

---

[26] Adopted on 1 July 1983.
[27] See Section D, Council of Europe Resolution 800 (1983) on the Principles of Democracy, accessible at <http://assembly.coe.int/Mainf.asp?link=/Documents/AdoptedText/ta83/ERES800.htm#1>.
[28] *Refah* (No 1), supra n 10, para 43.   [29] Ibid., para 72.

sphere or the constant evolution of public freedoms'.[30] Similar views are indeed held among some hard-line Islamists who argue that Islam and democracy are inherently opposed to each other. Such Islamists base their claim on the misconceived proposition that democracy is strictly 'the rule of Man' while the *shari'a* strictly promotes 'the rule of God'; but study of both classical and modern Islamic political thought would reveal this to be inaccurate both in theory and practice. There is a vast contemporary literature[31] on the relationship between Islam and democracy, aimed at establishing that the *shari'a* is not inherently anathema to liberal democratic principles as suggested by the Court. In its generic statement, the ECtHR ignored or was oblivious to that literature and to those other jurisprudential views. As rightly observed by Asef Bayat, 'there is nothing intrinsic in Islam, and for that matter any other religion, which makes them inherently democratic or undemocratic',[32] arguing that it is 'we, the social actors [who] render a religion inclusive or exclusive, non-vocal or pluralist, democratic or authoritarian'.[33]

While the *shari'a*, as the source of Islamic law and Islamic political thought, is divine in nature, its scope and application do certainly extend to the secular. With respect to applied law and applied political thought, the processes under the *shari'a* are essentially 'secularised', that is, transformed from the *shari'a*'s divine nature into a secular, temporal nature. Thus, in Islamic jurisprudence, the coverage of the *shari'a* is usually divided into the religious *(ibādāt)*, relating to acts of worship, and the temporal *(mu'āmalāt)*, relating to inter-human relations; even though both aspects still overlap, as they are all regulated by religious injunctions. While the injunctions relating to acts of worship are generally considered settled and unchanging, those relating to temporal inter-human relations, as derived by the earlier jurists from the Qur'an and *Sunna*, are more flexible and responsive to change according to time and circumstances. Matters relating to human rights and good governance fall principally within the sphere of temporal inter-human relations. Thus, while Islamic human rights instruments such as the Universal Islamic Declaration on Human Rights (UIDHR)[34] and the

---

[30] Ibid.
[31] See, eg, A Sachedina, *The Islamic Roots of Democratic Pluralism* (New York, 2001); K Abou El Fadl, *Islam and the Challenge of Democracy* (Princeton, 2004); A Soroush, *Reason, Freedom, and Democracy in Islam* (New York, 2002); JL Esposito, *Islam and Democracy* (New York, 1996); A Bayat, *Islam and Democracy: what is the real question?* (Amsterdam, 2009); JL Esposito and JP Piscatori, 'Democratization and Islam', (1991) 55(3) MEJ 427.
[32] Bayat, *Islam and Democracy*, supra n 31, p 10. [33] Ibid., p 12.
[34] Adopted by the Islamic Council in London on 19/9/81; see <http://www.alhewar.com/ISLAMDECL.html>.

Cairo Declaration on Human Rights in Islam (CDHRI)[35] or the constitution of a Muslim majority state may be 'based on the Qur'an and *Sunna*'[36] and appear theocratic, the interpretation and application of their provisions cannot be rigid but must be flexible and responsive to the dynamics of time and place.

Historical evidence and classical works on Islamic political thought represent governance under the *shari'a* as not sacrosanct or divine, per se; rather it is temporal in nature and geared towards good governance and human welfare but is underpinned by God-consciousness to encourage accountability to the populace here and now and to God in the hereafter. A pertinent question is what happens where the ruling authority abuses power and rules contrary to the principles of good governance and human welfare. Will such ruling authority be left accountable to God only, perhaps in the hereafter? Quoting Khidr Husayn, Kamali has observed that 'Islam made it an obligation of the community to monitor the conduct of the head of state and his officials with a view to rectifying those who deviate, and alerting those who might be neglecting the duties with which they are entrusted'.[37] The inaugural address of the first Caliph, Abubakr, in which he encouraged the populace to monitor and correct him whenever he went wrong, is an indication of his recognition of this right.[38] Thus, from a *shari'a* perspective, governance is not a 'theocracy' as is often presumed, but rather a secular dispensation underpinned by God-consciousness. In a recent *fatwa*, the renowned Islamic jurist, Sheikh Yusuf al-Qaradawi, observed that '[t]he Islamic state is a civil one, like other governments in the modern world and the only difference is that it makes Islamic *shari'a* its reference'.[39]

The temporal nature of governance under Islamic political thought is also borne out by the earlier practice of Prophet Muhammad when he migrated to Medina in the seventh century (AD 622) and became the political head of the Medinan mini-state. He agreed to the formulation and adoption of a document that has come to be known as 'the constitution of Medina'[40] for

---

[35] Adopted by the Organisation of the Islamic Conference (OIC) in Cairo in 1990, accessible at <http://www.oic-oci.org/english/article/human.htm>.
[36] See, eg, the seventh paragraph of the foreword of the UIDHR, which provides that the Declaration is based on the Qur'an and the *Sunna*. See also the fifth preambular paragraph of the Constitution of Pakistan for a reference to the Qur'an and *Sunna*.
[37] See MH Husarn, 'Naqd Kitâb al-Islâm wa Usûl al-Hukm' (1925), p 89, trans. in MH Kamali, *Freedom of Expression in Islam* (Cambridge, 1997), p 52.
[38] See Kamali, *Freedom of Expression in Islam*, supra n 37, pp 49–57 for further examples.
[39] <http://www.islamopediaonline.org/fatwa/yusuf-al-qaradawi-shura-compatible-essence-democracy>.
[40] See M Hamidullah, *Majmu'ah al-Watha'iq al-Siyasiyah*, (Beirut, 1969), pp 41–47. For an English translation of the document, AD Al-Umari, *Madinan Society at the Time of the Prophet*, trans H

the temporal governance of the state, which recognised both the religious and the secular rights of the Muslim and non-Muslim residents of Medina. Although the divine revelation of the Qur'an was still ongoing at that time, the Prophet did not receive any divine revelation condemning the adoption of 'the constitution of Medina' for the temporal governance of the state. That early precedent of the Prophet in Medina represents a clear demonstration of constitutionalism, a positive step towards the recognition of the rights and duties of all people within the community, and a basis for peaceful coexistence. The individual clauses are impressive in themselves: accommodating the Prophet's 'secular' role as arbiter and spokesman. The political concept of *siyasa shar'iyya*[41] was also developed by early Islamic jurists around the eleventh century as a means of responding to the secular and dynamic nature of governance under the *shari'a*. The Islamic principles of governance are therefore not static as presumed by the ECtHR in the *Refah* case; rather they must and do respond to the needs of time within the relevant provisions of the *shari'a*.

The *shari'a* (ie the Qur'an and the *Sunna*) does not actually specify any particular form of governance, but, rather, provides general relevant social and political values that can be used positively to promote effective governance in modern times. In relation to democracy the Qur'anic concept of *shūrā* (consultation) in Qur'an 42.38 is now the springboard for promoting democratic governance and public participation in many Muslim majority states: 'Better and more enduring is God's reward to those ... who obey their Lord, attend to their prayers *and conduct their affairs by mutual consultation*'. Bayat has noted that '[i]n contrast to advocates of [an] incompatibility thesis others tend to present an *inherently* democratic spirit of Islam and claim it as a religion of tolerance, pluralism, justice and human rights', citing the view of Rashid al-Ghonoushi, for example, that 'Islamic rule is by nature democratic'.[42] In a recent interview with *Le Mode diplomatique*, Rashid al-Ghanoushi observed that 'Islam has a strong democratic spirit inasmuch as it respects religious, social and political differences. Islam has never favoured a monolithic state. Throughout their history Muslims

---

Khattab, (Virginia, 1995), vol 1, pp 107–10. See also M Hamidullah, *The First Written Constitution in the World* (Lahore, 1981); WM Watt, *Islamic Political Thought* (Edinburgh, 1980), pp 130–4; A Bulac, 'The Medina Document' in C Kurzaman (ed), *Liberal Islam, A Sourcebook* (Oxford, 1998), pp 169–78.

[41] *Siyasa shar'iyya* is an Islamic political principle that 'comprises all measures that bring the people close to wellbeing and move them further away from corruption, even if no authority is found for them in divine revelation and the *Sunnah* of the prophet', MH Kamali, *Principles of Islamic Jurisprudence* (Cambridge, 2003), p 355.

[42] A Bayat, *Making Islam Democratic: social movements and the post-Islamist turn* (Stanford, 2007), p 4; cf Esposito and Piscatori 'Democratization and Islam', supra n 31, 428.

have objected to the imposition of a single all-powerful interpretation of Islam. Any attempt to impose a single interpretation has always proven inherently unstable and temporary'.[43]

There are currently many scholars advancing this compatibility view. Yusuf al-Qaradawi is among the Islamic scholars who – alongside Islamic institutions – has endorsed democratic governance by reference to Qur'an 42.38 read in conjunction with Qur'an 3.159 in which Muhammad was specifically directed to consult the populace in their affairs: 'It was thanks to God's mercy that you dealt so leniently with them. Had you been cruel or hard-hearted, they would have surely deserted you. Therefore pardon them and implore God to forgive them. *Take counsel with them in the conduct of affairs* ... '[44] John Esposito and James Piscatori have rightly observed further that:

> In recent decades, many Muslims have indeed accepted the notion of democracy but differed as to its precise meaning. Muslim interpretations of democracy build on the well-established Qur'anic concept of *shura* (consultation), but place varying emphases on the extent to which 'the people' are able to exercise this duty. One school of thought argues that Islam is inherently democratic not only because of the principle of consultation, but also because of the concepts of *ijtihad* (independent reasoning) and *ijma'* (consensus). It is argued that, just as Islamic law is rescued from the charge of inflexibility by the right of jurists in certain circumstances to employ independent judgment and to secure agreement among themselves, Islamic political thought is rescued from the charge of autocracy by the need of rulers to consult widely and to govern on the basis of consensus.[45]

Esposito and Piscatori have made an important point of which the ECtHR must be made aware, which is that '[w]hether the word democracy is used or not, almost all Muslims today react to it as one of the universal conditions of the modern world. To this extent, it has become part of Muslim political thought and discourse. This fact must be appreciated by Western policymakers'.[46]

If leaders in the Muslim states did actually take counsel with their people in the conduct of affairs, as mandated by Qur'an 3.159, the people's choice would largely be for a democratic society that accommodated Islamic values as well as democratic pluralism. This is well reflected in the so-called

---

[43] <http://mondediplo.com/openpage/tunisia-islamist-leader-returns-from-exile-an>.
[44] 'Muslim World Needs Democracy, says Qaradawi', *Muslim News*, 8 July 2006, accessible at <http://www.muslimnews.co.uk/news/news.php?article=11311>. See also al-Qaradawi's website, accessible at <http://www.islamopediaonline.org/fatwa/yusuf-al-qaradawi-shura-compatible-essence-democracy>.
[45] Esposito and Piscatori, 'Democratization and Islam', supra n 31, 434.   [46] Ibid., 440.

'Arab Spring' in different parts of the Muslim world that started from Tunisia in December 2010. In Tunisia, Yemen, Libya, Egypt and elsewhere, demonstrators, opposition groups and even members of Islamic political parties combine Islamic slogans such as *'Allahu Akbar'* ('Allah is great!') with slogans of democracy and freedom in the different Muslim majority states. In Egypt, the religious authorities of Al-Azhar University, which is recognised as one of the most authoritative religious institutions in the Muslim world, also issued a *fatwa* in the wake of the Arab Spring, in which it proposes, *inter alia*, a democratic, constitutional and modern Egyptian state governed by the rule of law, in which human rights are respected and full protection and total respect guaranteed to other religions.[47] Such a *fatwa* demonstrates a clear acknowledgment of the temporal nature of governance under Islamic political thought, accommodating democratic participation and geared towards ensuring general human welfare and human rights.

ISLAMIC LAW AND THE EUROPEAN CONVENTION ON HUMAN RIGHTS

So we move on from *shariʿa* and democracy to our other pair: Islamic law and the ECHR. Concerns regarding the relationship between Islamic law and human rights are usually focused on criticisms of Islamic criminal law and of the rights and status of women and minorities under traditional Islamic law.[48] As with the *shariʿa*, so with Islamic law: a historical perspective here would certainly result in some incompatibilities between Islamic law and the ECHR as interpreted by the ECtHR; but the scope of incompatibility will be greatly reduced and the areas of tensions much more easily resolved where Islamic law is construed in an evolutionary sense. There is abundant theoretical and practical evidence to establish that Islamic law – as rulings derived from the *shariʿa* through *fiqh* – has not actually been inherently immutable, but has adjusted to the factors of time and circumstances since its inception, particularly in respect of temporal matters pertaining to inter-human relations (*muʾāmalāt*) where human rights issues arise, in contrast to matters relating to religious observances and acts of worship *(ibādāt)* which are relatively fixed. Among many jurisprudential principles of Islamic law depicting its evolutional and flexible nature both in theory and practice, one maxim is that Islamic legal

---

[47] <http://www.ft.com/cms/s/0/56ac8782-9dbe-11e0-b30c-00144feabdc0.html#ixzz1Qhql4qVM>.
[48] *Refah* (No 1), supra n 10, para 72.

rulings may change with relevant changes in time and place within the context of the *shari'a*.[49]

An evolutionary perception of Islamic law has already resulted in the re-evaluation of some of the traditional rulings that apparently conflict with modern human rights norms in some Muslim countries.[50] Such evolutionary interpretations are well justified within the context of the overall objectives or the higher intents of the *shari'a* (*maqāsid al-shari'a*), which are understood by both the classical and contemporary Islamic jurists to be the promotion of human welfare/benefit (*maslahah*) and prevention of harm (*mafsadah*).[51] Ibn Qayyim al-Jawziyyah, the renowned thirteenth/fourteenth century Islamic jurist of the Hanbali School of jurisprudence stated in that regard that:

> Islamic Law is structured and founded upon wise purposes and the best interests of God's servants both in this world and the next. The Law is pure justice, pure mercy, pure benefit, pure wisdom. Hence, anything which embodies injustice rather than justice, cruelty rather than mercy, harm rather than benefit, or folly rather than wisdom does not originate from the Law, even if it happens to have been interpolated therein by means of interpretation.[52]

Although some Muslim states and commentators continue to advance a strict historical perception of Islamic law and political theory, which may be practically problematic in relation to the ECHR, there is currently a strong wave of scholarship advocating the evolutionary interpretation of Islamic law in ways that would help realise the humane objectives of the *shari'a* in the modern world consistently with modern objectives of promoting human rights and fundamental freedoms generally.[53]

In a similar vein, I argue strongly in this chapter that Islamic law is not inherently inimical to most of the rights guaranteed under the ECHR. Much depends on which perception is adopted between the historical and evolutionary interpretations of the *shari'a* in response to different challenges and circumstances of time and place.

---

[49] This is expressed as *Lā yunkar taghayyur al-Ahkām bi taghayyur al-Azman* ('change in legal rulings with the change in times is not deniable'); see, eg, Maxim 39 of the Maxims of Islamic Jurisprudence in the *Majallah*, accessible at <http://www.ummah.net/Al_adaab/fiqh/majalla/index.html>.
[50] See, eg, the new Moroccan Family Code (Moudawana) adopted on 5 February 2004, accessible at <http://www.globalrights.org/site/DocServer/Moudawana-English_Translation.pdf>.
[51] For some contemporary writings on *Maqāsid al-Shari'ah*, see, eg, J Auda, *Maqasid al-Shari'ah as Philosophy of Islamic Law: a systems approach* (London, 2008); GE Attia, *Towards Realization of the Higher Intents of Islamic Law: Maqāsid al-Shari'ah: a functional approach* (London, 2007).
[52] I Qayyim al-Jawziyyah, *I'lām al-Muwaqqi'īn an Rabb al-Ālamīn*, vol 3 (Cairo, 1968), p 3, trans in Attia, *Towards Realization*, supra n 51, p 7.
[53] Cf MA Baderin, 'The role of Islam in human rights and development in Muslim states' in J Rehman and SC Breau (eds), *Religion, Human Rights and International Law* (Leiden, 2007), p 324.

BUT WHO SPEAKS FOR ISLAM?

The question is often asked, who has the authority or competence to decide which interpretation of the *shariʿa* to adopt in particular circumstances?[54] Confusion usually arises from the fact that there is no equivalent of the papacy in Islam, which is often taken to mean that there is no central authority in Islam generally. But the lack of a 'papacy' does not necessarily translate into lack of a process for determining authority or decision-making in Islamic legal and political thought. Even though there may be differences of opinion on most issues in Islam, there is a clear jurisprudential process for reaching and identifying a binding authoritative position on different issues under Islamic law.

The starting point for addressing the question of authority and competence is Qurʾan 4.59, which enjoins Muslims: 'Obey God and obey the Prophet and those charged with authority among you, but if you differ in anything among yourselves, refer it back to God and His Prophet, if you believe in God and the Last Day; that is best and most suitable for final determination.' Obedience to God and the Prophet becomes obedience to the Qurʾan and the *Sunna*; obedience to those charged with authority becomes obedience to 'the rulers or the scholars', who must in turn show that their ruling is in accordance with the Qurʾan and the *Sunna*.[55] Rulings under Islamic law are of three main categories: theological, political and legal. A non-binding theological opinion *(fatwa)* is given by a qualified theologian *(mufti)* either *suo moto* or on consultation either by individuals to guide them in making decisions on personal religious matters, or by the political authority to guide it in making binding political decisions of state, or by the judicial authority to guide it in making binding legal decisions in cases brought before it.

Traditionally, there are five main schools of Islamic jurisprudence with established juristic principles and processes for extracting rulings from the Qurʾan and the *Sunna*. The differing opinions on particular issues held by the scholars/jurists of the established schools of jurisprudence are all considered to be legitimate and valid and a source of God's benevolence to the Muslim community. The community is free to choose and follow any one of those opinions, which would range from 'liberal' to 'hard-line'. A particular school's opinion can be considered as the better opinion on an

---

[54] See, eg, JL Esposito and D Mogahed (eds), *Who Speaks for Islam? What a billion Muslims really think* (New York, 2008); M Ahmed, D Reetz and TH Johnston, *Who Speaks for Islam? Muslim grassroots leaders and popular preachers in South Asia* (Washington, 2010); K Abou El Fadl, *The Great Theft: wrestling Islam from the extremists* (New York, 2005).

[55] ABK Zaidan, *Individual and the State* (Kuwait, 1983), pp 90–1.

Shari'a *law and secular democracy* 89

issue at particular times and under particular circumstances. Thus, the individual is free to choose between the different theological/juristic opinions on personal matters, while the political and judicial authorities are similarly free to choose between theological/juristic opinions to guide them on matters of state and on legal matters respectively, all taking into consideration the circumstances of place and time. The relevant Islamic legal principle on this point, as contained in the classical sources, is: *hukm al-ḥākim yarfaʿ al-khilāf*, meaning: 'the ruling authority's (political or judicial) decision resolves the differences of opinion on particular matters'. This is with particular reference to temporal matters (*muʾāmalāt*).

This chapter urges, then, that the political and legal authorities exercise their authority on the basis of the 'liberal' Islamic theological/juristic opinions that would enhance good governance and human rights of the populace.[56] Such an approach is already being adopted in Muslim countries such as Morocco, Malaysia and others.

CHALLENGING TRADITIONAL ASSUMPTIONS

We have been asking whether a political system based on the *shari'a* can really be compatible with secular democracy, and have focused on the *shari'a* and its requirements. At issue as well, of course, is the definition of 'secular democracy'. The *shari'a* would certainly be more compatible with secular liberal democracy where this is understood as a political process for the guarantee of good governance, the rule of law, human rights and democratic pluralism, than where it is understood strictly as conformity to the ideology of 'secularism' completely opposed to religion and the exercise of religious beliefs in the public sphere. Such an ideology was an object of concern to the Archbishop of Canterbury too in his lecture, as he discussed the standing and liberties of all religious believers.

The debate is often framed in the terms of an absolute, post-Enlightenment dichotomy: *shari'a* and Islamic law, it is said, are religious precepts that must be confined strictly to the private domains of its adherents; democracy and human rights are secular precepts that must, to the exclusion of any religious precepts, regulate the public domain. But such simplistic dichotomies only reveal some aspects of modern societal realities while masking others.[57] Elizabeth Hurd has observed that '[a]s it stands,

---

[56] A similar view is advanced in El Fadl, *The Great Theft*, supra n 54.
[57] See, eg, ND Rosiers, 'Introduction' in Law Commission of Canada, *New Perspectives on the Public–Private Divide* (Vancouver, 2003), pp vii–xviii.

secularism arrogates to itself the right to define the role of religion in politics, [and] [i]n doing so, it shuts down important debates about the moral bases of public order and incites a backlash against its hegemonic aspirations'.[58] For example, in *Leyla Sahin v Turkey*, the Grand Chamber of the ECtHR suggested that the need to protect secularism constituted, per se, a legitimate aim, under the terms of Article 9(2) of the ECHR, to restrict the liberty of a Muslim woman to wear a headscarf in university, even though she believed that 'by wearing the headscarf, she was obeying a religious precept and thereby manifesting her desire to comply strictly with the duties imposed by the Islamic faith'.[59]

In today's world, it would be extraordinarily simplistic to propose that 'the religious' could be completely separated from 'the secular', with the former completely locked up within presumed individual and private spheres while the latter monopolises supposed general and public spheres. Religious precepts continue to seep into the public sphere in most modern societies; and conversely democratic and human rights principles are continually being called upon to regulate the traditionally private sphere and to reduce the span of the truly 'private'. The claimed distinction between private religion and public democracy and human rights is not just an ingenuous separation. Nathalie Rosiers has observed that 'like all socio-legal constructs, the public–private divide is a concept that can be manipulated' and that it does 'influence the power dynamics between people'.[60]

The point has also been made that '[i]n a certain sense, the best confirmation of the validity of the deprivatisation of religion can be found in the heartland of secularisation, that is, in Western European societies, [where] religion has certainly returned as a contentious issue to the public sphere of European societies'.[61] Talal Asad has noted that secularism is no longer to be construed as a 'simple matter of absence of "religion" in the public life of the modern nation-state',[62] but should rather be understood as 'a concept that brings together certain behaviours, knowledges, and sensibilities in modern life'.[63] Conversely, as religion and religious precepts, including *shari'a* and Islamic law, claim a greater role in the public sphere,

---

[58] ES Hurd, 'The political authority of secularism in international relations', (2004) 10(2) EJIR 235, p 237.
[59] *Leyla Sahin v Turkey* (2007) 44 EHRR 5 (GC), paras 116, 78.
[60] Rosiers, 'Introduction', supra n 57, p xvi.
[61] J Casanova, 'Public religions revisited' in H de Vries (ed), *Religion: beyond a concept* (New York, 2008), p 101.
[62] T Asad, *Formations of the Secular: Christianity, Islam, modernity* (Stanford, 2003), pp 5–6.
[63] Ibid., p 25.

they cannot in practice be immune from the modern secular challenges of democracy and human rights.

We must pay still further attention to the terms of the debate. It is often framed strictly in relation to promoting multiculturalism and to accommodating the cultures of Muslim emigrants now settled in the West. These terms fail to appreciate that there is today a growing number of Western Muslim converts[64] who are culturally 'Western' yet believe in *shari'a* and Islamic precepts as necessary aspects of their adopted religious faith. For such Muslims, questions of multiculturalism or of their 'accommodation' in the West are irrelevant; for them, the debate is more appropriately about the scope and limit of their right to religious freedom within a democratic system and under the ECHR. Here is a critical test of the guarantee of religious rights under the ECHR. Widespread assumptions are well captured by Malcolm Evans and Peter Petkoff in their observation that under international law generally 'religious rights are only seen and interpreted in the context of a conflict (Cold War, clash of civilizations, terrorism, etc) ... It appears that outside of the context of conflict and tension, there is no legal tool for interpretation of religious rights'[65] in a more objective way. With specific reference to the ECHR, they further argue that:

> Increasingly, religious manifestation is seen as permissible only to the extent that this is compatible with the underpinnings of the ECHR system, these being democracy and human rights. The Court today seems to identify democracy and human rights with tolerance and pluralism and is apt to construe any forms of religious manifestation which do not manifest those virtues as posing a threat to these central values.[66]

This presumption contextualises Muslims' religious liberty under the ECHR in a particularly restrictive way. What could otherwise be perceived as a legitimate human rights claim for Islamic religious liberty is instead seen as a threat. It has been argued that there is, in fact, a negative treatment of Islamic precepts in ECtHR jurisprudence; Islam is apparently perceived as a danger to the right to freedom of religion and belief rather than as itself deserving that right.[67] This can be very problematic for an objective discourse on freedom of religion generally under the ECHR.

---

[64] See, eg, MAK Brice, 'A minority within a minority: a report on converts to Islam within the United Kingdom (Swansea, 2010), accessible at <http://faith-matters.org/images/stories/fm-reports/a-minority-within-a-minority-a-report-on-converts-to-islam-in-the-uk.pdf>.
[65] Evans and Petkoff, 'Secularism', supra n 12, p 15.   [66] Ibid.
[67] Danchin, 'Islam in the secular *nomos*', supra n 4, p 37.

CONCLUSION

It is doubtful whether Muslims in Europe are asking for a wholesale introduction of the application of traditional Islamic criminal law, as is often claimed by critics of the *shariʿa* and Islamic law. The argument is rather for a formal recognition of aspects of the *shariʿa* relating to Islamic personal law in 'aspects of marital law, regulation of financial transactions and authorised structures of mediation and conflict resolution', just as indicated by the Archbishop of Canterbury.[68] It is essential to highlight that some of these aspects of *shariʿa* and Islamic law are already operating either formally or informally in the UK and other European countries. For example, a so-called '*shariʿa*-compliant' Islamic banking and finance system is currently operating side by side with the conventional banking system in London and elsewhere. A 2007 policy paper issued by the Robert Schuman Centre for Advanced Studies noted that while 'Islam all too often resonates negatively in Europe, with a great part of non-Muslim public opinion uncomfortable with Islamic culture and values', yet 'Islamic finance is thriving in Europe, and many major European banks perceive it as a profitable opportunity to generate new business rather than as a threat to existing business'.[69] In the UK, the Financial Services Authority has recognised and supported the initiative within the provisions of the general financial laws and regulations. The Islamic banking and finance system does not operate as an imposition of *shariʿa* precepts on anyone, whether Muslims or not, but is a matter of choice – a choice which is, incidentally, being taken up even by non-Muslims for ethical reasons.

There are as well a number of so-called *shariʿa* councils and tribunals currently operating, mostly informally, in the UK and providing Islamic mediation to Muslims on a voluntary basis.[70] I submit that a formal recognition of such institutions would facilitate their regulation, which would ensure, among other things, the adoption and maintenance of good practices and alternative access to justice for many Muslim women in the UK who might prefer an Islamic settlement of their disputes to litigation in the civil courts.

We can see how wise was one commentator to observe that the question of mere compatibility can be the wrong question to pose; for, as we have

---

[68] Supra p 32.
[69] R Wilson, 'Islamic finance in Europe', RSCAS Policy Papers 2007/02 (European University Institute, 2007), accessible at <http://www.eui.eu/RSCAS/WP-Texts/07_02p.pdf>.
[70] See, eg, the Muslim Arbitration Tribunal, accessible at <http://www.matribunal.com/>.

seen, with this emphasis the debate in the West 'centres almost exclusively on one side of the equation, Islam, as if the other side, democracy, is free from complexities'.[71] The question of compatibility and the debate to which it gives rise are, however, not likely to go away. That confirms the importance of the approach adopted in this chapter: to interrogate the traditional assumptions that have often made the debate one-sided in the past; and to provide a contextual understanding of the *shariʿa* and Islamic law, which I hope will encourage a more objective and pragmatic debate of the question in the future.

---

[71] A Bayat, *Islam and Democracy*, supra n 31, p 9.

CHAPTER 6

Dignity and religion

Christopher McCrudden

The chapters in this section of the book have analysed the current debates over the approach taken by the European Court of Human Rights (ECtHR) in the *Refah* case,[1] and to some extent in the *Sahin* case.[2] A key, but seldom identified, *future* problem in the interpretation of the European Convention on Human Rights (ECHR) in the context of Islam and Muslim religious practices and beliefs is the problematic role of the concept of 'dignity' in that debate.[3] The ECtHR has failed to articulate an understanding of dignity that comes close to being persuasive, yet British courts rely on this 'thin' conception as a central plank in their current approach to examining the compatibility of some manifestations of religious beliefs with the ECHR, and Islam may be significantly affected by this in the future.

To be protected by the ECHR, beliefs must be 'worthy of respect in a democratic society and ... not incompatible with human dignity'.[4] The ECtHR has struggled with cases involving claimants' religious beliefs that may be seen to adopt a view of women's proper role and behaviour that differs from that of Western society. There is a danger here of creating human rights outlaws. But as Lord Walker has said, 'in matters of human rights the court should not show liberal tolerance only to tolerant liberals'.[5] There is a basis for more than mere tolerance: in due recognition of the dignity of both parties to the case.

Whereas the ECtHR's understanding of what is 'worthy of respect in a democratic society' in this context has been subject to severe criticism which I shall not rehearse, what is likely to be considered 'incompatible with human dignity' by the ECtHR and the British courts in religion cases has

---

[1] *Refah Partisi (Welfare Party) v Turkey* (No 2) (2003) 37 EHRR 1 (GC).
[2] *Leyla Sahin v Turkey* (2007) 44 EHRR 5 (GC).
[3] For an extended discussion of the concept of dignity, see C McCrudden, 'Human dignity and judicial interpretation of human rights', (2008) 19 EJIL 655.
[4] This test is set out in *Campbell and Cosans v United Kingdom* (1982) 4 EHRR 293, para 36.
[5] *R (Williamson and Others) v The Secretary of State for Education and Employment* [2005] 2 AC 246, para 60.

passed almost without significant notice. My purpose in this brief intervention is to initiate a conversation on this, hitherto under-analysed, aspect of these cases.

ABSOLUTE AND QUALIFIED RIGHTS

The ECHR contains several different kinds of rights, or at least rights with different weights. So, we can distinguish those rights, such as the right to be free from torture, the right not to be held in slavery and the right to life, as rights that have considerable weight. In the case of torture and slavery, we even say that the right is 'absolute' in the sense that the right has such weight that no other consideration is sufficiently important for it to trump that right. Other rights, in particular such rights as the right to a private life, the right to freedom of speech and the right to freedom of assembly, are structured so that other considerations can be taken into account in determining whether that right has been breached. In that sense, these rights are qualified rather than absolute. The right to freedom of religion is partly of the first and partly of the second type. Article 9(1) of the ECHR provides:

Everyone has the right to freedom of thought, conscience and religion; this right includes freedom to change his religion or belief and freedom, either alone or in community with others and in public or private, to manifest his religion or belief, in worship, teaching, practice and observance.

The right to 'freedom of thought, conscience and religion', therefore, has two dimensions: 'freedom to change his religion or belief' which is not subject to any limitation (we might say it is an 'absolute' right), and freedom to manifest his religion or belief, which is a 'qualified' right, subject to limitations set out in Article 9 itself:

Freedom to manifest one's religion or beliefs shall be subject only to such limitations as are prescribed by law and are necessary in a democratic society in the interests of public safety, for the protection of public order, health or morals, or for the protection of the rights and freedoms of others.

The way in which this limitation provision is drafted (limitations must be 'necessary in a democratic society') has led the ECtHR to interpret this and equivalent provisions as requiring a test of 'proportionality' to be satisfied by states wishing to restrict these rights: that is, the Court considers if the purpose of the limitation of the right is legitimate, and if the limitation is necessary for attaining the purpose, and if the measure strikes a proper balance between the purpose and the individual's right that is being restricted. 'Qualified' rights are thus highly contextualised, requiring judgments to be made about how the right is to be exercised in particular situations.

The difference between the two sets of rights ('absolute' and 'qualified') should not, however, be exaggerated. In the case of the prohibition against torture, what constitutes 'torture' involves a complex analysis that can be highly contextual. And, on the other hand, the approach that has generally been adopted in interpreting the 'qualified' rights has been to adopt an approach that creates a broad *prima facie* right which must be protected unless the state can justify restrictions on that right. In this way, the ability to interfere with these rights is considerably more limited than might at first sight appear to be the case if the text is read in isolation from the jurisprudence of the Court importing a 'proportionality' analysis into the interpretation of the restrictions.

There are, of course, general exceptions that are provided for in the ECHR, such as the ability of a state to effectively opt out of certain rights in time of war or other public emergency that threatens the life of the nation, but even this exception is constrained both in terms of the limited set of rights from which states are able to derogate under these circumstances (not from torture or slavery, for example), but also by process requirements that ensure a degree of transparency in the operation of the derogation. So too, in the case of the 'political' rights guarantees, Article 16 of the ECHR provides that these rights do not impose limitations on the ability of states to restrict the political activities of aliens. Whilst important, however, the drafting of these provisions makes it clear that such permitted restrictions are regarded as limited and confined. Thus far, the structure of the ECHR makes it relatively clear that a rough hierarchy of human rights is adopted, depending on whether or not – and the degree to which – 'balancing' of the *prima facie* right against other considerations is permitted.

AVOIDING THE PROPORTIONALITY TEST

It is crucial, however, that the exercise of the rights protected is not, in general, dependent on any assessment of the moral worthiness of the individual claiming the right. In the practice of human rights, it is well known that the person claiming a right is sometimes, perhaps often, a highly dubious character. Despite this, it is not the case that the right not to be tortured, for example, is dependent on the person not being a terrorist, or the right not to be enslaved is dependent on the person not being an illegal alien. In general, also, the motive of the person claiming the right is not relevant to whether the person's rights are regarded as being breached. It is not the case, therefore, that the fact that a claimant has a political motivation in claiming the right is relevant in determining that his right to a private life has been breached.

In some circumstances, however, the drafters of the ECHR envisaged that the rights they were protecting might have to be restricted in a much more radical way than we have previously identified: that is, there are circumstances where the moral worthiness of the person claiming a right, or their motivation in choosing to exercise a right, *should* be taken into account. In this way, the drafters attempted to address what was identified as the problem with the Weimar Republic: a liberal state was undermined using democratic means. For this reason, Article 17 of the ECHR provides:

Nothing in this Convention may be interpreted as implying for any State, group or person any right to engage in any activity or perform any act aimed at the destruction of any of the rights and freedoms set forth herein or at their limitation to a greater extent than is provided for in the Convention.

This is the instantiation in the Convention of the controversial idea of 'militant democracy', where the state is permitted to restrict the rights of those who would seek to restrict the rights of others. And in the immediate post-Second World War period, one did not have to look far to see that such dangers loomed large. A resurgence of Nazism in Germany, or the success of Stalinist Communism in France and Italy was by no means impossible. Outside these key examples, however, 'militant democracy' has been rightly regarded with a considerable degree of suspicion, and the Court has seldom overtly referred to it, let alone explicitly relied on it. The reason is obvious: to allow the state easy access to such a provision could end up undermining, rather than protecting, the rights in issue.

The major exception to the general restraint which the Court has exercised in relying on Article 17 is in the area of so-called 'hate speech', where the theory of 'militant democracy' is much in evidence. These cases usually involve a claim by far-right individuals or groups that their right to freedom of speech has been breached because their ability to disseminate racist speech has been restricted, or a situation in which Holocaust-deniers are imprisoned for denying aspects of the Holocaust. (In Europe Holocaust denial is punishable in Austria, Belgium, the Czech Republic, France, Germany, Lithuania, Poland, Romania, Slovakia, Spain and Switzerland.) The Court has consistently denied these claimants a remedy, and has done so in two, somewhat different, ways. The first approach is to rely explicitly on Article 17, enabling the Court to conclude that although the right to freedom of speech or assembly had been breached, Article 17 denied the claimants the ability to access the Convention remedies.[6]

In several cases, the Court has held that the speech in issue simply does not come within the ambit of Article 10 because it is not the type of expression to which Article 10 applies.[7] It is important to note precisely what is *not* happening in such cases. It is not the case that the Court finds a *prima facie* breach of Article 10, and then proceeds to find that breach justified. Instead, the Court closes off access to the justification stage (in which the State has the onus of justifying the restrictions) and limits the ambit of the *prima facie* right itself. The claimant does not even get to first base, to use a baseball metaphor. The reason appears to be that the Court is unwilling in these cases even to engage in the type of proportionality analysis that it would normally undertake.

In general, however, the Court will not use Article 17 to close off an Article 10(2) assessment, even in cases where alleged hate speech is at issue.[8]

The technique of restricting the ambit of the *prima facie* right in order to avoid having to engage in a proportionality analysis is also apparent in the context of the Court's interpretation of freedom of religion. Two approaches are evident.

Establishing interference

The first is the well known restrictive approach to the interpretation of what constitutes an 'interference' in the 'manifestation' of a religious belief, where the Court denies that the challenged restriction constitutes an interference because the claimant had the opportunity to manifest the belief in circumstances other than the one where he chose to do so.[9] Lord Bingham, in *R (On the Application of Begum (By Her Litigation Friend Rahman)) v Headteacher, Governors of Denbigh High School*, noted 'a

---

[6] See, inter alia, *Jersild v Denmark* (Ser A) no 289 (1995).
[7] See, inter alia, *Garaudy v France*, App no 65831/01 (2003); *Norwood v United Kingdom*, App no 23131/03 (2004). A similar approach is taken to Article 11: *WP and Others v Poland*, App no 42264/98 (2004).
[8] *Vejdeland and Others v Sweden*, App no 1813/07 (2012).
[9] See, inter alia, *Stedman v UK* (1997) 23 EHRR CD 168; *Kalak v Turkey* (1997) 27 EHRR 552; *Jewish Liturgical Association Cha'are Shalom Ve Tsedek v France* (2000) 9 BHRC 27; *Aktas, Bayrak, Gamaleddyn, Ghazal, J Singh, R Singh v France*, App nos 43563/08, etc: cf *R (On the Application of Begum (By Her Litigation Friend Rahman)) v Headteacher, Governors of Denbigh High School* [2007] 1 AC 100, para 25 per Lord Bingham and para 50 per Lord Hoffman ('Article 9 does not require that one should be allowed to manifest one's religion at any time and place of one's own choosing ... people sometimes have to suffer some inconvenience for their beliefs').

coherent and remarkably consistent body of [European] authority which our domestic courts must take into account and which shows that interference is not easily established'.[10] The test adopted by the ECtHR stipulates that 'alternative means of accommodating a manifestation of religious belief' have 'to be "impossible" before a claim of interference under Article 9 could succeed'.[11]

Again, note what is *not* being done in these cases: the Court, in denying that the claimant's right was breached, is not denying it because other considerations outweighed the *prima facie* right stated in Article 9(1). That would have required a proportionality analysis. Nor does the Court explicitly draw on the 'militant democracy' approach and rely on Article 17's protection; to over-use Article 17 would let a potentially nasty genie out of the bottle, and unbalance the structure of the Convention.[12] Rather, the Court denies that even the *prima facie* right is breached.

It is not particularly puzzling that the Court is uneasy about relying on Article 17; what is more puzzling is why the Court appears so unwilling in Article 9 cases to engage in the proportionality analysis that it would regard as second nature in the context of other rights.[13] This unease is nowhere explicitly explained by the Court, but an inkling of why judges may be uneasy about applying proportionality in freedom of religion cases is given by Justice Sachs of the South African Constitutional Court in the *Christian Education South Africa* case,[14] where he identifies the problem of the incommensurability of rights and other values as particularly present in the freedom of religion context: 'The most complex problem is that the competing interests to be balanced belong to completely different conceptual and existential orders. Religious conviction and practice are generally based on faith. Countervailing public or private concerns are usually not and are evaluated mainly according to their reasonableness.'[15]

Beliefs not 'incompatible with human dignity'

The second restriction that is now increasingly apparent in the interpretation of the freedom of religion by the British courts has been the development of

---

[10] *Begum,* supra n 9, para 24.   [11] Ibid.
[12] For a discussion, see H Cannie and D Voorhoof, 'The abuse clause and freedom of expression in the European Human Rights Convention: an added value for democracy and human rights protection?', (2011) 29 *Netherlands Quarterly of Human Rights* 54.
[13] According to the most recent authoritative study of proportionality, it 'is a central feature of human rights according to the Convention', A Barak, *Proportionality: constitutional rights and their limitations* (Cambridge, 2012), p 184.
[14] *Christian Education South Africa v Minister of Education* (CCT 4/00) [2000] ZACC 11.   [15] Para 33.

a threshold requirement as to what constitutes a belief that qualifies for protection in the first place. Here, an approach is taken that is similar to that adopted in the hate-speech cases. To be protected, beliefs must be 'worthy of respect in a democratic society and ... *not incompatible with human dignity*'. This is the test set out in *Campbell and Cosans v United Kingdom*.[16] Thus, on the basis of this test, where a belief is considered to be inconsistent with 'human dignity', it does not come within the ambit of Article 9's protection.

The 'dignity' test is not uncontroversial, and is itself not fully tested. For example, when the ECtHR adopted it in *Campbell and Cosans*, the Court developed the test in the context of interpreting the limits of philosophical 'convictions' in Article 2, Protocol 1, under which the State shall respect the right of parents to ensure their children's education in conformity with the parents' own religious and philosophical convictions. The Court was not developing the test explicitly as a set of criteria by which to judge major world religions for the purposes of protection under Article 9. Some British judges have also expressed concern with the *Campbell and Cosans* threshold test. Rix LJ has said that '[r]eligion is a controversial subject and there would be many who would argue that undoubted religious convictions are not worthy of respect or are not compatible with human dignity. It is in part to guard against such controversy that the Convention guarantees religious freedom.'[17] Lord Walker has also said, and this more generally, that 'the requirement that an opinion should be "worthy of respect in a 'democratic society'" begs too many questions.'[18]

This threshold test has proven increasingly popular in the English courts when dealing with difficult freedom of religion cases. It was accepted and applied in *R (Williamson and others) v Secretary of State for Education and Employment*, on corporal punishment in some Christian schools, by Lord Nicholls,[19] who held that '[t]he belief must be consistent with basic standards of human dignity or integrity'. This was expressly also accepted by Lord Walker, despite his reservations,[20] and Baroness Hale,[21] who also made clear her view that the 'dignity' test did not only apply to philosophical beliefs and did apply to religious beliefs. Lord Nicholls applied this threshold in the context of Article 3, which forbids torture and inhuman or degrading treatment or punishment: 'Manifestation of a religious belief, for instance,

---

[16] (1982) 4 EHRR 293, para 36.
[17] *R (Williamson and Others) v The Secretary of State for Education and Employment* [2002] EWCA Civ 1925, para 151.
[18] *Williamson*, supra n 5, para 60.   [19] Ibid., para 23.   [20] Ibid., para 64.   [21] Ibid., para 76.

which involved subjecting others to torture or inhuman punishment would not qualify for protection.' Subsequently, however, the concept of dignity has been used as a threshold test well beyond the context of Article 3. Mrs Ladele, a marriage registrar and Christian, refused to officiate at civil partnership ceremonies between two homosexuals, a refusal based on her religious beliefs. In the Court of Appeal in *Ladele v Islington London Borough Council and Liberty (Intervening),* Lord Neuberger MR regarded this dignity test as 'support[ing] the view that Mrs Ladele's proper and genuine desire to have her religious views relating to marriage respected should not be permitted to override Islington's concern to ensure that all its registrars manifest equal respect for the homosexual community as for the heterosexual community'.[22]

In the ECtHR in *Sahin*, the Grand Chamber draws on a similar approach. Although it begins paragraph 108 with praise for a view of democracy that 'does not simply mean that the views of a majority must always prevail',[23] and espouses the view that 'a balance must be achieved which ensures the fair and proper treatment of people from minorities',[24] this approach quickly evolves into a decision that the 'dialogue and . . . spirit of compromise',[25] on which democracy is said to be based, involves 'concessions on the part of individuals or groups of individuals which are justified in order to maintain and promote the ideals and values of a democratic society'.[26] Given that the Court accepts that the restriction on the wearing of Islamic dress was based on the Turkish state's policy of 'secularism' and 'equality' which 'may be considered necessary to protect the democratic system in Turkey',[27] the conclusion was clear, at least to the Court: that an 'attitude that fails to respect [the principle of secularism] will not necessarily be accepted as being covered by the freedom to manifest one's religion and will not enjoy the protection of Article 9'.[28] From a starting point of compromise, the Court moves swiftly to uphold the state's principled refusal of any compromise.

The use of the 'human dignity' threshold test (and the same can be said for 'democracy') thus appears to be attractive both to the British courts and to the ECtHR. It is attractive mainly because the ECtHR has held that all rights protected by the ECHR derive from the meta-principle of 'dignity'. If that is the case, then (according to the Court) these rights should be

---

[22] [2009] EWCA Civ 1357, para 55. At the time of writing (April 2012), the author was junior counsel acting for Ms Ladele in her application to the European Court of Human Rights.
[23] *Sahin v Turkey*, supra n 2, para 108.   [24] Ibid.   [25] Ibid.   [26] Ibid.   [27] Ibid., para 114.
[28] Ibid.

interpreted in the light of what 'dignity' requires. It is, theoretically at least, a small step from this proposition to the further proposition that any right that is to be interpreted cannot be used in a way that is incompatible with 'dignity'. When coupled with a strategy that does not define 'dignity' explicitly, the courts have considerable discretion in how the term will be used, and how it will evolve.

The application of what I shall call this 'human dignity' threshold test is likely to be particularly problematic in the context of Islam, and the more particularly given the extension of the dignity test to encompass aspects of equality in *Ladele*. The potential for trouble is well illustrated in the cases in which the Court has struggled to deal with claims by those who espouse Islamic religious beliefs that may be seen to adopt a view of women's proper role and behaviour that differs from that of Western society. The cases dealing with the wearing of Islamic dress by women demonstrate these difficulties. The creation of a group of individuals or groups that are literally outside the protection of human rights law because of their views, human rights outlaws, strikes me as both dubious in principle and highly likely to be counter-productive in practice.

To its credit, the ECtHR has dealt with the recurring problem of *terrorism* not by excluding those connected with it from the protection of the ECHR but rather by showing that there was a legal and democratic route open to the redress of grievances, and this was one of the significant factors in the gradual weaning of those involved off the use of gun and the bomb. So too, courts in Europe, both at the European and domestic levels, have in general been highly sceptical of US attempts to create a category of detainees (perhaps not incidentally, *Islamic* detainees) that is outside the protection of the Geneva Conventions. Yet in the cases dealing with Islamic religious activity, we see the ECtHR adopting a somewhat similar approach, by creating a category of religious believers whose beliefs are not even recognised as being worth balancing for the purposes of the protection of Article 9. That cannot be right, not least because there is an alternative.

THE 'HUMAN DIGNITY' THRESHOLD TEST

The Court has been right in not relying on Article 17; it has, however, been wrong in not developing the tool of proportionality in such a way as to enable it to deal with these claims without compromising its principles. In this respect, the German, Canadian and South African courts provide a considerably better model of how to address these difficult cases, not least because they have identified human dignity as underpinning the claims of *both* those who are seeking to restrict religious practices, *and* those who are seeking to manifest their religious beliefs. As Justice Sachs said in *Christian Education South Africa*, 'The right to believe or not to believe, and to act or not to act according to his or her beliefs or non-beliefs, is one of the key ingredients of any person's dignity. . . . religious belief has the capacity to awake concepts of self-worth and human dignity which form the cornerstone of human rights.'[29] This use of 'dignity' thus enables a degree of commensurability to be identified between the values to be balanced in situations where there is an apparent clash of rights protected. The solution is one that is most compatible with advancing 'dignity'. Neither side of the debate is ruled out of court, there are no 'outlaws', and respectful attention is given to the claims of both parties.

The Canadian and South African courts have not, however, stopped there. In addition, they have developed two approaches to the application of proportionality that the ECtHR has so far shown too little appetite to embrace. The first is the importance of evidence. Because 'dignity' attaches to both sides of the debate, each right side's carries significant weight. Restrictions on either right should be considered to be justified only after a close analysis of the facts of the case. One might have supposed that one of the features that marks courts out as different from legislatures is their meticulous (some non-lawyers might say obsessive) attention to facts and evidence. Yet the cases I am considering here are noticeably thin when it comes to the Court's analysis of the relevant facts, and its attitude to evidence can charitably be described as cavalier. In *Sahin*, for example, as Jennifer Westerfield points out, 'Turkey presented no evidence at all that the wearing of the headscarf in schools is inconsistent with its principle of secularism', nor 'significant evidence that wearing the headscarf contravenes the principle of equality', and yet the Court still accepts its assertions on both issues.[30]

The second Canadian and South African approach is an approach to the interpretation of rights and interests that attempts to create the maximum space for rights by, seemingly paradoxically, requiring both sides in the dispute not to push their rights or interests to the limit. The German Constitutional Court has termed this the principle of 'practical concordance':[31]

---

[29] *Christian Education South Africa*, supra n 14, para 36.
[30] JM Westerfield, 'Behind the veil: an American legal perspective on the European headscarf debate', [2006] AJCL 656, 657. See also the dissenting judgment of Judge Tulkens in *Sahin*, supra n 2, para 4 in which she states, in criticism of the majority judgment: 'only indisputable facts and reasons whose legitimacy is beyond doubt – not mere worries or fears – are capable of . . . justifying interference with a right guaranteed by the Convention.'
[31] German Constitutional Court, 12 May 1987, *Classroom Crucifix Case*, BverfGE 93, 1, 1 BvR 1087/91, C.II.3a.

This conflict among various bearers of a fundamental right guaranteed without reservation, and between that fundamental right and other constitutionally protected objects, is to be resolved on the principle of practical concordance, which requires that no one of the conflicting legal positions be preferred and maximally asserted, but all given as protective as possible an arrangement.

Both rights carry significant weight. They should therefore both be protected to the greatest extent possible, and this requires that each be accommodated to the greatest extent possible by the other. Only by each side 'backing off' from making claims that assert its interests to the limit can this be accomplished.

As Lucy Vickers has written:

> This involves a recognition that the rights are not reconcilable, and yet that a *modus vivendi* must be found. If this is to be achieved, it will require an approach by the courts which is fact and culture dependent. One disadvantage of such a fact sensitive approach is that predicting the outcome in any particular case becomes difficult as so many interests are being weighed in the balance. However, the advantage of such an approach is that it can provide consistency in terms of clear procedural safeguards, to ensure that restrictions on religious freedom, and exceptions to the non-discrimination principle are only imposed after proper consideration of the varied interests at stake, in the cultural and political context of the particular member state.[32]

She continues, referring to the role of the courts engaging with this approach, that their role

> is not so much to determine exactly where the equilibrium between the rights ... to equality and the rights of religious groups to religious freedom and autonomy is to be found. Instead its role is to establish clear procedural safeguards so as to ensure that the correct issues are considered in the proportionality equation.[33]

Several prominent freedom of religion judgments in which this approach plays a central role illustrate this approach in practice. In *Multani*, for example, the Canadian Supreme Court struck down the order of a Quebec school authority that had prohibited a Sikh child from wearing a *kirpan* to school; the Court considered that the 'minimal impairment' element of proportionality required the state to satisfy the Court on the basis of evidence that a reasonable accommodation of the religious practice could not be achieved.[34] In *Christian Education South Africa*, Justice Sachs (giving the judgment of the Court) stated:

---

[32] L Vickers, 'Religion and belief discrimination in employment: the EU law' (European Commission, 2007), p 5.
[33] Ibid., p 5.   [34] *Multani v Marguerite-Bourgeoys* (2006) SCC 6, paras 51–53.

The underlying problem in any open and democratic society based on human dignity, equality and freedom in which conscientious and religious freedom has to be regarded with appropriate seriousness, is how far such democracy can and must go in allowing members of religious communities to define for themselves which laws they will obey and which not. Such a society can cohere only if all its participants accept that certain basic norms and standards are binding. Accordingly, believers cannot claim an automatic right to be exempted by their beliefs from the laws of the land. *At the same time, the state should, wherever reasonably possible, seek to avoid putting believers to extremely painful and intensely burdensome choices of either being true to their faith or else respectful of the law.*[35]

The power of this approach is evident in these cases, not least because whether or not one agrees with the result in any particular case,[36] at least the reasoning is considerably more transparent than in the ECtHR, and it is usually determined on the facts and the context rather than on the basis of ungrounded and sweeping statements of principle.

DIGNITY, DISCRIMINATION AND REASONABLE ACCOMMODATION

This approach is by no means incompatible with the ECHR jurisprudence on religion. First, the ECtHR has identified dignity as the basis for freedom of religion, although this analysis is noticeably absent from the Islamic cases. Indeed it is extraordinary that, given its recent prominence in ECtHR jurisprudence, the concept is never mentioned in the *Sahin* or in the *Refah* cases.

Second, the need to accommodate religious beliefs was the basis for the approach that the Court took in *Thlimmenos v Greece*,[37] a case that is also noticeably absent from the judgments on Islamic cases. The applicant was a Greek national. He had, due to his religious beliefs as a Jehovah's Witness, disobeyed an order to wear military uniform. He had been imprisoned. He was then refused an appointment as a chartered accountant on the basis of the criminal conviction. He argued that the legitimacy of such refusal should be made dependent on the nature of the offence in question, and of the motives behind it. The ECtHR adopted the concept of reasonable accommodation, in the context of this claim of discrimination on grounds of religious belief. The decision held that Article 14 of the ECHR,

---

[35] *Christian Education South Africa*, supra n 14, para 35 (emphasis added).
[36] Indeed in *Syndicat Northcrest v Amselem* [2004] 2 SCR 551, 2004 SCC 47 the Canadian Supreme Court split on precisely the issue of whether both sides had compromised enough.
[37] (2000) 31 EHRR 15 (GC).

forbidding discrimination on religious (or many other) grounds, requires member states not only to treat equal cases equally, but also to treat unequal cases differently. Formally neutral provisions may thus be considered as discrimination under the ECHR. Paragraph 44 of the judgment provided:

> The right not to be discriminated against in the enjoyment of the rights guaranteed under the Convention is also violated when States without an objective and reasonable justification fail to treat differently persons whose situations are significantly different.

Another way of putting what is essentially the same point is that Greece breached Article 14 read with Article 9 when it failed to reasonably accommodate the consequences of the claimant's assertion of his religious beliefs.

The ECtHR has adopted the concept of reasonable accommodation in the context of disability under Article 14. Switzerland levied tax for exemption from military service on a man with disabilities who, because of his disabilities, could not carry out compulsory military service. In *Glor v Switzerland*,[38] the Court held that the Swiss Government had violated Mr Glor's rights under Article 14 read with Article 8 (guaranteeing the right to private and family life). The Court held that the Swiss authorities failed to provide reasonable accommodation to Mr Glor in finding a solution that responded to his individual circumstances. There is nothing in *Glor* to suggest that the concept of reasonable accommodation does not also reflect a willingness to apply the concept of reasonable accommodation in the context of religion. Indeed, *Thlimmenos* itself is an example of such an application. Such 'practical concordance', respecting the dignity and rights on both sides of a debate, is to be welcomed; and could bring more securely under the ECHR's wing those Muslim citizens who currently risk being made outlaws from its protection. The application of 'reasonable accommodation' in Article 9 cases is now the subject of considerable debate within the ECtHR, with different judges taking different stances, and the outcome is uncertain.[39]

---

[38] App no 12444/04 (2009).
[39] Contrast *Jakóbski v Poland*, (2010) 30 BM Rc 417, App no 18429/06 (2010) and *Gatis Kovalkovs v Latvia*, App no 35021/05 (2012) (both of which can be seen as implying recognition of reasonable accommodation in freedom of religion cases) with *Sessa v Italy*, App no 28790/08 (2012) in which the majority appeared to reject the application of the concept of reasonable accommodation in Article 9, but with a strong dissent from Judges Tulkens, Popovic and Keller.

Legal pluralism: should English law give greater recognition to Islamic law?

CHAPTER 7

Family law: current conflicts and their resolution

Elizabeth Butler-Sloss and Mark Hill

Should English law be giving greater recognition to Islamic law? The question is widely discussed; but we must tread with caution. This is an area of particular importance and sensitivity. The matter is not well understood in the public at large and the printed media in particular, as the fallout from the Archbishop of Canterbury's lecture on the subject bears witness.[1] From our own perspectives, respectively as a former family judge and a scholar of law and religion,[2] we reflect on the relationship between English family law and families who live in the UK and are British citizens, but who have their own separate culture, family traditions and religious system, which may have an impact upon their family disputes.

ENGLISH FAMILY LAW

English family law is entirely based upon statute law and the decisions of judges interpreting those statutes. Marriage and divorce remain matters exclusively for the civil law of this country. (Whilst the Church of England is empowered to solemnise matrimony, and legally obliged to do so in the case of parishioners, its ministers act as civil registrars on behalf of the state for these purposes.[3]) The jurisdiction of the civil courts on ancillary matters

---

[1] For the lecture and commentary on the fallout from it, see R Griffiths-Jones, 'The "unavoidable" adaption of *shari'a* law – the generation of a media storm', supra pp 9–19 and R Williams, 'Civil and religious law in England: a religious perspective', supra pp 20–33.
[2] Baroness Elizabeth-Butler Sloss was appointed as a Justice of the High Court, Family Division from 1979 to 1988 and served in the Court of Appeal from 1988 to 1999. Created a Life Peer in 2006, she speaks in the House of Lords on matters of family justice. Professor Mark Hill QC specialises in ecclesiastical law and religious liberty. He is an Honorary Professor at the Centre for Law and Religion at Cardiff University, Convenor of the Interfaith Legal Advisers Network and President of the European Consortium for Church and State Research.
[3] See *Parochial Church Council of Aston Cantlow v Wallbank* [2004] 1 AC 546, which considered the extent to which component parts of the Church of England might be public authorities for the purposes of the Human Rights Act 1998. Lord Hope of Craighead observed at para 61: 'The relationship which the state has with the Church of England is one of recognition, not of the devolution to it of

within divorce proceedings, such as the upbringing of children, cannot be ousted.[4]

English law, then, applies to all cases where the parties come to the English court for adjudication upon divorce, domestic violence,[5] financial disputes, determination of matters of residence and contact with the family, and other 'specific issues'. The religious and cultural tradition of the parties in an English court may, and often will, be relevant to their approach to the issues between them; but English law, and only English law, applies.

Now if the members of a family choose in a dispute to invoke the help of their own religious tribunals, there is no reason why those tribunals should not assist the family. The two major religious communities with their own separate legal tribunals are the Muslims with *shari'a* councils and the Jews with the Beth Din. A divorcing couple – both parties being of sound mind and properly advised, neither being under any sort of compulsion – might choose to reach a provisional settlement on financial arrangements and on the children's upbringing, a settlement that might well be facilitated by the mediation of the parties' lawyers, the Beth Din or a *shari'a* council. The English court is likely to say, 'Why interfere with the settlement?' The court may well endorse the settlement. So the intervention of the tribunals *may* be very influential. But for the settlement's enforcement the terms of the settlement must pass under English law through the English courts; the decisions of religious tribunals on matters of family law are not recognised in the English courts, nor can they be enforced.[6]

The Family Justice Review established by the government under the chairmanship of David Norgrove published its final report in November 2011.[7] A premium is placed upon parties resolving disputes away from the court arena. Resort, or at least exposure, to mediation or to other forms of dispute resolution is to be encouraged before a dispute may be permitted to move into the family court. In this regard, the potential for the various faith communities to provide assistance in dispute resolution, either within their formal council or tribunal structure or more informally, is not to be ignored.

---

any of the powers or functions of government'. However, as Lord Nicholls of Birkenhead noted, 'some of the emanations of the [Church of England] discharge functions which may qualify as governmental. Church schools and the conduct of marriage services are two instances' (para 13).

[4] Matrimonial Causes Act 1973, s 34; Children Act 1989, s 10.
[5] The criminal law may also be invoked in cases of domestic violence.
[6] Disputes of this nature may not be the subject of binding arbitration under the Arbitration Act 1996; see I Edge, 'Islamic finance, alternative dispute resolution and family law: developments towards legal pluralism?', infra pp 125–31.
[7] Accessible at <http://www.justice.gov.uk/downloads/publications/policy/moj/family-justice-review-final-report.pdf>.

There is, then, no question of the jurisdiction of English secular courts being delegated or ceded to the courts or tribunals of religious organisations whether on a formal or ad hoc basis. This was never the suggestion of the Archbishop of Canterbury, nor of Lord Phillips of Worth Matravers, subsequently President of the United Kingdom Supreme Court, when he spoke at the East London Muslim Centre in 2008.[8] Reflecting on the Archbishop's lecture, Lord Phillips concluded:

> It was not very radical to advocate embracing *shari'a* Law in the context of family disputes, for example, and our system already goes a long way towards accommodating the Archbishop's suggestion. It is possible in this country for those who are entering into a contractual agreement to agree that the agreement shall be governed by a law other than English law. Those who, in this country, are in dispute as to their respective rights are free to subject that dispute to the mediation of a chosen person, or to agree that the dispute shall be resolved by a chosen arbitrator or arbitrators. There is no reason why principles of *shari'a* law, or any other religious code, should not be the basis for mediation or other forms of alternative dispute resolution. It must be recognised, however, that any sanctions for a failure to comply with the agreed terms of the mediation would be drawn from the laws of England and Wales. So far as aspects of matrimonial law are concerned, there is a limited precedent for English law to recognise aspects of religious laws, although when it comes to divorce this can only be effected in accordance with the civil law of this country.

In a Parliamentary Written Answer later in 2008, Bridget Prentice, Parliamentary Under-Secretary in the Ministry of Justice, responded to a request as to what guidance the Ministry had issued in respect of rulings of religious authorities in matrimonial disputes. She answered:

> We do not issue any guidance on the validity of fatwas or other rulings by a religious authority because there is no need for such guidance. *Shari'a* law has no jurisdiction in England and Wales and there is no intention to change this position. Similarly, we do not accommodate any other religious legal system in this country's laws. Any order in a family case is made or approved by a family judge applying English family law. If, in a family dispute dealing with money or children, the parties to a judgment in a *shari'a* council wish to have this recognised by English authorities, they are at liberty to draft a consent order embodying the terms of the agreement and submit it to an English court. This allows English judges to scrutinise it to ensure that it complies with English legal tenets. The use of religious courts to deal with personal disputes is well established. Any member of a religious community has the option to use religious courts and to agree to abide by their decisions but these decisions are subject to national law and cannot be enforced

---

[8] Lord Phillips of Worth Matravers, 'Equality before the law', address to the East London Muslim Centre, 3 July 2008, [2008] L & J 75; see further infra pp 286–93.

through the national courts save in certain limited circumstances when the religious court acts as arbitrator within the meaning of the Arbitration Act 1996. Arbitration does not apply to family law and the only decisions which can be enforced are those relating to civil disputes. Religious courts are always subservient to the established family courts of England and Wales.[9]

This represents an accurate and anodyne statement of English law, although it was badly misreported in the press at the time.[10]

THE ROLE OF RELIGIOUS COURTS

In 2009–11 Cardiff University undertook research on this subject and presented its findings at a symposium 'Britain's Religious Courts: Marriage, Divorce and Civil Law' in May 2011.[11] The project was given unprecedented access to proceedings in the London Beth Din, a *shariʿa* council in Birmingham and the Catholic National Tribunal for Wales. The research concluded that all three religious courts strongly encourage the parties to obtain a civil divorce before they engage in religious proceedings, recognising that the law of the state takes priority and that it is in no one's interest to have a 'limping marriage'.[12] The Catholic tribunal will not entertain an application for an annulment until a civil divorce has already been obtained. Also of interest is the fact that three-quarters of Muslim *nikah* marriages are not recognised in English law.[13] The Cardiff study strongly suggests that there is no desire on the part of the tribunals to

---

[9] Written answer on 23 October 2008 to question of Michael Penning (Shadow Minister, Health) to the Secretary of State for Justice, from Bridget Prentice (Parliamentary Under-Secretary, Ministry of Justice).

[10] It might usefully be noted here that in a recent decision of the United Kingdom Supreme Court, an arbitration clause in a commercial agreement was upheld which required any dispute under the agreement to be determined by three respected members of the Ismaili community: *Jivraj v Hashwani* [2011] UKSC 40. The argument that it amounted to unlawful discrimination in the provision of services on the grounds of religious belief was expressly rejected. The decision is instructive as it underscores the importance which the English courts now attach to the consensual alternative dispute resolution using religious leaders applying religious principles. Note also 'Belief in Mediation and Arbitration' (BIMA) established in 2011 as a facility for providing mediators and arbitrators skilled in addressing disputes with a religious dimension: see <http://bimagroup.org/>.

[11] The research was carried out by Cardiff Law School in conjunction with Cardiff University's Centre for the Study of Islam in the United Kingdom. It was funded by the Arts and Humanities Research Council and the Economic and Social Research Council.

[12] Note that the Divorce (Religious Marriages) Act 2002 introduced a new section 10A into the Matrimonial Causes Act 1973. This permits a party to a pending divorce to apply for the grant of a decree absolute to be delayed until a *get* has been secured from the Jewish authorities. The 2002 Act is sufficiently widely drafted to allow similar provision to be made for other religions but, to date, none has invited the Secretary of State to do so. See further R Griffith-Jones, 'Religious rights and the public interest', infra p 201.

[13] On the conditions for such recognition, see Edge, 'Islamic finance, alternative dispute resolution and family law', supra n 6.

which they had access to expand their jurisdiction or to supersede the State's authority. They see themselves as providing a service to the faithful whilst recognising and affirming the parties' citizenship as residents in the wider society.

The keynote address at the symposium was given by a distinguished family judge, Sir Andrew McFarlane.[14] He helpfully provided an overview of what the Archbishop of Canterbury had actually said in his lecture, as opposed to what he was reported as having said. The Archbishop identified three issues or difficulties which might arise if greater prominence were given to religious fora in the resolution of family disputes. These included the following:

Recognition of a 'supplementary jurisdiction' (for example the jurisdiction of a church tribunal) in some areas, but especially family law, could have the effect of reinforcing elements which are repressive or retrograde and which may have particularly serious consequences for the role and liberties of women, for example with regard to forced marriage. There is a real problem in giving authority to a religious court to determine certain matters finally and authoritatively, one being that to do so may deprive members of that religious community of the rights and liberties that they would otherwise be entitled to enjoy as citizens. Dr Williams, after teasing the issues out, considered that such difficulties might be addressed if we are prepared to think about the basic ground rules that might organise the relationship between jurisdictions in an open manner that did not give any 'blank cheques' to unexamined systems that may have an oppressive effect.[15]

For those, therefore, who practise in the family courts, the status and weight to be afforded to determinations of religious bodies is both topical and controversial.

McFarlane spoke at length about the courts' concern for children, whose welfare is paramount under the Children Act 1989. He emphasised that the determinations which family courts make about children are not made in isolation. Each decision is fact specific and takes into account all features concerning the multilayered environment in which the child is growing up, including religious, ethnic, racial and other matters. As he candidly identified:

In those parts of our jurisdiction which have large micro-communities, quite where the balance lies in welfare terms between recognising and accepting the traditional norms of other cultures within a society and judicial system based on European traditions and values is, and will remain, one of the greatest problems facing family

---

[14] AE McFarlane, '"Am I bothered?" The Relevance of Religious Courts to a Civil Judge', Keynote Address by The Honourable Mr Justice McFarlane, Justice of the High Court, Family Division, subsequently reproduced at (2011) 41 *Family Law* 946.
[15] Ibid.

courts in the twenty first century. It is necessary for the court to adapt the exercise of evaluating each child's welfare, and the factors in the welfare checklist that have to be considered, to the circumstances of the individual child.[16]

In particular with children, the English court will always want to investigate the circumstances and satisfy itself that any agreement relating to the children's custody and maintenance is fair and in the best interests of the children. The requirement that the welfare of the child is paramount has become the mantra of the family courts. Individual cases may well require consideration of religious features as part of the background, and it may well be that the determinations of religious courts and tribunals will be relevant, though not determinative, when such issues are considered in the family court.[17]

There are several examples of the family courts' engagement, with care and sensitivity, in matters where the religious or other cultural heritage of a child is in issue.[18] This affects more than just cases of Muslim families. In a claim which went to the House of Lords, in which Christian parents challenged a prohibition on corporal punishment of their children whilst at school on the basis that their religious beliefs required such punishment as part of the disciplining of their offspring, Baroness Hale of Richmond expressed the following concern. The case concerned judicial review proceedings in the Administrative Court where the welfare principle is of no application. Baroness Hale, however, sought to alert the court to the relevance here too of the welfare principle:

---

[16] Ibid.

[17] The Canadian experience outlined by M Boyd, 'Ontario's "*shari'a*" court: law and politics intertwined; infra pp 176–86, is highly instructive in this regard.

[18] Here are just two examples, in both of which McFarlane himself was involved. *A (Leave to Remove: Cultural and Religious Considerations)* [2006] EWHC 421 (Fam): Y, a nine-year-old Shia Muslim, would become tribal 'mantle-head' of over 4,000 families in Iraq – a position bringing high status and significant economic advantage – if (and only if) he was brought up and educated for the role by his father, H. Should his mother, S, be allowed to take him to Holland, where she had siblings, to live there with her new husband Mr A-S and herself? Judgment: Yes. Since Y was already living with S and Mr A-S in the UK, his future role as mantle-head was already forfeit; and his father's ongoing denigration of his mother was distressing him deeply. *Re S (Children) (Specific Issue Order: Religion: Circumcision)* [2004] EWHC 1282 (Fam): A Jain father and Muslim mother separated when their daughter R was nine and son K was eight. The children had until then, in a predominantly Jain home, had 'the best of both [religious] worlds'; the parents had achieved this by pretending at the mosque, for several years, that the father was Muslim. The children were now based with their mother, who sought the court's permission to have K circumcised, so that he – and in consequence R and their mother – could play a full part in the Muslim community. The father objected: he feared that the children would lose their links with their Jainism and with himself. Judgment: K was not (until he was competent to make the decision for himself) to be circumcised. The court would not sanction the parents' deception of the mosque; and it was in the children's best interests to continue to enjoy 'the best of both worlds'.

This is, and has always been, a case about children, their rights and the rights of their parents and teachers. Yet there has been no-one here or in the courts below to speak on behalf of the children. No litigation friend has been appointed to consider the rights of the pupils involved separately from those of the adults. No non-governmental organisation, such as the Children's Rights Alliance, has intervened to argue a case on behalf of children as a whole. The battle has been fought on ground selected by the adults. This has clouded and over-complicated what should have been a simple issue.[19]

The courts can be faced with particular issues, when considering determinations by religious authorities: if there is doubt, for instance, whether the welfare of the children had been paramount in the determination, as such welfare in practice is understood by English law;[20] or if there is doubt whether the testimony of a man and a woman – in this case, of the husband and the wife – had been given equal weight.[21] Perhaps more fundamental is the further perception that submission to religious courts and tribunals can be coercive and therefore that the voluntary element – essential in the different setting of binding arbitration – is lacking. The process, so it is suggested, is undermined by the possibility that one, or perhaps both, of those engaging in the process is an unwilling participant.

CONCLUSION

Increasingly pluralism within society and the appreciation of the multi-faceted nature of human identity has consequences for family courts which operate, not in rarefied isolation, but in the harsh and demanding realities of the real world. They have shown themselves adept at addressing the myriad

---

[19] *R v Secretary of State for Education and Employment and Others* [2005] UKHL 15, per Baroness Hale of Richmond at para 71.

[20] For the prevailing views on the custody of children after divorce in the schools of Islamic jurisprudence, see D Pearl and W Menski, *Muslim Family Law* (third edition, London, 1998), p 411: in *Hanafi* law, the mother retains the right of custody until age seven for boys and nine for girls; in *Maliki* law, until puberty for boys, marriage for girls; in *Hanbali* law, until age seven for both boys and girls, after which the child is given a choice between either parent; in *Shafi'i* law there is no fixed limit and the child is, on attaining discretion, given a choice between either parent. For flexibilities, see ibid., pp 412–25.

[21] On the testimony of women: 'When you enter into transactions involving a debt for a fixed period [in the future], reduce it to writing. And let a scribe write it down between you in fairness ... And bring two witnesses from among your men. Should there not be two men, then a man and two women of the women that you choose to be witnesses; if the one of the two errs, the one may remind the other.' – Qur'an 2:282, tr. MH Kamali, *Freedom of Expression in Islam* (Cambridge, 1997), pp 66–8. Kamali emphasises that this concerns only contracts where payment is immediate but delivery is postponed and that in the final clause the dual can refer to two men or to two women; he notes too that women in Muhammad's time were more frequently illiterate than men and were not customarily engaged in commercial or judicial transactions.

novel questions which arise in cases concerning the upbringing of children. They have shown an awareness of and a sensitivity to religious sensibilities and of the nature of Islamic identity within the context of British citizenship. There is scope for family courts to take into account matters of *shariʿa*: the religious element can be a significant part of the parent's, family's or child's experience. As McFarlane observes, 'I am interested in seeing the individual human beings in a family case in a rounded way because of the impact that these individuals have with respect to the individual child whose welfare is my paramount concern'.[22] However, as McFarlane also firmly stated, family judges are not – nor should they be – subservient to or reliant upon the determination of a religious court.

[22] McFarlane, '"Am I bothered?"', supra n 14.

CHAPTER 8

Islamic finance, alternative dispute resolution and family law: developments towards legal pluralism?

Ian Edge

INTRODUCTION: THE ARCHBISHOP'S LECTURE IN FEBRUARY 2008

The application of Islamic law[1] generally in the UK has become a publically contentious issue since early 2008 when Dr Rowan Williams, then Archbishop of Canterbury, gave his lecture, 'Civil and Religious law in England: a Religious Perspective'.[2] The lecture was intended to be a consideration of the religious aspects to the question posed early on by the Archbishop: 'what level of public or legal recognition if any might be allowed to the legal provisions of a religious group'?[3] In attempting to answer this question the Archbishop recognised that it applied to all religious groups, but as the lecture was the foundation lecture for a series of debates on 'Islam in English Law,' his concern was predominantly with the issues thrown up by the fact that a very sizable Muslim community was now living in the UK[4] with very different cultural and religious allegiances from those of the majority of the population.

I would like to acknowledge my deep appreciation and thanks to Robin Griffith-Jones for his unfailingly courteous but sharp-eyed and clear-headed comments and suggestions for this chapter which have undoubtedly enhanced the original. Any remaining errors are entirely my own.

[1] The terms 'Islamic law' and '*shari'a*' create problems of definition. For the purposes of this chapter, I will refer to 'Islamic law' as those rules of Islamic law which Muslims follow and apply in the contemporary world and '*shari'a*' as the traditional rules of Islamic law found in the medieval textbooks of the various Sunni and Shia schools of Islamic jurists.

[2] The Archbishop was taken to task by the media for advocating the inevitability of the application of Islamic law in Britain. This was not based upon his lecture, which was cautious and careful to state that all religious norms had to take second place to English secular law, but to a line in a radio programme recorded before the lecture; see Robin Griffith-Jones, 'The "unavoidable" adoption of *shari'a* law – the generation of a media storm'; supra p 13.

[3] Supra p 20.

[4] The figures from the 2001 census were 1.54 million in England and Wales and 40,000 in Scotland giving a total of approximately 1.6 million. The figures from the 2011 census are not yet available. S Gilliat-Ray suggests a figure of 2.4 million for 2009, *Muslims in Britain: an introduction* (Cambridge, 2010), p 117.

The Archbishop outlined what he saw as the 'broader issues around the rights of religious groups within a secular state'[5] but he recognised that 'there remains a great deal of uncertainty about what degree of accommodation the law of the land can and should give to minority communities with their own strongly entrenched legal and moral codes'.[6] In essence the Archbishop outlined his idea that the state should consider moving beyond the present legally positivist system, which he characterised as an 'unqualified secular monopoly',[7] to a system in which there would be some form of accommodation of religious or cultural norms. He saw individuals in modern society as having multiple and sometimes overlapping allegiances and castigated as 'very unsatisfactory' the view that 'to be a citizen is essentially and simply to be under the rule of the uniform law of a sovereign state in such a way that any other relations, commitments or protocols of behaviour belong exclusively to the realm of the private and of individual choice'.[8] Thus, in his view, the state fails in its central purpose of communicating with, and including, all its citizens if it fails to recognise the 'other' within its midst who may want to order some of their affairs in a different way from the majority. As long as these different cultural or religious norms did not 'deprive members of the minority community of rights and liberties that they were entitled to enjoy as citizens'[9] then the system should accommodate them by providing for a liberty of choice. By this accommodation individuals would be able to choose whether they wanted certain limited matters to be dealt with by secular or by religious principles. The Archbishop made clear (in the question and answer session that followed the lecture)[10] that he was not advocating 'parallel systems'[11] of courts and tribunals, but speaking 'about how the law of the land most fruitfully, least conflictually, accommodates practice'. The areas the Archbishop specified as suitable for this accommodation were 'some aspects of marital law, the regulation of financial transactions and authorised structures of mediation and conflict resolution', and possibly inheritance; whereas he accepted that there should be no accommodation in the cases of criminal law, polygamy and forced marriage.

THE LECTURE OF LORD PHILLIPS IN JULY 2008

Less well known, but almost as important, was a lecture entitled 'Equality before the Law' which the then Lord Chief Justice, Lord Phillips of Worth Matravers, first President of the Supreme Court of the UK, gave at the East

---

[5] Supra p 21.   [6] Supra p 21.   [7] Supra p 31.   [8] Supra p 23.   [9] Supra p 26.
[10] Accessible at <http://www.templechurch.com/PublicDiscussions/documents/ArchbptextwithQandA.pdf> and (2008) 10 Ecc LJ 262, pp 275–82.
[11] (2008) 10 Ecc LJ 262, p 276. Suitable areas, supra p 32.

London Muslim Centre on 3 July 2008, five months after the furore generated by the Archbishop's speech.[12] Lord Phillips began by referring to his own personal family history: his grandparents, Sephardic Jews, had emigrated from the increasingly restrictive and inimical state of Egypt to the freedom of England at the beginning of the twentieth century. From this, his aim was to show how English law had developed historically into a system in which the courts offer the same justice to all who come before them regardless of gender, race, creed or religion. In doing so, he defined the approach of English law as being based upon the concept of liberty and quoted Lord Donaldson as saying: 'The starting point of our domestic law is that every citizen has a right to do what he likes unless restrained by the common law or by statute.'[13] It was this freedom, Lord Phillips stated, that allowed people to exercise their religions freely; and concomitantly there could be, and indeed there already is, some accommodation for dispute resolution in accordance with religious principles based upon the consent of the parties. Nevertheless, like Dr Williams, Lord Phillips was adamant that any accommodation could only be within the confines of English law by stating that 'those who come to live in this country must take its laws as they find them'.[14]

THE REACTION OF THE LABOUR GOVERNMENT

The Labour government of the day was clearly concerned by the attention that the topic was attracting and strove to reassure the public that there was no intention by the state to apply Islamic law in any form. The then Justice Minister Bridget Prentice on 23 October 2008 announced clearly to Parliament, in answer to a question about matrimonial disputes, that 'the shari'a has no jurisdiction in England and Wales and there is no intention to change this position'. Further, on 29 October 2008, the then Lord Chancellor Jack Straw addressed the Islamic Finance and Trade Conference in London:

> As a Government, it has always been our aim to extend opportunity and prosperity to all – to all parts of the country and to all different communities. This is not about preferential treatment. It is about fairness. This is not about political correctness. It is about respect ... This is the thinking which underpins our approach to shari'a law. Of course those who live in this country will always be governed by English law and will be subject to the jurisdiction of English courts ... Speculation abounds on this point, so let me say once again: there is nothing whatever in English law that

[12] [2008] L & J 75. [13] In *Attorney General v Observer Ltd* [1990] 1 AC 109, 178. [14] Supra n 11.

prevents people abiding by *shariʿa* principles if they wish to, provided they do not come into conflict with English law. There is no question about that. But English law will always remain supreme, and religious councils subservient to it. It is worth me stressing that nothing has changed to the law or to the Government's position. There has been press comment suggesting that the ability to apply to an English court for a consent order for a *shariʿa* ruling is somehow a new development. It is not. We have not changed the position on *shariʿa* law established by the previous government in 1996 and nor will we do so. The position remains as before: there is no room for parallel legal systems. Regardless of religious belief, we are all equal before the law.[15]

The position of the Government therefore seemed clear: there was no intention for the foreseeable future to create separate systems of religious courts in the UK that would be officially recognised.[16]

It is the argument of this chapter that the Archbishop was mistaken to propose the accommodation of religious practices if the result would be the creation of any form of legal pluralism in the UK. I argue that legal pluralism is not acceptable as a blueprint for the future accommodation of the UK's religious practices. Accommodation for religious practices should only be by recognition of such practices by the state and by their inclusion within laws promulgated by the state. Indeed the freedom and flexibility of English law already admits the application of Islamic law in a number of areas for Muslims in Britain. In Islamic financial transactions and alternative dispute resolution, particularly arbitration, two of the legal areas mentioned by the Archbishop, English law already incorporates aspects of Islamic law into state law. Family law is the one important remaining area where there is a need to provide for further inclusion into state law notwithstanding the unfounded fears and criticisms of some groups.

THE PRESENT POSITION IN RELATION TO ISLAMIC FINANCE

Islamic financial transactions are recognised and enforced as valid in English law in a number of circumstances and the Islamic financial industry in the UK is one of the fastest growing and innovative in the then global market.[17] Under the former Labour government, Ed Balls, the then Economic Secretary to

---

[15] Accessible at <http://www.justice.gov.uk/news/sp301008a.htm>.
[16] There remains an official system of Christian religious courts (the Consistory Courts and the Court of Arches) which predate the Reformation and which are now formally recognised in primary legislation under the Ecclesiastical Jurisdiction Measure 1963. Although originally they had jurisdiction over marital and inheritance matters, they now deal primarily with changes to the fabric and ornaments of consecrated church buildings of the Church of England.
[17] See E Housby, *Islamic Financial Services in the UK* (Edinburgh, 2011).

the Treasury, said in a speech on 30 January 2007 that the aim of the Treasury was to make the UK 'a global centre for Islamic Finance' and explained that 'since the Bank of England's first Working Party in 2002 and the Finance Act 2003, when the Government started shaping the tax and regulatory framework to allow for the development of Islamic Finance products, the market has grown from strength to strength'.[18] Referring to the change made to stamp duty to facilitate the market in Islamic mortgages, he said: 'In 2003 we removed the double stamp duty land tax charge on *murabaha* and *ijara* based mortgages enabling at a stroke the explosion in Islamic home finance.'

In this case English law was amended, via the Finance Act 2007,[19] in order to ease the development of Islamic mortgages which work on the basis not of a single transfer of title (from vendor to purchaser) but of two transfers (from vendor to Islamic bank and at the end of the mortgage from Islamic bank to purchaser). Without an amendment to the tax regime, Islamic mortgages would be subject to the payment of two amounts of stamp duty and hence less competitive. The *quid pro quo*, however, is that recent Finance Acts have provided for the taxation of Islamic financial transactions and by so doing have accepted them into mainstream banking. This is not done purely out of a desire to assist the Muslim community; the prime reason for the Treasury's actions is clearly economic. The Treasury has now set up a special unit dedicated to understanding (and proposing taxation of) new Islamic instruments. The promotion of Islamic finance is undoubtedly good for the British economy and numerous Islamic banks have been set up on the back of this Treasury support.

Such banks are licensed to operate as UK institutions and the transactions they enter into are ultimately governed by English law no matter how they are designated. Two decisions of the English High Court[20] and the Court of Appeal[21] held that the English courts applying the Contracts (Applicable Law) Act 1990 will not accept a choice of law clause in a commercial contract which seeks to apply only Islamic law or the *shari'a* to such a contract. The Contracts (Applicable Law) Act 1990 incorporated the Rome Convention into English law and the English courts have now held effectively that the Convention only provides for territorial choices, not

---

[18] See http://webarchive.nationalarchives.gov.uk/+/http://www.hm-treasury.gov.uk/newsroom_and_speeches/speeches/econsecspeeches/speech_est_300107.cfm.

[19] Finance Act 2003, ss 72, 73. The provisions were extended by the Finance Act 2005 c5 to equity sharing arrangements, and to profit sharing agreements by the Finance Act 2006, ss 95–8.

[20] *Islamic Investment Company of the Gulf (Bahamas) Ltd v Symphony Gems NV* [2002] All ER (D) 171 (Feb).

[21] *Shamil Bank of Bahrain v Beximco Pharmaceuticals Ltd* [2004] EWCA Civ 19.

personal or religious, of law. (The Rome Convention was replaced by the Rome I Regulation, 2009.) Thus, although an accommodation already exists to some extent in the area of Islamic financial transactions, in that certain specified Islamic financial transactions are recognised and permitted by English law and taxation, public policy still prevents the creation of an Islamic financial instrument in England that is expressly said to be solely governed by Islamic law or *shariʿa*.

THE PRESENT POSITION IN RELATION TO ALTERNATIVE DISPUTE RESOLUTION

In the second area of suggested accommodation, alternative dispute resolution, it is already possible for Muslim parties to submit some of their civil (but not criminal) disputes to determination by mediation or arbitration according to Islamic procedures or to the application of Islamic law (or *shariʿa*) as adopted by various Islamic (or *shariʿa*) councils or tribunals. Parties may by agreement give to arbitral tribunals a greater flexibility as to the law which the tribunal may apply to determine the submitted disputes than parties have by law in drafting a choice of law clause in an ordinary commercial contract to be applied by the courts.

As to the law that may be applied by an arbitral tribunal, section 46(1) of the Arbitration Act 1996 provides that an arbitral tribunal may decide a dispute (a) in accordance with the law chosen by the parties as applicable to the substance of the dispute or (b) in accordance with such other considerations as are agreed by the parties. Subsection (b) clearly permits an arbitral tribunal in England to apply legal rules other than those that are strictly territorial, which would include the application of the rules of a religious law (with the agreement of both parties). In this way Islamic law (or *shariʿa*) principles could be applied by an arbitral tribunal with the clear agreement of the parties.

Any arbitral award decided upon Islamic law (or *shariʿa*) principles would then be enforceable in the courts in the same way and subject to the same defences and challenges as an ordinary arbitral award. The Arbitration Act 1996 is straightforward as regards enforcement: the award of an arbitrator (or arbitral tribunal) following a proper reference to arbitration is enforceable by leave of the court in the same manner as a judgment of the court.[22] Generally an English court will enforce an arbitral award without considering its merits. This is the case for all arbitrations. There are no special provisions for the awards of religious tribunals in general or for Islamic or *shariʿa* tribunals in particular.

---

[22] Arbitration Act 1996, s 66(1).

The enforcement of any arbitration award by an English court is subject to challenge as to substantive jurisdiction[23] where it is claimed that the arbitral tribunal acted outside its powers, and as to substantive irregularity,[24] which would include failure to comply with the general rule of procedure that the tribunal should act fairly and impartially giving each party a reasonable opportunity to put their case.[25] Thus any limitation by a *shari'a* tribunal as to the weight to be accorded to a person's testimony based upon their sex or religion would most likely fall under this heading and result in the award being unenforceable.

In any event, a court has a general duty to consider that an arbitral award complies with public policy and is in the public interest. Thus, the Court of Appeal in the case of *Soleimany v Soleimany*[26] refused to enforce an award of the Beth Din applying Jewish law where the underlying transaction involved the commission of illegal acts in Iran. The arbitral tribunal was entitled to disregard the underlying illegality of the parties' acts but the award would not be enforced by the English courts.

The requirements of public policy would also certainly mean that an English court would not enforce any arbitral award that failed to comply with the provisions of the Human Rights Act 1998 and the European Convention on Human Rights (ECHR). For example, the overriding objective of the so-called Muslim Arbitration Tribunal that the tribunal should act in accordance with Qur'anic injunctions and Prophetic practice as determined by recognised Schools of Islamic Sacred law[27] must be read subject to the public policy limitations outlined above.[28]

A number of recent High Court cases in England have considered such Islamic dispute settlements and one has recognised[29] and one refused[30] recognition according to compliance or non-compliance with the requirements of the Arbitration Act 1996.

Faith-based arbitration often concerns mixed issues of law and religion, where the parties particularly want to choose an arbitrator familiar with their religion. Such arbitration in the UK seemed to have been dealt a fatal blow when the Court of Appeal in July 2010 in the case of *Jivraj v Hishwani*[31]

---

[23] Arbitration Act 1996, s 67. [24] Arbitration Act 1996, s 68. [25] Arbitration Act 1996, s 33.
[26] [1999] QB 785. [27] See Procedural Rules of the Muslim Arbitration Tribunal, section 1.
[28] Of course, it may be that enforcement may not be sought outside the religious community in which the religious tribunal is based and there is anecdotal evidence that faith-based arbitral awards are sometimes enforced within a religious community by the threat of naming and shaming within the community and by removal of religious privileges.
[29] *Bhatti v Bhatti* [2009] EWHC 3506 (Ch) (strictly an arbitration within the Ahmediyya community).
[30] *Al-Midani v Al-Midani* [1999] 1 Lloyds Rep 923. [31] [2010] EWCA 712.

struck down an arbitration clause that provided that the arbitrators had to be members of the Ismaili community as being contrary to the Employment Equality (Religion and Belief) Regulations 2003, which make it an offence for an employer to discriminate on grounds of religion. Apart from the contentious finding that an arbitrator was an employee,[32] the decision prohibited parties from overtly providing in an arbitration clause that an arbitrator should have to follow a particular religion. The legislation has an exemption provision but the Court of Appeal chose not to apply it. In April 2011, however, the Supreme Court[33] unanimously overruled the Court of Appeal and decided that the Regulations did not apply to arbitrators because they were not employees; this was because, most importantly, an arbitrator 'does not perform those services or earn his fees for or under the direction of the parties'.[34] Hence there is nothing to stop parties providing for a religion-based condition for appointment to arbitrator.

Finally, the Arbitration Act provides[35] that the rules of law relating to the matters which are not capable of settlement by arbitration (the issue of arbitrability) continue to apply to all arbitrations. Thus, certain matters may not be the subject of arbitration. There is no exhaustive or prescribed list, but these include crimes and any other public law matter including family law matters.

Most legal issues of family law are public law issues and are therefore also considered not to be capable of arbitration. This includes dissolution of marriage, by divorce or nullity, and orders relating to the upbringing of children. Mediation, entirely different from arbitration, is supported by the general law as an ideal mechanism to be used in issues concerning the distribution of the family financial resources upon separation or dissolution of a marriage. (Some *shari'a* tribunals fail to make the distinction between arbitration and mediation.) Any supposed 'arbitration award' on such matters may be considered by an English Family Court determining issues of financial relief but the 'award' will carry little weight (still less will it be determinative) if it fails to take account of the generally applicable rules of family law.

This was made very clear in the aftermath of the Archbishop's lecture when it was suggested in some quarters (mainly in the tabloid press) that the Arbitration Act 1996 permitted binding arbitration in family law matters. The government stepped in very firmly to quash any such notion. Elizabeth

---

[32] The Court of Appeal equated an arbitrator to a plumber, accountant or lawyer (paras 16 and 19) all of whom provide services for hire. All of these, however, can be scrutinised in their performance and sacked if they deviate from agreed processes and procedures. This cannot as easily be said of an arbitrator.
[33] [2011] UKSC 40.   [34] See para 40.
[35] See Arbitration Act 1996, s 81(1)(a). Settlement agreements as a result of mediation (see below) are enforceable as contracts, not as arbitration awards under the Arbitration Act.

Butler-Sloss and Mark Hill have quoted the answer of the then Minister of Justice, Bridget Prentice, to a written question on 23 October 2008 by Michael Penning MP as to what guidance the Ministry of Justice issues on the validity of *fatwas* or other rulings by religious authorities in the determination of matrimonial disputes.[36] The government's position was reiterated by Lord Bach in the House of Lords on 24 November 2008 in answer to a question put by Lord Lester of Herne Hill whether English courts may refuse to give effect to a consent order embodying the terms of an agreement reached by the parties to a family dispute in a *shari'a* council, rabbinical court or other religious body, on grounds of public policy. Lord Bach, Government Whip, said:

It is the function of the court to question any order which appears unfair irrespective of the process through which the parties to a family dispute reached that agreement and, if appropriate, to refuse to make the order requested . . . this applies to agreements reached by parties having gone through religious councils as well as any other process. The Government have no plans to amend the provisions of the Arbitration Act 1996. Arbitration is not a system of dispute resolution that may be used in family cases. The issue of enforcement of an arbitrated decision only arises in civil disputes.[37]

More recently, on 7 June 2011, Baroness Cox introduced into the House of Lords the 'Arbitration and Mediation Services (Equality) Bill', which indicates the level of concern in some quarters over the rise of religious tribunals in the UK and their unfettered and unregulated activities. The Bill sought to add two clauses to the Arbitration Act 1996: first, to state expressly that any criminal or family matter cannot be the subject of arbitration proceedings;[38] and, second, to prevent an arbitration agreement or process from discriminating against women in giving less weight to a woman's evidence than to a man's, in the unequal division of an estate on intestacy as between male and female children and in according to women fewer property rights than men.[39] The Bill would also require public officials to inform individuals that polygamous marriages are without legal protection and may be unlawful,[40] would make it easier for a court to set aside an agreement negotiated under possible duress[41] and would make it a criminal offence falsely to purport to exercise a judicial function on any matter which

---

[36] Supra p 110; HC Deb col 562W.
[37] See HL Deb 24 November 2008 Col 246W. A number of authors – among them, eg, K Moore, *The Unfamiliar Abode: Islamic law in the United States and Britain* (Oxford, 2011), pp 104–5 – persist in maintaining, quite wrongly, that the use of *shari'a* tribunals in the UK has been given official sanction by the UK Government.
[38] See the Bill, s 4. [39] See the Bill, s 3. [40] See the Bill, s 1. [41] See the Bill, s 5.

is within the jurisdiction of the criminal or family courts.[42] The Private Member's Bill had its second reading on 19 October 2012.[43]

Given that family law matters may not be the subject of binding religious arbitration in the UK the question then remains as to how the judicial system regards and deals with issues of Islamic law that may arise. It is this third legal area of family law that the Archbishop referred to in his lecture that is the major concern of this chapter and with which I deal in the next section.

THE PRESENT LEGAL POSITION IN THE UK IN RELATION TO RELIGIOUS FAMILY LAW

As far as English law is concerned, all matters of domestic family law are governed by statute and the common law. Questions in relation to the validity and status of marriage, divorce, the residence, custody and maintenance of children and ancillary relief are all dealt with solely and exclusively by specially designated family law judges in the Family Division of the High Court and in the County Courts. These judges are generally former practitioners in family law and so have considerable expertise in the intricacies and complexities of family law but are also sympathetic to the predicaments of the parties who come before them. English law considers, as a matter of public policy, that these areas of family law should be subject to the sole jurisdiction of an English family law judge applying a unified and single set of legal principles to all regardless of race or creed. This is an example in practice of Lord Phillips's view that everyone is and should be equal under the law.

At present English family law does permit some divergence on religious grounds. This is seen most clearly in the area of marriage where the Marriage Act 1949 accepts a number of different marriage ceremonies as creating a valid marriage. Two conditions are (almost) universal: (i) the ceremony must be held in a place authorised for the celebration of marriages[44] and (ii) either a licensed registrar or a person authorised to act as a registrar or as the registrar's substitute must be present to register the

---

[42] See the Bill, s 7.
[43] The UK Government's stance may also be compared with that of Ontario in Canada, as charted and analysed by M Boyd, the author of 'the Boyd Report', in 'Ontario's "*shari'a* court": law and politics intertwined', infra pp 176–86.
[44] As a minor exception to this, the Marriage Act 1983 permits the marriage of housebound or detained persons at their place of residence.

marriage. Thereafter different conditions apply to marriages celebrated under the various different forms.

Section 5 of the Marriage Act 1949 provides that there are four methods by which a marriage may be solemnised according to the rites of the Church of England, the most common being after the publication of banns. By a singular act of pragmatism the religious ceremony has incorporated a provision for registration and the officiating clergyman or clergywoman acts as registrar for the purposes of registration.

Two other religious traditions are expressly provided for in the legislation: the Society of Friends (or Quakers)[45] and those professing the Jewish religion.[46] (In the second case both parties must be Jewish.) In these two cases certain religious officials are authorised by the state to act as registrars at marriages conducted according to their respective religious rites.[47] The official is, respectively, the local registering officer for the Society of Friends and the secretary of the husband's synagogue.[48] As a result, those marrying according to Anglican or Quaker rites and Jews undertaking a Jewish ceremony are not required to go through a separate civil marriage; the religious marriage, duly registered, is recognised by the state as creating a valid English marriage.[49] One feature of these rules will be of particular value later in this discussion: the marriages of Jews and Quakers are not confined to registered buildings.[50]

Section 26 of the Marriage Act 1949 provides for marriages to be solemnised under certificates of a superintendent registrar; this comprises the majority of all other marriages. There are provisions for a wholly secular civil marriage in a Register Office[51] (or licensed approved premises since the Marriage Act 1994[52]), where religious symbolism is prohibited and where either the registrar or other authorised person will register the marriage.

Provisions for marriage are available to non-Anglican Christian churches and to other religions, if the place of the ceremony is registered for marriages and if the 'trustees or governing body' of the place nominate an 'authorised person' to act on behalf of the superintendent registrar to register the marriages held there.[53] Thus a Roman Catholic Church can become a

---

[45] See Marriage Act 1949, s 26(1)(c).   [46] See Marriage Act 1949, s 26(1)(d).
[47] Marriages according to the usages of the Society of Friends and according to Jewish rites were already excluded from the terms of Lord Hardwicke's Act of 1753.
[48] See Marriage Act 1949, s 53.
[49] This is completely at odds with the French system of laicism in which only a civil ceremony of registration creates a valid marriage. Such a system however has the advantages of logic and simplicity.
[50] See Marriage Act 1949, s 26(c) and s 26(d).   [51] See Marriage Act 1949, s 26(1)(b).
[52] See Marriage Act 1949, s 26(1)(bb).
[53] See Marriage Act 1949, s 43 and s 53(e). On the off-putting and sometimes inappropriate requirements for a building's registration, see A Bradney, 'How not to marry people', (1989) 19 *Family Law* 408.

registered building for the purposes of the Marriage Act 1949 and there is evidence that Roman Catholic priests are being nominated as 'authorised persons' for the registration of marriages. But lamentably few other religious communities seem to have used this route for ensuring that their marriage ceremonies are recognised under the law of the land. Perhaps one of the main reasons for this is that to be valid any marriage ceremony in a registered building must conform to the rites of a civil marriage, the words of which must be in the English language and are not always considered appropriate. Some Muslims, for example, believe (erroneously) that the words of an Islamic marriage must be in Arabic; other religions require the words of marriage to be in a language other than English with which the parties are more familiar. In such cases a marriage is not at present possible in the UK. Furthermore, to be a valid English marriage the words of marriage must be said in the presence of the other party and by each party. This may create problems in a Muslim marriage: the sexes, including the bride and groom, may be (but are not always) separated during the marriage ceremony; and the consent of the bride is in some traditions given on her behalf by her guardian.

The imams or heads of some mosques might be understandably reluctant to register their building of worship for the celebration of marriages where marriages – perhaps polygamous, perhaps involving a party under the English law's age of consent – are taking place that are valid under Islamic but not under English law. But the reason for non-registration may be simpler. It should be emphasised that an Islamic marriage (and indeed a Jewish marriage) is a purely civil contract; it is not a 'sacramental' solemnisation such as is familiar within Christian traditions. Any overtly religious component is optional. As a result, the venue for an Islamic marriage ceremony takes on a less important role and a home (which is not generally admissible as a permissible venue for a marriage recognised by English law except in the case of housebound or detained persons) is as appropriate as a mosque for the contract's simple formalities. Only a small proportion of Islamic marriages in the UK are in fact contracted in a mosque; many are contracted at home or in the offices of a *shari'a* council. There is therefore little reason for a mosque's imam or head to go through the (sometimes burdensome) process of registration, and such registration may still only bring a few extra Islamic marriages within the purview of English law.

The result is that there are many Muslim couples undertaking only an Islamic marriage in England who will not be considered as being married according to English law so that they will not be able to call upon the English courts if the marriage breaks down, except in respect of issues relating to their children. Their situation is acute as the parties cannot obtain a divorce from the English courts and hence the courts also have no jurisdiction to award financial relief except, again, in relation to any children. This is a source of great concern as a large proportion of the Muslim population in Britain falls, in consequence, outside the protections of the English family law system; and this inevitably impacts disproportionally upon Muslim women.

The English courts have over the years sought to find practical solutions to this problem within Muslim and other religious communities. Where parties have lived together as husband and wife in a monogamous union for a long period of time and have brought up children, at all times believing themselves to be married in accordance with religious tenets, the English family court may try to recognise the union. In *Gereis v Yagoub*, a ceremony of marriage took place in a Coptic Orthodox church in London. The priest was not properly authorised and none of the proper procedures for a valid English marriage had been complied with. The parties cohabited on the assumption that there was a valid marriage and it was only when one party sought to obtain a divorce that the status of the marriage needed to be considered. The English judge held that the marriage was a marriage, albeit void, on the ground that the parties had intentionally gone through a Christian ceremony of marriage but which unbeknownst to them was in disregard of the formalities of the Marriage Act 1949. Importantly, since it was a (void) marriage jurisdiction was available for the English court to award matrimonial relief to the wife.[54]

In *Chief Adjudication Officer v Kirpal Kaur Bath*[55] the parties were married according to Sikh religious rites (and by no other ceremony) in a Sikh temple in London in 1956 and had lived together as husband and wife, bringing up two children, for thirty-seven years until the husband died in 1994. Unbeknownst to the parties the Temple was not registered until 1983. The widow's claim for a pension on the basis of her husband's contributions (made as a supposedly married man) was rejected by the DSS on the basis that she was not married. Two of the judges in the Court of Appeal, using the ancient common law principle of marriage by cohabitation and repute, stressed that it would be inequitable not to recognise the marriage. The Court went to remarkable lengths to make possible the recognition. Evans

---

[54] [1997] 1 FLR 854. Robert Walker LJ in *Chief Adjudication Officer v Kirpal Kaur Bath* [2001] FLR 8, at 22 suggested that 'some reliance' might have been placed on the Christian character of the ceremony; Hughes J in *A-M v A-M (Divorce: Jurisdiction: Validity of Marriage)* [2001] 2 FLR 6 thought the judgment may have been 'merciful'. In *Leigh v Hudson* [2009] EWHC 1306/ EWCA Civ 144, by contrast, the couple had been warned by the Christian priest in a penthouse in South Africa that without the relevant formalities the marriage would not be valid; it was declared to be a non-marriage (as distinct from a void marriage) and therefore Miss Hudson was unable to make a claim for ancillary relief. For non-marriages, infra p 129.

[55] *Kirpal Kaur Bath*, supra n 54.

LJ went so far as to say that as there was no clear evidence that the Temple had not been registered or the celebrant licensed then he would make presumptions in favour of both facts; while Walker J (with whom Schiemann J agreed) merely held that there was insufficient evidence to rebut the presumption without going into details. In both cases the judges referred to public policy in choosing to recognise a marriage created by what they called an irregular ceremony which was of long standing and had borne children.

If in general the courts were to recognise such ceremonies as sufficient to bring about a 'void' marriage, so founding jurisdiction in the Family Court to grant a decree of nullity, the Family Court would have jurisdiction to grant financial relief to the parties and particularly to the wife. But the courts have tended to resist such recognition. In 2001 the problem of unregistered Islamic marriages led to the creation of a new category, of 'non-marriages': in *A-M v A-M* Hughes J concluded that the couple were in a non-marriage in that the Islamic ceremony in London 'in no sense purported to be effected according to the Marriage Acts, which provide for the only way of marriage in England' (paragraph 24); it could not therefore found jurisdiction for nullity.[56] The judge looked nonetheless for an equitable solution: he accepted that in the complex circumstances, the wife could rely on the presumption of marriage arising from twenty years' cohabitation and reputation. This decision, however, turned on its own unusual facts, because there was an evidential basis for saying that a ceremony of marriage could have occurred abroad in a manner authorised to take place without the wife's knowledge or presence. It was nevertheless held in *Al-Saedy v Musawi* that the 'presumption of marriage' arising from long cohabitation and reputation of being married cannot generally apply to 'validate' a known and identified ceremony which had failed to create any marriage at all.[57]

In 2009, in *AAA v ASH*,[58] a British Muslim father sought to have an unregistered Islamic ceremony of marriage that had taken place in England recognised so that he could be afforded rights of parental responsibility over his child born of the marriage. The couple had chosen not to pursue an Islamic

---

[56] *A-M v A-M*, supra n 54, followed by Park J in *Gandhi v Patel* [2001] EWHC 473 (Ch). *R v Bham* had introduced the notion, under similar circumstances, of a 'purported marriage', [1966] 1 QB 159. See R Probert, 'When are we married? Void, non-existent and presumed marriages', (2002) 22 OJLS 398 generally on the status of marriages in English law.
[57] *Al-Saedy v Musawi* [2010] EWHC 3293.
[58] *AAA v ASH, The Registrar General for England and Wales, The Secretary of State for Justice, The Advocate to the Court provided by the Attorney General* [2009] EWHC 636 (Fam). The couple knew from the start that their particular *nikah* (unlike that of the husband's brother) was not recognised as a valid marriage under English law (paras 8, 44, 48, 50, 69).

marriage in a mosque with a registration that would have been recognised under English law. Their cohabitation, after the private Islamic ceremony, was too brief to give rise to a presumption of marriage. The marriage was therefore declared by the judge to be under English law a 'non-marriage'; matrimonial relief was therefore not possible, and the father had no real rights at all (except those of an unmarried but no longer cohabiting parent).[59]

In 2011, in *G v M*, otherwise *El Gamal v Al Maktoum*,[60] in relation to an unregistered Islamic marriage which took place in a private house in or around 2007, the judge presumed in both parties belief that they were contracting a marriage valid under English law, so as to permit an application to issue a petition for nullity without a marriage certificate. After a trial of the evidence in December 2011, Bodey J concluded that the unregistered Islamic marriage ceremony was a 'non-marriage' in line with his previous decision of *Leigh v Hudson* so that the wife's petition for nullity failed.

Finally and most recently (September 2012), an English court came more closely than ever before to recognising an unregistered Islamic marriage in *MA v JA* [2012] EWHC 2219. Here Moylan J held that an Islamic marriage which had taken place in a mosque that was registered for the purpose of marriages but where the relevant authorised person did not perform the ceremony so that the marriage was not subsequently properly registered although there was a written marriage contract was to be treated as a valid English marriage. The circumstances that weighed heavily with the judge were that the parties had intended to marry under English law (albeit in a Muslim ceremony) and so had chosen the mosque deliberately with this in mind; the parties had been told that the marriage would be recognised by English law by the Chairman of the mosque; and an authorised person was present during the ceremony although he did not actually perform the ceremony.

The English courts, then, are all too aware of the problems associated with unregistered religious marriages and may, in deserving cases, attempt to find ways to get around the legal problems that those marriages create. To stretch existing concepts of law, however, leads to uncertainty in the law's application. The long-term solution would be to facilitate the recognition of Islamic marriages in England. This would most easily be effected by a simpler method of authorising (not buildings at all but only) *persons* whose presence as state-registered registrars would be sufficient at Islamic (and indeed at all other religious) weddings to have the marriage

---

[59] English law does not have a concept of a putative marriage as some other jurisdictions (such as California) do.
[60] [2011] EWHC 2651 (Fam); [2011] EWHC 3763. For *Leigh v Hudson*, supra n 54.

recognised under English law.[61] This would at a stroke assist those who are often the most vulnerable members of society.

THE PRESENT POSITION IN RELATION TO OTHER AREAS OF FAMILY LAW

It may be argued that if Muslim marriages are accepted then English law will also have to accept Islamic divorces, polygamy and Islamic rules affecting children. This is not necessarily so. As regards the three religious traditions accorded special privileges in the Marriage Act 1949, none of them claims that any special rules should apply on divorce which they accept as a secular act of the state with which the religious authorities cannot interfere.[62] Although marriage is a personal act of two parties, its legal effects are more widely felt and as a matter of public policy the state and the courts become involved in its outcome and its dissolution. It creates a status *in rem*[63] which affects third parties and it then becomes a matter of public policy and interest which requires the state to intervene to consider all the ramifications of divorce. It is therefore a clear rule of English law that all divorces in England must be obtained in the English family courts which will apply English law.[64]

As regards the Jewish faith, although Jewish marriages are recognised by English law, Jewish divorces are not. Thus, practising Jews will obtain both a secular and a religious divorce, so that either party may thereafter contract a second valid religious marriage. There are various Jewish tribunals in the UK, known individually as a Beth Din, which consider issues relating to Jewish law and among them Jewish divorce.[65] The problem of the *agunah* ('chained') woman has plagued modern Jewish society. Jewish law requires a Jewish husband to divorce his wife by giving a paper of release known as a *get*;[66] this document he must give of his own free will and, subject to some very unusual exceptions, he cannot be forced by a Jewish court to do this;

---

[61] This has been the situation in Scotland since 1977. See the Marriage (Scotland) Act 1977 as amended in 1980. See the Scottish case of *Aneeka Sohrab v Sulman Khan* (2002) SLT 1255 for a case where an Islamic marriage in a mosque in Glasgow was held a nullity for failure to comply with the procedures laid down in the 1977 Act.
[62] Jewish religious divorces are dealt with by the Beth Din. Quakers accept civil divorce as ending a Quaker marriage.
[63] See GC Cheshire and PM North *Private International Law* (thirteenth edition, London, 1999), p 704.
[64] See Family Law Act 1986, s44 and Rules 77 and 78, AV Dicey, JHC Morris and L Collins *The Conflict of Laws*, (fourteenth edition, London, 2006)
[65] See *Berkovits v Grinberg* [1995] Fam 142 and B Berkovits, 'Transnational divorces: the Fatima decision', (1988) 104 LQR 60.
[66] Ibid.

thus, a husband who wants to prevent his wife from marrying religiously a second time may simply refuse to give her a *get*. The Divorce (Religious Marriages) Act 2002 was enacted to provide a sliver of relief to such a Jewish wife. Where a Jewish husband seeks to divorce his Jewish wife in the secular English family courts, she may apply to stay the proceedings until such time as he has given her the *get*. The Act may be extended to other religious groups by statutory instrument made by the Lord Chancellor[67] but no such Statutory Instrument has yet been made.[68]

There is therefore no logical or legal reason why accepting a more liberal test for the validity of Muslim marriages (or indeed those of any other major religious group) should necessarily lead to the application of religious divorce law.

A similar view may be expressed with the argument in relation to polygamy.[69] The institution of marriage is a public right created by private means. The state has an important interest in defining the rights and duties of the parties to the marriage (particularly where there are children) and of ensuring its ordered dissolution. When the Archbishop himself was asked in the question and answer session that followed his lecture whether he accepted that Muslim men should be permitted to exercise a right of polygamy in England, he said unequivocally that 'because most aspects of our public law assume, as axiomatic, certain attitudes to the rights of women which are not readily compatible with the practice of polygamy, I cannot really see this as an option'.[70]

This does not mean that English law does not recognise polygamous marriages at all. English law now recognises polygamous marriages in some circumstances in contradistinction to the position in the nineteenth and early twentieth centuries when even foreign polygamous marriages were not accepted or recognised at all as being contrary to English public policy which only recognised the Christian notion of a monogamous and indissoluble marriage.[71]

---

[67] See Divorce (Religious Mamepes) Act 2002, s 1(1), which adds a new section 10A to the Matrimonial Causes Act 1973. The provision for extension to other religions is in s 10A(6).
[68] In the case of *Kandeel v Hands* [2010] EWCA Civ 1233 the argument that it was discriminatory for the 2002 Act only to apply to the Jewish religion was rejected. The Court of Appeal held that the 2002 Act provided a legislative mechanism for religious usages other than Jewish ones to become prescribed by the Act which was considered perfectly reasonable.
[69] Strictly a male marrying more than one wife is known as polygyny whereas a woman marrying more than one husband is known as polyandry. Polygamy refers to the two terms. In lay terms, polygamy refers to what should be known as polygyny. That term has been accepted into case law and statute with that meaning and so this chapter will use that terminology accordingly.
[70] See supra n 10.
[71] See *Hyde v Hyde* [1866] LR 1 PD 130, which defined marriage in the classic phrase of 'the voluntary union for life of one man and one woman to the exclusion of all others' at p 133 per Sir JP Wilde (later Lord Penzance).

This lack of recognition applied even to Islamic marriages abroad (even if they were actually monogamous) because the husband had the capacity to take a further wife or wives under that foreign law: this was the so-called 'potentially polygamous marriage' which was caught by the restriction created by the English common law.

Thus, for many years the English courts denied any relief to Muslims living in England who had been married abroad according to Islamic law even if they were married monogamously. This meant hardship for Muslims living in England as they could not seek divorce in the English courts. Furthermore, as their marriage was not recognised, the wife and children could not inherit as legitimate heirs or have any legal rights in English law. Gradually however the law changed; first the courts began to recognise foreign Islamic marriages for some purposes and eventually in 1972 statute permitted Muslims married abroad to seek matrimonial relief from the English courts albeit only if monogamously married.[72] The final vestiges of this rule however did not disappear until 1995.[73] Public policy had over this period changed and so since 1995 English law has assimilated an actually monogamous Muslim marriage (foreign or English) to the status of any other monogamous English marriage while still maintaining the refusal to recognise an actually polygamous marriage entered into in the UK. For example, a person who has decided to make England his or her permanent home, whatever their nationality, and so becomes domiciled in England, has no future capacity under English law to enter into an actually polygamous marriage.[74] This causes some problems for Muslims from South Asia who have made their home in England, and so have become domiciled in England, but who nevertheless return and enter into an actually polygamous marriage in their country of origin. It also causes problems for Muslim women born in the UK who enter actually polygamous marriages outside the UK as a second wife. Under English law, such a marriage is void as the wife does not have any capacity to enter into it but at least the wife will thereby have access to matrimonial relief following a decree for nullity. The reason why such a person is advantaged over a wife of an unregistered Islamic marriage in the UK is that the marriage was entered into abroad so that conflict of law rules come into play. It is however another example of how inequitable the failure to recognise unregistered

---

[72] Matrimonial Proceedings (Polygamous Marriages) Act 1972 now re-enacted as Matrimonial Causes Act 1973, s 47 and amended by the Private International Law (Miscellaneous Provisions) Act 1995.
[73] At least as regards potentially polygamous marriages: see the Private International Law (Miscellaneous Provisions) Act 1995.
[74] See Matrimonial Causes Act 1973, s 11(d).

Islamic marriages that take place in the UK is, in that the English domiciled wives of actually polygamous marriages outside the UK may get financial relief (after a decree of nullity) whereas the actually monogamous wives of unregistered Islamic marriages in the UK are denied such rights.

As regards dissolution of marriage, English law accepts and enforces foreign divorces including Islamic divorces as long as they comply with the provisions of the rules on recognition of foreign divorces now found in Part II of the Family Law Act 1986. *Talaq* divorces by a Muslim husband may be recognised under the Act but only if they satisfy the stringent conditions that generally require the husband to have maintained substantial connections with the country in which the *talaq* takes place.[75] Recognition may be refused if the family judge considers that the wife has not been properly notified of the proceedings or that she has not been given an opportunity to be part of the proceedings or that recognition is manifestly contrary to public policy, but this rarely applies in the case of Islamic divorces.[76]

Another important area of law in which Islamic law is permitted to play a role in England is inheritance. English law is one of the most liberal in terms of testamentary power giving a person almost complete freedom when it comes to making a will. The power has only relatively recently been reduced by giving dependents a right to seek an order for their continued support.[77] In this regard, the Archbishop had no reason to introduce as a problem the position of Muslim widows. English law, through its completely flexible law of wills, enables a testator to disinherit any of his heirs or alternatively to prefer any one of them at the expense of the others. This liberality means that Muslims may organise succession to their estate in accordance with Islamic law principles by means of making a will. In such a will, a Muslim testator may discriminate between heirs favouring sons over daughters in accordance with Islamic law rules. It may be said that this is wrong and that the English courts should intervene to stop such practices but, if English law accepts that a testator has complete freedom to prefer one heir over another, or even validly leave the whole of their estate to a cat's home to the exclusion of all the heirs, it is difficult to see why an English court should intervene as a matter of public policy in the case of a so-called Islamic will. Providing,

---

[75] See Family Law Act 1986, s 46(1) and (2) for the rules that apply to overseas divorces obtained by way of proceedings and those obtained other than by way of proceedings respectively. What is to be accepted as 'proceedings' has been extensively and liberally interpreted by the courts: see *El Fadl v El Fadl* [2000] 1 FCR 683, recognising a *talaq* in Lebanon, and *MA v JA* [2012] EWHC 2219 recognising a *talaq* in Saudi Arabia.
[76] See Family Law Act 1986, s 51(3).
[77] See the Inheritance (Provision for Family and Dependants) Act 1975.

therefore, for the application of the rules of inheritance of Islamic law to apply in a will in this way does not and should not contradict English public policy.[78]

THE POSSIBILITY OF CHANGE

As is evidenced above, English law already accords considerable freedom to apply Islamic law in one's private relations in England though subject always to public policy which has changed and continues to change in tune with alterations in society's values. It is possible to foresee further changes and their benefits in the near future. We have seen how the requirements for solemnisation of a valid marriage in England could be simplified: without any reference to the venue or its registration for marriages, individuals within a recognised community could be nominated as 'authorised persons' who would act at the ceremony as or on behalf of registrars.[79] This may not be easy to achieve in the UK's Muslim community. Authority within the Muslim community, as the Archbishop appreciated, is fragmented; and heavy state regulation might be resented, particularly if it involved standards and qualifications, drawn up by the government, to which the community's authorised persons must adhere. But it is hard to see these as insurmountable problems.

Such acceptance of registrar-based marriages would certainly be the one constructive change that would bring Muslims within the jurisdiction of the English courts and indicate the state's willingness to include Muslims within the scope of mainstream English family law. Such acceptance would leave unchanged the rules governing divorce. Muslims married under English law would need a civil divorce granted by the English courts and could also, quite separately, want an Islamic divorce that would free

---

[78] This is of course different from a case of intestate succession where the rules of English law are of mandatory applicability which do not comply with Islamic ideas of inheritance. Baroness Cox's 2011 Bill, s 3(2), would seek to make it expressly clear that no arbitration agreement or process could make an award on the basis of an unequal distribution based solely on gender. The intestacy rules are subject always to the heirs coming to a different agreement post-death. Presumably the courts would enforce such an agreement if it were shown to be a completely voluntary arrangement between persons of full capacity who were cognisant of the legal repercussions.

[79] In the Jewish faith this process is for the most part under the control of the Board of Deputies of British Jews, but the Marriage Act 1949, s 67, also refers to the West London Synagogue and the Liberal Jewish Synagogue and those connected to them, so that a multiplicity of authorities does not seem impossible to countenance. Any such regulation would be subject to the difficult question of deciding whether a particular faith is worthy of the designation 'religion'. For such proposals for a 'celebrant based' system of marriage, drafted by the Labour government in 2002 (and incorporating recommendations from the Church of England), see N Lowe and G Douglas, *Bromley's Family Law* (tenth edition, Oxford, 2007), pp 63–4.

them to marry again in a religious marriage ceremony. One could even extend the provisions of the Divorce (Religious Marriages) Act 2002 to Muslims (and other faiths) so that the obtaining of a decree absolute of secular divorce could be stayed by a Muslim wife until her Muslim husband gave her an Islamic divorce.[80]

Islamic councils and tribunals might also play a role in aiding the process of dissolution of marriage. Section 1 of the Family Law Act 1996 lays down principles to be adhered to on marriage breakdown and was meant to be prefatory to a system of mandatory mediation in family matters. This was never achieved in practice; but the English family courts still encourage the use of voluntary mediation of marital disputes and in cases of marital breakdown mediators may assist in the creation of a separation agreement that the courts can endorse with the minimum of fuss. The use of mediation in family cases was in November 2011 given further support by the Report of the Family Justice Review.[81]

Sir Jim Lester MP, at the time of the passing of the 1996 Act, said in Parliament: 'Mediation is essentially a private and informed decision-making process and that is its strength. However because of that it does not include the safeguards of due legal process. Therefore it requires high standards of training and practice to secure the participation of both parties.' The Family Law Protocol of 2006 provides for best practice in all aspects of private family law disputes and has a number of sections dedicated to how such mediations should be effected. One of its most important recommendations is that the mediators are properly qualified and there are now a number of recognised bodies that accredit family mediators. There is every reason therefore to promote the use of mediators from the Muslim community in relation to the breakdown of Muslim marriages. Such mediation could be by individual Muslim mediators or through procedures laid down by existing Muslim institutions. One such institution comprises the Conciliation and Arbitration Boards which have been set up by the members of the Shia Ismaili community under the auspices of the Aga Khan Foundation. These Boards are established around the world for the use of members of the Ismaili community and have had considerable success particularly in the field of family mediation. This is mainly because each

---

[80] For the differences between the Battei Din and the *shari'a* councils, see R Griffith-Jones, 'Religious rights and public interest', infra p 201.
[81] For the Final Report of the Family Justice Review 2011, see <http://www.justice.gov.uk/downloads/publications/policy/moj/family-justice-review-final-report.pdf>.

National Board has a wide voluntary membership, including both women and men, and they have developed and encouraged an excellent programme of training in the techniques of mediation as well as providing a basic knowledge of the legal rules applicable in family law in the states in which they operate. In many countries the Ismaili system is now held up as a model of Islamic mediation.[82]

If mediation results in a separation agreement then, of course, those agreements must be considered and ratified by an English family law judge who will want to be assured that the agreement has been voluntarily entered into and complies with English family law, particularly in relation to any provisions relating to children. It seems unlikely that an English judge will acquiesce in the application of the child custody rules of Islamic law which often, though not always, remove custody of children from a mother at an early age, or when she remarries; but there seems no reason why such an agreement should not include payment of Islamic dower (*mahr*) as part of the financial arrangements on divorce.[83]

IS IT LEGAL PLURALISM?

Legal pluralism has become, like multiculturalism, a symbol of the modern age. It is a highly contested concept, attracting much debate and acrimony, and its definition often depends upon the background and ideological orientation of the author.

There are a number of different ways in which existing nations around the world may be said to have a pluralistic legal system. In a federal system each individual state has its own legal system although they may be subject to areas of uniform federal law and a single overarching court authority. This is the paradigm case of the US and Canada where common law and civil law systems exist side by side. It is also partially true of the UK which comprises the separate legal systems of England, Wales (until recently part of the English legal system), Scotland and Northern Ireland, all of which are subject to the Supreme Court in London. In federal systems there are often complex legislative competencies at regional and state levels. The UK is also now part of a proto-federal European structure; it is therefore also subject to European law and has accepted the ascendancy of European courts in some

---

[82] See M Keshavjee, *Dispute Resolution among Muslims in the Diaspora* (doctoral thesis, SOAS, 2009).

[83] *Mahr* is a sum of money payable by the Muslim husband to his wife and is a mandatory effect of a valid Islamic marriage. See R Mehdi and J Nielsen (eds), *Embedding Mahr in the European Legal System* (Copenhagen, 2010).

areas of law. Law in the UK is therefore a patchwork of different laws and courts with their own separate competences but ultimately each court or tribunal is accorded its role by means of the sovereign power of Parliament.

This then leads to a consideration of those states where different sources of legal rules are recognised within a legal system. This generally takes one of two forms: (i) where, within a state, enclaves with separate legal rules may operate; and (ii) legal systems which sanction or enforce different systems of legal rules in state-wide but separate and parallel court systems. This normative state of affairs is sometimes described as state legal pluralism or official legal pluralism. Many states operate such a system of legal pluralism, even though it is not always acknowledged or appreciated.

Examples of the first type would include Canada where the First Nations as indigenous and aboriginal Peoples of Canada are recognised as having their own sphere and enclave of legal competence just as some Native Indian tribes do in the US within their reservations. A more recent example would be the creation of the common law legal enclave of the Dubai International Financial Centre within Dubai and the UAE.[84] Examples of the second type are more numerous and include many of the states of Asia and Africa (and increasingly elsewhere) which openly accept that a number of parallel legal systems (or rules in certain areas) may operate within the state and be sanctioned by it. In particular, many of these states accept that, in the area of family law, ethnic or religious communities may operate their own rule systems with official legal effect. Thus marriage, divorce, inheritance and other matters dealing with personal status may be regulated by the rules of that particular community on the basis of the sanction of the state.

In some countries the state courts themselves apply these different rule systems whereas in other countries legal issues are dealt with by courts or tribunals within the community of people concerned whose decisions are accorded the force of law or are enforceable within the state system. As an example of the former, in Egypt all the religious courts were abolished in 1955 so that the state courts now deal with all personal status issues even though the state recognises that a number of different religious legal systems may be applicable. As an example of the latter, Syria still maintains religious courts for those religious communities (fourteen in number) which the state recognises and their decisions are enforceable in the state courts in the same way as other first instance decisions. In some ways it could be said that whereas such states are pluralistic (in accepting the presence within the state

---

[84] For First Nations, see C Bell and RF Paterson, *Protection of First Nations Cultural Heritage: laws, policy and reform* (Vancouver, 2009); for Dubai, see <www.difc.ac> and <www.difccourts.ae>.

of different legal systems) the legal systems themselves are not pluralistic, merely consisting of different systems of rules that rarely conflict or overlap.

Western states have generally unified and centralised their legal systems so as to remove the multiplicity of such courts. England still maintains religious courts for the Church of England but with a severely circumscribed jurisdiction. Other European countries have abolished such courts completely. There has been, however, in recent years a realisation that the rules of minority ethnic and religious communities ought to receive state recognition particularly as exceptions to the application of certain state rules: for example, by accepting religious methods of animal slaughter or allowance for religious dress[85] or, as we have seen, by providing for special tax rules to promote religious types of contract. In a sense this is not making the state pluralistic but merely accepting that state law should accommodate as much as possible the desires of minorities to be governed according to their religious or cultural norms provided always that they are applied within the strictures of state law.

Another type of pluralism, known as unofficial or non-state legal pluralism, seeks to maintain that the rules which a particular religious or ethnic community follows, even though not given any state recognition, produces legal norms which the state should acknowledge. Its proponents see this as a purely descriptive state of affairs in which more than one legal or cultural order operates within a given social field; legal pluralism, therefore, is seen simply as a statement about social reality in that people may be subject to or may follow more than one rule system. Only one of these systems is generally given state recognition; the other or others are acknowledged for a mixture of religious and cultural reasons. Religious communities such as Jews or Muslims abide by practices which they accept as obligatory but which are not enforced by the state. There may even be parallel or equivalent adjudicatory mechanisms which the particular community may choose to call 'courts'. In the case of the Jewish community in the UK the Battei Din have operated outside the official state system for many years and, as we have seen, were given some recognition in the Divorce (Religious Marriages) Act 2002 where a High Court judge may refuse a civil divorce if one party is refusing to give the other a religious, Jewish divorce.

---

[85] Jewish and Islamic slaughter methods are exempt from provisions in the Welfare of Animals (Slaughter or Killing) Regulations 1995 that require stunning, and certain specific methods are laid down in accordance with the EU Directive 93/119/EC. The Regulations were amended in 1999 to ensure that Jewish or Islamic slaughtering is only carried out in licensed premises. The Motor Cycle Crash Helmets (Religious Exemption) Act 1976 permits Sikhs to wear turbans without a crash helmet when riding a motor cycle.

Much of the literature of legal pluralism, by invoking a wide definition of 'law', seeks to include all of these various types of legal pluralism as valid and equal components in any legal system. This is argued most forthrightly by John Griffiths[86] who distinguishes (in non-neutral language) the 'strong' pluralism recognised by an empirically accurate analysis of society from a 'weak' pluralism discerned by scholars who, it is claimed, are blinkered by the ideological delusions of legal 'centralism' or positivism. 'Law', properly understood in the sense of strong pluralism, 'is the self-regulation of a "semi-autonomous social field"[87] ... A situation of legal pluralism – the omnipresent, normal situation in human society – is one in which law and legal institutions ... have their sources in the self-regulatory activities of all the multifarious social fields present, activities which may support, complement, ignore or frustrate one another.'[88] Griffiths ignores the coercive, mediatorial and unifying roles – all of them vital to a society's well-being – of positive state law.

Griffiths's view as developed by Masaji Chiba[89] has been taken up by such authors as Werner Menski who has spoken of the rules and norms of the Muslim community in England as forming a new system of law which he calls *angrezi shariʻat*[90] (Urdu for 'English *shariʻa*') or English Muslim law and which he maintains should be accorded recognition alongside state law in the UK. The terminology itself could mislead those who encounter it: *angrezi shariʻat* is not a term used within the Muslim community, and negates the commonly accepted premise of the *shariʻa* that it is a universal system even though there are many interpretations of it.[91] More substantively, such recognition would require a homogeneity of purpose, institutions and rules in the so-called English *shariʻa* which is sadly lacking in the UK's Muslim community. The interpretations of the Shia community and the Sunni community are very different, disabling from the start any sense of unity; and there are many different views within the UK's Sunni community as to which *shariʻa* rules are or should be applicable in the UK. The *shariʻa* rules applied by the various Muslim communities in the UK cannot therefore be thought of as the application of a single system with a clear set of agreed rules.

---

[86] J Griffiths, 'What is legal pluralism?', (1986) 24 JLP 1.
[87] See SF Moore, *Law as Process: an anthropological approach* (London, 1978) who posits this idea
[88] Griffiths, 'What is legal Pluralism?', supra n 86, 38–9.
[89] See M Chiba, *Asian indigenous Law in Interaction with Received Law* (London, 1986) and *Legal Pluralism: towards a general theory through Japanese legal culture* (Tokyo, 1989).
[90] See D Pearl and W Menski, *Muslim Family Law* (third edition, 1998), chapter 3, 'Muslims in Britain' and particularly pp 58ff.
[91] This is the doctrine of difference or *ikhtilaf*. The Prophet Muhammad said in a number of *hadith* that difference of opinion is for the Muslim community's benefit.

Developments towards legal pluralism? 141

A final difficulty should be mentioned, of a different kind. The *shariʿa* rules applied by the different Muslim communities among themselves in the UK often have their basis in the unreformed traditional rules of *shariʿa* which are almost nowhere applied in the Islamic world because important reforms and amendments (at least in personal status matters) have become almost universal. The *shariʿa* rules applied by Muslim communities in the UK therefore may be more conservative and restrictive than those currently applied in the Islamic countries from which Muslim immigrants to the UK have migrated.

For any application of religious law to have a truly long-term and meaningful effect in society it must in some way be recognised and applied by the state. There are two main ways by which this may be done: either as a completely parallel and separate system or as an accommodation within an existing system. The second case may result in a transformation either of the religious system or of the system into which it is grafted.

In the last part of his lecture, the Archbishop referred to a work[92] by an Israeli academic, Ayelet Shachar, who recommends that members of religious communities be given the right to consent to certain civil disputes being heard by religious tribunals whose decisions would then be recognised and enforced by the state. Shachar's academic posts have been in the US and Canada; but she herself confirms that the true origins of her book date back to her own childhood in Jerusalem. Underlying her work is a comparison with the states of Israel and the Levantine Middle East where the tribunals of certain religious communities are recognised as possessing jurisdiction in relation to many family and personal status matters that are determined by religious laws. But the resultant babel of laws and decisions does not create certainty or efficiency, particularly where there are inter-community marriages and transactions. Inheritance disputes for example can easily extend for generations.

Examples of uncertainty and inefficiency produced by states with parallel legal systems are legion.[93] States which have adopted or operate a judicially pluralistic system often experience considerable problems at the overlap of the various jurisdictions. In Malaysia there are frequent clashes between the civil courts and the *shariʿa* courts as to jurisdiction, most recently on the issue of religious conversion.[94] Even where a state, such as Egypt, applies separate systems of family law within a unified court system, there are still problems. For example, an Egyptian Copt converting to Catholicism has

---

[92] A Shachar, *Multicultural Jurisdictions: cultural differences and women's rights* (Cambridge, 2001).
[93] See MB Hooker, *Legal Pluralism: an introduction to colonial and neo-colonial laws* (Oxford, 1975) for the colonial heritage in many African and Asian states.
[94] See M Adil, *The Malaysian State and Freedom of Religion: a conceptual analysis with particular reference to apostacy* (doctoral thesis, SOAS, 2005).

been held by the Egyptian courts to be entitled to divorce his Coptic wife by Islamic *talaq* even though he was not a Muslim because he now belonged to a different Christian sect from his wife; Coptic law, therefore, could no longer apply, so that Islamic law applied by default.[95] This opens a route for Coptic husbands for the dissolution of their Coptic marriages which would otherwise be dissoluble on very few grounds.

There has been a call in some quarters of the Muslim community for separate Islamic courts to be established in the UK applying Islamic law.[96] It is said that multiculturalism inevitably leads to legal pluralism where two systems of law operate within the same territorial space but have different jurisdictional bases,[97] or that the right to freedom of religion in the ECHR includes a right to have a separate system of Islamic courts for the Muslim community.[98] There is no support in the UK government for separate systems of courts and probably little within the wider Muslim community itself, many of whose members have sought to live in England to escape the mandatory application of *shari'a* law.[99] There is then little call to explore the practical problem at which we have glanced above: Islamic law is not a single monolithic system of rules so that no single tribunal could be set up in the UK which would be accepted by all Muslims nor could any single set of Islamic rules be drawn up that would be acceptable to all.

CONCLUSION

Neither the Archbishop nor Lord Phillips advocated that the *shari'a*, or indeed any other religious system of law, should apply in the UK as a separate system of legal rules with its own officially sanctioned courts and tribunals. This is as well the position of the UK government that has, as we can see from the work of Sebastian Poulter, remained unchanged since the 1970s.[100] What each did agree was that there should be some accommodation made to religious communities within the existing legal framework and supported by legislation. The state would therefore continue to determine the extent to which religious norms were to be applied.

---

[95] See M Berger, 'Conflicts law and public policy in Egyptian family law: Islamic law by the backdoor', (2002) 50 AJCL 555.
[96] S Poulter, *Ethnicity, Law and Human Rights: the English experience* (Oxford, 1998) particularly chapter 6 which refers to the frequent calls by the Union of Muslim Organisations of the UK (UMO) for a separate system of Islamic Personal Law in the UK in the 1970s and 1980s.
[97] See Pearl and Menski, *Muslim Family Law* supra n 90, pp 74–5.
[98] See Poulter, *Ethnicity, Law and Human Rights*, supra n 96, chapter 3, 'Human Rights and Minority Rights'.
[99] See supra pp 110, 118–9 on the reaction of the Labour government.   [100] See supra n 96.

As to the existence and use of religious tribunals in the UK, neither the Archbishop nor Lord Phillips advocated a separate and parallel system of religious tribunals; they merely brought to public notice the use of such tribunals in areas of English law that were already amenable to mediation or to arbitration, and suggested that they be regulated by the state to ensure parity and adherence to existing legal rules based upon the ECHR and the Human Rights Act. Such tribunals would require consent by both parties to all parts of the process. Standards or codes of conduct would need to be drafted to ensure that the members of such tribunals understood the limited framework of English law within which they were allowed to function. Registration of religious tribunals might be problematical in the absence of a single authority representing Muslims in Britain. There already exist a number of areas of law where religious norms have been accepted as applying and accommodated within the present legal system in England. This has so far been accomplished with a minimum of fuss and publicity. What is called for is the further assessment, cogent and reasonable, of those areas of the *shari'a* which can be easily accommodated within the existing system; and the most obvious place to start would be the recognition of unregistered Muslim marriages in the UK.

CHAPTER 9

Judging Muslims

Prakash Shah

The current discussion of Muslim law and its relevance for British jurisdictions has largely bypassed the activity of the official courts. Whatever accommodation may or may not be given to Muslim law within British legal systems, judges in British courts and tribunals will need to ensure that greater attention is paid to the religion and mores of Muslim communities. Indeed, there is already evidence that British judges have had to reckon, and increasingly so, with issues of cultural specificity and expertise when cases involving Muslims come before them. In this chapter, I outline some of the tensions between legal traditions in such cases. The focus is on issues of marriage and divorce, and the argument centres on the need for a greater flexibility in judicial decision-making when Muslim cases come before courts.

The moral deficiency of those who subscribe to non-Christian religions is a well-established – and still endemic – theme in Western culture. Those who follow 'false religions' are morally suspect and, since it is assumed that action follows doctrine, their actions bear out the falsity of their doctrines. Modern secularism, although it purports to transcend the bias of particular religions, has not abandoned this theme, and it survives and reproduces through other, ostensibly non-religious, secular tests.[1] The underlying theme is clear and evident in the ways in which Western legal orders are responding to the presence of Muslims. Muslims, for their part, have not been able to formulate coherent responses to societal or legal pluralism, and generally assume that others should accept the centrality of their Islamic doctrines.[2] It may therefore be argued that neither the West nor its Muslims are fully prepared to respond to the globalisation, migration and pluralism

---

The research leading to this article was performed within the framework of the RELIGARE project. This project received funding from the European Commission Seventh Framework Programme (FP7/2007–2013) under grant agreement number 244635.

[1] SN Balagangadhara, *The Heathen in his Blindness: Asia, the West, and the dynamic of religion* (New Delhi, 2005).
[2] B Parekh, *Europe and the Muslim Question: does intercultural dialogue make sense?* (Amsterdam, 2007).

of contemporary times. Instead, each side manoeuvres with the aim of asserting the moral superiority of its own doctrines. This chapter takes these blockages to pluralist thinking as givens, and assumes that there is nonetheless a willingness to overcome them.

It is as well to start this discussion with a definition. References here to the legal tradition of Muslims are to an internally plural set of normative assumptions which refer not only to doctrinal Islamic prescriptions but also to the customs and conventions that operate within each distinct Muslim community and even family. Indeed, one could contemplate a finer-grained study which brings into greater focus the mechanisms of individuals' decision-making. Muslim law, then, should not be reduced to a doctrinal legal order, much less to a legal system with fixed rules about real life situations. This then raises the question, to whom should judges listen when attempting to construe the nature of the normative assumptions that individuals bring with them to courts, and how they should respond to them. In the attempt to assess the normative reality of Muslims one has to be careful not to give overriding attention to doctrinal prescriptions of Islamic jurists. Evidence of judicial activity in Muslim legal history and in contemporary times shows that Muslim judges have also used Islamic doctrines as but one set of criteria when making decisions, and generally to clothe in such doctrines decisions essentially reached on the basis of wider considerations of justice.

Linked to the presumption of moral deficiency is the fact that discussions on Islam and Western legal systems are largely based on stereotypes of gender relations within Muslim communities.[3] Discussions draw on the long-standing Western assumption that Muslim women are an oppressed group who do not enjoy equal civil rights under Islamic law or within Muslim communities. While there is no doubt that many types of disadvantages are suffered by Muslim women, we are not yet in a position to assess accurately how gender relations are functioning within British Muslim communities. We hardly research men; and we do not know how Muslims, whether men or women, use the law except through reported cases or the anecdotal evidence we come across as individual researchers. Are these anecdotes informing our theoretical viewpoints on men's and women's lives in Muslim communities and on their use either of *shari'a* or of official courts and laws?

---

[3] S Razack, *Casting Out: the eviction of Muslims from Western law and politics* (Toronto, 2008); S Fernandez, 'The crusade over the bodies of women', (2009) 43 *Patterns of Prejudice* 269.

We cannot assume that women are ill-informed nor that men are well-informed about their respective rights under official law and Islamic law. More often than not, both women and men appear to be confused, while trying to use legal norms and mechanisms instrumentally to further other social goals. Women appear to be just as likely as men to use their options under religious law, perhaps even more so, if the largely female customer base of the *shari'a* councils is anything to go by. There is also anecdotal evidence that Muslim women often cleverly use English law to make the best for themselves, and sometimes even take advantage of the ignorance of such women's lives among the legal system's personnel who may be moved to pity by the personnel's own stereotypes of the 'oppressed Muslim woman'. This is familiar 'code-switching,' which members of all minorities use to varying extents, and which members of the majority culture rarely see through because they are not themselves required to navigate in the same ways.[4] There are also instances of men who, because their immigration or other status is insecure, have less bargaining power than women. Men can also be 'forced' into a marriage.

Some judges have grasped that we must not be led unwittingly by stereotypes, and have even become super-conscious about the potential for the law to stereotype and act Eurocentrically. In a case concerning care proceedings brought by a local authority because an Iraqi Kurdish girl was effectively forced into a marriage by her parents, Munby J (as he then was) said:

We must guard against the risk of stereotyping. We must be careful to ensure that our understandable concern to protect vulnerable children (or, indeed, vulnerable young adults) does not lead us to interfere inappropriately – and if inappropriately then unjustly – with families merely because they cleave, as this family does, to mores, to cultural beliefs, more or less different from what is familiar to those who view life from a purely Eurocentric perspective.[5]

Support comes for that perspective in the concurring opinion of the Russian judge, Anatoly Kovler, in two major cases decided by the European Court of Human Rights (ECtHR), which underline that the issues are of relevance to the wider public order of Europe. The first is the *Refah Partisi (the Welfare Party) v Turkey* (No 2):[6] the Turkish government had closed an

---

[4] R Ballard, *Desh Pardesh: the South Asian presence in Britain* (London, 1994).
[5] *Re K (A Local Authority) v N* [2005] EWHC 2956 (Fam), para 93. The statement was more recently cited by Munby LJ himself in *In the Matter of A (A Child) (No 2)* [2011] EWCA Civ 12, para 33, and adopted by Sir Christopher Sumner in *London Borough of Brent v S* [2009] EWHC 1593 (Fam), para 24.
[6] (2003) 37 EHRR 1 (GC).

Islamic political party partly on the grounds that the party would, if it ever had the power, establish a plurality of legal systems (among them, an Islamic system) which would threaten to destroy Turkey's secular democracy; the party challenged the closure. Although that case is cited as the standard reference point to support the incompatibility of European human rights law and the *shari'a*, Judge Kovler stated:

> I also regret that the Court ... missed the opportunity to analyse in more detail the concept of a plurality of legal systems, which is linked to that of legal pluralism and is well-established in ancient and modern legal theory and practice ... Not only legal anthropology but also modern constitutional law accepts that under certain conditions members of minorities of all kinds may have more than one type of personal status ... Admittedly, this pluralism, which impinges mainly on an individual's private and family life, is limited by the requirements of the general interest. But it is of course more difficult in practice to find a compromise between the interests of the communities concerned and civil society as a whole than to reject the very idea of such a compromise from the outset ... This general remark also applies to the assessment to be made of *shari'a*, the legal expression of a religion whose traditions go back more than a thousand years, and which has its fixed points of reference and its excesses, like any other complex system. In any case legal analysis should not caricature polygamy (a form of family organisation which exists in societies other than Islamised peoples) by reducing it to ... 'discrimination based on the gender of the parties concerned'.

In the more recent case of *Serife Yigit v Turkey*,[7] the Court had to decide whether the state had correctly refused a woman entitlement to a widow's pension because she had not gone through a civil marriage even though she had gone through an Islamic marriage. Judge Kovler stated:

> I think it would have been wiser to refrain from making any assessment of the complexity of the rules of Islamic marriage, rather than portraying it in a reductive and highly subjective manner in the short section entitled 'History' ... where what is left unsaid speaks louder than what is actually said .... I would like to see the European Court of Human Rights take a more anthropological approach in the positions it adopts, by 'not just exploring difference, but exploring it differently' ... Otherwise, the Court is in danger of becoming entrenched in 'eurocentric' attitudes.

The advocacy of more anthropologically-informed, legally pluralistic and non-Eurocentric perspectives may still be at the margins of legal thought in Europe and yet be more conducive to justice, as we shall see, than the still-prevailing legal techniques.

---

[7] App no 3976/05, Judgment of 2 November 2010.

MARRIAGE: THE REGISTRATION OF *NIKAH*

Muslims in the UK tend not to contract the Muslim marriage contract, *nikah*, in a mosque; they can marry practically anywhere, including at home. There is no requirement that the marriage contract be reduced to writing and no necessity that an imam act as celebrant. Marriage is not a sacrament and state involvement is not required.[8] (At all costs, one should avoid the paradigm of marriage's Church-based solemnisation when thinking about official recognition of Muslim marriage.) But there is still a widespread assumption that an adaptation of English norms and mechanisms will suit Muslims well. We must free ourselves from this illusion, to let other and more suitable possibilities open before us.

First, it may do no harm to encourage mosques to facilitate official registration when a *nikah* is contracted so that parties are protected under English law. Those Muslims who lack solid community links in Britain and are likely to be in greatest need of such protection may well be more likely to marry in a mosque. (We may think in particular of transients who have only few or very recent connections with British society.) Registration could be linked in to the planning process for mosques and thereby arranged in advance. Such a proposal would still have at least two practical problems to overcome. A mosque will often not have planning permission in its early stages of establishment; its administrators will apply only later for permission for its use as a mosque. And those seeking planning permission run into problems with local authorities which prefer mosques to be located away from residential areas; Muslim communities tend to prefer mosques within their residential area and within walking distance, and there is some empirical evidence that it is more difficult to obtain planning permission for mosques than for other religious buildings.[9]

Such mosque-registraton might however divert us from a more fruitful solution: *to recognise the* nikah *itself, regardless of any registration, as conferring the official status of marriage upon the parties*. To some extent, judges have conferred such recognition through the principle of presumption of marriage as a result of long cohabitation.[10] It is a cause of concern that in

---

[8] For discussion of the doctrine, history and contemporary developments, see D Pearl and W Menski, *Muslim Family Law* (third editon London, 1998); J Tucker, *Women, Family and Gender in Islamic Law* (Cambridge, 2008).

[9] R Jones, 'Planning law and mosque development: the politics of religion and residence in Birmingham', in P Shah (ed), *Law and Ethnic Plurality* (Leiden, 2007), pp 127–44.

[10] *Chief Adjudication Officer v Kirpal Kaur Bath* [2000] 1 FLR 8 (marriage of a Sikh couple); *A-M v A-M (Divorce: Jurisdiction: Validity of Marriage)* [2001] 2 FLR 6 (marriage of a Muslim couple).

Scotland, where the presumption of marriage was more embedded and allowed judges some flexibility, this principle was removed by section 3 of the Family Law (Scotland) Act 2006 just as the English courts had begun to use it particularly in ethnic minority cases. English judges are not always ready to accept that rights may follow a *nikah*, a refusal with potentially unjust consequences.[11] It is all the more heartening that some judicial decisions show an increased awareness of the importance, from a social perspective, of *either* upholding a Muslim marriage *or* deciding firmly that it has ended. In one such case, surrounded by uncertainty as to the effectiveness of an alleged divorce pronounced in Pakistan, Thorpe LJ explained the considerations that had motivated Wood J in the lower court to clarify and expedite matters by ordering that the validity of the divorce be decided by proceedings in a Pakistani court within a certain timeframe:

> He went on to observe that given that both of the parties were of Pakistani origin and both still have family in that jurisdiction, it would be a matter of grave consequence to the wife were the court in this [UK] jurisdiction too lightly to uphold the husband's application, which would demonstrate that the wife had, for a period of some years after the dissolution of the marriage, been cohabiting with the husband under the same roof and holding herself out to be his wife. So the importance of a profound investigation to ensure justice to the wife was at the heart of the judge's reasoning.[12]

One might nonetheless quibble with the reasoning here of Wood J on two grounds. First, the reasoning assumes that the matter be decided so that the families' *Pakistani* branches may rest assured of the couple's status; but this ignores the importance to such families settled in *Britain* that the matter be brought to resolution. This point underscores the trans-jurisdictional reality of Muslim communities: just because a person is in Britain, he or she is not necessarily any less attached to the conventional understandings surrounding marriage. It seems increasingly artificial therefore to separate out the social significance of what happens in Britain and in another jurisdiction such as Pakistan. Second, and perhaps more fundamentally, it remains open to question how important the perceptions of the community would be in

---

[11] In *AAA v ASH, The Registrar General for England and Wales, The Secretary of State for Justice, The Advocate to the Court provided by the Attorney General* [2009] EWHC 636 (Fam), a father was denied custody rights over his child after splitting from the child's mother with whom he had had a *nikah*. The judge so held even though the father had been allowed to enter himself as the father in the birth certificate. See also *El Gamal v Al Maktoum* [2011] EWHC B27 (Fam). For further discussion of these cases, nn 10–11, see I Edge, 'Islamic finance, alternative dispute resolution and family law: developments towards legal pluralism?', supra pp 129–30.

[12] *Abbassi v Abbassi & Another* [2006] EWCA Civ 355, para 10.

such a case, since Muslims are by now largely used to the state law operating at odds with their own community's understanding of the legal relations between parties to a marriage, and have learnt to navigate around the obstinacy of state laws. It would have been helpful to emphasise, not that the parties and their families would find themselves socially compromised by an English court's position on the status of their marriage, but rather that the state's law is failing to keep up with the legal understandings shared by the parties and is thereby causing other dysfunctional effects to follow.

Many Muslims do not register marriages under English law; to encourage mosques to act as places of registration may only go some way to ensuring legal security for Muslims. Evidence from specialist practising solicitors suggests that up to 70 per cent of their case work might involve non-registered Muslim marriages. The reasons why Muslims do not register are many: a kind of politically motivated defiance of the official system of registration ('Islam provides for all our needs'); ignorance of the official law ('I thought my marriage was recognised by common law'); the perception that it is the 'husband's role' to ensure registration or indeed to refuse to register; and the fact that legal systems 'back home' (ie in the countries of origin) do recognise unregistered marriages. Registration may also be omitted because of its other consequences: one can obtain extra state benefits if one does not declare one's partnership or marriage or declares oneself as a single parent. Some might go for a *nikah*-only marriage because they cannot register, given official obstacles such as the 'permission to marry' requirement in immigration law in force since 2005.[13] Such restrictions drive marriage further 'underground'.

A key issue therefore is how to bring under the umbrella of state law Muslims who do not register their *nikah*-marriages, and we should seriously consider whether a *nikah* itself should suffice. Other jurisdictions are able to function without an all-encompassing registration law. India has long accepted non-registered marriages as officially valid (and not just for Muslims). Moves have recently been made there to encourage registration; legislation by individual Indian states still does not make registration a precondition of validity, but appears to be designed to facilitate the later

---

[13] The requirement for a 'certificate of approval' was introduced in the Asylum and Immigration (Treatment of Claimants, etc) Act 2004 and the UK has recently been found in violation of the ECHR because of its discriminatory effects in *O'Donoghue and Others v United Kingdom* [2011] All ER (D) 46 (Jan). Discrimination was found particularly because the requirement did not apply to marriages solemnised in an Anglican Church. The scheme was finally abolished with effect from 9 May 2011, but its abolition has met with concerns about marriages being contracted solely for immigration purposes: Home Affairs Committee, 'The work of the UK Border Agency', ninth report, (November 2010–March 2011), para 25.

production of proof of marriage.[14] However, if a marriage's validity is contested, it can still be proved by other evidence, and the Indian courts have traditionally been more flexible in establishing the existence of marriage than the English courts which rely on such conditions as 'long cohabitation'. Evidently, over the past few decades, English law has become more flexible in how a marriage can be solemnised although the core element of registration has been retained.[15] Can we envisage making marriage in the UK more flexible, with proof of marriage adequately furnished, when necessary, in ways other than registration?

The Scottish Court of Session has, on a quite different trajectory, already gone behind registration to invalidate a marriage in which (according to the court) the couple lacked the intention to marry at registration according to the Scottish law's understanding of marriage; in the couple's intention, it was a subsequent *nikah* (which was not in fact ever contracted) that would make them husband and wife.[16] This is a very narrow basis on which to have invalidated the marriage; it requires Muslims to intend a relationship as contemplated by Scottish civil law without reference to Islamic law whereas, in socio-legal reality, Muslims are likely to be contemplating more than one legal order. Meanwhile, British officials and judges have regularly to construe the validity of a *nikah* when the marriage has been conducted abroad. In those cases in which I have been involved as an expert, British officials and courts appear in practice to be insisting on evidence of registration in foreign jurisdictions where there is no need for such registration or where no registration exists; thus the courts are misapplying accepted rules of private international law.[17]

---

[14] Eg the Maharashtra Regulation of Marriage Bureaus and Registration of Marriages Act 1998, s 10 and the Gujarat Registration of Marriages Act 2006, s 13.

[15] Marriage (Registration of Buildings) Act 1990 (deleting the requirement to have a separate building as a registrable place of worship) and Marriage Act 1994 (allowing the use of 'approved premises' other than religious buildings or local authority registries). The 1994 Act still rather unrealistically contemplates a total separation of the 'secular' and religious ceremonies by stipulating that 'No religious service shall be used at a marriage on approved premises ... ' Guidelines issued by the Registrar General under the Marriage Act 1994 (para 7) follow this: 'Marriages on approved premises may be followed by a celebration, commemoration or blessing of the couple's choice, providing that it is not a religious marriage ceremony and is separate from the civil ceremony. However, if a religious blessing were to regularly follow marriage ceremonies on particular premises, or be considered part of the service being offered on the premises, there may well be a religious connection which would breach the requirements and lead to the local authority having to consider revoking the approval.'

[16] *H v H* [2005] SLT 1025. The man had been delaying going through a *nikah* once the registration had been accomplished and was in a relationship within another partner; there were grounds to suspect that he had gone through the marriage registration process to secure his immigration status.

[17] P Shah, 'When South Asians marry trans-jurisdictionally: some reflections on immigration cases by an "expert"' in L Holden (ed), *Cultural Expertise and Litigation: patterns, conflicts, narratives* (London, 2011), pp 35–52, and see Pearl and Menski, *Muslim Family Law*, supra n 8, p 171.

We therefore appear to have got into knots about the issue of marriage and registration. The Christian presuppositions of the official legal order make it difficult to understand that marriage actually means different things to different groups of people. Marriage already, within social reality and according to religious understandings, has quite different associations attached to it depending on the specific circumstances and backgrounds of the parties to it. A *nikah* is indeed not the same as a Western marriage; but should the way in which Muslim communities understand the former simply be dismissed or be assimilated to Western norms? Universalised Western assumptions appear to be hampering people in deciding what forms of relationships are appropriate for them. Instead, state law needs to be made more flexible to respond to their diverse circumstances in a realistic manner, while also bringing within the scope of official law a whole swathe of relationships currently existing unofficially. Since the acceptance of nuptial agreements by the UK Supreme Court, it seems only logical to extend to Muslims the principle that parties' choices be respected.[18] This will also help judges approach their tasks without needing recourse to what sometimes reads like tortuous logic because their hands have been tied.

DIVORCE

The making of marriage in the well established Muslim communities is not generally an individualistic matter, although the *shari'a* and its contemporary proponents often present it as such. And so it is with divorce. In social reality divorces tend to be complicated and non-individualistic in nature. Wider kinship involvement can often be expected and it is in the kinship sphere that the first attempts at resolution of differences and/or agreement to divorce will be tried. Often the significant members of the kinship groups will not be in favour of the couple splitting; such a split would tear apart finely concluded inter-familial arrangements, with the involvement of all kinds of honour and financial issues. In some British Muslim communities, marriages not uncommonly occur between cousins; families will often be closely tied in to all other kinds of relationships and would not favour divorce.[19]

---

[18] *Radmacher (formerly Granatino) v Granatino* [2010] UKSC 42. Indeed, anecdotal evidence from expert legal practitioners suggests that judges can be persuaded to respect the terms of a marriage settlement in a *nikah* contract.

[19] A Shaw, 'Kinship, cultural preference and immigration: consanguineous marriage among British Pakistanis', (2001) 7 JRAI 315; K Hasan, 'The medical and social costs of consanguineous marriages among British Mirpuris', (2009) 29 SAR 275.

Judging Muslims

Women may well be consulting *shariʿa* councils because kinship dispute resolution mechanisms have not favoured divorce, or because they have not worked, or because they are not sufficiently effective for the aggrieved party to be satisfied with their outcome, or because the aggrieved party is attempting to bypass them altogether.[20] Many marriages, being arranged on the basis of other concerns, may not have been well planned to take into account the spouses' compatibility, while transnational marriages and the consequent experience of immigration restrictions complicate the picture further.[21] Some people may already be in a relationship with a third party and a marriage could be arranged in order to bring that other relationship to an end, with deleterious consequences for the marriage itself. We have recently learnt that gay men can also be pressured into marriage.[22]

In *shariʿa* councils, Muslims find a Muslim framework of dispute resolution that is culture- and religion-friendly, unlike the secular legal system which seems time-consuming, unfriendly and unable to take into account cultural and religious factors. The secular system potentially involves much cost, even if it might ultimately offer – and especially to women – a 'better deal'. Since the formation of *shariʿa* councils in the 1980s, divorce has been the mainstay of their work. Meanwhile, more than 90 per cent of official divorces in the courts are uncontested and are reduced to a paper exercise under the so-called 'special procedure'. So the more *general* reality of divorce in Britain seems to be, as much as possible, consensual. Muslims may not be that different in this regard.

Although contemporary discussions about divorce under Islamic law tend to focus on the *talaq* (unilateral divorce issued by a husband), in reality more divorces among Muslims than acknowledged could be consensual, whether initiated by a woman and involving some compensation from her (*khul*) or agreed between the spouses (*mubaraat*). It may well suit the men (for reasons of dignity, assets or for other reasons) to appear opposed to any divorce and allow the woman to make the first move. Divorces issued by Islamic *ulama*, now often handled in Britain by *shariʿa* councils, are *faskh* divorces although they are often confusingly also called *khul*.[23] As on many

---

[20] Having said that, Bano's research shows that family members may have a role in persuading women to go to *shariʿa* councils for a divorce. See, eg, S Bano, 'Muslim family justice and human rights: the experience of British Muslim women', (2007) 1 JCL 1. Bano does not however pursue the issue of the role of kinship in divorce further.

[21] See, in particular, R Ballard, 'Inside and outside: contrasting perspectives on the dynamics of kinship and marriage in contemporary South Asian transnational networks' in R Grillo (ed), *The Family in Question: immigrant and ethnic minorities in multicultural Europe* (Amsterdam, 2008), pp 37–70.

[22] A Hill and K McVeigh, 'Gay men become victims of forced marriages', *The Guardian*, 1 July 2010.

[23] For terminological confusions and overlaps, which may have something to do with differences among Islamic legal school traditions and geographical regions, see Pearl and Menski, *Muslim Family Law*,

other questions of law, there remain divergent views among Muslims about whether a divorce issued by a secular official court may be legitimately regarded as a divorce under Islamic law.

We need more research into the seemingly increasing rates of Asian divorce in the UK, and must ask to what extent Muslims conform to that trend.[24] If it is the case that many Muslim divorces are in reality *mubaraat* divorces then there is little that the official courts can or will do unless a particular problem is drawn to their attention; then there enter all the unwanted consequences of its becoming a contested and expensive divorce with the involvement of lawyers who rarely understand what has gone on between the parties. There is a larger point here: the official system may indeed be rigorously premised (unlike, we are to assume, *shari'a* councils) on the protection of the vulnerable party, but this system also seems designed to avoid recourse to its own elaborate procedures; it reduces things to a paper exercise in a staggering majority of cases. Such a system can even lead to cases in which, years later, it is claimed that there was no real acknowledgement of service of the divorce papers because, perhaps, such matters had been left to be dealt with by another family member.[25]

Judges in the official courts should be allowed to deal more flexibly with different scenarios. Judges can be hamstrung by the assumption, among legislators and others, that they must be dictated to correctly in order to reach the outcome desired. The focus should be on empowering judges to appraise with confidence the cultural and religious background of any case before them in a sufficiently holistic manner and so to make decisions according to their view of a just outcome. Indeed, it is arguable that much of family law legislation already allows space for judicial discretion, under the umbrella of general principles such as a child's interests being paramount, or under broad principles of matrimonial relief. If the question is what sort of

---

supra n 8, pp 283–6 and Tucker, *Women, Family and Gender in Islamic Law*, supra n 8, pp 84–100. For a discussion of how these conceptual distinctions might affect how *shari'a* councils in Britain could justify an end to a marriage, see J Bowen, 'How could English courts recognize *shariah*?' (2010) 7.3 USTLJ 411.

[24] Among the stray reports on the trend, see L Greenwell, 'They look straight through me', 1 February 2006, accessible at <http://news.bbc.co.uk/1/hi/uk/4669284.stm>.

[25] See *Akhtar v Rafiq* [2006] 1 FLR 27 where the High Court had to void a decree absolute eleven years after it had been pronounced because the wife, who did not read English (and was in fact illiterate), had started divorce proceedings anew claiming that she had never thumb-printed the original acknowledgement of service. Luckily for the husband, who had remarried and had five children with his second wife, the question of potential prosecution was dismissed by the judge as the husband was held to have acted on the advice of his solicitors. 'Reading between the lines', however, one gets the impression that the first wife could have known she was divorced given that they were cousins and her father had provided the address in Pakistan for service of papers.

'family meeting' took place before a person came to the official court, or what a *shari'a* council did before the court was approached, or whether the token *mahr* payment should be supplemented by a larger maintenance award, the judge should be encouraged to ask the right questions and to take into account all that went on beforehand. Along the way, there may be several culture-specific issues to which the judge needs to be alert. Families and married couples come in different shapes and sizes, and the assumption that a one-size-fits-all solution can be found for all Muslims – let alone for everyone in Britain – should be avoided.

Indeed, existing divorce legislation leaves much room for judges to manoeuvre, and there are examples of judges using their powers creatively and with some finesse. Even before the Divorce (Religious Marriages) Act 2002, it was the judges who were responding to the plight of Jewish women, moving to penalise the husband for obstinately withholding the Jewish *get* divorce.[26] There are Muslim equivalents also: in a case concerning an Iranian couple, for instance, Baron J made a lump sum order of £35,000 for the wife in ancillary relief proceedings, with a potential additional payment of £25,000 if the husband failed to grant the wife a *talaq* within a specified time.[27] Such judges have already been responding to the facts and circumstances in real-life cases; they need to be given better ways to do so either through new legislation which gives them greater flexibility or through the provision of fuller information to the courts. The point is to stop being overly prescriptive. We hardly understand what goes on within Muslim families and we are certainly not in a position to devise 'intelligent legislation' except to the extent that it allows judges to use their discretion to do justice. All too often we are coming from within a narrow 'sectarian', politically correct, agenda be it from a human rights, feminist, Deobandhi or other perspective. This is an ill-advised basis on which to devise plurality-conscious legislation.

CONCLUSION

This chapter has been a plea for more attention to be paid to the role of judges in the process of developing the law with respect to cases involving Muslims. It is presumed that Muslim cases cannot simply be shunted off to *shari'a* councils and that judges will face a continuing stream of cases in

---

[26] *N v N (Jurisdiction: Pre Nuptial Agreement)* (also known as: *N v N (Divorce: Judaism)*) [1999] 2 FLR 745; *O v O (Jurisdiction: Jewish Divorce)* [2000] 2 FLR 147.
[27] *A v T (Ancillary Relief: Cultural Factors)* [2004] EWHC 471 (Fam).

which they will be asked to reckon with Muslim legalities at various levels. Working within a complex matrix involving law, religion and culture, they cannot avoid doing so. We might still ask what we expect to happen if British judges take Muslim legalities more seriously. We would still not expect the legal behaviour of Muslims necessarily to conform to the British courts' views. Muslims are more than likely to continue to use all of their legal options by going to *shari'a* councils, by going abroad, by shopping among various fora, and so on, in order to obtain what they see, sometimes selfishly, as the optimal outcome. This is the reality of contemporary globalisation and legal pluralism. Thus the job of British courts and the wider legal order should be to keep legal options open to Muslims and yet encourage and guide Muslims to behave honourably.

CHAPTER 10

From Muslim migrants to Muslim citizens

Shaheen Sardar Ali

INTRODUCTION

This chapter attempts some answers to the question whether the UK ought to adopt a pluralistic legal system. I will reflect upon various perspectives on the subject advanced in academic literature, and will suggest that the critical question underlying this debate is not simply about popular perceptions of Islam and Islamic law, both among Muslim migrants themselves who are now British citizens and in the non-Muslim majority population. It is in reality about the phenomenon of Muslims as permanent 'features' on the British societal landscape; their engagement or lack of it with the mainstream institutions of state, law and society; their rights and responsibilities as equal citizens; the commonalities and differences of Islamic law vis-à-vis the prevalent legal system; and the likely impact in the event of its recognition and application in this jurisdiction.

The question therefore is a much deeper and more complex one than meets the eye. The line of argument I propose (and have proposed for some time) is the following: the starting point of this discussion must be to develop a list of priorities where there is a real or perceived divergence of thought or action between British Muslims and the majority non-Muslim population, to interrogate each issue honestly and sincerely, and to explore possible mechanisms for reaching a consensual resolution. Unless there is the will to define and address the difficult issues confronting us, all parties to the debate will (as has been the case until now) fail to reach a satisfactory resolution.

I initiate the discussion by placing it in the context of how I, a Muslim woman born in a far-away mountain village in the north west of Pakistan, first heard about the United Kingdom (or Vallieth, or simply London, or England as it was commonly called in Pakistan). Long before 9/11 and the invasion of Iraq and of Afghanistan, long before the present bloody conflicts in my beloved Swat and the North West Frontier Province of Pakistan,[1] I remember my childhood in the Swat Valley. People used to go on very long journeys by sea to 'Vallieth' – to England. My earliest recollection of this far-away place is of stories told me, when I was four or five, by one of my great-uncles, who had actually *been* to Vallieth for six months. He told us the two most important things to remember about Vallieth. First, if you want tea you must call it (and here please imagine a strong Pathan accent), 'cuppa tea'. We all duly took that to heart. 'And the second thing,' he went on, 'that I want you all to remember is this: if only they would recite the *kalima* – "There is no god but God, Muhammad is the Messenger of God" – then they would be better Muslims than you and I.' We were of course amazed; so he repeated it. That was the best of Vallieth. This very good Muslim thought that the British had values and norms so close to our own hearts that we could say: 'All you need is to recite the *kalima* and we will all be home and dry.'

How different the atmosphere and environment are today. There is very little conversation about these common Muslim and (non-Muslim) British norms so valued by us all, and much more about the (in)famous 'clash of civilisations' rhetoric that has followed us especially since the 9/11 tragedy. On all sides people are tying their value systems in to their own favoured political and social norms and veiling them in the garb of religion. In the words of Bassam Tibi, we are experiencing 'the double process of religionisation of politics and of the politicisation of religion'.[2] It is after all, an easy political trick to place all the bad things in the economy, society and indeed the whole world at the doorstep of religion. It was the Jewish people in the not too distant past who bore the brunt of popular contempt; then came the Irish Catholics from across the sea as the next wave of undesirables, only to be replaced by Muslims today as the cause of all evil.

'Should the UK adopt a pluralistic legal system?' If we are to discuss such a question with any hope of making honest and sincere progress, there are some basic prerequisites that we need to have in place. The first on my list is this: *we have got to have a dialogue between equals*. We cannot have one set of people talking down to the other. The second is *a willingness to engage*, not to talk at each other or through each other or over each other, but to engage respectfully between knowledge systems of East, West, North and South. The third would be *to distinguish between the notions of shariʿa* (as the

---

[1] Now re-named Khyber Pukhtunkhwa.
[2] B Tibi, 'Islam and Europe in the age of intercivilizational conflict, diversity and challenges' in M-C Foblets (ed), *Islam and Europe: challenges and opportunities* (Leuven, 2008), p 63.

overarching set of norms and principles informing Islamic law and practice); *usul al-fiqh* (jurisprudence or principles of law), *aman* (protection afforded by the state to minorities) and *qanun* (state promulgated legislation). (I will come back to these terms in a moment.) And finally, I ask us to acknowledge that all major world religions have always had a streak of patriarchy in them. I will be analysing some of the patriarchy in modern British Islam. But it is not peculiar to Islam. Islam, Christianity, Hinduism and Judaism – all have a similar streak in them. But in all of them there are as well multiple and diverse interpretations of the religious texts, some of them truly equitable and human-friendly. These are my prerequisites for a constructive dialogue between our communities that will benefit us all.

As you can tell already, I have a serious objection to the manner in which the dialogue on Islamic law, British Muslims, the UK and its legal system has in general been carried on. It has been an action and reaction, in offensive and defensive mode. There has been a divide which there need not have been, an 'either–or' approach in which each side seems set to undermine the other.

Most important here is the need for us all to change our departure points. As a British Muslim, I do not want this debate to be held on the fringes and margins of society. I want it to be raised fair and square within the understanding that all of us have equal citizenship rights in this country. I want the debate on the multiple identities and multiple norms that inform me – whether legal, ethical or moral – to be undertaken on the understanding that I am an equal citizen of this country. To pick up a few areas of Islamic family law and to park them away from the mainstream, for discussion in the shadows, is to insult my equal status and equal rights as a British Muslim woman in this country. We shall see that it is also, with respect, an evasion of the real issues that confront Muslim communities in this country and an omission that lies at the doorstep of government and society as well as of British Muslims.

I ask myself why does discussion on *shari'a*, Islamic law and the English legal system always take its departure from those areas of Muslim law that are contested and controversial and the subject of debate and discourse *within and between Muslim communities themselves,* and that have been throughout Muslim history? Why is such discussion of Islamic law confined to a very small, restricted area, to the exclusion of the ethical, moral and universal norms that inform the religious traditions of us all? Just one example: why is polygamy always thrown in, with the line, 'This is Islamic family law'? Polygamy is contested within Islam and is the exception rather than the norm in Muslim societies; there has always been a huge resistance to it. Another example would be divorce, so often tabled now as an area for which, it is said, Muslim communities are asking for a parallel legal system. I will come back to this. Let me here just remark that such a supposed request would be alien to Islamic tradition itself. Marriage in Islam is a civil contract. Yes, it has religious undertones and overtones. But in which Muslim country is it that men and women in Muslim communities arrange marriage and divorce outside that country's legal system? Why is an English Muslim couple less Muslim for accepting, in their divorce, the jurisdiction of the English courts?

It is all too easy for communities to pigeon-hole each other.[3] Neither 'host' nor Muslim communities are homogeneous or monolithic in their composition. It is often the most extreme and stereotypical forms of culture and religion that become stark and visible binaries proclaiming themselves as 'authentic' representations of groups and communities. Added to this is the question, whose is the authoritative voice within the Muslim community itself. This has always been a contested site in Muslim history but in a non-Muslim jurisdiction it assumes critical importance. Who speaks and for whom? The answer determines which further questions are posed, by whom and to what end and purpose. The host communities have to be aware of the multiplicity of interpretations and diversity within Muslim communities and vice versa. Further, it is important to take on board the fact that culture, custom and even understandings of religion change and evolve. European Muslims live Islam in their own present context and this is very different from the manner in which it is practised in the various countries of origin.

Most if not all Muslim immigrants come from undemocratic, class-based, hierarchical communities where there is very little participation of the citizens with the state. The state and her functionaries are hardly accessible and accountable. Most immigrants have previously had little chance to confront anyone remotely connected to government or in positions of 'formal' authority. The approach of immigrant communities in Europe has been to keep their heads down and get on with their work. This disengaged attitude has led to a dangerous gap between 'host' and Muslim migrant communities and must be addressed.

---

[3] For a fuller presentation of the argument that follows, S Sardar-Ali, 'Religious pluralism, human rights and Muslim citizenship in Europe: some preliminary reflections on an evolving methodology for consensus' in T Leonon and J Goldschmidt (eds), *Religious Pluralism and Human Rights in Europe* (Antwerp, 2007), pp 57–79.

In any setting, a serious attempt has to be made at defining what constitute issues of culture and tradition and what may be described as emanating from religion. In the case of Muslim migrant communities this assumes a crucial dimension because, in the articulation of 'identity', culture is also elevated to the status of religious belief and hence becomes non-negotiable. A number of problems arise within Muslim communities thanks to the fact that they structure their lives around cultural and linguistic identities but perceive these to be central to and to represent their religious identity. Further, inadequate language skills have inhibited (and continue to inhibit) interaction with the host communities and institutions.

How might the discussion of *law* be a helpful part of this dialogue? In my work I attempt to discover or construct a space in which two different knowledge systems – classical Islamic jurisprudence and contemporary 'Western' research methodology – can both be at home. On the one hand, classical Muslim jurisprudence restricted itself to an interpretative analysis of a text without questioning the text itself, or without attempting to extend it to apply to contemporary situations. The process of law-making is particularly fraught with tension. Some Muslim scholars will argue that a law based upon the Qur'anic text is divine since its source is divine. Others, including myself, would take the view that as soon as human intervention enters the domain of law-making, the law-making no longer remains divine; the law is a human-made endeavour to interpret and understand the divine text and must be distinguished from it. On the other hand stands 'Western' scholarship, based on reason and argumentation; to mount challenges to existing theory, ideology or philosophy is integral to sound scholarship. How does one approach these seemingly incompatible knowledge systems with a view to generate a common understanding and resolution of issues?

A final point regarding the prerequisites for consensus building relates to terminology in European languages that has no exact translation in Arabic and other languages spoken by Muslim communities. 'Secularism' highlights my point. The term itself has led to a conceptual (as well as socio-political and ideological) gap between the 'Western' and non-Western world in general and Muslim communities and jurisdictions in particular. 'Secular' is often understood in Muslim communities as 'un-Islamic' or 'in opposition to religion (Islam)', rather than as 'non-religious and neutral with respect to religion and to particular religions'. A discourse in which laws, rights and obligations are presented within an avowedly 'secular' framework invites protests from Muslim communities from the start. We might even ask if secularism is now perceived as akin to and as a new form of colonialism. This becomes more plausible if Muslims come to believe that liberal democracy and its secular jurisdictions are set not in religion-free soil but on a bedrock of solid Christian norms.

STATEMENT OF THE PROBLEM

I start by mapping out the lines of thought I hope to explore here. Large-scale voluntary and permanent settlement of Muslims in a diaspora of 'non-Muslim' countries was unknown before the second half of the twentieth century. Where can we find guidance in the classical Islamic tradition to the obligations of such Muslims and to the practices and accommodations that the host communities might come to value in the welcome they give to such Muslims? First, for the obligations of Muslims. We find that Islamic jurists, early in the life of Islam, ceded their legislative role to the polity's powers; and Muslims who have to live under non-Muslim rule are urged to obey the law of the land in which they are. There is nothing new in Muslims' obedience to local laws made by a secular power. Second, for the obligations that might be undertaken by the host communities. Here we look to the conditions of the *dar al-sulh*, the Abode of Peace classically offered to non-Muslims living in Muslim territory; and I will propose the creation of a mirror-image of these conditions, for modern Muslims living in non-Muslim territory.

MANIFESTING THE SIGNS OF ISLAM: MUSLIMS IN EUROPE

First, then, for Muslims living in non-Muslim territory. Classical Islamic law does not provide a uniform or clear indication of whether and under what conditions it is permissible for a Muslim to migrate to such territory, voluntarily and permanently.[4] The most tolerant view allowed a Muslim to accept *aman* (protection) from non-Muslim governments and to reside temporarily under such a government's power. The acceptance of such *aman* was subject to certain conditions: the most important was that the Muslim be able to 'manifest signs of Islam' whilst residing in the non-Muslim territory.[5]

The most common argument advanced in favour of the modern, permanent emigration to non-Muslim states is *darura* or necessity, in the sense of

---

[4] There was little call for it; B Lewis, 'Legal and historical reflections on the position of Muslim populations under non-Muslim rule', (1992) 13 JIMMA 1, 6.
[5] Ibid., 6–7.

economic necessity.[6] If we can expound an 'Islamic' rationale for Muslim migration to contemporary Europe, and so can show that European Muslim migrant communities are living in their newly chosen homelands in a manner that does not clash with their religious obligations, we will add a dimension to their identity; they can be both European citizens and Muslims simultaneously, just as other persons may be Christian or Jewish and European. They will not be trapped in an 'either–or' situation. A shared space would thus be visible and open for developing common values and interests.

As Muslims, these immigrants believe in seeking guidance within the Islamic tradition but they are also painfully aware of the near-absence of learned discourse and writing on the subject from which to find guidance and on which to build. Whatever guidance is available lies in the work of jurists which is centuries old and has not evolved with time and place. The arrival of Muslims in Europe has confronted these Muslims (and the host communities) with the realisation that human beings have multiple identities and are governed by plural and often conflicting norms. European Muslims have both a Muslim and a European identity (in addition to their ethnic, racial and linguistic identity). Likewise, the host communities have a European as well as various other identities, whether based on religion or other markers. Plural legalities, multiple 'belonging' and affiliations to religious, cultural and territorial communities are important aspects to European Muslim-ness.

CLASSIFICATION OF EUROPE AS *DAR AL-HARB*, *DAR AL-ISLAM* OR *DAR AL-SULH*

In this setting should we, as European Muslims,[7] still point towards an exclusive and exhaustive division of the world into *dar al-harb*[8] (territory of

---

[6] Others have attempted to use the *hijra* of the Prophet to Medina in support of their voluntary migration to Europe. (Literally the term denotes migration. In the context of the Islamic tradition it means migration of the fledgling Muslim community from Makkah to Medina to escape persecution of the Makkans and signals the start of the Islamic calendar. Prior to this *hijra*, Muslims also migrated to Ethiopia to escape cruel treatment at the hands of their non-Muslim Makkan compatriots.) Modern migration to Europe, it has to be said, is generally incongruous with the Medinan *hijra*; that movement was necessitated by the Prophet and his followers leaving behind a non-Muslim, antagonistic environment whereas Muslim immigrants to Europe leave behind them, in most cases, a Muslim country.

[7] I am consciously adopting the term 'European Muslims' in this chapter rather than saying Muslims in Europe. In this approach I am inspired by and follow the viewpoint advanced by AA An-Na'im, 'Global citizenship and human rights' in MLP Leonon and JE Goldschmidt (eds), *Religious Pluralism*, supra n 3, pp 13–55.

[8] This consists of all states and communities outside the territory of Islam. Its inhabitants were called *harbis* or people of the territory of war, M Khadduri, 'Islam and the modern law of nations', (1956) 50 AJIL 358.

war) and *dar al-Islam*[9] (territory of Islam/Muslim country) as prescribed by *as-siyar* or Islamic international law?[10] Or do the countries of Europe today fall into an intermediate classification known as *dar al-sulh*, territory of peace?[11] If so, what are the consequences for European Muslims?

Some scholars are of the opinion that *as-siyar* is synonymous with *jihad* which in their view represents a religiously sanctioned aggressive war to propagate or defend the faith of Islam. Hence the world can only be classified as *dar al-Islam* and *dar al-harb*. According to Majid Khadduri, this dichotomy stems from the belief that Islam emerged in the seventh century as a conquering power with world domination as its goal;[12] he argues that the notions of Islamic international law were bound to be in keeping with its mission of proselytisation of the whole of humankind.[13]

This dichotomy has been challenged by a number of scholars including Mahmassani, Hamidullah and Agha Shahi who are of the view that Islam only permits war in self-defence and is not inherently aggressive in nature. They argue that with the expansion of Islamic jurisdictions *as-siyar* developed into a regime of international law, as Muslims increasingly came into contact with other equally powerful societies. The Islamic state was indeed meant to sustain itself and expand territorially through waging *jihad*, but this did not always mean going to war. Muslim states had to acknowledge the *de jure* existence and legitimacy of other communities and states.

Gamal Badr attempts to place this tripartite notion of the world (ie *dar al-harb*, *dar al-Islam* and *dar al-sulh*), in the historical perspective of Islam which he says passed through three stages of unequal duration as presented below:

1. The age of expansion, where Islam embarked on its mission of winning the whole world and transforming it into *dar al-Islam*. Muslim jurists of the time presented the world falling outside the domain of Islam as

---

[9] *Dar-al-Islam* denotes territories under Islamic sovereignty. Its inhabitants were Muslims by birth or conversion, and people of the tolerated religions (Jews, Christians and Zoroastrians) who preferred to remain non-Muslims and paid the special tax (*jizyah*). See M Khadduri, 'Islam and the modern law of nations', supra n 8; also S Mahmassani, 'International law in the light of Islamic doctrine', (1966) 117 *Recueil de Cours* 201, 250–2; M Hamidullah, *Muslim Conduct of State: being a treatise on siyar...* (Lahore, 1977).

[10] See for instance, J Busuttil, 'Humanitarian law in Islam', (1991) 30 MLLWR 113; R Mushkat, 'Is war ever justifiable? A comparative survey', (1987) 9 Loy LA Int'l & Comp L Rev 227.

[11] The terms, *dar al-ahd* (country of treaty), *dar al-aman* (country of security), *dar al-darura* (country of necessity) may also be explored and have similar connotations, as the discussion in this section will attempt to show. This section draws upon my paper, 'The concept of *jihad* in Islamic international law', (2005) 10 JCSL 321.

[12] M Khadduri, *War and Peace in the Law of Islam* (Baltimore, MD, 1955), pp 51–4.

[13] Khadduri, 'Islam and the modern law of nations', supra n 8, 358–9.

dar al-harb. These mutually exclusive territories were considered to be in a state of perpetual belligerency. Truce was permitted but its duration was restricted to ten years.[14] This age lasted for over a century after which it became clear that the objective of carrying Islam to the four corners of the world was unattainable.

2. The age of interaction saw the main change in legal thought in the rationale for waging war against non-Muslims. In the earlier period, war against disbelievers was justified by the mere fact of their disbelief. Later jurists however, placed more emphasis on the disbelievers' hostility to and aggression against Islam as a rationale for maintaining a dichotomous world order. Badr suggests that it was in this age of interaction that the dichotomy of *dar al-Islam* and *dar al-harb* was replaced by a tripartite division of the world by the inclusion of *dar al-sulh*. The *dar al-sulh* is comprised of those states which, while not recognising the authority of the Muslim state over them, are not hostile and entertain friendly relations with it.

3. The age of coexistence or the third age of Islamic international law is roughly conterminous with contemporary international law. In this age, maintaining a state of peace has come to be more widely recognised as the 'normal' relationship between Muslim and non-Muslim states, and treaties of amity need not be confined to a fixed duration. A further distinction that is relevant here is the fact that there is no single 'Islamic' or 'Muslim' state but a number of political entities in the international community that have a predominantly Muslim population. Likewise, there is no single 'other' *dar al-harb* territory but numerous independent states (and groups of states such as the European Union) where the dominant population is comprised of non-Muslims.

A broad definition of *dar al-Islam* is 'any territory whose inhabitants observe Islamic law'. Europe's colonial age called for the criterion to be defined more closely. Under colonial rule, were Muslims able freely to fulfil their religious obligations? One test was whether Friday and Eid[15] congregational prayers could be held in a jurisdiction; on this test alone, British India was considered by Muslim scholars as *dar al-Islam*.[16] Other tests include, for

---

[14] Cf the ten years' peace stipulated in the Treaty of Hudaybia between Muhammad and the Makkan Quraish tribe, 628 CE. See GM Badr, 'A survey of Islamic international law', (1982) 76 *Proceedings of the American Society of International Law* 56.

[15] The two major feasts of Muslims. The first, *eid al-fitr*, falls after the month of *ramadan* (fasting month); and the second, *eid al-adha*, is celebrated after the annual pilgrimage to Makkah known as *haj*, which is obligatory for Muslims once in a lifetime.

[16] A Rahim, *Muhammadan Jurisprudence* (Lahore, 1995), pp 396–7.

example, the ability of Muslim inhabitants to comply with the five pillars of Islam (reciting the *kalima*; *salat* or the five daily prayers; fasting; *haj*; and *zakat*[17]) and the availability of *halal*[18] meat. A state, then, may be regarded as part of *dar al-Islam* if Muslims can fearlessly implement and observe the five pillars of Islam and believe that their life, property and honour are protected by the state. On the basis of this analogy, might we even argue that Western states (of Europe, the US and Canada) qualify for consideration as *dar al-Islam*?

To do justice to this question, we must acknowledge the countervailing argument of the late Zaki Badawi. He argued that, in the classification of the world, *dar al-Islam* or *dar al-harb* are political rather than religious concepts: *dar al-Islam* and *dar al-harb* are distinguished from each other by the polity's power (or lack of power) to implement *shari'a*.[19] If this is right, then some Muslims might argue that most countries, whether Muslim-majority or not, would qualify as *dar al-sulh* since Muslims are able to fulfil their five pillars there with a degree of confidence and protection but the political power is either unable or unwilling to implement principles of Islamic law (*shari'a*). This argument as well dissolves, in practice, much of the distinction between *dar al-Islam* and *dar al-harb* and places modern Europe in *dar al-sulh*.

In all that we have said so far, however, have we created any space for *secularity*?

FROM DIVINE *SHARI'A* TO *QANUN* VIA *SIYASA SHAR'IYYA*: CREATING SPACE FOR SECULARITY?

Early in Islamic history, the *fuqaha* (jurists) receded from law-making and the political authority/ies took to themselves the role of law-making in the public sphere without much protest from the jurists. Thus human endeavour at legislating had the effect of distancing it from *shari'a* perceived as divine; and a neutral, secular, non-religious arena was created where religion played a less pronounced role. The gap between the theory and practice of

---

[17] The annual voluntary offerings obligatory upon Muslims, subject to certain conditions. Normally a Muslim beyond a certain level of income gives 2.5 per cent of his/her annual savings to deserving people (rules are laid down for who is 'deserving' of *zakat*).
[18] Food is either permitted (*halal*) or prohibited (*haram*). Meat of permitted animals however must be slaughtered in a particular manner for it to qualify as *halal* meat. *Zabiha* is the meat of an animal slaughtered in the prescribed manner. Lamb, cow and chicken meat is *halal*, that is, permitted, but if not slaughtered in the prescribed manner is not *zabiha*.
[19] Z Badawi, 'New *fiqh* for minorities', in I Yilmaz (ed), *Muslim Laws, Politics and Society in Modern Nation States: dynamic legal pluralism in England, Turkey and Pakistan* (Aldershot, 2005), p 39.

shariʻa became apparent, a gap that was continually being filled by state-sponsored law-making (including codification during the Ottoman Empire). This process of law-making is known as *siyasa sharʾiyya* and the law thus made as *qanun*.[20]

We have now found space outside the distinction between *dar al-Islam* and *dar al-harb* in the neutral – and dare we say *secular?* – *dar al-sulh*. We have found *siyasa sharʾiyya*, ready for application there. Might the stage be set for European Muslims to discover, through a reconstructive dialogue, a space for their citizenship and their multiple belonging and identities?

Let us explore this possibility in more detail. First, what are the rules of engagement, as outlined in *as-siyar*, regarding Muslims residing permanently and voluntarily in non-Muslim territories?[21] And second, what can or should the rules of engagement be that the modern secular state observes in relation to such Muslim citizens? I will propose a mirror-image of *dar al-sulh*: what was once a safe haven for 'protected' non-Muslim people residing within Muslim territory becomes applicable to Muslims as 'protected' populations within Muslim-minority Europe.

Islamic law recognises the presence of non-Muslim states in peaceful relations both with Muslim states and with a Muslim minority. That these states have the authority to make laws for regulating these minorities is also evident.[22] It is accepted that European Muslims are subject to the laws of their newly acquired homeland; a number of mechanisms exist in Islamic jurisprudence to inform and facilitate such interaction and residence, including the concepts of duress (*ikrah*), necessity (*darura*) and public welfare (*maslaha*).[23] Under the strict principles of Islamic law that agreements must be honoured (in the Latin West, *pacta sunt servanda*), Muslims are required to fulfil their obligations to the state which has offered them protection. They are subject to all legal regulations of the host country as long as they are living within its territory. Hamidullah in his well-argued treatise *Muslim Conduct of State*, makes the point that 'in general, Muslims temporarily residing in a foreign country are recommended very strongly . . . to behave in an exemplary and law abiding manner; to observe fully the conditions of their permit or passport and to refrain from any act of treachery'.[24]

---

[20] M Baderin, *International Human Rights and Islamic Law* (Oxford, 2003), pp 52–3.
[21] Badawi, 'New *fiqh* for minorities', supra n 19, p 39.
[22] Hamidullah, *Muslim Conduct of State*, supra n 9, p 130.
[23] Badawi, 'New *fiqh* for minorities', supra n 19, p 39. K Abou El-Fadl, 'Islamic law and Muslim minorities: the juristic discourse on Muslim minorities from the second/eighth to the eleventh/seventeenth centuries', (1994) 1 *Islamic Law and Societies* 141.
[24] Hamidullah, *Muslim Conduct of State*, supra n 9, p 128.

The obligations of Muslims residing outside *dar al-Islam* are reduced where necessary. If the law of the land requires that they undertake any act classed as un-Islamic, on their return to *dar al-Islam* they will not be liable for prosecution. Muslim law is intensely personal, and a *hadith*[25] of the Prophet Muhammad is said to have ordered non-resident Muslims to observe Muslim law wherever they might be. But there was the proviso that this depended upon the liberty of observance enjoyed in other states.[26] Hamidullah[27] also makes the point that, despite the general rule of adherence – wherever a Muslim may be – to Islamic law, local reality has to be taken on board and into consideration.

And conversely, what might or should be required of the host countries, to make the space for Muslim minorities to live as equals in rights and dignity? We turn to principles of Islamic law developed for non-Muslims living within *dar al-Islam*, and ask if their mirror-image might be applied to European Muslims. For the protection of non-Muslims in *dar al-Islam* there is a well-developed jurisprudence.[28] Islamic law protects such non-Muslims' right to life, property, honour and liberty of conscience or religion, whether they are citizens of *dar al-Islam* or resident aliens there.[29] Non-Muslim citizens of *dar al-Islam* are not liable to pay *zakat*, and are exempt from conscription into the armed forces. The *jizyah* (tax) is to be exacted from men, not from women. If a non-Muslim willingly undertakes military service in *dar al-Islam*, he is exempted from the *jizyah*; also exempt from this payment are children, unemployed males, the sick and infirm, as well as those of a wage below a certain threshold. The *dhimmis* (protected non-Muslims) belonging to the revealed religions may and ought to participate in the civil and political affairs of the state and offer themselves for administrative positions.[30] Graveyards of non-Muslims should be respected and protected from damage. A further important regulation regarding non-Muslim minorities is that litigation relating to what has been described in colonial terminology as 'personal status', is assigned to and decided by co-religionists in accordance with their religious law.[31] Hamidullah also urges non-Muslims in Muslim states 'not to imitate the Muslims in dress or other social manifestation'.[32]

---

[25] *Hadith* is the record of the Prophet Muhammad's words and deeds known as *sunna*.
[26] Hamidullah, *Muslim Conduct of State*, supra n 9, pp 119–20.   [27] Ibid., p 121.
[28] Including Hamidullah, Mahmassani, Khadduri and others who in turn rely upon scholars from the classical period of Islamic jurisprudence.
[29] Hamidullah, *Muslim Conduct of State*, supra n 9, p 111.
[30] Eg, an envoy of the Prophet Muhammad was a non-Muslim.
[31] Hamidullah, *Muslim Conduct of State*, supra n 9, p 111, and accompanying footnotes.
[32] Ibid., pp 117–18.

Might we now employ the principle of reciprocity, and argue that the rules governing non-Muslims in Muslim territory as protected individuals could be used as 'indicators' in constructing some ground rules for European Muslims as citizens of the countries they have chosen to make their home? An important proviso, however, is to be noted. Bearing in mind the contemporary nature of our discourse and the lack of continuity of scholarship amongst Muslims, the application of rules for *dhimmis* must be evaluated and examined in light of the contemporary discourse and requirements of human rights and citizenship.

We have reached our first and more theoretical conclusion: under the conditions we have outlined, Muslims can live as full and equal citizens, loyal to Islam, in secular Europe. But how will this play itself out in practice? What place in this scenario is there for the systems of leadership and mediation already in place within Britain's Muslim communities? It is time to explore the role of so-called Muslim institutions in diasporic communities in Europe, the institutions' impact on second and third generation Muslims and the perceptions of Muslims – and of these institutions – within the host communities.

'ISLAMIC INSTITUTIONS' AND 'ISLAMIC AUTHORITY': A CRITICAL ANALYSIS

As noted above, most European Muslims fifty years ago had limited intellectual skills and their educational and language levels were poor, to say the least. They obviously felt vulnerable and insecure and sought out familiar persons and places. This led to close-knit migrant communities living near to a mosque, a place where Muslims enjoyed some degree of familiarity and social interaction. They felt the need for an imam or someone to give the call to prayer, lead prayers and generally take charge of the mosque. This led to the 'import' of imams from countries of origin of Muslim communities. 'Religious' leaders, in the sense in which Christianity and other religions understand the concept, are alien to Islam which has no organised clergy. European governments, however, with limited understanding of this fact, created and supported religious leaders/imams; so they created an institution and religious hierarchy where none existed before. In Pakistan for instance and other countries of South Asia, the mullah or imam (sometimes the terms are used interchangeably) is assigned tasks in the mosque that are mostly of a housekeeping nature. These include cleaning the mosque, making sure there is water for ablutions, that the call to prayer is made, that prayer mats are rolled out and so on. It is relevant to make the point here that this person is at the lower levels of the socio-economic ladder and is dependent for his subsistence on the community he serves. In my own village, *talibs* or religious students, living in mosques and assisting the mullah/imam, would come round twice a day to the houses and ask for *wazeefa* (in this case translated as food, usually left-overs). The *talibs* would then take the food to the mosque where they would have their meals. A mullah/imam of the mosques was usually given a small piece of land to till for food for his family or a small shop/kiosk where he would trade in merchandise typical of a 'corner shop' and so support his family.

On arrival into Europe, these 'religious' leaders were elevated by the host community to the rank and position of religious leaders and provided with all the paraphernalia accompanying the position. They were thus placed in a position of power and authority that was unthinkable in their country of origin. The Muslim communities sponsored imams from their own native villages and small towns; these were people who were not very educated, either in secular or religious knowledge. Further, and most importantly, they had never ventured out of their village or town and so lacked exposure to other religious and cultural traditions. They did not speak the language of their new home nor were they able to converse with second generation Muslims who had grown up in Europe and related to it. The results are clear and before our eyes. Rigid and inflexible interpretations of the Qur'an, attributing all the evil of the world to non-Muslims, became a given in sermons and lectures of these mullahs/imams. Political wranglings followed. An important dimension of our discourse is for both Muslim and host communities to realise this grave misunderstanding regarding religious leaders in Islam and the damage it has done to inter-community as well as intra-community relations.

MUSLIM *SHARI'A* COUNCILS: FRIEND OR FOE? EMERGING PLURAL LEGALITIES IN EUROPE

Is the position more promising in the *shari'a* councils? These have been termed as 'internal regulatory frameworks',[33] 'complex informal networks',[34] 'new *ijtihad*'[35] and are perceived as an emerging parallel legal system in Europe.[36] Just as there are wide variations among the Muslim

---

[33] D Pearl and W Menski, *Muslim Family Law* (third edition, London, 1998), p 396.
[34] S Poulter, *Ethnicity, Law and Human Rights* (Oxford, 1998), p 61.
[35] Badawi, 'New *fiqh* for minorities', supra n 19, p 3.
[36] In this section, I will confine myself to an account of Britain.

communities residing in Europe, so there is an equally diverse manifestation of 'Islam' and 'Islamic law' within these bodies and structures set up for informal dispute resolution.[37]

The *shari'a* councils undertake a range of functions including mediation, reconciliation, issuing divorce certificates to Muslim clients and producing expert reports on matters of Muslim family law and other matters. These institutions locate themselves in migrant Muslim communities within the communities' power structure and at the intersection of society and state. They are unofficial, extra-legal entities providing advice and assistance on family matters to the Muslim communities.

The history of the *shari'a* councils in the United Kingdom can be traced to the 1970s and 1980s. They were established in close alliance with mosques and were said to represent a shift 'within the migrants' self-perception from being sojourners to settlers'.[38] Their establishment also represents a reluctance to recognise or trust Western, secular law when it comes to family matters and the belief that secularism is necessarily un- or anti-Islamic. Although we do not have a precise figure for the number of *shari'a* councils, there are presently between sixty and seventy in the United Kingdom.[39]

The need for *shari'a* councils was felt by Muslim communities in family matters. The English courts have exclusive rights over divorce and over custody and guardianship orders. Likewise, the state declares that marriages must be registered under the law of the land. Muslim communities have thus been confronted with a real difficulty: they are required to subscribe to the law of the country they have made their home; simultaneously, they do not wish to do or seem to be doing anything that is un-Islamic. The *shari'a* councils thus came in handy for giving advice on both parts of this dual identity and for fulfilling its Islamic requirements.

The working of the *shari'a* councils and their impact on the lives of Muslims in Britain are however not very salutary. First and foremost, there arises the question of the legitimacy of these institutions within Islam, within the countries of origin and within the host countries. Does Islamic law require a parallel institution in the presence of a mainstream court structure? In the case of *dhimmis* as protected people, there existed a provision for religious minorities to have their own co-religionists sitting

---

[37] For this section, I gratefully acknowledge and draw upon the work of S Bano, *Complexity, Difference and 'Muslim personal Law': rethinking relationships between shari'a councils and South Asian Muslim women in Britain* (doctoral thesis, University of Warwick, 2004).
[38] P Lewis, *The Function, Education and Influence of the 'Ulama in Bradford's Muslim Communities* (Leeds, 1996).
[39] See Bano, *Complexity*, supra n 37, p 117 and accompanying footnotes.

in court to hand down judgments in family matters. But in a neutral, secular public space, are these separate and parallel legal systems required at all? Further, since there is no clergy in Islam and no single authority to present a unified representation of Islamic law, is it in the interest of justice and equity that a *shari'a* council be given such unlimited powers to determine matters of personal law? Some clear (if unsettling) answers are offered, I suggest, by current practices in countries of origin and by the working in Britain of the *shari'a* councils.

Countries of origin (eg, Pakistan, Bangladesh, India) do not acknowledge or recognise the *shari'a* councils as legal entities. Any decision, certificate or ruling from such councils, unless accompanied by a decision from an official institution, is rejected by authorities in these countries. One of the reasons for this non-recognition is the fact that state practice in Muslim countries has itself become based on *siyasa shar'iyya*. Marriage, divorce, custody and guardianship issues have become codified and institutionalised and regulated by the state and are no longer a matter of private concern. A ceremony of marriage is conducted by an official of the state in Pakistan known as the *nikah* registrar (marriage registrar). He has to be present and sign the marriage contract and register it in his official records. There is abundant case law in Pakistan and elsewhere in Muslim jurisdictions where unregistered marriages have caused problems to parties. In Muslim communities in Britain there are numerous instances of deliberately unregistered marriages conducted by so-called 'religious' leaders. This situation has left women vulnerable to abuse. There are notorious cases in which women have been 'divorced' and thrown out of the marital homes. On their seeking support from the social services, they have been told that their marriage is not registered and therefore they do not qualify for assistance as a 'wife.' Here is an important step which *shari'a* councils and mosques can immediately undertake: the person conducting the 'religious' ceremony of marriage should demand to see in advance a certificate of the civil ceremony. Mosques can already be licensed as official places where civil marriage ceremonies may be conducted and certificates provided.

The graver violation of the rights of Muslim women takes place where the marriage has been dissolved at the instance of the wife by a court of competent jurisdiction in the host country (in this case Britain). The husband can refuse to accept the divorce as 'Islamically' valid and can keep the woman in a 'limping marriage'.[40] Philip Lewis in his narrative

---

[40] Pearl and Menski, *Muslim Family Law*, supra n 33, p 396, use this term; cf W Menski, *Angrezi Shariat: plural arrangements in family law by Muslims in Britain* (unpublished paper London, 1993).

on the lives of Bradford Muslims describes how *pirs* or religious persons are inundated by community members asking for guidance on whether an Islamic marriage registered under English law and dissolved by the same law without the husband's approval is dissolved under Islamic law.[41] Many husbands thus abuse the system to their wife's detriment by not pronouncing *talaq*.[42]

The *shari'a* councils of Britain are often approached by the now ex-wife to seek the 'Islamic' divorce. But their working methods are clearly based upon the insecurities, the ignorance and the lack of confidence of the Muslim communities in general and of their women in particular. One of the objectives of the *shari'a* councils is to provide assistance to Muslim women in a safe, secure environment; for it is said that these Muslim women are reluctant to speak about such intimate and personal matters to 'strange' men. It is then surprising that the *shari'a* councils are all male organisations whose members are in the eyes of Muslim women a group of 'strangers'.[43] Further, a woman who is desperate to be acknowledged as an 'Islamically' divorced woman is at the mercy of the husband and the negotiating powers of the *shari'a* council. She has to pay a fee to initiate her case and the negotiation may end up demanding money or other privileges in return for the husband declaring *talaq* in the presence of the *shari'a* council. If the erstwhile husband refuses to be persuaded to pronounce the *talaq*, there is nothing that the *shari'a* council can do to force him to do so. Finally, the *shari'a* councils, in 'difficult' cases, usually make the woman opt for *khula*[44] which means giving up her *mahr*[45] in return for dissolution of the marriage. This step is highly disapproved of; where the wife has a legitimate claim to divorce, she is not required to relinquish her *mahr*, which may indeed be her sole economic resource after divorce.

The matter of imams and of *shari'a* councils therefore forms part of an important agenda for a dialogue between host and Muslim communities. These institutions have emerged due to a vacuum within the state institutions, which have failed to understand and provide space for accommodating the concerns of Muslims. Rather than confront and mount a challenge from within the system, Muslim communities have preferred the option of

---

[41] Lewis, *Bradford's Muslim Communities*, supra n 38, p 83.
[42] Ibid., p 120. Dissolution of marriage at the instance of the husband is known as *talaq*.
[43] A few, rare exceptions have emerged over the years. For instance in the Birmingham Sharia Council, Amra Bone has been a judge since 2005.
[44] Dissolution of marriage at the instance and request of the wife, usually by returning the marriage gift or *mahr* received from the husband at the time of marriage.
[45] *Mahr* is a sum of money or other property given by the husband to the wife at the time of the marriage as part of the marriage contract, or pledged to be given to her on demand or on the dissolution of the marriage by death or divorce.

creating parallel, albeit unofficial structures for resolving their family disputes. This does not bode well for Muslim women in particular, nor for inter-community relations and citizenship rights in general.

FROM MUSLIM MIGRANT TO MUSLIM CITIZEN: SOME REFLECTIONS ON THE CONTOURS OF A FRAMEWORK FOR CONSENSUS

I suggest that Europe be construed as *dar al-sulh*, a neutral territory of peaceful coexistence between Muslims and non-Muslims. As protected persons under a pact of citizenship (through naturalisation), Muslim migrants become transformed into Muslim citizens. By accepting citizenship of Europe, Muslim migrants accept and undertake to abide by laws, rules and regulations of their new homeland. At the level of Islamic law, this approach is valid because *siyasa shar'iyya* legitimated *qanun* or law-making by political authority in Muslim jurisdictions. This opens up *dar al-sulh* as a space for citizenship rights.

Samina Yasmeen[46] makes the point that issues confronting Muslims in the diaspora may be addressed by looking at the linkage between migration and citizenship. She emphasises that citizenship is more than a legalistic concept. It has a strong operational element: as a citizen, one interacts, engages with and participates in the personal, market, public and political sphere of the civil society of one's chosen home.[47] The ease with which the immigrants operate in their new environment determines to large extent their relationship to their new homeland. Muslim migrants' levels of ease and comfort can be raised once they engage in a common, neutral space as equal citizens of a country and with their multiple identities intact.

Bhikhu Parekh[48] makes the point that 'immigrants bring different ways of understanding and organising life. Their views and values converge and diverge at various points with those of the receiving communities. Commonalities should be explored and consolidated; differences debated and resolved.' According to Parekh, calls for a dialogue between communities are effective only if the receiving liberal society considers its cultural framework as one among many, rather than as the sole embodiment of all

---

[46] S Yasmeen, 'Muslim migrants living in non-Muslim States: building peace and harmony', (2001) 1 *Islamic Millennium Journal* 43.
[47] Ibid., 45.
[48] B Parekh, 'Europe, liberalism and the "Muslim question"' in T Modood, A Triandafyllidou and R Zapata-Barrero (eds), *Multiculturalism, Muslims and Citizenship: a European approach* (London, 2006), pp 197–8.

that is best. That Muslim communities can coexist with others does find resonance within the Qur'anic framework, when the Qur'an calls for respect for multiple religious traditions: 'To you your religion, to me mine' (Qur'an 109.6).

If this is the case, what might be the difficulties in this engagement? The first and greatest difficulty arising from the Islamic perspective is the fact that there is no single resolution or viewpoint regarding the position of Muslims in non-Muslim territories; nor is there a uniform approach regarding the treatment of non-Muslims under Muslim rule. Divergent approaches and viewpoints characterise the debates of earlier jurists leading to confusion and multiple understandings of the issue. That there is no official clergy in Islam is often cited as an advantage, but in the present case it can lead – and has led – to problems. The most fossilised and conservative interpretations are often adopted as the authoritative position and accepted by host communities as the definitive 'Islamic' position on the subject.

Can Muslim communities ever arrive at a mutually acceptable position on parameters of engagement with their host communities and as equal citizens of Europe? On the part of the host communities, can there be an acceptance of the fact that Muslim migrants are now indeed citizens of Europe and have some basic rights and obligations within a human rights framework? If so, is Europe able to tolerate diversity within its citizens and not interpret visible manifestations by some Muslims as a danger to European civilisation?

CONCLUSION

We have been concerned here with the law itself. But I should draw back, in closing, from this concern. In Coventry, where I live, one of the wards which has the highest Muslim population has also one of the worst health indicators in this country; the maternal and the infant mortality rates are the highest in England and Wales. *That* is where the value systems of Islamic law, the English legal system and human rights all converge. We should be starting with questions of empowerment, health, education and access to resources, empowering Muslim men and women to come in to the mainstream of life in this country. Then of course other issues – of law and engagement with legal systems – will follow.

CHAPTER 11

Ontario's 'shariʿa court': law and politics intertwined

Marion Boyd

We will be dealing with the major issues and the current realities of family law arbitrations in Ontario. Many conflicting reports are in circulation; it is important to have before us a sequential account.

Family law in Canada is a shared jurisdiction between our federal government and our provincial governments. The division of powers is set out in the British North America Act 1867 and was confirmed in our Constitution Act 1982. Section 91 of the 1982 Act sets out the areas subject exclusively to the Canadian Parliament: these include criminal law, marriage and divorce. Section 92 sets out the areas that fall exclusively within the authority of the provincial legislatures: these include, within each province, the solemnisation of marriage, property rights and civil rights.

The federal Divorce Act applies not only to married people who want a divorce, but also to the custody, access, child and spousal support claims that they make as part of that divorce. Ontario law, under the Family Law Act 1990 and the Children's Law Reform Act 1990, applies to all other family law matters, including separation (as distinct from divorce) of married or unmarried couples and support and custody where no divorce is sought, and at both separation and divorce the division and possession of property, restraining orders and related issues of child protection and enforcement orders.

Inheritance is also a provincial matter. Where there is a will, the wishes of the testator apply. However, an excluded surviving spouse may make application for herself or himself and any dependent children under the Family Law Act if the net property of the deceased spouse is greater than that of the surviving spouse. Where a person dies intestate, the Succession Law Reform Act 1990 comes into play: all children of the deceased, whether born in or out of wedlock or whether natural or adopted, are eligible for support from the estate if they are still dependent and for a share in the estate if they are not; a surviving legal spouse is entitled to a preferential share of the estate.

Given the division of jurisdiction on family law and inheritance matters, Canadian family law differs substantially from one province to another, particularly with respect to division of property. For example, as a condition of confederation, Quebec is governed by the Civil Code, based on the French Napoleonic Code and the notion of patrimony. The Ontario Family Law Act explicitly provides in its preamble for a strong emphasis on the equal rights and obligations of both spouses, particularly with respect to responsibility for their children. In Quebec law, arbitration of family law matters is expressly forbidden but mediation is mandatory. In Ontario in 2004, when the use of arbitration for family law disputes became an issue, arbitration was not included in either the Divorce Act 1985 or the Ontario Family Law Act 1990; although both statutes explicitly encouraged mediation, neither required it.

Section 27 of our Constitution requires us not only to permit but to enhance the capacity of multicultural communities in our land. In a very real sense we already have some pluralistic notions in our legal system and we have an ongoing constitutional obligation to honour multicultural aspirations.

Canadians have always been able to use arbitration as an alternative dispute resolution to settle matters without court intervention. The statute governing arbitration was adopted from British law in the 1890s and was available except in Quebec as the basis for arbitrating family law and inheritance matters, both in a religious and in a non-religious context. But the act was by the late twentieth century woefully out of date. In 1990, the Uniform Law Commission of Canada proposed a model law which was subsequently adopted in Ontario and seven other provinces. The Arbitration Act 1991 recognised the increased legitimacy of arbitration when two parties to a dispute freely and voluntarily agree to abide by the decision of a third party. The Act limited the court's supervisory power to set aside arbitration decisions when a properly executed arbitration agreement had been made and it allowed for the enforcement of an arbitration award by the Court.

One point should be made here which will be important later: under the Arbitration Act, as it was before the revisions that were made in the light of my report, there was for the arbitrators absolutely no qualification spelt out in the law. An arbitrator could be anybody upon whom the two parties agreed. The person did not necessarily know Canadian law at all, nor even Islamic law; one of our leading Islamic scholars said during the 2003–5 debate that there was probably only one person in our province who had a sufficient knowledge of Islamic law to be qualified to apply it.

In 2003, an organisation called the Islamic Institute of Civil Justice announced publicly that it was setting up a '*shari'a* court' in Ontario under the auspices of the Arbitration Act, implying that 'recent' changes to the Act made it possible to enforce binding arbitration and that Ontario's court no longer had oversight with respect to arbitrated settlements. (One problem for the Muslim community, a precipitating factor in the community's asking for consideration of *shari'a*-based arbitration, was that neither our Ontario superior courts nor the Supreme Court would uphold the contract around *mahr*. This has subsequently changed.)

Syed Mumtaz Ali, the main proponent of the Institute, suggested in media reports that the existence of an Islamic *shari'a* court required all 'good Muslims' to settle their disputes only in that forum. Mumtaz Ali was already known as a proponent for a separate identity for Muslims in Canada, similar to that allowed constitutionally for Francophone and Aboriginal Canadians. A public storm ensued. It became clear that the previously existing faith-based arbitration services, which had been offered for years by Jewish, Muslim and Christian agencies, were completely unfamiliar to most Canadians. The impression was given that the Ontario government had handed over special powers to enable Muslims to settle legal issues without reference to Canadian or Ontario laws and that all the perceived injustices observed in Islamic countries governed by *shari'a* laws were about to be visited on Muslim Canadians. Of particular concern, of course, was the unequal treatment of women under *shari'a* law. Those who had fled Islamic states were convinced that the use of arbitration for family law was the thin edge of the wedge whose ultimate goal was a separate political identity for Muslims in Canada, where *shari'a* law would eventually prevail in both civil and criminal matters. There was a huge public pressure on the government to intervene to prevent the Institute from proceeding. Much of the protest was frankly Islamophobic and very hurtful in the wake of 9/11.

At the time I was co-chair of the Law Society of Upper Canada's Access to Justice Committee and a member of its Equity and Aboriginal Affairs Committee. As the regulator of lawyers, and now also of paralegals, the Law Society was under some pressure to intervene in this issue. As an ardent feminist and a Protestant woman of faith, I was deeply concerned about the issue's divisive impact on individual women and on our multicultural and multireligious communities. As the misinformation propagated by the media increased, I offered advice to my successor, the then Attorney General, that this storm was not going to subside unless the concerns were aired, the issues clarified and some constructive compromise developed. To my surprise (and somewhat to my dismay) I was then asked to head up a Review of the Arbitration Act, to consult with affected individuals and communities, and to report my findings to the government.

My report, entitled 'Dispute resolution in family law: protecting choice, promoting inclusion'[1] (191 pages long and including 46 recommendations) was submitted to the government in December 2004. To the loud dismay of the opponents, I recommended that the government continue to allow arbitration of family law matters and that they allow these arbitrations to be carried out under religious laws if the parties freely agree to do so. However, I also recommended sweeping changes to all family law arbitrations as follows:

- That arbitration agreements be included in the provisions of the Family Law Act, be contemporaneous with the dispute, be in writing, signed and witnessed, and be voidable by the court on the same grounds as other domestic contracts or agreements;
- That the court must approve any domestic agreement entered into by a minor child;
- That the court be able to set aside any arbitration award which is unconscionable, where it does not reflect the best interests of children, where a party did not have or waived independent legal advice, where the parties do not have a copy of the arbitration agreement and a written decision including reasons, and, with respect to faith-based arbitration, where a party had not received a statement of the principles to be used in the faith-based arbitration before signing the arbitration agreement;
- That regulatory powers be added to the Arbitration Act to require arbitrators to maintain written records of issues, evidence, form of law, decision and reasons, to maintain those records for at least ten years, to include in any agreement an explicit statement that judicial remedies specified in the Arbitration Act or the Family Law Act cannot be waived and to include either a certificate of Independent Legal Advice or an explicit waiver of Independent Legal Advice.
- That minimum requirements for the training and education of arbitrators be put in place and that there be a process for ongoing evaluation and oversight of arbitrations;
- That the parties in any arbitration be separately screened to determine issues of power imbalance between them to ensure that both parties are agreeing voluntarily to arbitration and understand the nature and consequences of entering into the process.
- That public legal education in family and inheritance law as well as community development in multicultural communities be put in place to ensure that vulnerable parties have a better understanding of family law and dispute resolution options.

---

[1] Accessible at <http://www.attorneygeneral.jus.gov.on.ca/english/about/pubs/boyd/>.

One of my chief concerns was to have mandatory education requirements – minimal though they may be – for arbitrators, and to require arbitrators to tell possible clients on what principles they were going to form the arbitration. This became an important part of the revisions subsequently made by the government by regulation to the Arbitration Act.

The quality needed in an arbitrator is a very strong commitment to the rule of law and to natural justice. The training courses that are now running in Ontario are precisely on these things: on fair and equitable procedure and on a clear understanding that Canadian rules of evidence apply. The requirement, then, is not that the person is a religious leader or an expert in one form of law or another. Arbitration was set up not to replace the courts but to offer in problem-solving another dimension for those who do not want to go through the court process but want somebody they can trust to give a neutral decision. The Arbitration Act offers people the opportunity to come to a decision themselves on an arbitrator whom both of them can trust to make a decision fairly and equitably in their particular case.

I entirely understand the fears expressed by many opponents of arbitration that this private means of resolving family disputes may disadvantage vulnerable people, in particular women, and possibly erode hard-won equity rights over time. However, although we sought out examples of egregious wrongs resulting from arbitrations, the review body received no reports – even anonymous or by hearsay – to confirm that these fears were valid in our province given that religious arbitration had been going on for a long time. Nonetheless, the apprehension of so many people must be taken into account by a responsible government. The unregulated nature of arbitration left the whole process open to abuse. We respected the argument of those opposed to arbitration in family law that decisions would become private and that any kind of behaviour could then follow without judicial oversight. We ourselves, on the same principle, had no wish to have the decisions sealed; sealed decisions would allow no way of judging what the overall impact over time of arbitrated settlements might be on the erosion of civil rights.

The government had clearly hoped that my findings would quiet the storm of controversy. While those in favour of family law arbitration were delighted and relieved that I did not recommend scrapping the whole process, those opposed to arbitration – and more particularly those opposed to faith-based arbitration – became even more vociferous. Fuelled by misinformation, the media continued to pummel the government daily. The controversy became very heated. Ontario was criticised around the world for permitting Islamic law to victimise our citizens.

We should be clear who was opposed to my recommendations. The most vociferous group was led by a woman named Homa Arjoman, an Iranian-born citizen of Canada who gathered together a huge collection of people who were seriously fearful of what they saw as a creeping recognition by Canadian officials of the very worst cultural practices rather than of actual religious law. Most of those people, however, were also adamant secularists and framed their arguments in a way that was (unfortunately) quite demeaning for anyone coming from a position of faith. They made strong comments that only the secular law should apply, that everyone should have to go through the courts, there should be no alternative dispute resolution because of their fear – their legitimate, genuine and passionate fear – that the rights of others would be destroyed in that process.

The second group, a very articulate coalition of women, was made up of three groups: the members of the Canadian Council of Muslim Women identify as faithful Muslims and act politically for the rights of Muslim women within their community; the National Association of Women in the Law is a group of very knowledgeable women which has done wonderful work throughout Canada on women's rights and has made representation in many fora; and, third, the National Immigrant Women's Coalition. The view of this coalition, led by the National Association of Women in the Law, which at that point was based in Quebec and led by Quebec lawyers, was that arbitration – which is not allowed in Quebec – should not be allowed anywhere in Canada. Why not? Because the power differential between women and men can never be overcome in that private system. (As a former Attorney General – and so the object of much of such women's fury over the courts' historical behaviour with respect to women's rights – I was slightly surprised to hear that argument come from that source; women in the law know very well that the treatment of women's equality in our own courts is far from perfect.) They argued that authority, rather than being safely handed over to liberal people who understand the context of Muslim life in Canada, could in fact be hijacked by people who want to impose values that are completely contradictory to our Canadian law.

We also heard from many Muslim women who *did* want arbitration to continue, but who were also for the most part very strongly of the opinion that there had to be some measures taken to balance out the power between the parties going for arbitration. Suggestions for public legal education, community development, pre-screening for issues of domestic abuse or power imbalance – these came primarily from those women and from the feminists who supported them.

The people most vociferous in favour of arbitration tended to be lawyers. Many lawyers in Canada had begun turning to arbitration as a way of reaching quicker resolution. Clients were more likely to go along with a decision of which they felt they were part; they were less likely to lodge the serial court complaints raised when people feel that a settlement has been imposed upon them and that their story has never been told. Then of course there were the groups such as the groups lobbying for fathers' rights who wanted arbitration to be completely free from the government's regulation, because they understand very well that in those circumstances, without any monitoring, they would have the opportunity to erode the equality rights of their partners. They were surprisingly frank about their advocacy for arbitration and what they hoped to see accomplished by it.

Then there were the people inflamed on this issue by very serious misinformation about our whole legal system. Everyone involved in the system came away feeling that we have not done a good job of helping people understand the law in our country and how it applies. For example, the Canadian Council of Imams did not understand that there is no such thing as an illegitimate child in Ontario; a lot of their presentation was concerned with the care and protection of 'illegitimate' children who are not in Ontario law illegitimate at all. There was also, at the start of the discussion, a lot of misunderstanding over the possible implications of family law arbitration for the criminal law. There is a small group in Canada that wants to see a full *shari'a* regime for both civil and criminal matters; but there was absolutely no one in the mainstream speaking in favour of such a *shari'a* regime for the criminal law. (Only one person argued for it before the review body; the other proponents of religiously based arbitration wanted us to ignore the idea and to concentrate on civil law.) It is important to remember here the division of powers in Canada: the federal government is responsible for all criminal law and the same criminal code gets applied across the country, although enforcement and prosecution are the responsibility of each province. As a province we have no jurisdiction over criminal law; in our work for the review, therefore, the criminal law did not arise.

Eventually and unfortunately on 11 September 2005 the Premier of the province blurted out to a reporter that he would put an end to religious arbitration in Ontario. It was a brilliant political manoeuvre; the heat on the government eased abruptly. But it was, in my view, bad public policy. The Ministry of the Attorney General was left to fashion a legislative and regulatory response.

The decision was to implement virtually all the legislative and regulatory recommendations from my report but to make faith-based arbitration awards advisory only; that is, they would not have any force in law. Citizens would still be able to choose faith-based arbitration, but the awards would not be enforced by the courts. If one or more party to an arbitration dislikes the decision of a religious tribunal, they can begin their case again in the civil courts without encumbrance. Summaries of arbitral decisions and of the basis on which they are reached now have to be made available for monitoring by the Ministry of the Attorney General. But if the parties choose to follow the decision of the arbitrator, the courts may in fact never even know that the arbitration took place.

As before, civil divorces are only available through the federal Divorce Act and the federal courts; religious divorces can continue through religious courts as they did before. We should dwell for a moment on religious divorces. The Supreme Court has upheld the principle that a divorce settlement that is in any way conditional upon the subsequent granting of a religious divorce has no place in law. The work that led to this result is instructive. The Coalition of Jewish Women for the *Get* in Canada, having worked throughout the late 1980s, got legislation to this effect put in place in the Divorce Act 1989 which was then adopted in our Ontario Family Law Act.[2] The provision is similar to that of the UK's Divorce (Religious Marriages) Act 2002, but in Canada it applies to all religions. The clause was promoted by a group of very determined Jewish women whose major concern was that if they remarried their children would not be Israeli citizens. They are the same group or an off-shoot of the group that worked in England. Some of the women from the Coalition of Jewish Women for

---

[2] Ontario Family Law Act 1990, s 2(4)–(6): '(4) A party to an application under section 7 (net family property), 10 (questions of title between spouses), 33 (support), 34 (powers of court) or 37 (variation) may serve on the other party and file with the court a statement, verified by oath or statutory declaration, indicating that, (a) the author of the statement has removed all barriers that are within his or her control and that would prevent the other spouse's remarriage within that spouse's faith; and (b) the other party has not done so, despite a request. (5) Within ten days after service of the statement, or within such longer period as the court allows, the party served with a statement under subsection (4) shall serve on the other party and file with the court a statement, verified by oath or statutory declaration, indicating that the author of the statement has removed all barriers that are within his or her control and that would prevent the other spouse's remarriage within that spouse's faith. (6) When a party fails to comply with subsection (5), (a) if the party is an applicant, the proceeding may be dismissed; (b) if the party is a respondent, the defence may be struck out.'

the Get were talking with the Muslim groups of women about what might be accomplished; they traded techniques. That may have been one of the most important outcomes of the whole discussion, and offers an example to follow: when women have a strong belief, they can make changes both within their community and to the mainstream law.

Four years have passed, as I write, since the Family Law Amendment Act was passed in Ontario and there is still no clear evidence of how it has impacted religious people seeking faith-based arbitration. I believe that faith-based arbitration will continue and that, since it will operate outside the law, there is no guarantee that individual rights will be respected and that coercion will not prevail. Some of the existing arbitration services, which had operated prior to this whole process, appear to be content to have their decisions considered advisory. For example, the Ismaili Conciliation and Arbitration Board and the Jewish Rabbinical Courts had already been operating in that fashion in provinces where family law arbitration is not allowed. In granting divorces, the Superior Court of Justice continues as before to be loath to interfere with agreements reached by the disputants through mediation, arbitration or self-designed separation agreements. Only when an agreement is egregious or when children's best interests may not be respected will the Court intervene. To my knowledge, none of the religious organisations has yet challenged the amendments to the new Acts and there is no evidence of increased appeals to the court.

The whole controversy did open a debate about the role of multiculturalism in Canada. This open dialogue has helped many to understand the value of diversity in our society and to appreciate the tensions that underlie any form of accommodation. The overt prejudice and racism expressed during the process caused many people to re-examine their attitudes and actively to seek ways to come together. Many Muslims have committed to providing programmes within their communities to foster a sense of Canadian citizenship. Many Canadians, previously unaware of arbitration as an alternative dispute resolution method available to them, are now choosing arbitration as a faster, cheaper and less adversarial way to settle their personal issues. There is some suggestion that arbitration should, in the future, become the norm, with only very contentious issues ever needing a full court hearing. The government has worked with legal and community groups to provide public legal education on family law in many languages and in many communities to the benefit of all. The Ministry's website now includes a thorough explanation of family law, what options there are and how to access assistance; there is clear information about arbitration as an option and the limits on faith-based arbitration are outlined.[3] The regulatory requirements for arbitration are laid out so that consumers have some measure of quality control and protection.

In my report, I heeded the advice of the vast majority of respondents (whether they were for religious arbitration or not) to maintain the availability of family law arbitration but to recommend measures to ensure that arbitrators act appropriately under Canadian and Ontario law, that there is an appropriate oversight by the courts, that parties are not coerced into arbitration, that parties are not allowed to waive their basic rights, and that arbitration orders can be effectively enforced through the court. I believe that, with such legislation and regulation in place, with intensive public legal education about rights and obligations under family law, and with co-operative community development efforts aimed at including – and I cannot stress this enough – minority citizens in our civil society, allowing faith-based arbitration would not only provide everyone with a choice of dispute resolution methods but would bring under the umbrella of our laws those who will otherwise operate outside them.

I am convinced that people of faith, who believe that their faith requires them to eschew the secular courts, will always seek faith-based dispute resolution. The issue for me is not whether the dominant culture allows such normative rules and practices of minority ethnic and religious communities to continue, but rather how we can include these people so that their rights and freedoms as citizens are not swallowed up by hegemonic cultural norms. I believe in Ayelet Shachar's concept of multi-dimensionality, that we all have many identities simultaneously: we are citizens of our state but we may also define ourselves by gender, sexuality, age, race, language, ethnicity, religion and so on.[4] In a liberal democratic and multicultural society like Canada, it is *citizenship* that allows membership in the minority community to take shape. Commitment to individual rights lies at the core of the legal and political organisation of any liberal democracy and underpins freedom of information and expression, and the rights of minorities to enter legitimately into dialogue with the broader society. It is illogical and untenable to claim minority rights in order then to entrench religious or cultural orthodoxies that seek to trample the individual rights of select others; accommodation of cultural

---

[3] Ontario Ministry of the Attorney General, Family Law Information Centre Locations, accessible at <http://www.attorneygeneral.jus.gov.on.ca/english/family/infoctr_locations.asp>.
[4] A Shachar, *Multicultural Jurisdictions: cultural differences and women's rights* (Cambridge, 2001). Shachar's argument is discussed by Rowan Williams, 'Civil and religious law in England a religious respective', supra pp 27–32 and by R Griffith-Jones, 'Religious rights and the public interest', infra pp 188–94.

difference should not extend this far. Rather tolerance and accommodation must be balanced against a firm commitment to *individual* agency and autonomy. It is my view that including faith-based arbitration as a choice of dispute resolution and making arbitrations subject to the law of the land is a win/win proposition; it is, in the terminology used by Shachar and taken up by the Archbishop of Canterbury, a 'transformative accommodation'.

Accommodation or conflict: trajectories in the United Kingdom

CHAPTER 12

Religious rights and the public interest

Robin Griffith-Jones

'TRANSFORMATIVE ACCOMMODATION': RETROSPECT

Dr Rowan Williams, then Archbishop of Canterbury, aimed in 'Civil and Religious Law' 'to tease out some of the broader issues around the rights of religious groups within a secular state, with a few thoughts about what might be entailed in crafting a just and constructive relationship between Islamic law and the statutory law of the United Kingdom'.[1] It is time to revisit the Archbishop's own – tentative and provisional – suggestions for the future. Dr Williams drew upon the work of the legal theorist Ayelet Shachar:[2]

> It might be possible to think in terms of what [Shachar] calls 'transformative accommodation': a scheme in which individuals retain the liberty to choose the jurisdiction under which they will seek to resolve certain carefully specified matters, so that 'power-holders are forced to compete for the loyalty of their shared constituents' ... Hence '*transformative* accommodation': both jurisdictional parties may be changed by their encounter over time, and we avoid the sterility of mutually exclusive monopolies. It is uncomfortably true that this introduces into our thinking about law what some would see as a 'market' element, a competition for loyalty as Shachar admits.

This competitive element calls for some attention. Neither Shachar nor the Archbishop was offering a detailed blueprint for action. To clarify the conditions to which Shachar's suggestion might give rise, we do well to follow Shachar's own response to the pressures put by the events of recent years upon the theory she advances in *Multicultural Jurisdictions*.

Shachar confronts a central problem of multiculturalism. A liberal society may well hope, in accordance with the West's understanding of human rights, to accommodate the minority cultures at home in it, allowing (and

---

[1] Supra p 21.
[2] A Shachar, *Multicultural Jurisdictions: cultural differences and women's rights* (Cambridge, 2001), p 122.

even encouraging) such minorities to foster their own traditions in accordance with their own principles. But how is such a liberal society to accommodate the practices and principles of minorities whose norms do not conform to the West's understanding of human rights? In particular, how are the rights of women to be protected in any minority communities that are perceived by the liberal majority to be improperly patriarchal and androcentric? Must women in such communities be faced with a stark choice, forgoing either their culture or their rights?

Shachar proposes the introduction of joint governance and so of competition to the legal provision made for various carefully defined sub-matters within a polity. This will 'make power-holders more accountable to their constituents'. For given a group traditionally self-contained and closed to outside influence,

the onus is [in the light of the alternative(s) available] on group leaders to respond to 'alternative' voices within the group, and thus lead to the internal transformation of the group's *nomos*. If they systematically fail to address the concerns of group members who bear a disproportionate burden of the costs of [multicultural] accommodation, and these members are granted at least minimal (educational or material) resources through the state's exercise of authority in its designated sub-matters, then these 'peripheral' members can, perhaps for the first time, pose a real threat of selective exit. The group and the state now engage in a competitive relationship where the result of failure to address their constituents' needs can lead to the strengthening of the other power-holder.[3]

Shachar's book was warmly reviewed as a valuable contribution to legal theory. Commentators observed, nonetheless, that she had given little attention to the practical difficulties to which her proposal would give rise.[4] The women in greatest need of such partial 'exits' from the procedures of their own culture are the women least likely to have, in practice, knowledge of – let alone genuine, easy access to – the state's alternatives.[5] (Even such partial exit is itself a drastic measure; it is hard to be sure how realistic such a threat from an endangered woman would be or would be perceived to be.) Shachar does not address the hard cases: there will be areas such as education over which both the state and the group are likely to seek control; will the state (as stronger than the minority groups) simply decide on and impose the demarcation of

---

[3] Ibid., pp 124–5.
[4] 'A weakness ... is the abstract and theoretical character of her elaboration', R Pierik, 'Multicultural jurisdictions: review', (2004) 32(4) *Review in Political Theory* 585, 589.
[5] EJ Mitnick, 'Individual vulnerability and cultural transformation', (2002–3) 101 Mich L Rev 1635, 1656–60. On the same theme, more generally: SM Okin, '"Mistresses of their own destiny": group rights, gender and realistic rights of exit', (2002) 112 *Ethics* 205. Cf SM Okin, 'Feminism and multiculturalism', (1991) 108 *Ethics* 661: how girls are affected if they internalise the values of a culture that does not value women's autonomy.

responsibilities? The allocation will not depend on 'the justifications that each provides for its preferred position in governing a specific sub-matter', but upon the state's greater power.[6] In the division of principal responsibility for different sub-matters, Shachar assumes between state and group just the consensus whose absence gives rise to the problems she sets out to solve.[7] Can the state that has already let its vulnerable members be exposed to danger really be depended on to offer them better?[8]

Shachar herself has returned to the theme in several papers. She holds a post in Canada (Toronto), and has responded at length to the highly politicised debate over the proposed Muslim Court of Arbitration in Ontario, of which we have heard more from Marion Boyd, 'Ontario's "*shari'a* court" : law and politics intertwined' (supra pp 176–86). Leading the preparations for the Muslim Court was the Canadian Society of Muslims. Its president, Syed Mumtaz Ali, laid down a striking and contentious challenge: once the court was in place, Muslims would be faced with the choice, 'Do you want to govern yourself by the personal laws of your religion, or do you prefer governance by secular Canadian family law?'[9] Here, in a phrase of Shachar's, is a strong 'reactive culturalism' in response to the perceived dangers of assimilation to the West's secular agenda.

At the time of the dispute itself in Ontario, Shachar proposed three procedural emendations to the state's Arbitration Act to secure the rights of women under any such Muslim Court:[10] 'to introduce a requirement of mandatory and independent legal advice for each party *before* entering the binding arbitration process'; 'to permit a non-governmental organisation to act as amicus curiae to assist women, in making their choices', and 'to file a written affidavit confirming the consultation session and the choices made by each party with a civil registration authority or local court'. In order to ensure that a woman had not been pressured or frightened into supposed loyalty to her culture, Shachar proposed a mandatory review of any family-law arbitration settlement prior to its becoming binding.

---

[6] M Deveaux, 'Political morality and culture: what difference do differences make?', (July 2002) 28 STP 503, 512, 517; cf B Parekh, 'Review', (2002) 96(4) *APSR* 811.
[7] M Mookherjee, 'Feminism and multiculturalism: putting Okin and Shachar in question', (2005) 2(2) JMP 237, 241.
[8] Mitnik, 'Individual Vulnerability', supra n 5, 1658.
[9] 'Interview: a review of the Muslim personal/family law campaign', first published August 1995, accessible at <http://muslimcanada.org/pflfaqs.htmll>. See A Shachar, 'Religion, state and the problem of gender: new modes of citizenship and governance in diverse societies', (2005) 50 McGill LJ 49, 62.
[10] Shachar, 'Religion, state and the problem of gender', supra n 9, 75–7. For the comparable proposals in the Boyd Report itself, see M Boyd, 'Ontario's '*shari'a* court': law and politics intertwined', supra pp 179.

Returning to the topic three years later, Shachar outlined the lessons to be learnt from Ontario: entry into a secular agreement (with a religious aspect), she argued, would offer better protection to women than entry into a community-based, semi-private tribunal with binding authority over consenting members; *ex ante* regulatory control would be preferable to *ex post* judicial review; voluntary agreement by faith-based tribunals to comply with statutory restrictions ('self-restraint') would be preferable to imposition by state fiat.

Shachar's original proposal has in these later presentations been transformed. Under the pressure of events, of Syed Mumtaz Ali's expansionism and of a state constitutionalism that would concede nothing which might endanger women, we might wonder if Shachar's 'transformative accommodation' has come to occupy no more than a niche, tightly regulated and supervised, within the state's (untransformed) system.[11] The prospect of competition had in Ontario driven a deeper wedge between the protagonists. The state, under Shachar's own consequent recommendations, would accommodate no claimants to jurisdiction who were not 'transformed' in advance into public and binding compliance with the state's norms.

Dr Williams included 'aspects of marital law' among those areas in which he believed that some 'transformative accommodation' could fruitfully be undergone. He spoke strongly of the need to foreclose any dangers of 'reinforcing in minority communities some of the most repressive or retrograde elements in them, with particularly serious consequences for the role and liberties of women'. We are not the first to wonder, nonetheless, if the Archbishop's outline of supplementary tribunals had been tested for the dangers to which such tribunals might expose women if the tribunals were not exposed to full regulatory supervision by the state.[12] *Shari'a* councils can be reluctant to concede a divorce, even where the wife alleges violence by her husband; Samia Bano has reported cases of women's exposure, within such mediation, to the husbands at whose hands the women have, by their own account, suffered violence or threats of violence.[13]

---

[11] Cf A Shachar, 'Privatizing diversity: a cautionary tale from religious arbitration in family law', (2008) 9 *Theoretical Inq. Law* 573, pp 598–602. For further analysis of constitutionalism's self-defence against any perceived sources of competition, R Hirschl and A Shachar, 'The new wall of separation: permitting diversity, restricting competition', (2008–9) 30 CLR 2535, pp 2552–4 in relation to Ontario.

[12] A valuable survey in M Malik, 'Muslim legal norms and the integration of European Muslims', RSCAS Policy Paper 2009/29 (European University Institute, 2009), accessible at <http://cadmus.eui.eu/handle/1814/11653>: on multicultural vulnerability, pp 18–21; on *shari'a* councils, Muslim family arbitration, etc, and the possible pressures upon women, pp 21–3.

[13] S Bano, 'In pursuit of religious and legal diversity: a response to the Archbishop of Canterbury and the "*shari'a* debate" in Britain', (2008) 10 Ecc LJ 282; S Bano, 'Shari'a councils and the resolution of matrimonial disputes: gender and justice in the "shadow" of the law' in RT Thiara and AI Gill (eds), *Violence against Women in South Asian Communities* (London, 2009), pp 182–210.

Dr Williams spoke of 'something like a delegation of certain legal functions to the religious courts of a community'. In order to prevent vexatious claims:

> There needs to be access to recognised authority acting for a religious group: there is already, of course, an Islamic *Shari'a* Council, much in demand for rulings on marital questions in the UK; and if we were to see more latitude given in law to rights and scruples rooted in religious identity, we should need a much enhanced and quite sophisticated version of such a body, with increased resources and a high degree of community recognition.

If such questions as 'the provision for the inheritance of widows' is to be subject to 'directly binding enactments by religious authority', the rights of the more vulnerable members of that religious community must clearly be protected. Shaheen Sardar Ali has asked how is the state to be confident that both parties are in such cases 'free' to choose this subjection to religious authority. We need further to press the question that has come to dominate Shachar's proposal: who shall regulate the enhanced – and strikingly powerful – version of a *shari'a* council? The state, we must assume, would still be the authority responsible for defining the conditions which would constitute such freedom; and the state would retain the power to investigate possible infringements of that freedom and of other rights, and to overturn such settlements as either procedurally or substantively had not, in the state's view, honoured them. The questions that so vexed Ontario remain as pertinent as ever; and the supplementary jurisdiction, as refined in the light of these questions, would be coming once more under the aegis of the state's courts and regulation.[14]

It is striking that Shachar cites Malaysia as a state with a successful arrangement of multiple jurisdictions. The bar set for the competition between jurisdictions in Malaysia is high: a person's conversion to – or with more difficulty from – Islam. This hardly opens any sub-domains of legal provision, for the benefit of the vulnerable and without damaging repercussions, to competition between Islamic and civil law. Where conversion of one party to a marriage does lead to such competition, lasting contention has followed. The Ong Report[15] of 1971 drew attention to 'married individuals, nearly always men, [who] converted to Islam only to

---

[14] English law, as we are seeing throughout this book, tenaciously insists on the use of *lex fori* in family (as opposed to civil) justice. The civil law jurisdictions of Continental Europe, by contrast, routinely apply (not *lex fori* but) the system of law most applicable to the parties before the court ('applicable law').

[15] HT Ong, 'Malaysia: Report of the Royal Commission on Non-Muslim Marriage and Divorce Laws' (1971).

escape their obligations under their existing marriages.'[16] This becomes a problem of competency: Muslims' family matters are under the jurisdiction not of the High Court but of the Syariah Court. (Such jurisdictional questions have also arisen over the conversion of adults and of children, the custody of children and inheritance.[17]) The courts are not complacent. In *Tang Sung Mooi v Too Miew Kim* the then Supreme Court dismissed the argument of the former husband who converted to Islam after his divorce but before relief was settled; he claimed to be free from the jurisdiction of the High Court to which his former wife, still a non-Muslim, had appealed for division of assets and maintenance.[18] But if this is the level and character of competition recommended by Shachar, it is hard to imagine its incorporation into English life.

In one important respect, the Archbishop himself refined Shachar's expectations for transformative accommodation. The Archbishop had in mind the UK's communities of religious believers living in some tension with the legislature and the courts; by such accommodation, 'both jurisdictional parties may be changed by their encounter over time, and we avoid the sterility of mutually exclusive monopolies' (p 32 above). Shachar was writing with a different emphasis: on those religious believers who are most vulnerable to oppression within their own religious culture.

From the viewpoint of Christians and of non-believers in today's UK, the vulnerable believers most likely to come to mind – rightly or wrongly – are Muslim women.[19] But are there victims within the churches themselves? Shachar writes of the 'reactive culturalism' of groups that respond to external or internal pressure for change by a defensive reinforcement of familiar and conservative norms. The 'peripheral' members of the group then find themselves facing, more starkly than ever, a choice between their culture and their rights. An analyst might diagnose just such reactivism in

---

[16] The Law Reform (Marriage and Divorce) Act 1976 failed to bind such men upon divorce to honour the full obligations imposed by their pre-conversion, non-Islamic marriages; see <http://malaysianchristian.files.wordpress.com/2007/06/mccbchst-protest-note-june-2007.pdf>.

[17] Conversion of an adult, *Lina Joy v Majlis Agama Islam Wilayah Persekutuan* [2007] 4 MLJ 585; of children, *Subashini Rajasingam v Saravanan Thangathoray* [2008] 2 MLJ 147. Custody: *Shamala Sathiyaseelan v Dr Jeyaganesh C Mogarajah* [2004] 1 CLJ 505, 2 CLJ 416, 3 CLJ 516. Inheritance: *Latifah bte Mat Zin v Rosmawati bte Sharibun* [2007] 5 MLJ 101. I am grateful to Paul Garlick QC for alerting me to these difficulties and these cases.

[18] [1994] 3 MLJ 117. Zaleha Kamaruddin kindly briefed me on the problem and on the case as opening a route to its solution, now in 'Current legal routes to division of matrimonial property upon conversion' (2010), accessible at <http://ikim.gov.my/v5/index.php/imagesweb/file/index.php?lg=1&opt=com_article&grp=2&sec=&key=2109&cmd=resetall>. Cf Z Kamaruddin, 'Insights into the inter-relationship and the associated tension between shari'ah and civil family law in Malaysia', (2008) 6 MLJ 76.

[19] P Shah warns against such an assumption, supra p 146.

the churches – and just such a difficult choice for their homosexual members – when a church refuses to employ a gay youth officer[20] or refuses to administer Holy Communion to an openly gay man[21] or (taking such reaction to a new level) if it withdraws all social services to a capital city for fear of contributing to the pensions of gay couples.[22] It is not clear, in such examples of believers with multiple affiliations, that the churches are undergoing a transformation in order to compete for the loyalty of their more vulnerable constituents; on the contrary, they are (in the defence of their beliefs and principles) using their power to resist the liberalism of the state which would, on the state's account, benefit those constituents.

We may seem, thus far, to be facing a frustrating dead-end. It is time to look for alternative routes. What follows is only one side of a conversation: a view of the present position and of its possible development from a layman far more closely aligned with the life of English than of Islamic law. Dr Williams identified a real danger: that everything can be too easily seen from the comfort of a hegemonic culture, complacent in its own virtues and blind to its own faults; so that its members look for nothing but the assimilation of more recently founded communities to their own 'host' culture's norms and expectations. We will be saved from this pitfall by the voices of our partners in this conversation in this book itself. For the rest of this present chapter we continue the search launched by Dr Williams for 'a pattern of relations in which a plurality of diverse and overlapping affiliations work for a common good'.

THE ALTERNATIVE: A STERILE STAND-OFF?

In 1998 the third edition of David Pearl's *Muslim Family Law*,[23] written with Werner Menski, sketched such a stand-off as Dr Williams warned of. They drew attention to the value that British Muslims put on the legal norms and practices of Islam, to the informal legal provision they were making for themselves in the face of the English courts' apparent reluctance to have any regard for those norms and practices, and to the resentment to which this reluctance was giving rise. Pearl and Menski argued that it was neither honest nor helpful to imagine that British Muslims would – and

---

[20] *Reaney v Hereford Diocesan Board of Finance*, (2008) 10 Ecc LJ 131.
[21] 'Netherlands gay protest over Catholic communion snub', *BBC News* 28 February 2010.
[22] C Pope, 'DC same-sex marriage Bill: an imposing agenda', *The Washington Post*, 12 November 2009; elaboration from the Archdiocese accessible at <http://blog.adw.org/2009/11/dc-same-sex-marriage-bill-an-imposing-agenda>.
[23] D Pearl and W Menski, *Muslim Family Law* (third edition, London, 1998).

arrogant to assume they should – give up their reverence for and adherence to *shari'a*. In Menski's phrase, an 'English *shari'a*', *angrezi shariat*, is growing up largely out of the sight, supervision or regulation of the English courts. If we set the Archbishop's approach to one side, we may seem to be left with nothing more than a rebarbative stand-off between the state and informal, 'underground' regimes of local community tribunals.

Menski himself, as expert witness in a case to which we shall return, vividly described the premises upon which the law is administered in Bangladesh. His account helps those of us brought up under English law to acknowledge how different the premises and practices of the law can be in a Muslim-majority country.

> In situations of conflict, it was always the position in Pakistani law and remains the position in Bangladeshi law today that the traditional Muslim law as God-given law co-exists with, but ultimately prevails over, the statutory civil law. The statutory law of Bangladesh, in turn, subtly seeks to avoid such conflict by constantly adjusting its written provisions almost imperceptibly to the outsider's eyes to the letter and spirit of the traditional *shari'a* law ... The Law Commission of Bangladesh ... decided in July 2005 that Bangladesh could not have a Uniform Civil Code, if that meant that state-made law would become superior to the Quran-based Islamic law.[24]

It is not surprising if British Muslims with such presuppositions find the English courts alien.

How alien might be more readily seen in the light of a summary statement by Munby J which has become widely known:

> Although historically this country is part of the Christian west, and although it has an established church which is Christian, I sit as a secular judge serving a multi-cultural community of many faiths in which all of us can now take pride, sworn to do justice 'to all manner of people' ... So the starting point of the law is an essentially agnostic view of religious beliefs and a tolerant indulgence to religious and cultural diversity ... All [religions] are entitled to equal respect, whether in times of peace, or, as at present, amidst the clash of arms.[25]

There are Christian leaders too who feel marginalised by this ethos. In 2011 Lord Carey, Archbishop Williams' predecessor, submitted a witness

---

[24] W Menski, Expert Testimony in, *KC, NNC v City of Westminster Social & Community Services Department, IC (a protected party, by his litigation friend the Official Solicitor)* [2008] EWCA Civ 198, para 58 and Addendum 76.

[25] *Sulaiman v Juffali* [2002] 1 FLR 479, para 47. Cicero, *Pro Milone* 4.9: 'Silent enim leges inter arma.' Famously denied in England by Lord Atkin in *Liversidge v Anderson* [1942] AC 206 (HL(E)), 244 (in rebuttal of Lord Macmillan): 'In England, amidst the clash of arms, the laws are not silent.' Munby LJ returned to the theme in R *(Eunice Johns and Owen Johns) v Derby City Council* [2011] EWHC 375 (Admin), paras 38–53.

statement to the Court of Appeal in *McFarlane*.[26] Mr McFarlane, working for the counselling-service Relate, had refused on the grounds of his Christian beliefs to offer psycho-sexual counselling to same-sex couples; he had been dismissed. Lord Carey insisted that Christian faith and love are not discriminatory: 'the desire of the Christian is to limit self destructive conduct by those of any sexual orientation and ensure the eternal future of an individual with the Lord'. Recent decisions of the courts have illuminated 'insensitivity to the interests and needs of the Christian community' and 'a lack of sensitivity to religious belief' (on *Ladele*).[27] 'The fact that senior clerics of the Church of England feel compelled to intervene directly in judicial decisions and cases is illuminative of a future civil unrest'; that is a remarkable warning.

Lord Carey therefore asked for Mr McFarlane's appeal to be heard 'under the direction of the Lord Chief Justice and a freshly constituted five member Court of Appeal'. He continued:

Further, I appeal to the Lord Chief Justice to establish a specialist Panel of Judges designated to hear cases engaging religious rights. Such Judges should have a proven sensitivity and understanding of religious issues and I would be supportive of Judges of all faiths and denominations being allocated to such a Panel. The Judges engaged in the cases listed above should recuse themselves from further adjudication on such matters as they have made clear their lack of knowledge about the Christian faith.

We must wonder how such judges would have proved that sensitivity and understanding: by prior judgments, presumably, which had satisfied a Christian lobby. Lord Carey was near to proposing a court designed to satisfy the requirements of a particular section of the community: this would be 'transformative accommodation' indeed. Lord Carey looked forward to seeing judges sensitive to other faiths too. It is perhaps ironic that Lord Carey had in 2008 made clear that Dr Williams' 'conclusion that Britain will eventually have to concede some place in law for aspects of

---

[26] On appeal from EAT 0106/09/DA.
[27] Lord Carey may not have had the opportunity to study the judgments in *Ladele v Islington London Borough Council and Liberty (Intervening)* at the Employment Appeal Tribunal [2008] UKEAT/453/08 1912 and in the Court of Appeal [2009] EWCA Civ 1357. Elias J, EAT at 15: '[f]undamental changes in social attitudes, particularly with regard to sexual orientation, are happening very fast and for some – and not only those with religious objections – they are genuinely perplexing. In that context, there seems . . . to be some virtue in taking a pragmatic line if it is lawful.' Lord Neuberger MR in the Court of Appeal at 60 quoted Sachs J in *Christian Education South Africa v Minister of Education* (CCT 4/00) [2000] ZACC 11, para 35: 'the state should, wherever reasonably possible, seek to avoid putting believers to extremely painful and intensely burdensome choices of either being true to their faith or else respectful of the law.' Ms Ladele's case was heard in the European Court of Human Rights (App no 51671/10), 4 September 2012.

shariʿa is a view I cannot share'.[28] But once appropriate judges were selected for cases that needed a sensitivity to Islam, Lord Carey would surely have to expect *shariʿa* law to make a contribution to the courts' reasoning and judgments.

The response of Laws LJ was robust: 'The conferment of any legal protection or preference upon a particular substantive moral position on the ground only that it is espoused by the adherents of a particular faith ... is deeply unprincipled ... The individual conscience is free to accept such dictated law; but the State, if its people are to be free, has the burdensome duty of thinking for itself.'[29] Munby and Laws LJJ serve laws that acknowledge no reliance on God or his commands for their validity. The contrast with Islam is acute.

In 2011 the importance of specifically Christian values was reasserted in *Lautsi*, before the Grand Chamber of the European Court of Human Rights (ECtHR).[30] The presence of crucifixes in the classrooms of Italian state schools had been challenged, as infringing two non-Christian pupils' rights under the principles of equality and of religious freedom. The Italian Administrative Court and then the Consiglio di Stato rejected the complaint. The Consiglio concluded that:

in Italy the crucifix symbolised the religious origin of values (tolerance, mutual respect, valorisation of the person, affirmation of one's rights, consideration for one's freedom, the autonomy of one's moral conscience vis-à-vis authority, human solidarity and the refusal of any form of discrimination) which characterised Italian civilisation. In that sense, when displayed in classrooms, the crucifix could fulfil – even in a 'secular' perspective distinct from the religious perspective to which it specifically referred – a highly educational symbolic function, irrespective of the religion professed by the pupils. The *Consiglio di Stato* held that the crucifix had to be seen as a symbol capable of reflecting the remarkable sources of the above-mentioned values, the values which defined secularism in the State's present legal order.[31]

The Administrative Court had already countered any charge that this excluded non-Christians and any attempt to win similar recognition for other faiths: 'the logical mechanism of exclusion of the unbeliever is inherent in any religious conviction, even if those concerned are not aware of it, the

---

[28] 'Carey weighs into shariʿa law row', *BBC News* 10 February 2008.
[29] Laws LJ, *McFarlane v Relate Avon Ltd* [2010] EWCA Civ 880, para 24. At para 26: 'Lord Carey's statement also contains a plea for a special court. I am sorry that he finds it possible to suggest a procedure that would, in my judgment, be deeply inimical to the public interest.' It was in Aristotle and Kant that John Laws himself found the intellectual heritage he needed for his Mishcon Lecture, describing a good constitution in harmony with the sovereign autonomy of those who belong to it, 'The constitution: morals and rights', [1996] *Public Law* 622.
[30] *Lautsi v Italy* (2012) 54 EHRR 3.   [31] Ibid., para 16.

sole exception being Christianity', thanks to the priority of charity over faith (1 Corinthians 13.13).

The (small) Chamber of the ECtHR disagreed. Before the ECtHR's Grand Chamber ten governments, three Christian organisations (from Germany, France and Italy) and thirty-three MEPs intervened against the plaintiff; seven human rights organisations intervened on the other side. The Grand Chamber agreed with the Italian Government that the cross is a (merely) 'passive symbol'; its display then fell within the state's margin of appreciation. At the time of writing (summer 2012) it remains to be seen if this will become the fountainhead of a jurisprudential river flowing in favour of Europe's specifically and overtly *Christian* secularism.[32]

CO-OPERATIVE ACCOMMODATION: TRAJECTORIES?

Such grand cases and gestures should not obscure low-key, local initiatives within the UK's Muslim communities.

In August 2008, the Muslim Institute in London published a 'Muslim Marriage Contract'; it was endorsed by the Imams and Mosques Council, the Muslim Council of Britain, the Muslim Parliament of Great Britain and other organisations.[33] Its explanatory notes emphasise the procedure for a marriage's registration under English law.[34] The contract itself requires two witnesses; 'this requirement is gender/faith neutral'. The terms and conditions bind both parties not to abuse the other or their children 'verbally, emotionally, physically or sexually'. The husband binds himself to monogamy. In the event of divorce, both parties will accept the British courts' decision over the custody and care of children and over the division of property. We should admit the anecdotal evidence that this contract has not been widely used; despite its provenance, it may be too clearly an attempt to import English norms and procedures into Muslim marriage.

There has as well been opposition in more conservative Muslim communities to such exploratory co-operation. The contract puts aside

---

[32] For apparent bias in the ECtHR against non-Christian and non-mainstream religions, TJ Gunn, 'Adjudicating rights of conscience under the European Convention on Human Rights' in J van der Vyver and J Witte (eds), *Religious Human Rights in Global Perspective: legal perspectives* (Leiden, 1996), pp 327–8. For wider bias, R McCrea, 'Limitations on religion in a liberal democratic polity: Christianity and Islam in the public order of the European Union' (LSE Law, Society and Economy Working Papers 18/2007); for the immigration tests imposed in the Netherlands, Germany and France, ibid., pp 33–8.
[33] Accessible at <http://www.muslimparliament.org.uk/Documentation/Muslim%20Marriage%20Contract.pdf>.
[34] So the couple honours the contract with the state by obeying its laws; cf Qur'an 5.1, 17.34.

familiar and broadly accepted requirements for Islamic marriage, and proposes new ones that have no jurisprudential basis. The Islamic Shari'a Council (ISC), in defence of the familiar requirements, roundly criticised the contract.[35] The response illustrates the difficulties through which the government, in seeking out representative voices from widely divergent Muslim communities, is negotiating its way. (The ISC's forthright reaction, which might be described in Shachar's terms as an example of 'reactive culturalism', should not disguise the ISC's actual practice; the ISC argues for the importance of civil marriages to protect the parties to a marriage, and in particular the wife.) The ISC insists that the witnesses to a marriage between Muslims must be Muslim. Only one of the schools of Islam allows for women to be witnesses, and only inasmuch as two women may replace one of the two men. 'Allah allowed a man to marry four wives and no one has the authority to make illegal what Allah has made legal'; and this, in a society where 'the detestable habit of cohabiting with more than one woman occurs in the form of a wife and mistress or many girlfriends'. In relation to 'sexual abuse', the ISC's response asks: 'Are there any proposed constraints on matrimonial rights fulfilled between them?' In relation to submission to the decisions of a British court, 'it is a well-established principle that referring all types of disputes to Allah and his Messenger is a prerequisite for belief'; the ISC evokes the hypocrites, led far astray by Satan, who turn to false judges (Qur'an 4.60).[36]

Calls for the state's supervision of marriage – calls respected in the Muslim Marriage Contract – are prompted by fears that the balance of power is still often unequal between men and women in the UK's Muslim communities and that this imbalance must not be allowed to endanger the woman in any proposed marriage. (This is not to deny that men too have been forced into marriage.) In 2008 the Muslim Arbitration Tribunal (MAT) published a proposal, 'Liberation from forced marriages', which forthrightly addressed the problem of forced marriages; the MAT estimates that over 70 per cent of all marriages between an English citizen and a foreign national from the Asian sub-continent involve an element of force or coercion.

The MAT offered to help prevent such coercion. Important for our purposes was the offer to undertake a semi-statutory role. Here, we might think, is a *shari'a* body in an enhanced role as anticipated by Dr Williams;

---

[35] Accessible at <www.islamic-shari'a.org/ ... /isc-standing-on-the-marriage-contract/download.html>.
[36] For further reports of the ISC, cf C Dwyer Hogg and J Wynne-Jones, 'We want to offer *shari'a* law to Britain', *The Daily Telegraph*, 20 January 2008.

and here too is the question over regulation to which it gives rise. Third parties, according to the MAT's proposal, would be able to refer cases of apparent coercion to the MAT, 'on the basis that a community based court would be better placed to deal with the intricacies of the community issues'. MAT might visit the family of the British spouse, issue written warnings to the guilty parties, call upon 'senior members of the community' close to the British spouse, advise the victim on ways to terminate the marriage and in extreme circumstances liaise with the Entry Clearance Officer.

Here again is a careful proposal from within the Muslim communities designed to combat an acknowledged wrong. Several questions arise. With whose authority and under whose regulation would the MAT judges be given the right to enter other people's homes and alert the community's other members to possible coercion? Would the standards of evidence used in the MAT's declarations have to meet the standards of evidence (severely restricting hearsay) required in the English courts? If so, who would train and regulate the MAT judges; what appeal would there be from their procedures? MAT's proposal may strike an observer as an uncomfortable transplant of practices familiar from an autonomous neighbourhood with a clear local hierarchy to the UK's state-centred system of justice in which power is deliberately removed from the influence of local and personal agenda. It may not surprise us that the government has not taken up the suggestion; but here are some first substantive proposals whose practical details are ready to be assessed and refined.

Such initiatives would clearly benefit from closer collaboration between practitioners of English law and community organisations. There is on all sides information to be exchanged and understanding to be deepened. The public discussions at the Temple in 2008–9 and the subsequent meetings are just one extended example of such inchoate collaborations. (These paragraphs are written in grateful acknowledgement of those subsequent meetings: a series of round-table discussions, 2010–11, chaired by Stephen Hockman QC[37]) All of those involved can accept that they and all other protagonists have principles which their holders shall not compromise; questioned in more detail, the different protagonists would reveal divergent (and sometimes clearly conflicting) premises. But the emphasis within the process is rather on the resolution of particular problems, one by one; and developments are – by the time they come to public expression – likely to be

---

[37] The present law on civil marriage was discussed at these conversations and possible improvements proposed which at the time of writing (summer 2012) were being refined and submitted to government within the government's consultation on the issue. On the separate issue of forced marriages: the government announced plans to criminalise forced marriages, 8 June 2012.

light on theory. Indispensible is the growth of trust on two fronts: between Muslim leaders and the community of those who serve the English courts; and between the leaders themselves of different Muslim communities. Some proposals, in order to come to fruition, would need statutory emendation; some would depend on closer co-operation between community organisations than is yet in place; some would need both.[38]

We have glanced in earlier chapters at the proposal for the 'celebrant-based' registration of marriages.[39] Here is just such inchoate co-operation: exploratory, modest and subject to scrutiny by government. Muslim leaders and English lawyers are exploring together the permeable borderland between two highly developed legal traditions for the benefit, sought by everyone involved, of vulnerable members of the Muslim community.[40] The explorers are travelling through a single landscape with different equipment and with maps drawn to quite different projections and informed by different priorities. It may take time and effort to see that the same place is sometimes marked, *here* on this map and *there* on that, and that some parts of the two journeys can readily be shared, to the advantage of all the travellers. The reciprocal trust and respect won on these stretches of the road will encourage each party to look with greater care and appreciation at their new companions' map of others. None of this is to deny that through large parts of the landscape the roads that must be followed are marked out by the dominant group, and deviation is disallowed. And none of it denies that there may well be more maps in conflict with each other than will ever make for an easy journey.[41]

---

[38] Some thought has been given to the possible extension of the Divorce (Religious Marriages) Act 2002 to cover Islamic as well as Jewish divorces. But the jurisdiction of *shari'a* councils and Battei Din within their own communities is not parallel: a *shari'a* council can itself declare – and so create – an Islamic *faskh*-divorce; a Beth Din can only confirm what the husband has done, but can itself impose nothing.

[39] I Edge, 'Islamic finance, alternative dispute resolution and family law', supra pp 130, 135.

[40] As we explore such initiatives further, let us acknowledge one concern. The children and grandchildren of immigrants from the Indian sub-continent and East Africa who thirty years ago used to be designated by ethnic terms are now referred to by their *religion*. The Southall Black Sisters in particular argue that this trend gives unwarranted authority to specifically religious officials – male, conservative and unelected – within Britain's South Asian communities; P Patel and H Siddiqi, 'Shrinking secular spaces: Asian women at the intersect of race, religion and gender' in RK Thiara and AK Gill (eds), *Violence against Women in South Asian Communities* (London, 2010). Similar concerns are aired by S Sardar Ali, 'From Muslim Migrants to Muslim citizens', supra p 169.

[41] There is no prospect of the remission of any part of criminal procedures to *shari'a* courts. There is anecdotal evidence, however, of informal procedures, endorsed by the police. See *The Evening Standard*, 9 February 2008: Somali youths were arrested on suspicion of stabbing a Somali teenager. The victim's family told officers the matter would be settled out of court and the suspects were released on bail. A hearing (*gar*) was convened by a Somali youth worker, and elders ordered the assailants to compensate the victim. Uncles and fathers were there, contributed to the compensation and apologised for the wrongdoing. See further R Grillo, 'Cultural diversity and the law: challenge and accommodation' (Working Paper 09/14, Max Planck Institute for the Study of Religious and

These paragraphs are not written to gloss over the serious differences that remain to be addressed. Several have been aired in earlier chapters by Dominic McGoldrick and Shaheen Sardar Ali. Nor are we setting up a naive contrast between women's suppression in *shari'a* courts and their rescue under English law. On the contrary: Prakash Shah, whose chapter in this book studies the courts' understanding of Muslims, has in the past drawn attention to cases in which, he argues, Muslim women have not been treated fairly.[42] It is not surprising if, on all sides, we are in particular sympathy with our own historic culture; but we do well to recognise the bias. Many in the West are suspicious of patriarchal religion, typified (we suppose) by Islam; but women in Christendom have for centuries been subject to the spiritual, moral, and social authority of an exclusively male priesthood. Only recently and only in some churches has this come to seem odd, let alone unconscionable.

It is in court that different principles and practices come most clearly – and sometimes most painfully – to view. There may on occasion be a blunt conflict between English law and the law obtaining in a couple's former or other home. IC was a severely autistic man; in no area of his development did he show the skills that are to be expected of an average three year old. He suffered from echolalia: the tendency to repeat (without understanding) the last word he had just heard. He had been married over the telephone (in a conversation in which he could be prompted) to a woman, NK, in Bangladesh. There was no dispute that the marriage was valid both in *shari'a* law and in Bangladeshi civil law.[43] In the judgment of Wall LJ:

Ethnic Diversity, 2009), accessible at <www.mmg.mpg.de/workingpapers>, pp 28–9. The MAT website emphasises that MAT has no jurisdiction to try criminal matters. 'However where there are criminal charges such as assault within the context of domestic violence, the parties will be able ask MAT to assist in reaching reconciliation which is observed and approved by MAT as an independent organisation. The terms of such a reconciliation can then be passed by MAT on to the Crown Prosecution Service (CPS) though the local Police Domestic Violence Liaison Officers with a view to reconsidering the criminal charges ... The final decision to prosecute always remains with the CPS.' Muslim Arbitration Tribunal, 'Family Dispute Cases' (2008), accessible at <http://www.matribunal.com/cases_faimly.html>.

[42] For *R v Kiranjit Ahluwalia* [1992] EWCA Crim 1 and for *R v Zoora Ghulam Shah* [1998] EWCA Crim 1441 – two women who had been subjected to great cruelty – see P Shah, *Legal Pluralism in Conflict* (London, 2005), pp 83–6. The Court of Appeal itself described *Ahluwalia* as tragic, and ordered a re-trial on the basis not of provocation but of a diminished responsibility that had not been adduced at first instance. The Court had less sympathy for Zoora Shah, who had conspired to commit forgery, hired a hit man and when double crossed made false allegations of rape and theft. The Court accepted the importance of honour in her society and the possibility of retaliatory violence if she broke its codes, 'but her way of life was such that there might not have been much left of her honour to salvage', para 8 [d]. *Zoora* continues to be contentious.

[43] *KC, NNC v City of Westminster Social & Community Services Dept, IC* supra n 24, per Wall LJ at para 48; the following quotations are at paras at 44–6. The Court ruled that the marriage should be held not valid, and under the Mental Capacity Act 2005 prevented IC from going to reside in Bangladesh.

The appeal throws up a profound difference in culture and thinking between domestic English notions of welfare and those embraced by Islam ... To the Bangladeshi mind, ... the marriage of IC is perceived as a means of protecting him, and of ensuring that he is properly cared for within the family when his parents are no longer in a position to do so.

Menski, as expert witness, had also emphasised the importance attached to the avoidance of improper sexual relations. He invited the court to consider the case as one of private international law: the couple were married under Bangladeshi law.[44] But for the court, English law trumped other considerations. Both parties were both in danger of abuse. Wall LJ continued:

To the mind of the English lawyer, by contrast, such a marriage is perceived as exploitative and indeed abusive. Under English law, a person in the position of IC is precluded from marriage for the simple reason that he lacks the capacity to marry ... To the mind of the English lawyer, the marriage is also exploitative of NK, although the evidence is that she entered into it with a full knowledge of IC's disability.

The families acknowledged from the outset that the marriage might not work, and in that case would be ended; two families, then, were realising under Bangladeshi law an exploratory plan. Ralph Grillo has described the financial and social arrangements which Bangladeshi families expect to make around marriage.[45] The contract is in effect between not two individuals but two extended families. Such considerations, had they been brought before the Court, may not have deepened its sympathy; the Court might well have asked more pressingly whether the interests of the young woman NK were being subordinated to the broader interests of two families (interests, then, which did include her own) and their lives on two continents.

The Court in IC saw differences which Wall LJ could 'neither sidestep nor ignore'. But we should not assume that such differences are always visible in all their detail. In the dispute between Mohammed Uddin and Nazmin Begum Choudhury, the ISC had effected a *shari'a* divorce for Ms Choudhury from an Islamic marriage (not registered under English law)

---

[44] I am grateful for the access to Menski's full report to the Court.
[45] The significance of the case has been aired too by Grillo, 'Cultural diversity and the law: challenge and accommodation', supra n 42; R Ballard, 'Human rights in the context of ethnic plurality: always a vehicle for liberation?' in R Grillo, R Ballard, A Ferrari, AJ Hoekema, M Maussen and P Shah (eds), *Legal Practice and Cultural Diversity* (Farnham, 2009), pp 299–310, describes the roles and resilience of 'multi-generational corporate extended families' in communities of non-European origin (with a glance at *qurban*, 'sacrifice', including a person's voluntary sacrifice of interests in marriage for the benefit of the family). See now *XCC v AA, BB, CC and DD* before Parker J [2012] EWHC 2183.

that had not been consummated.[46] The ISC helps such women as Ms Choudhury by providing a 'no fault' divorce; the *mahr*, which normally reverts to the husband when the divorce is sought by the wife (a *khul'* divorce), is in such cases put by the ISC into an escrow account and, if it is unclaimed by the husband after six months, it is returned to the wife. When a marriage is dissolved before consummation and the wife has not refused to consummate, the wife can expect to keep half the *mahr*. The circumstances were disputed in this case, and the ISC made no proposal for the division of the assets given or pledged; the husband, then, still had the *mahr* (£15,000), which he had not yet paid. In the present case, however, there remained at issue further jewellery which Mr Uddin, the husband's father, said was worth over £25,000 and was now in Ms Choudhury's possession. Mr Uddin went to the civil court to recover it; Ms Choudhury counter-claimed for the unpaid *mahr*. The joint expert witness was the MAT's Shaykh Siddiqi, who advised (in an unexpected move) that the wife was entitled to the whole *mahr*. (It appears that neither Siddiqi nor the court trusted Mr Uddin's testimony about the other gifts and jewels.) Here was a negotiation of some complexity, now involving both a *shari'a* tribunal and an expert witness. The English courts will in the coming years undoubtedly be introduced piecemeal but ever more frequently to Muslim tribunals' subtle and divergent procedures. The advantages of the common law, forever adapting and evolving, will once more be clear.

Dr Williams wondered if competitive accommodation was the best or indeed the only way to overcome the stark alternatives facing serious and principled groups between cultural or state loyalty. We might choose instead, within the systems of the English law, lawyers and courts, to nurture a *co-operative* accommodation. We will then assert the value of a low-key and sustained construction of trust, will work with quiet persistence at practical and sometimes intractable concerns, and will deepen on all sides the reciprocal understanding and respect for which Dr Williams himself has so consistently and so powerfully argued.

---

[46] *Uddin v Choudhury* [2009] EWCA Civ 1205, discussed by J Bowen, 'How could English courts recognize *shariah*?', (2010) 7.3 USTLJ 411. Bowen points out (417–18) that South Asians moving to England 'brought with them ideas and habits about personal status that had been developed under British rule of the Indies.'

PART III
Responsibilities and rights

The creation of avoidable resentment, never mind avoidable suffering, does not seem like a positive good for any social unit; and the assertion of an unlimited freedom to create such resentment does little to recommend 'liberal' values and tends rather to strengthen the suspicion that they are a poor basis for social morality and cohesion . . . We may decide, as on the whole we have decided, that religion should not be protected by law over and above the ways we have just been summarising; but that does not close the moral question of what are the appropriate canons for the public discussion of belief . . . Rather than assuming that it is therefore only a few designated kinds of extreme behaviour that are unacceptable and that everything else is fair game, the legal provision should keep before our eyes the general risks of debasing public controversy by thoughtless and (even if unintentionally) cruel styles of speaking and acting.

– From the Archbishop of Canterbury's Lecture, 'Religious hatred and religious offence', in the House of Lords, 29 January 2008.

The paradox is that from the Western perspective we frequently see the Muslim world as powerful, aggressive, coherent and threatening. From the other side of the world, the Muslim world – or a great deal of it – sees us as powerful, coherent and threatening in very much the same way. Now, when those are the perceptions, you don't have a very fertile ground for critical, relaxed, long-term discussions of some legal and cultural issues.

– From the Questions and Answers following the Archbishop's lecture, 'Civil and religious law in England', 7 February 2008.

Freedom of speech, incitement to religious hatred: beyond the divide?

CHAPTER 13

Where to draw the line, and how to draw it

Sydney Kentridge

The discussion which follows between Tariq Modood and Albie Sachs raises fundamental questions about the right to freedom of speech. Their chapters are based on their debate at the Temple Church, which focused on (but was by no means limited to) the controversies which arose from Salman Rushdie's novel, *The Satanic Verses*, and from the publication in a Danish newspaper of cartoons satirising or mocking the Prophet and Islam generally. The novel and the cartoon undoubtedly caused grave offence to members of the Muslim faith. To what extent should law protect statements which are offensive to a not insubstantial section of the public? In particular should there be any limitation on speech or writing offensive to deeply held religious feelings? Does literary merit redeem a grossly offensive and insulting publication?

In the UK freedom of expression is not an absolute right. It must be balanced against other rights and such interests as national security and public safety. But in general freedom of speech in the UK encompasses the freedom to give offence to others, whether individuals or groups. Indeed, it has been said that at the heart of freedom of speech is the freedom to offend.

As to English law the European Convention on Human Rights (ECHR), which is incorporated now into English law, deals with both freedom of religion and freedom of expression. And what it says about freedom of religion is this: 'Everyone has the right to freedom of thought, conscience and religion; this right includes freedom to change his religion or belief and freedom either alone or in community with others and in public or private to manifest his religion or belief . . . '

The next clause on freedom of expression starts off by saying everyone has the right to freedom of expression. But, it continues, the exercise of these freedoms – since it carries with it duties and responsibilities – may be subject to such conditions or restrictions 'as are prescribed by law and are necessary in a democratic society' in the interests of (among other things) the prevention of disorder or crime, the protection of health or morals or the protection of the reputation or rights of others. As far as I am aware that is the only part of the ECHR which says anything about the responsibilities of citizenship. Also for good measure there is in England the Malicious Communications Act 1988 which makes it an offence to send out a communication of a grossly offensive nature.

A significant exception to this freedom of expression is what is colloquially called 'hate speech'. English law distinguishes hate speech from speech which is merely offensive. Under the Public Order Act 1986 it is an offence to use

> threatening, abusive or insulting words or behaviour with intent to stir up racial hatred or if in the circumstances racial hatred is likely to be stirred up.

Thus the prohibition is narrowly circumscribed. Stirring up hatred is a concept which goes well beyond offensiveness or insult. When it came to dealing with religion, Parliament was even more circumspect. The offence of stirring up religious hatred, created by the Racial and Religious Hatred Act 2006, requires threatening words or behaviour (abusive or insulting words or behaviour would not be sufficient), and there must be an actual intention to stir up religious hatred – a likelihood of its being stirred up is not enough to constitute the offence. This Act contains, in addition, an explicit protection of free speech. A section of the Act headed 'Protection of freedom of expression' reads as follows:

> Nothing in the Part shall be read or given effect in a way which prohibits or restricts discussion, criticism or expressions of antipathy, dislike, ridicule, insult or abuse of particular religions or the beliefs or practices of their adherents, ... or proselytising or urging adherents of a different religion or belief system to cease practising their religion or belief system.

Under the existing law, therefore, neither *The Satanic Verses* nor the Danish cartoons could be the subject of prosecution in this country. The discussion between Modood and Sachs raises the question whether the public good does not call for a rather wider protection of religious sensitivities. Both authors suggest that under existing law insufficient weight is given to the effect of insults to their religion on communities which in the current climate of opinion may be particularly vulnerable to discrimination or to violence. The deep feelings of hurt caused by 'merely offensive' publications should also, they suggest, be given greater weight. Both authors try to find, and to define, a distinction between a serious work of literature and an ephemeral, would-be humorous cartoon, both of which caused hurt to Muslims in the UK or elsewhere.

I would suggest that in considering such questions it may be useful to go back to the reasons why we recognise and promote the right of free expression.

One of the purposes of freedom of speech is to encourage the personal self-development of those who wish to express ideas or state facts, to the corresponding benefit of the recipients. This enriches society even if the ideas or facts stated are unwelcome and offensive to some. A second justification of the right is that truth is likely to emerge from the free and vigorous expression of conflicting views. As that great US judge, Justice Oliver Wendell Holmes, put it, 'the best test of truth is the power of the thought to get itself accepted in the competition of the market'. Another accepted purpose of freedom of speech is to enable voters in a democratic society to make choices between those who aspire to govern them and (I would add) between those who aspire to exercise not only political but moral or intellectual authority. Perhaps, then, in examining any seriously offensive speech, we should ask ourselves whether it is capable of furthering any of those objectives.

Now how all these provisions are to be reconciled is a problem on which the English courts have not yet said the last word. In fact, as far as I am aware, they have not yet said the first word. But it is an issue which has directly arisen in many other countries including South Africa.

It would hardly have been possible to find two authors better qualified than the two whose chapters appear below. Tariq Modood is the Founding Director of the University Centre for the Study of Ethnicity and Citizenship at Bristol University. Albie Sachs was from 1994 to 2009 a Justice of the Constitutional Court of South Africa. Under the new South African Constitution his Court has had to adjudicate on issues arising from the inevitable tension between freedom of speech and other important rights. In what I might be permitted to call a colourful career, he has been an advocate, a prisoner of the apartheid state, a teacher of law in Southampton and then improbably in Mozambique, the survivor of an assassination attempt, a draftsman of the South African Constitution and a judge, more or less in that order.

The insights of Modood and Sachs are based on a practical experience of these problems which it would be difficult to match.

A note: The Satanic Verses *and the Danish cartoons*
Robin Griffith-Jones

There follows just a sketch of the debates to which Tariq Modood and Albie Sachs refer in their chapters. I concentrate on *The Satanic Verses*, by Western standards a 'brilliant' work (in Sachs's phrase) such as the Danish cartoons are not.

THE SATANIC VERSES BY SALMAN RUSHDIE (1988)

The Satanic Verses[1] was published in the UK in September 1988. In January 1989 copies of the book were publicly burned in a demonstration in Bradford. A demonstration in Hyde Park delivered a memorandum of protest to Penguin's offices. Early in 1989 police in Pakistan killed five demonstrators protesting against the novel. On 14 February 1989 Ayatollah Khomeini issued a decree (*fatwa*) that Rushdie and the publishers had been sentenced to death. The next day a bounty was put by an Iranian cleric on Rushdie's head: $2.6 million for an Iranian to kill Rushdie, $1 million for anyone else. Twelve people were killed in rioting in Bombay; two bookshops in California were firebombed; two liberal Muslim clerics in Brussels were murdered for opposing the *fatwa*. In 1991 the novel's Italian translator was stabbed and its Japanese translator murdered; in 1993 Rushdie's Norwegian publisher was shot. In England the common law protected only the Christian religion by the ancient crime of blasphemy or blasphemous libel. The Court of Appeal in *R v Chief Metropolitan Stipendiary Magistrate ex parte Choudhury*[2] dismissed the attempt to bring Islam within

---

[1] For the story in at-Tabari, see WM Watt, *Muhammed at Mecca* (Oxford, 1952), pp 100–9. The version in the Qur'an reads: 'Why – for yourselves [you would choose only] male offspring, whereas to him [you assign] female' (Qur'an 53.21). In explanation: 'since the Meccan polytheists were in the habit of killing their female offspring, a practice vigorously condemned in the Qur'an, it was illogical as well as impious of them to ascribe daughters to God and to worship them as divine beings', M Ruthven, *A Satanic Affair* (London, 1990), p 38, citing M Asad, *The Message of the Qur'an* (Gibraltar, 1980), p 814 n 14. For the killing of infant daughters in pre-Islamic Arabia, S Rushdie, *The Satanic Verses* (London, 2006), p 118. Ruthven, *A Satanic Affair*, gives an account of the protests in the UK. On the debate over the novel, see, eg, D Cohn-Sherbok (ed), *The Salman Rushdie Controversy in Interreligious Perspective* (Lewiston, NY 1990), in particular the chapters by S Akhtar, P Weller and B Parekh; MM Ahsan, 'The "Satanic" Verses and the Orientalists' in MM Ahsan and AR Kidawi (eds), *Sacrilege versus Civility: Muslim perspectives on 'The Satanic Verses'* (London, 1991); D Pipes, *The Rushdie Affair: the novel, the Ayatollah and the West* (New Brunswick, NJ, 2003); A Teverson, *Salman Rushdie* (Manchester, 2007).

[2] [1990] 3 WLR 98, [1991] 1 QB 429, upheld on application to the ECtHR, Application 17439/90.

the purview of blasphemous libel in a case which claimed that Rushdie and Penguin had blasphemed against Islam by publishing *The Satanic Verses*.[3]

The chapter that caused the greatest offence described a dream of Gibreel Farishta ('Angel Gabriel'); its text was photocopied and widely distributed.[4] Gibreel, a film-star, is one of the novel's two protagonists. He was so mischievous as a child that his mother nicknamed him Shaitan ('Satan', p 91). He is in every way unstable. From the start he fears madness (pp 92, 189). There will be hopes that he is rebuilding the walls between dreams and reality (p 340); but the walls collapse. By the time of his later dreams he has been diagnosed as a paranoid schizophrenic and is under heavy medication (pp 428, 433–4).

Twice he dreams of 'Jahilia', a term used by Muslims to refer to the 'ignorance' or 'barbarism' that preceded the revelation of the Qur'an. The city's chief character is the prophet 'Mahound', a name for Muhammad used insultingly in the West.[5] At the start of the second Jahilia dream, Mahound has been in exile, but he is on the point of return. The poet Baal, who had mocked Mahound, is in fear for his life. He takes refuge in The Curtain, *Hijab*, a brothel of twelve prostitutes and an old madam.[6] The customers talk of little else than Mahound and his own twelve wives: '"*One rule for him,*" complains a grocer, "*another for us.*"' The prostitutes wonder if it would be good for business if they themselves mimicked the prophet's twelve wives. The youngest duly acts out the role of Ayesha with the grocer. From then on, life in The Curtain imitates life in the harem of Jahilia's great mosque. Baal takes on an ever more confident and masterly role; and the prostitutes decide to become his brides. 'The Madam married them all off herself, and in that den of degeneracy, that anti-mosque, that labyrinth of profanity, Baal became the husband of the wives of the former businessman, Mahound' (p 383). Baal finds himself writing the most beautiful poetry of his life. He has fallen in love with the youngest girl, Ayesha; and when with her – and only with her – he would find a heaviness come upon him: 'It is as if I see myself standing beside myself. And I can make him, the standing one, speak; then I get up and write down his verses' (p 385).

---

[3] On the Rushdie affair in general, R Webster, *A Brief History of Blasphemy* (Southwold, 1990), p 129; and now Rushdie's own account, S Rushdie, *Joseph Anton: a memoir* (London, 2012).

[4] The dreaming is emphasised, *The Satanic Verses*, supra n 1, pp 363, 370, 372, 376, 390, 393, 394.

[5] The novel admits as much: 'His name: a dream-name, changed by the vision. Pronounced correctly, it means he-for-whom-thanks-should-be-given, but he won't answer to that here ... Here ... he has adopted the demon-tag the farangis [unbelievers] hung around his neck ...', p 93.

[6] The *hijab* or veil is the facial covering worn by many Muslim women, and was the curtain behind which Muhammad's wives retired from public view. After the death of his first wife, Khadijah, Muhammad married twelve wives, of which Aisha was the youngest.

As protests against the novel gathered momentum, Rushdie wrote to the Indian Prime Minister Rajiv Gandhi. The letter was widely circulated.[7]

> I am accused of having 'admitted' that the book is a direct attack on Islam. I have admitted no such thing, and deny it strongly. The section of the book in question (and let's remember that the book isn't actually about Islam, but about migration, metamorphosis, divided selves, love, death, London and Bombay) deals with a prophet who is not called Mohammad living in a highly fantasticated city ... in which he is surrounded by fictional followers, one of whom happens to bear my own first name. Moreover, this entire sequence happens in a dream, the fictional dream of a fictional character, an Indian movie star, and one who is losing his mind, at that. How much further from history could one get?

One response may stand for many; Tariq Modood (infra p 223) will similarly emphasise the novel's coarsely erotic treatment of the sacred. The Tanzanian Ali Mazrui, speaking at Cornell, said in 1989:[8]

> The Western world understands the concept of treason to the State ... Now in Islam, there is a concept which can be translated as treason, not to the State but to the Ummah, to the religious community and to the faith ... Secular countries take an oath in defence of the constitution. The Koran, in this case, is the equivalent of the constitution. And this particular writer seems to have launched an attack against it. [Pakistanis in November 1988 were saying,] 'It's as if Rushdie had composed a brilliant poem about the private parts of his parents, and then gone to the market place to recite that poem to the applause of strangers, who inevitably laughed at the jokes he cracks about his parents' genitalia and he's taking money for doing it.'[9]

---

[7] From a letter to Rajiv Gandhi, October 1988, in L Appignanesi and S Maitland (eds), *The Rushdie File*, (London, 1989), pp 42–5 (43). Rushdie himself first spoke about the novel soon after its publication, in an interview published in *Sunday*, India, 18–24 September 1988, in Appignanesi and Maitland (eds), *The Rushdie File*, pp 40–1. He has since written further about the novel's character, its reception and its background: 'In good faith' and 'In God we trust' in S Rushdie, *Imaginary Homelands* (London, 1991); 'Is nothing sacred?', (1990) 31 Granta 97–110; and in *Step across this Line: collected non-fiction 1992–2002* (London, 2002), especially pp 324–5. In A Abdallah (ed), *For Rushdie* (New York, 1994), a hundred Arab and other Muslim writers (in Algeria, Bangladesh, Egypt, Iran, Morocco, Libya, Palestine, Turkey and elsewhere) write in support of Rushdie and of freedom of expression.

[8] Ali Muzrui, speaking at Cornell University on 1 March 1989, in Appignanesi and Maitland (eds), *The Rushdie File*, supra n 7, pp 220–8. Cf Z Badawi, *The Guardian*, 27 February 1989: 'What [Rushdie] has written is far worse than if he had raped one's own daughter. Muslims seek Muhammad as an ideal on whom to fashion our lives and conduct, and the Prophet is internalized into every Muslim heart. It's like a knife being dug into you – or being raped yourself.'

[9] GK Bhatti's play, *Behzti* (*Dishonour*), was also (in Sachs' terms, p 231 below) a serious reflection, deliberately provocative but constituting part of a serious debate within a community. The play's run was curtailed as a result of protests from the Sikh community; on the controversy, see D Nash, *Blasphemy in the Christian World* (Oxford, 2007), pp 34–6. The play became notorious for Min's rape (off-stage) by Mr Sandhu, the Chairman of the Gurdwara's Renovation Committee, in the Gurdwara. But it is the final scene that plays out the work's polemic and would have provided its most poignant experience: Min's disabled mother, for whom Min has been caring bitterly for years, has discovered

THE DANISH CARTOONS: *JYLLANDS-POSTEN* (2005)

On 30 September 2005, the Danish newspaper *Jyllands-Posten* printed a page of cartoons depicting the Prophet Muhammad. In the protests that have ensued over 130 people are believed to have been killed.[10] Anger remains on both sides: at the cartoons' offensiveness; and at the restraints to free speech imposed on the West by the fear of violence.[11]

In 2006 Flemming Rose, culture editor of *Jyllands-Posten*, wrote an article 'Why I published those cartoons':

> I commissioned the cartoons in response to several incidents of self-censorship in Europe caused by widening fears and feelings of intimidation in dealing with issues related to Islam ... The idea wasn't to provoke gratuitously – and we certainly didn't intend to trigger violent demonstrations throughout the Muslim world. Our goal was simply to push back self-imposed limits on expression that seemed to be closing in tighter.[12]

In his lecture on 'Religious Hatred and Religious Offence' in the House of Lords, 29 January 2008, Dr Rowan Williams, then Archbishop of Canterbury warned that 'the sound of a prosperous and socially secure voice claiming unlimited freedom both to define and to condemn the beliefs of a minority grates on the ear. Context is all.'[13] He would probably, in this case, have pointed out how small a minority the Muslims in Denmark are: 3.7 per cent of the population, 210,000 people.[14] There will never be agreement, across Europe's

---

that Mr Sandhu is a predatory serial rapist and has killed him with his own *kirpan*, the sword that symbolises Sikh warriors' resistance to oppression. Min is freed to go with the outsider Elvis, and is at last reconciled to her mother. The scene is titled, 'Resurrection'.

[10] The cartoons are readily accessible on the web.

[11] The most widely discussed cartoon, depicting the Prophet with a bomb for a turban, was by Kurt Westergaard. On 1 January 2010, Danish police shot and wounded at Westergaard's home a man described as a twenty-eight year-old Somali linked to an Islamist militia.

[12] *The Washington Post*, 19 February 2006. Cartoons continue to stir controversy. *Libération* ran a cartoon that showed Jesus wearing nothing but a condom; he is surrounded by bishops, one of whom is saying, 'He sure would have worn a condom'; in 2006 the Paris Court of Appeal upheld the lower court's judgment that the cartoon did not constitute an insult against a religious group, since the cartoon was intended to draw attention to the need for condoms in the fight against HIV/AIDS in Africa (R Uitz, *Freedom of Religion* (Strasbourg, 2007), 157). On 29 March and 3 April 2010, when the Roman Catholic Church was under widespread attack for its failure to prevent child abuse in its institutions, *Le Monde* ran one cartoon of the Pope sodomising a boy and another of a bishop with a small boy. In self-declared defiance of self-censorship several Swedish newspapers published, 18 August 2007, a series of drawings by Lars Vilks depicting Muhammad as a 'roundabout dog', a roadway installation familiar in Sweden. The French magazine *Charlie Hebdo* (whose cartoon-satires of Islam, 9 February 2006 and 3 November 2011, became well-known) satirised Muhammad and Islam on 18 September 2012 in response to protests against an anti-Islamic film widely publicised in the Muslim world at the anniversary of '9/11'.

[13] Accessible at the Archbishop's website www.archbishopofcanterbury.org/1561.

[14] Uitz, *Freedom of Religion*, supra n 12, p 163.

The Satanic Verses and the Danish cartoons

cultural and religious divides, on the appraisal of the cartoons affair; but as we look back on the Danish setting, the Archbishop's point is at least engaged.

SHIFTING STANDARDS

When Muslims were offended, a vigorous defence of free speech was mounted in the West on behalf of Salman Rushdie and *Jyllands-Posten*. Some ask whether the West has been so resolute when the use of such freedom has offended *Christians*. (Among the first such cases faced by the European Court of Human Rights (ECtHR) was *Otto-Preminger-Institut v Austria*.[15] The institute had attempted to show a film offensive to the religious sensibilities of the predominantly Roman Catholic and highly observant residents of the Tyrol. The Court upheld the ban.) In the UK the common law crime of blasphemous libel, protecting Christianity alone, was abolished in 2008. 'While the belated review of the UK domestic laws on blasphemy law undoubtedly represent a positive measure, disappointment has been expressed at the European human rights institutions for their apparent endorsement of a patently discriminatory law for such a sustained period of time.'[16]

I close this short note with a reminder how rapidly standards have changed in the West itself. Parekh has reminded us, in relation to Jesus, that in the West

> until the 1960s a strict protocol governed his depiction and it was considered disrespectful to portray his face on the screen. *The Last Days of Pompeii* (1935), *Quo Vadis* (1951) and *Ben Hur* (1959) show him only from afar or feature only his hand or foot. In *King of Kings* (1961), Jeffrey Hunter, who played Jesus, had to remove all bodily hair because it detracted from his divinity.[17]

The freedoms which we now regard as natural were, only two generations ago, unimagined.

---

[15] (1995) 19 EHRR 34.
[16] J. Rehman, *International Human Rights Law*, (second edition, Harlow, 2010), p 211. For the Christian secularism espoused in *Lautsi v Italy* (2012) 54 EHRR 3; (2010) 50 EHRR 42, see supra pp 197–8.
[17] B Parekh, 'The Rushdie affair and the British press' in Cohn-Sherbok, *The Salman Rushdie Controversy*, supra n 1, pp 71–95, 88.

CHAPTER 14

Censor or censure: maintaining civility

Tariq Modood

In discussion of free speech and incitement to religious hatred there is a tendency to draw an analogy with blasphemy. This becomes the point of departure or more than the point of departure. But I want to suggest that a better analogy, as a starting-point, is incitement to *racial* hatred or (in a slightly different but related challenge) the legal and other issues around Holocaust-denial.

Clearly there is sometimes a public order concern about the forms of dangerous speech that incite hatred. We recognise occasions on which the law has to intervene to stop people saying certain things or things in a certain way or saying those things in a certain time and place. For a classic illustration used by political theorists and others, take a situation in which there is a threat of immediate violence. Such a case is sketched by John Stuart Mill in *On Liberty*.[1] He is championing freedom of speech but he says:

> even opinions lose their immunity, when the circumstances in which they are expressed are such as to constitute their expression a positive instigation to some mischievous act. An opinion that corn-dealers are starvers of the poor, or that private property is robbery, ought to be unmolested when simply circulated through the press, but may justly incur punishment when delivered orally to an excited mob assembled before the house of a corn-dealer, or when handed about among the same mob in the form of a placard.

The crowd are outside the house of the corn-merchant, cannot afford to buy food for themselves and their families and are protesting about their hunger. The orator or demagogue says, 'There, that is the man who is responsible. The corn merchant lives in this house. He is in here.' The orator does not have to add, 'Go and get him' for us to know from the context that he is provoking the mob to violence. The demagogue here is threatening violence; and anyone framing legislation must clearly have such cases in mind.

---

[1] JS Mill, *On Liberty* (1859), chapter 3, in *On Liberty and other Essays* (Indianapolis, IN, 1956), pp 67–8.

I want to suggest, however, that when we think about legislation we go well beyond such threats of immediate violence. Let us tease out in more detail the rationale behind the current law.[2]

Where feelings run deep in a society, a climate of opinion can be exacerbated – or a climate of opinion can be created – in which victimisation or racial attacks may take place, or where some forms of speech or literature may create emotive perceptions of a group as an enemy within. Such speech or literature is likely to lead to acts of discrimination against this putatively undesirable group of people, although perhaps not to immediate violence. That is my point: perhaps not to *immediate* violence. The speech or literature is nevertheless likely to create fear in the vulnerable group. In mentioning this fear we introduce a new feature which complicates the initial picture of incitement which we drew from Mill's example of the corn-merchant. We start considering the effects not just on the emotions of the incited rabble but of its *targets*. What are the corn merchant and his family feeling, trapped inside with this baying mob outside? Fear, obviously; but the victims of such incitement are likely to undergo other and longer-term forms of distress.

For example (and now we are talking about real social-political cases), to taunt people of some backgrounds with images of slavery and of lynching is to remind those people of subjugation: 'This is how you were treated or your parents or ancestors were treated, and this is perhaps what *you* deserve. Do not feel cocky here; this is the treatment appropriate for you.' Similarly with racist materials that portray black people as simian, as of less than human intelligence and sensibility; and again with images, held aloft or put on a wall or banner in Northern Ireland, of Protestant victories over Catholics. And so on.

Only if we focus on the emotions of *victims*, of targeted groups and targeted people, can we understand the fact that eleven countries in the European Union have legislation against Holocaust-denial, with the offences typically punished by prison sentences of some years.[3] No one has ever suggested that the literature of Holocaust-denial would lead to immediate violence. But it would, we all recognise, have a very distressing effect on some people: in particular on people whose family histories are tied up with the Holocaust, almost certainly on Jewish people more generally, and probably on others. Such literature also poses the danger of legitimising the particularly gross

---

[2] This rationale in relation to the incitement to religious hatred is also discussed in other countries. For further details, see T Modood, 'Muslims, incitement to hatred and the law' in J Horton (ed), *Liberalism, Multiculturalism and Toleration* (Basingstoke, 1993); reproduced in the collection, T Modood, *Multicultural Politics: racism, ethnicity and Muslims in Britain* (Edinburgh, 2005).
[3] In Europe Holocaust-denial is punishable in Austria, Belgium, the Czech Republic, France, Germany, Lithuania, Poland, Romania, Slovakia, Spain and Switzerland.

dictatorship of the Nazis as having been just another political regime. My point is this: when we specify what is wrong with incitement, we think about its effect on the victims and not just on those who are incited.

Among the effects that we might anticipate and which we might attempt in our legislation to prevent are the emotional reactions in the victims that may lead *them* into violent responses. So we are working to prevent both the violence of the victimiser and violent responses from the victim. This too is, of course, a public order concern, but is again not apparent in the image of incitement with which I began.

Incitement to hatred, then, involves not just the danger of immediate violence, but the production as well of a climate of opinion or emotions, or the exploitation of that climate; not just the arousal of certain hatreds in the dominant group but also a fear and humiliation in the victim group that can lead in turn to conflict and violence. These dangers all inform any agenda for the prevention of incitement to hatred.

An objection might be raised here, that everything we have said so far is about protecting people, not their religious beliefs. Yes, that is exactly my concern: protecting people not religious beliefs. But the people in question may be people marked by religious identity: Roman Catholics in Northern Ireland, for instance; Jewish people, as I have already mentioned; and in relation to this chapter, Muslims in Britain.

Now what if a group of religious people, let us say some Muslims (and this is close to a real example), are connected to aspects of their faith with such deep emotion that disrespectful attacks upon it will cause them the kind of distress that is caused to other groups by reference to images of black bestiality or by Holocaust-denial? Add to this a set of domestic and geopolitical circumstances in which these Muslims – and here we might include as well Muslims who are less intense in their religion – feel that they are being targeted and harassed as culturally backward, as disloyal and as terrorists, in short as not belonging in the UK, as unwanted and under threat. And is not that, if somewhat briefly and over-simply stated, the Britain in which we are living? And will that not explain the explosions of protest, anger and violence sparked by *The Satanic Verses*, for example, or more recently to the cartoons of the prophet Muhammad published in *Jyllands-Posten*?[4]

---

[4] See the debate, GB Levey and T Modood, 'The Danish cartoon affair: free speech, racism, Islamism, and integration', (2006) 44(5) Int Migr 3; and GB Levey and T Modood, 'Liberal democracy, multicultural citizenship, and the Danish cartoon affair' in GB Levey and T Modood (eds), *Secularism, Religion and Multicultural Citizenship* (Cambridge, 2009). Some particulars are given by R Griffith-Jones, 'A note: *The Satanic Verses* and the Danish cartoons' supra pp 211–5.

I am not justifying everything that was done in the name of those protests. I am pointing to certain chain reactions and to the need for us to understand how they may be prevented. Of course certain Muslims (let us call them 'extremists'), in their responses to *The Satanic Verses* and the cartoons, exploited the situations, feelings and ignorance of other Muslims. That is true; but there would have been nothing to exploit without the deep significance of these feelings to those other Muslims. Some people undoubtedly worsened the situation. But they could do so only because some Muslims think as they do about the prophet Muhammad's centrality to their sense of the sacred, of their faith and of the dignity of that faith.

At this point we can appreciate that not only should there be some legislation to curb incitement to religious hatred, but that in some cases and contexts the legislation may touch directly on religious feelings and beliefs and so may indeed appear to be protecting those feelings and beliefs, such as the intense devotion for the prophet Muhammad found amongst some Muslims. Such legislation then may seem to *privilege* those feelings and beliefs. But this would not be accurate. The legislation may come to have such a secondary consequence but that would not be its *purpose*; its purpose would be protection against incitement to religious hatred in the wider meaning of incitement that I have been elaborating.

This may seem to be putting Islam, alone of all religions, above all censure or criticism; but I do not want any religion to enjoy such a privileged position. We just need to acknowledge that what hurts different people – often re-opening the historical wounds that they already bear – varies over place and time: it may be racial slurs, or bigotry in Northern Ireland, or anti-semitism. And now Muslims are very much in the frame. What hurts them is historically contingent; and we need to respond to such hurt, as it arises. If certain actions are likely to provoke Muslims in ways that are harmful to their status as fellow and equal citizens and that are likely to lead to conflict, then there is a problem we need to address. Islam is not being privileged here. It is just a contingent fact (if it is accepted as a fact) that some actions hurt some Muslims just as other actions – which we acknowledge for this reason to be reprehensible – hurt other groups.

No religion should be protected from criticism. But how is that criticism to be stated? There are ways of criticising the actions of some Jewish people or of the Jewish state that might be considered racist, and there are ways of making the same criticisms that are not racist. Here it is not a matter of protecting Islam or Muslims from criticism but of the *kind* of criticism that will be permitted. Should others enjoy the right of mocking and ridiculing and hurting religious people to the point where some such people lose their self-control? Should that right take priority over the endeavour – of higher priority to me – to create a society in which mutual respect and civic equality prevail over people's right to castigate, ridicule and offend?

This of course raises the question, who shall be the arbiter of what is offensive? Shall it be the religious community that is the subject matter of the material in question? In answer I would emphasise again that we are not dealing primarily with a theological decision over blasphemy to be made by Islamic scholars, but with equality of respect and dignity. We see people feeling hurt and humiliated and reacting in aggrieved and angry ways. It is only civil to ask what has affected them in this way, and to seek to reduce the hurt. The pain of the victim, therefore, will indeed be one criterion of what should or should not be admissible. It will not be the only criterion; we will want to investigate the circumstances, to clarify what is really at issue and whether those who are hurt are running together in their grievance a number of concerns. And there may also be questions of other people's rights, to be balanced against the hurt. But my argument runs with the grain of the understanding reached by the criminal justice system on racial and (in the work-place) sexual harassment: the lead is often given by what the victim thinks. If the victim thinks he or she is harassed there is a presumption of harassment. Such presumption does not decide the matter, but the matter must then be investigated and aired. It is for such a principle that I am arguing.

Let me, however, make two qualifications that address the issue of limits. The first concerns a distinction between freedom of enquiry and freedom of expression. Mill and many libertarians who followed his lead have wanted to argue for freedom of expression in every social and intellectual sphere. Even if an opinion is wrong, Mill argued, present and future generations lose by its suppression

> the clearer perception and livelier impression of truth, produced by its collision with error ... The beliefs which we have most warrant for have no safeguard to rest on but a standing invitation to the whole world to prove them unfounded ... Since the general or prevailing opinion on any subject is rarely or never the whole truth, it is only by the collision of adverse opinions that the remainder of the truth has any chance of being supplied.[5]

These arguments place a value upon truth; they are arguments for the freedom of *enquiry*. Yet non-propositional expression is not – or at least may not be – a contribution to enquiry or to truth. So we may want to

---

[5] Mill, *On Liberty*, chapter 2, supra n 1, pp 21, 26, 64.

re-affirm the freedom of enquiry in relation to people's religions and faith, including of course Islam, without thereby entitling people to express their views about Islam in any offensive or insulting way that they like. As we know from our experience, almost every day of our life, there are gracious ways and there are aggressive ways of making a point. I want then to place freedom of enquiry on a higher level than freedom of expression. We may sometimes need to curb freedom of *expression* for the reasons I gave earlier about incitement, whereas freedom of *enquiry* should be curbed, if at all, only under very severe circumstances.

My second point about limits is this: in thinking about incitement to hatred and how to limit and prevent it, it may be more important to censure than to censor. The law is a very blunt instrument, and its capacity to deal with opinions and expressions is extremely limited. We cannot expect the law to do a lot of work where the issue is respect for people as people, including religious people as religious people. That does not imply that everything should be perfectly acceptable on which the law is silent. There need to be limits to avoid disrespect, offence and provocation, and to prevent fear and humiliation. These limits are exercised through personal and institutional self-restraint. (By institutional self-restraint, I mean such restraint as editors of newspapers have to exercise in their professional, editorial capacity.) Most of the ways in which we show courtesy, civility and respect for each other as fellow citizens are through ordinary behaviour where the law is silent, where the law leaves the space for us to be either offensive or civil.

Let us go back to the two examples we have mentioned: *The Satanic Verses* and the cartoons. A certain kind of education took place between those two affairs, an *education of sensibility* in what is offensive – gratuitously insulting – to Muslims. When some Muslims first protested about *The Satanic Verses* (published in 1988), the reaction of many people in this country – and most noticeably of people contributing to the serious media – was almost supercilious. What, they asked, was all the fuss about; the book was just a novel; Muslims should get over it and live with it. Most Muslims, of course, had not read the novel. They knew of it from garbled hearsay or photocopied extracts. But on all sides they heard prestigious and influential and literary people praise the novel and ask whether Muslims knew how to read a book. Now that was really insulting, and caused more hurt than the novel itself. Muslims heard both that novelists should be able to portray the Prophet however they liked and that any Muslims who could not see this novel's merits were culturally low and backward and lacking in sensibility.

The British reaction to the cartoons (published in 2005) was quite different. Those cartoons, originally published in a Danish newspaper, were reproduced in newspapers in several other countries — Germany and France for instance — as a kind of political declaration. The papers were taking a stand; they were insisting on their right to publish cartoons that offended Muslims. But not a single British newspaper — right-wing, left-wing or in the centre — published the cartoons. All the papers in Britain thought that the cartoons were unworthy of reprinting, that they would do harm and, in particular, that they would, without satisfying any particular principle, damage the good relations that should exist between Muslims and non-Muslims. In this there is a more general lesson to be learnt: that editors should exercise responsible judgment which may include a decision not to publish certain things. When the leaders of society and of institutions, alive to what is hurtful, exercise self-restraint, then the law can be minimally and rarely exercised. So an important principle is coming centre-stage: to censure rather than censor.

I would suggest that of *The Satanic Verses* and the cartoons, *The Satanic Verses* was by far the more serious affair. Of the twelve cartoons that were published, some were only mildly offensive, some were innocuous and one was even poking fun at the very exercise. We assumed (perhaps because we did not see them) that they were all offensive when they were not. There was one that I would say was racist: the cartoon that became famous, of a bearded man with a turban that was an old-fashioned cannon-ball bomb with a burning wick. Nothing in that cartoon showed that it was of Muhammad, but it was clearly of a Muslim. Its point was, I think, that Muslims are terrorists or that, at least, there is something about Muslims and terrorism that goes together. It was not, then, a remark about the prophet Muhammad as such but a remark about Muslims; and on this basis it was effectively 'racist'. Imagine a cartoon of the prophet Moses (recognisable by his carrying the two tablets of the law) surrounded by money-bags. I am thinking of some of the cartoons from *Der Stürmer* from the 1920s and 1930s in Germany.[6] The cartoonist would be making a statement not about Moses but about Jews; and on that basis it would be offensive and racist. That was the character of the cartoon with the turban-bomb.

---

[6] An anti-Semitic illustrated magazine produced by the Nazis. 'The semi-pornographic *Stürmer* was effectively the private vehicle of the Franconian Gauleiter Julius Streicher ... A sort of news of the sewers, it specialised in anything of a salacious nature ... Streicher claimed it was the only paper Hitler read from cover to cover', M Burleigh, *The Third Reich: a new history* (Basingstoke, 2000), p 210.

Should such a cartoon therefore have been banned? Not necessarily. There are some forms of racism that it is better to live with. But they should be censured. And that brings me back to *The Satanic Verses*, and the grounds for seeing the novel as a far more serious hurt for Muslims: there was no censure. At the time of the Danish cartoons a strong current of opinion in the media ran against their publication: the cartoons were offensive and improper and should not be circulated. Nobody had said that about *The Satanic Verses*. This is not to set aside the novel's content. Of course Muslims do not like being thought of, in the terms encouraged by the cartoons, as terrorists. But *The Satanic Verses* introduced various forms of what most people (not just Muslims) regard as vulgarity. The eroticisation of the sacred in *The Satanic Verses* was far more hurtful then anything in the cartoons.

In the face of *The Satanic Verses*, it was that sense of humiliation, of being (as it were) culturally naked, that was so hurtful to Muslims. At first there was nobody of any authority, nobody who might be a respectable voice of Britain, who acknowledged why Muslims were hurt or who questioned the novel's propriety. When at last important figures in the Church of England and the Roman Catholic Church began to moderate the debate, they did not call for the novel to be banned but they did at least publicly recognise why Muslims were hurt. Those opening months were so serious because nobody could see – as they *could* see seventeen years later when the cartoons were published – why Muslims were offended.

I am not so naive as to believe that all the editors who chose to not reprint the cartoons did so only out of respect for Muslims. At the very least some may have had mixed motives. Some may have been more concerned about the safety of their staff and premises, for example. I am unhappy that some Muslim protestors have created fear of reprisals, even murder, in relation to issues of respect and disrespect. Without seeking to justify intimidation, threats and violence of that sort, we should bear in mind that force and violence often, even if only by a minority of activists, accompany passionate protests against perceived injustice. This is true of demonstrations by students, trade unionists, animal rights activists, CND and others. One consequence is that public discussion often focuses on the behaviour of the protestors rather than an evaluation of their grievance. Another is that if people in power accede to the demands of the protestors it can be unclear whether they were persuaded by the force of argument or merely to avoid further violence. Nevertheless, it is the case that moral learning, political reform and violent protests can be part of a related dynamic and play a part in effecting justifiable social change.

Albie Sachs makes an important point about *The Satanic Verses* and the importance of its publication: the novel is a move towards Muslim self-reflection. Of course I support such self-reflection (as I support freedom of enquiry) and I value any contribution to it. I value too the enquiry into Islam that is shared with non-Muslims. But here I want to exercise my distinction between freedom of enquiry and of expression. Would a less offensive portrayal, even within fiction, undermine the enquiry? Why can the enquiry not be conducted in less hurtful ways?

I do believe that there should be legislation against incitement to religious hatred, as we now have in Great Britain and which we have had in Northern Ireland for some time. But I would put the weight upon censure. In relation both to *The Satanic Verses* and to the Danish cartoons, this is more appropriate. We do not necessarily want to prohibit actions by law, but we should be censuring people who, we think, are being gratuitously offensive. We may well be condemning at the same time the behaviour of some protestors against the offence. To decide whether something shall count as offensive or not, we do not ask whether those protesting against it are even more offensive. They may well be; they may be threatening to kill those who have offended them. But what caused the original offence is not thereby rendered inoffensive. Indeed our failure to censure now may create social divisions that will be more difficult to heal in the future and may require *more* not *less* legislation, legislation that may mean *less* not *more* freedom in the future.

CHAPTER 15

In praise of 'fuzzy law'
Albie Sachs

My term as a judge has come to its end. I have been able to reflect on what I was doing for fourteen years. How did I arrive at decisions? The judgments, as read, appear to proceed very logically: I say what this case is about, I set out the facts, state the legal principles that apply, and apply them to the facts to get a particular result. But all that is retrospective. Usually the very last sentence I would write was: 'This case raises questions about ...'. Only after I had been through all the turmoil, the wriggling, the going backwards and forwards, the wrestling with the material, did I get a sense of what the core issue was. In this chapter too I start off with the approach I would normally take to a legal issue presented to me as a judge. But whereas in writing a judgment I had ultimately to rationalise it all and come to a final determination, in a chapter such as this I can throw out certain ideas and propositions, and leave the conclusion open.

I begin with the instincts that I think any judge has when first coming across a case. These are not simply personal predilections. They are instincts based on decades of experience in a particular area, both conscious and to some extent unconscious. They have been shaped by a life spent in law, in litigation, in thinking about law, in seeing how law evolves and how one's own thought has evolved. I start here with what appears to be a contradiction. The idea of banning and prohibiting *The Satanic Verses* in the United Kingdom, I find horrific. The idea of permitting the publication of the Danish cartoons in England, I find horrific. What separates the two? What values are involved? Then I proceed from thinking about these concrete situations to determine why my instincts push me in one direction or another.

We had a case in South Africa with an apparent conflict between freedom of speech on the one hand, and statements, on the other, which were extremely hurtful to a section of the community that is defined by its culture and religion. (These statements should indeed have been offensive to everybody in the community¹). The case was based on a complaint made by the Jewish Board of Deputies to the South African Broadcasting Complaints Committee about a broadcast by a Muslim community radio-station in which the speaker, who in fact had come from the UK, had said that only 1 million Jews had died under the Nazis, most of them through infectious diseases such as typhus. He questioned the legitimacy of the state of Israel. And he spoke of the effect – as if it was common knowledge – that Jewish control of banking throughout the world has had on global economic development.

At stake was whether or not the broadcasting licence of the Muslim community radio should be suspended or revoked; this was not, then, a criminal prosecution. The regulations, that had been hastily adopted with the advent of our democracy, gave very broad criteria for suspending or revoking community licences, and included the phrase, communications which could be 'offensive to . . . any section of a population.'² If you made such communications you could be called upon to desist, and if you did not desist you could lose your licence. It was a case that caused me acute personal alarm. I felt so intensely about Holocaust-denial that I wondered if I could sit in judgment (in the words of my judicial oath) 'without fear, favour or prejudice'. The knowledge that large sections of my family were wiped out, and that if Hitler had arrived in South Africa I would have been targeted, is visceral and deep. I was wondering if I should not recuse myself. On the other hand, I was wondering if precisely because of that I should be there. Perhaps my opinions and historical and personal experience *should* be part of the mix, particularly as I was sitting in a collegial court where different approaches would intermingle to produce a richer result.

As it turned out, we did not reach the substantive issue of Holocaust-denial, and I was not required to make a decision on the facts of the case. We felt that the regulation was so vague (in speaking of anything that could be 'offensive to any section of a population') that it did not satisfy the test for being a reasonable limitation on freedom of speech. A reasonable limitation should have some precision; it should give some guidance so that people affected would know what they could and could not do.

---

¹ *The Islamic Unity Convention v The Independent Broadcasting Authority and Others* [2002] ZACC 3.
² Code of Conduct for Broadcasting Services, Clause 2(a) (in the Independent Broadcasting Authority Act, 153 of 1993, Schedule 1): 'broadcasting licensees shall . . . not broadcast any material which is indecent or obscene or offensive to public morals or offensive to the religious convictions or feelings of any section of a population or likely to prejudice the safety of the State or the public order or relations between sections of the population.'

The then Deputy Chief Justice (later Chief Justice) of South Africa, Pius Langa, made some comments about the way in which issues like this should be treated. He spoke firmly and strongly about the importance of freedom of speech. For us in South Africa this is not just an abstract notion or a good idea. We have known censorship, banning orders and every kind of restriction on freedom of speech. And so the battle for democracy, dignity and the suffrage was inseparable from the battle for a voice, for the right to criticise and denounce existing power. We also had a period where Christian National Education was imposed upon people without giving them a choice; certain versions of Calvinism, contested by many Calvinists themselves, were being imposed as an orthodoxy on large sections of South African society. So the space for openness and challenge was more than just a right, it was central to the vitality of our society. The sense of freedom to speak out – the sense that nothing was taboo – was very profound.

So Langa spoke about freedom of speech as integral to democracy, the freedom in particular to criticise the institutions of power in society, to give people individual voices and to have a community that is alive and expressive:[3]

As to its relevance to a democratic state, the Court has pointed out that freedom of expression '... lies at the heart of a democracy. It is valuable for many reasons, including its instrumental functions as a guarantor of democracy, its implicit recognition and protection of the moral agency of individuals in our society and its facilitation of the search for truth by individuals and society generally. The Constitution recognises that individuals in our society need to be able to hear, form and express opinions and views freely on a wide range of matters ...'[4]

Langa quoted the judgment in *Mamabolo*: 'it could actually be contended with much force that the public interest in the open market-place of ideas is all the more important to us in this country because our democracy is not yet firmly established and must feel its way.'[5] But Langa made clear too that speech can be extremely wounding:

The pluralism and broadmindedness that is central to an open and democratic society can, however, be undermined by speech which seriously threatens democratic pluralism itself. Section 1 of the Constitution declares that South Africa is founded on the values of 'human dignity, the achievement of equality and the

---

[3] *The Islamic Unity Convention v The Independent Broadcasting Authority and Others*, supra n 1, paras 24–5.
[4] Quoting *South African National Defence Union v Minister of Defence and Another* [1999] ZACC 7, para 7.
[5] *S v Mamabolo* (CCT 44/00) [2001] ZACC 17, para 37.

advancement of human rights and freedoms.' Thus, open and democratic societies permit reasonable proscription of activity and expression that pose a real and substantial threat to such values and to the constitutional order itself.

In South Africa race had been powerfully used to treat the majority of the population almost as subhuman. And together with race went demeaning stereotypes. To describe a section of the population, in the new South Africa, as being close to apes, for example, could threaten the whole country with disintegration. It touched on historic wounds. It touched on continuing forms of superiority and inferiority, advantage and disadvantage. It went to the very heart of our new constitutional order. It was denying dignity and common citizenship and the sharing of society. It violated the notion that the law was there to protect people – not only from violence and from exclusion from pubs and schools and boarding houses – but also in their dignity as members of society, as members of communities sharing historical experiences, beliefs and world views. We feel this deeply and strongly in South Africa because we know how a little spark can ignite a flame that leads the whole society to combustion.

Race and religion often go together. So the protection of racial and religious communities from degrading attacks would be a constitutionally protectable interest to be placed in the balance with freedom of speech. The balancing has to be done on a contextual basis and questions of proportionality become extremely significant. What somebody says in a pub when he is drunk, rude and abusive, might not carry the same threat to the integrity of the society as something published in a newspaper or something said over the radio where a licence is given subject to reasonable conditions being placed on the use of limited airwaves. There is no getting away from a proper scrutiny of the context or from proportionality when seeking specific solutions to specific cases. Contextual reasoning is the opposite of categorical reasoning. You do not arrange a hierarchy of rights in whose terms you say one right is intrinsically superior to another. Freedom of speech cannot be said to trump the right to human dignity, nor the contrary. They should be reconciled, wherever possible. And if in a particular situation some degree of clash is unavoidable, the context, looked at in the light of the deep values of an open and democratic society, must decide which right must prevail to what extent and in what manner.

Let me move on to another case that worried me in a similar way.[6] Once again it was not a clash between right and wrong, but between right and

---

[6] *Port Elizabeth Municipality v Various Occupiers*, South African Constitutional Court (CCT 53/03) [2004] ZACC 7.

right. It flowed from an eviction order given at the behest of the Port Elizabeth Municipality, responding to a demand by some thousands of overwhelmingly white suburbanites living in comfortable homes in a very upmarket portion of Port Elizabeth. There was some vacant land nearby owned largely by these suburbanites, and on that vacant land about fifteen African families had set up little shacks. These families said in effect that they would move if they were given a home somewhere else. The crisis for me was this. I, Albie Sachs, had been in the freedom struggle which had aimed to enable people to overcome the consequences of dispossession; could I now as a judge be a party to ordering the dispossession of people whose only home was a little shack on vacant land, in favour of people who already had their homes, and for whom this was spare land? Yet I had sworn an oath to uphold the law 'without fear, favour or prejudice'.

As it happened, the tension that I felt inside myself was replicated in the Constitution. This has both a property clause that protects the right not to be dispossessed of property, and a clause on the rights of the homeless which include the right that no one be evicted from their home without a court taking account of all relevant circumstances.[7] A law was passed that the Court which considered the relevant circumstances must decide what is just and equitable.[8] Not very helpful! Is it just and equitable to allow people to erect shacks on someone else's property? Is it just and equitable to evict homeless people on surplus land?

The dilemma actually forced me to think my way through my intellectual and moral crisis. I got some help from the German Constitutional Court, in the second abortion case heard there in 1993.[9] The minority said that there are some legal questions to which there is not a 'correct' answer. Abortion was such an issue: there are the rights of the growing, developing foetus and the competing rights of the mother who is bearing that child. This does not mean that the court cannot give an answer; the court must provide a definitive response to the legal question raised. But it is important not to

---

[7] The South African Constitution, s 25, provides that 'no one may be deprived of property except in terms of law of general application, and no law may permit arbitrary deprivation of property.' Section 26(3) provides that: 'no one may be evicted from their home, or have their home demolished, without an order of court made after considering all the relevant circumstances.'

[8] The Prevention of Illegal Eviction from and Unlawful Occupation of Land Act 1998, s 6.

[9] *Port Elizabeth Municipality v Various Occupiers*, supra n 6, para 38, citing opening words by the Vice-President of the German Federal Constitutional Court and the presiding judge in its second senate (Judges E-G Mahrenholz and B Sommer), reported in 'Die Entscheidung des Bundesverfassungsgerichts zum Schwangerschaftsabbruch vom 28 Mai 1993', *Juristenzeitung*, 7 June 1993, para 43, as translated and quoted by VZ Smit in 'Reconciling the irreconcilable? Recent developments in the German law on abortion', (1994) 3 Med LR 302, para 30.

claim that through logical reasoning the court can find the legal solution; rather, the court uses the instruments available to balance out the competing interests as well as it can. This eloquently illustrates certain inherent limitations of the law; some legal dilemmas cannot be resolved, they can only be managed more or less well. As the judges said:

> Legal regulation of the termination of pregnancy strikes to the innermost core of human life and touches fundamental questions of human existence. It is characteristic of the human condition that sexuality and the desire to bear children do not coincide. Women have to bear the consequence of this divergence ... Any regulation of the termination of pregnancy raises questions about the sphere of inviolable autonomy of the individual on the one hand, and the right of the state to regulate on the other; here the legislature finds itself at the limit of its capacity to regulate in any way an aspect of human life. It can introduce a better or worse regulation, but it cannot 'solve' the problem; in this sphere the state can no longer be confident that it can lay down the 'correct' legislation.

Similarly I found that in *Port Elizabeth* there was not a *correct* answer. Yet the Court ultimately had to pronounce. The appropriate response, as I saw it, was deliberately to fudge the issue as an abstract question of rights, and consciously to sharpen the search for a solution that would be practical, participatory and equitable. The answer lay not in the Court providing an outcome, but in the Court determining how the best outcome was to be achieved, namely, through meaningful engagement and mediation. It is not just and equitable to evict people if there has not been a judicially controlled attempt to get the parties to find a mutually acceptable solution. In that case, then, the procedural aspect linked up with the substantive aspect, and the eviction fell away. And the role of the Court moved from that of declaring who was in the right to that of managing a complicated, difficult social situation that was extremely threatening to society and that had a symbolic value going well beyond the particular facts of the case.

I would see something similar in respect of the intractable problem of freedom of speech as it clashes with the rights of communities not to be deeply wounded in their souls. Instead of looking for a correct answer, I would seek to find a correct *approach*, always bearing in mind the actual context and the real impact on those affected.

Let us look at some different contexts. If Indonesia passed a law prohibiting deeply insulting attacks on Christians, I would applaud it. Why? Because I know that Christian churches have been burnt, Christians have been killed and that statements which appeared to have been mere words with no immediate follow-through created a climate of hostility in which murder was committed.[10] Again, if India had a similar law I would say it was a good law. It would be part and parcel of Indian 'secularism' which protects the freedom of people to adhere to their faiths, to be in their communities without fear of being marginalised, discriminated against, injured and maybe even – in their enemies' most extreme expression of hatred – murdered.

Why, then, would I say that *The Satanic Verses* should *not* be censored? It is not simply that it is a brilliant piece of literature, well within the literary canon. More important, it represents a serious set of reflections that were deliberately provocative but constituted a supremely intelligent part of a serious debate within Islam. Salman Rushdie was viewed with particular hostility because he was seen as an apostate; but the debate was a debate within a community, and that kind of debate should be protected. It is particularly important that there be openness within our different communities.

The cartoons, by contrast, were intensely demeaning to a very vulnerable section of the population. An immigrant community was struggling to find its place within a broader society that was frequently intolerant; it was a community subject both to gross and to very subtle forms of discrimination. The cartoons were deeply wounding; they were attacking people right at the heart of their self-definition and identity. At issue, in my eyes, was not religious freedom so much as equality and citizenship. The significance of living in a multiracial, multicultural society was being profoundly undermined. The cartoons were a deliberate provocation, unintelligent and crude, intended not to advance reflection but to be aggressive, abusive and insulting. It formed part of an Islamophobic cultural matrix that led to a tit-for-tat response, and became an inflammatory part of the very fire that needed to be extinguished. Here the law can continue to set a public standard, to make a statement about citizenship and values and what matters in society; for that reason I would support some kind of a law that would make it impossible to disseminate the Danish cartoons. Does that mean invoking the criminal law? Not necessarily. There can be civil restraining orders; only if the restraints were violated would the perpetrators' conduct become punishable. One needs an area of flexibility and appropriateness in the remedy.

But how in practice could we distinguish in law between *The Satanic Verses* and the cartoons? If the law is to be involved, how would a law be

---

[10] Among incidents in Indonesia are those reported on 9 August 2010, 12 September 2010 (with the trial of those accused, 31 December 2010) and 11 February 2011.

drafted that would have restricted publication of the cartoons but not of the novel? First, in relation to a law that would criminalise blasphemy in England, I would revert to my opening paragraph and apply the principle of what I have unabashedly referred to as Albie's tutored intuitions. I would say there should be no such law. (I would not speak about blasphemy in a country that identifies itself as Muslim. That is very much an internal public order question that the citizens of that country have to determine for themselves.) In the UK the blasphemy law related to a society in which an orthodoxy of religion was imposed upon the whole of society; so the blasphemy law protected only Christianity. One could blaspheme against Islam, Judaism or Hinduism without any penalty. Such a law, re-enacted, would be discriminatory in itself. But more generally, the crime of blasphemy does not belong to the open and democratic society that the UK aspires to be. The central issue is not blasphemy, it is equality and citizenship. Religion, thanks to the dogmatism that frequently lies at its very core, may be regarded as stifling rational discussion. To challenge core beliefs – or even peripheral ones – is a key aspect of freedom of conscience. For its part, true faith survives critical argument, however speciously or offensively advanced. There should be no law that privileges any particular faith or world view or suffocates critiques made of any existential orthodoxy.

How would a law look, then, that would simultaneously permit restraints on the cartoons and protect the publication of *The Satanic Verses*? First we must consider the process to be followed in adopting such a law. Its formulation is not just a question for a political party to decide on its own, asking itself what would secure the greatest support from the electorate. Nor is it just for legal advisers to come out with a clever legal device. It is for all those who have an interest and a stake in such a law to participate in an attempt to achieve a consensus. What best reconciles the different and at times competing values and interests involved? How can we try out the different formulations? Negotiation and dialogue are absolutely vital in an area such as this. Much current estrangement comes precisely from attempts (even benevolent attempts) by government to find solutions and impose them on people for their own good.

Next we would have to determine what are the constitutional values at stake: why would I myself feel that certain constitutional values should protect *The Satanic Verses* in its particular context, and not the Danish cartoons? Judges are not blind to the realities of the world in which they live. They know roughly what is going on, and do not need expert evidence on most of these issues. It would not be sufficient simply to refer to the redeeming artistic value of the expression (the argument used in such

In praise of 'fuzzy law'

cases as *Lady Chatterley's Lover*).[11] Pornography did not become permissible because it was high art; anti-semitic tracts with horrendous implications would not become acceptable because they were couched in the prose of club-going gentlemen and not chanted by street-gangs. The assessment would have to be based on the extent to which the communication is demeaning to a section of the community identified through its religion, race, colour or ethnic origin – the traditional targets of discrimination and abuse.

And so I am giving a fuzzy answer in defence of the principles of fuzziness, suggesting there should be no clear legislative answer but rather a flexible legislative response based on a methodology that acknowledges the interests involved, that focuses on broad-based engagement and that offers a range of legal interventions, with penal sanctions entering the scene only as an ultimate penalty for violation of reasonable and proportionate civil interventions.

We may be left with an uneasy feeling that surely nobody has the right not to be offended; freedom of expression must surely be freedom to say things that offend people. But this depends on the nature of the offence. If people are under attack because they are black or Jewish or Catholic or Irish, the law does have a role to play. This is not just a question of subjective well-being. We live in a world of genocide and of violence and of hatred that has international repercussions. (I write here as a South African; we know from our own experience how deep these things can be.) The law should back up certain standards that are central to the kind of country in which most of us would like to live, a country based on its citizens' dignity and mutual respect. And if people are under attack for their political, literary or cultural views, or for their old age or youth or size (or for a whole range of other factors)? Such objects of attack do not, I think, go to the heart of the society in which we live, and should not be subject to forms of legal intervention and restraint.

Here are two anecdotes. I offer them simply as vivid examples of the offence that can be casually but *corrosively* caused. There is a South African cricketer named Amla, who has a beard. He is very proud to be a Muslim. A match-commentator, thinking he was off-mic, said at one moment that

---

[11] Under the Obscene Publications Act 1960: 'Section 4(1) A person shall not be convicted ... if it is proved that publication of the article in question is justified as being for the public good on the grounds that it is in the interests of science, literature, art or learning, or of other objects of general concern. 4(2) It is hereby declared that the opinion of experts as to the literary, artistic, scientific or other merits of an article may be admitted in any proceedings under this Act either to establish or negative the said ground.'

the terrorist had taken another catch. Why was Amla a terrorist? Because he wore a beard identifying himself as a Muslim. Then the commentator phoned Amla to apologise. He said he was sorry, he had not realised he was still on the air. *That* was his apology. Amla took it very well (or he pretended to take it very well), but such labelling and stereotyping is demeaning.[12]

I remember a man who played the tuba in the Vienna Art Orchestra (it was a jazz orchestra) who happened to be African–American and huge. He said he hated being in New York because when he walked down the street he had to smile at everybody, to sing or to whistle, just to show that he was not going to rob anyone. How awful it is to be looked on in one's own country – all the time, day and night, night and day – as a threat, an enemy, something hostile and something subversive, just because one is who one is. And that is the world in which we live.

A third story, familiar to most of us, comes from a different context and speaks in favour of flexibility and negotiation. For years a well-known political figure in Northern Ireland denounced popish plots. He was publicly violating the text of a law that made it a criminal offence to say what he did:

A person who uses threatening, abusive or insulting words or behaviour, or displays any written material which is threatening, abusive or insulting, is guilty of an offence if (a) he intends thereby to stir up hatred or arouse fear; or (b) having regard to all the circumstances hatred is likely to be stirred up or fear is likely to be aroused thereby.[13]

He was never prosecuted. Eventually he came into government with his former enemies, abandoned the rhetoric of religious conspiracy and became part of a new shared dispensation. Though the law was on the statute books, it had not been applied. That is not always bad. The fuzziness came from the law's non-application, where application, it was felt, might give rise to more problems than would non-application.

I am aware of the need not to control thought and not to control expression, and aware that the expression which matters the most is the expression that is challenging. How then can the law intervene appropriately,

---

[12] *The Guardian*, 8 July 2008.
[13] Statutory Instrument 1987 No 463 (NI 7): The Public Order (Northern Ireland) Order 1987, Part III: Stirring up Hatred or Arousing Fear, s 9(1). For the definitions: '*Meaning of "fear" and "hatred"*. 8. In this part "fear" means fear of a group of persons in Northern Ireland defined by reference to religious belief, colour, race, nationality (including citizenship) or ethnic or national origins; "hatred" means hatred against a group of persons in Northern Ireland defined by reference to religious belief, colour, race, nationality (including citizenship) or ethnic or national origins.'

without unduly inhibiting the public vitality that goes with freedom of speech? The answer for me is that there are areas of the law – habeas corpus, no torture, no capital punishment – where the law has to be absolutely precise, unforgiving and clear; in these areas fuzziness would be dangerous. But as we have seen throughout this chapter there are other areas of law where categorical line-drawing is harmful, where fuzziness – rooting the debate in its specific context, applying principles of proportionality to the turbulent mix of constitutional values at play, encouraging as much participation as possible by those most directly affected and maintaining the virtue of open-endedness with regard to outcomes – where such fuzziness is good.

Religion, the state and the meaning of *'jihad'*

CHAPTER 16

Towards an Islamic society, not an Islamic state
Abdullahi An-Na'im

I will approach the meaning and relevance of *jihad* in the modern context by trying to clarify the relationship between religion (Islam in this case) and the state. At the end, I will offer some direct responses to questions about *jihad* and related matters. Since what I am about to say may be surprising, in one way or another, I ask readers to bear with me and try to keep an open mind. In any discourse, preconceptions can by a curious process become so dominant that they start to be taken almost as facts of nature, though actually they are only parts of a human endeavour to understand. There are such preconceptions on all sides in the current debates about religion and the state. Discourses on any subject, including religion, are generated and shaped by the context, conditions and history out of which they emerge; and there is nothing eternal or divine about anything human.

It may also be pertinent to note that I am writing throughout from an Islamic perspective. Whatever I write of my obligation and my conviction, I believe to be my obligation as a Muslim, born of my conviction as a Muslim.

There is a first point to make clear: there is not a single mention of the concept of a state either in the Qur'an or in the *Sunna* of the Prophet. So whatever understandings Muslims may have of the state's character and however necessary or expedient any such character may seem to be, these Muslims' views are not mandated by scriptural sources. Any view that a Muslim may have about the state is therefore part of his or her understanding of the general obligation of Muslims to abide by *shari'a* (and there is no doubt in my mind that as a Muslim I am bound by *shari'a*). The question is this: whether a Muslim should expect the state to enforce *shari'a* or not? To that question my answer is 'No'; the state cannot and should not enforce *shari'a*. We need to introduce two further factors into our discussion before I expand on this overall position.

First, we must acknowledge the post-colonial context in which Muslims live today. Muslims throughout the world now live under territorial so-called 'nation-states' which are European in origin, and Muslims also live with conceptions of law that are European. Through our colonial experiences, we have come to live by the European notion of the state as an hierarchical, centralised, bureaucratic and political institution, and by the conception of law as positive law coercively enforced by the state. These concepts of the state and law are not consistent with Muslims' pre-colonial experience. So the question facing us in the present post-colonial era is this: do we revert to something we imagine about pre-colonial conditions, or do we make the best we can of what we have today as the so-called nation state or territorial state?

And for the second preliminary: we must address the ambiguous interdependence between the so-called secular and religious domains. Each is commonly defined in contrast to the other: what is secular is what is not religious; and what is religious is what is not secular. (In this contrast the individual is likely to be opposing the 'secular' to his or her own understanding of religion, whatever that religion may be.) It is still harder to attain, as we must, a clear understanding of a 'secular' state or to define the secularity of such a state, without reference to this contrast with a religious state.

To return now to my main proposition: I maintain that the state can never be religious.[1] To claim that the state is or can be religious is conceptually false, historically unprecedented and in practical terms untenable today. As a political institution the state is incapable of having a religion; conceptually, therefore, it is not possible for the state to be 'religious'. Historically there is no precedent in Muslim history for an Islamic state. And today such a state is impracticable in view of the profound diversity and interdependence of Muslim and non-Muslim populations.

I hasten to add that this is nothing to do with the obligation of Muslims to observe *shariʿa* as a matter of personal religious obligation. My objection here is to the notion that the state can legitimately be the instrument of the enforcement of *shariʿa*. *Shariʿa* as such cannot be coercively enforced by the state precisely because Muslims must obey *shariʿa* out of their own conviction and with a genuine intent to comply, in order to be accountable for their practice. So whatever the state enforces is not *shariʿa*. The religious nature of *shariʿa* requires it to be a matter of personal practice and conviction.

We need, in other words, to *separate* Islam from the state; that is, not to permit the state to claim the sanctity of Islam. The fact that some states

---

[1] I have presented this position in detail in AA An-Naʿim, *Islam and the Secular State: negotiating the future of shariʿa* (Harvard, 2008).

claim to be Islamic is not sufficient reason to concede the claim. The state cannot be Islamic; whenever the claim is made, the ruling elites are using the state institutions to enforce *their* view of Islam. When we see the position in those terms we can see how dangerous it is to concede the claim that the state can be Islamic.

Two objections may be raised here. First: surely the Qur'anic verses about penal sanctions demand the institution of an Islamic state for their implementation? No, they do not. Since we are partners in the state with people who would disagree with our personal religious convictions, we cannot base the penal law of the state on these convictions. My personal religious practice as a Muslim is my responsibility, but all matters of public policy and legislation must be mediated through civic reason. This means that the criminal and contract laws of a country are to be enacted by virtue of their consistency with civic reason; that is, they are to be based on reasons which can be debated openly and freely by all citizens at large, without reference to religious conviction. This applies to Muslim-majority countries too. To impose law based on our religious convictions as Muslims denies the right of equal citizenship to those among the citizens – including other Muslims – whom we have not persuaded to share these convictions. Whether it is criminal punishment (*hudud*), interest banking (*riba*) or any issue, Muslims can call for legislation or public policy through civic reason, and not by virtue of our religious beliefs. If as a Muslim I want to have *hudud* crimes punished as such, I cannot argue for such punishment in terms of my religious conviction in a state which I share with others who do not share that conviction.

I can, then, imagine a situation where a democratically elected parliament could enact a punishment like the *hudud*-punishment for theft or extra-marital sexual intercourse. It is difficult to oppose this possibility if one takes the principle of democratic governance seriously. However, since such legislation is not enacted as *shari'a*, a matter of religious mandate or command, it could in many countries be challenged as unconstitutional (such challenge may not be possible in the UK because of the sovereignty of Parliament); and legislation that does not claim religious sanctity can, regardless of the possibility of constitutional challenge, be repealed or amended through the democratic process.

In fifteen hundred years of Muslim history – through all of which Muslims have read the *hudud*-verses of the Qur'an – we are hard pressed to find instances of *hudud* enacted and enforced by a state's centralised administration of justice. There are today more than forty countries – more than a quarter of the nations represented in the United Nations – in which

Muslims are the majority. These countries have been independent, to some degree or another, for five or six decades or more. In how many of them have the *hudud* been enacted as the penal law of the country? Ask this about the comprehensive and systematic enactment and enforcement of *shariʿa* in any country, including Saudi Arabia, Iran, Sudan or Pakistan where the *hudud* are claimed to be the law of the land. Even if the historical record may be difficult to verify, the current record clearly shows that the vast majority of independent Muslim-majority states have not chosen to impose *hudud* as a matter of Islamic imperative for the state to enforce. The fact is that *shariʿa* has very little role, if any, in the legal systems in almost all Muslim majority countries around the world. So, let us be honest and candid here.

The choices people make about the law to apply and the life to live and their relations with other people are really what drives them and their own personal understanding of what Islam means to them. Change happens in society before it happens theologically. People make choices and then the theology follows the society. And this has been as true about Christians and Christianity as it has been true about Muslims and Islam.

A second objection may be raised to my denial that the state can be Islamic. There are collective addresses in the Qurʾan, such as, 'All you believers do this and do that.' Surely, then, believers must establish an Islamic state in order to ensure universal conformity? No. Believers of course need to have a state; a state is a political necessity for any society. But Muslims have always disagreed, and will continue to disagree, about what being 'Islamic' means. This has two consequences. First, what the state does should not be called *shariʿa* because it can only be *shariʿa* according to some understandings and not others; and, second, the state should be neutral, so that people can debate what *shariʿa* means to themselves and can live accordingly. As a Muslim I celebrate the fact that (at least amongst Sunni Muslims) we do not have an institutional hierarchy that pronounces what *shariʿa* is. To be a Muslim, I *need* a secular state.

On the other hand, there *is* a connectedness between Islam and politics, for there is a distinction between politics and the state. The 'politics' of a community or society is the government of the day, but 'the state' refers to the institutional continuity within and by which all citizens are served equally, without regard to their religious belief or lack of it. This distinction enables us to separate religion and the state, while accepting and regulating the relationship of religion and politics.

On this analysis, although the state can never be religious, it may not be secular enough. My definition of a secular state is this: a state that is neutral regarding religious doctrine and that does not take a position on religion or belief. I accept that by my definition the UK itself may (even if only in its symbols of state) be non-secular. This in itself bears out my point that the secular nature of the state is the product of an historical, contextual process. Britain is a largely secular state in a way that is peculiar to Britain, a way that emerges out of Britain's own history, traditions, and religious and other institutions. The US is a secular state, but in a way that is different from Britain's. In fact, among those states which are accepted as secular, no two states are identical in the *way* in which they are secular.

The point is that the state must be neutral regarding religion. That is, the state cannot deal with me *other* than by virtue of my citizenship. My religious affiliation has nothing to do with the state. It is not the business of the state to differentiate among its citizens on the basis of their religious affiliation. We now see in Europe a tendency to treat Muslims as a community of believers in a way very similar to that in which the Ottoman Empire used to apply the 'millet' system to non-Muslim communities. People's affiliation to a religious community becomes the means by which they and the state interact. So the French or the German state seeks so-called 'counterparts', the heads of the Muslim community. This is ironic. The Europe that dismantled the Ottoman Empire in the name of citizenship is now denying such citizenship to believers by accepting that the state can deal with believers by reference to their belief. There should be no accommodation here, on either side. The state should not deal with communities or with individuals other than by virtue of their citizenship, without reference to their religious affiliation; and citizens should interact with the state on the basis only of their citizenship.

Now one aspect of the state's obligations is to respect religious conviction. And the questions of identity and of cultural practices to which such conviction gives rise should be addressed in the same way in relation to all citizens. No distinction at all should be made on the basis of the particular religion to which any citizen is affiliated. Some of the controversies that I have recently observed about Muslims – doubts, for instance, about Muslims' loyalty to the state – are reminiscent of the suspicion to which Roman Catholics used to be subjected, where their loyalty to the state was cast into question by their religious affiliation and their presumed loyalty to some other entity. Present-day Muslims, whether in majority or minority situations, should relate to the state as citizens and should demand that the state relate to *them* as citizens, and not by reference to their religious affiliation.

So we can return to some of the principles I mentioned at the start of this chapter. Do Islamic values and fidelity to *shariʿa* remain an obligation for

Muslims? Yes, but outside state institutions. It is up to communities to organise themselves in civil society and to conduct their affairs according to their convictions *subject to the law of the land*, which is uniform and equally applicable to all citizens without any distinction.

Does *jihad* remain an obligation for Muslims everywhere? And does such *jihad* oblige a Muslim to strive to bring about an Islamic society or an Islamic state? Now there is a difference between striving for an Islamic society and establishing an Islamic state. Any meaning of *jihad* – which in my view *must* be non-violent – may have to do with promoting Islamic values in society; but *jihad* cannot impose the obligation to establish an Islamic state, which is incoherent conceptually and impossible practically. *Jihad* means to me a striving to comply with my obligations as a Muslim non-violently and in civil society, and not through state institutions.

There has been a history of violent *jihad*. It is time to be more explicit and methodologically more careful in our analysis of *jihad*. We need not just a counter-claim on behalf of non-violence, but a hermeneutical or theological argument to counter the historical acceptance of violence as integral to the notion of *jihad*. In other words, we need both a principled and hermeneutically coherent Islamic argument against violent *jihad*, as well as engaging political factors affecting practice. On this second count, for instance, people are often violent and intolerant of difference when they are or perceive themselves to be under attack. The task in which the wider society can play a constructive role is to assure people not only rhetorically but institutionally and as a matter of policy that they are welcome as equal citizens. So we will enable the Muslims among us to bring out tensions within their own history and tradition, and to let these be debated openly. Let the wider society help people come to terms with these issues. I write this as a Muslim: let Muslims come out with a strong statement – and more than that, with a systematic, coherent, methodologically sound statement – denouncing the violent element that we have had in the historical understanding of *jihad*.

The riposte can be made that there are surely extreme situations which justify a community's use of force in self-defence or in defence of principle. (Such situations can arise in any society; the oppression suffered under Hitler is just one overwhelming example.) And the doctrine of *jihad* in historical Muslim discourse is probably equivalent to the doctrine of just war in the Christian tradition; so there is some equivalence in that regard. But we now stand under the United Nations Charter as a global community. We can – and must – create conditions and institutions under which the need to resort to violence in defence against oppression is minimised.

In my belief as a Muslim, religious or moral obligation never justifies the use of violence. I reject violence, both as a matter of principle and because I do not believe that violence is a productive force in society. But I do retain the right, and sometimes the obligation, to undertake peaceful, non-violent dissent. (This is to follow the examples of Mahatma Gandhi and Martin Luther King.) It is part of my obligation as a citizen to maintain the moral integrity with which I hold my convictions, including the right and the obligation to oppose what I believe to be an unjust law. I would undertake such opposition openly, accepting full responsibility for my action and its consequences. There is a permanent need for citizens to maintain the courage and strength of their convictions, to oppose any law which they believe to be unjust.

Debates about such issues as non-violent resistance, distinctions between violence and other forms of forceful struggle, and the theory and practice of passivism, can be approached from a variety of religious and philosophical perspectives. These debates are not specific to Islam, although Muslims should be able, if they wish, to engage in them from their religious perspective. The point here is that not every law that is enacted by a secular state will be just or reasonable; and therefore the right and obligation to resist non-violently will remain. Through the twentieth century and in our own lifetimes, all round the world secular states, whether fascist, Marxist or nationalist, have used secular law to oppress their own citizens, and aggressively attack other states. In such situations people find it necessary to *resist*. It is precisely in order to maintain the integrity and justice of the state that we must stand by our convictions. The state is not always right or just simply because it is the state. It is citizens who make the state right and just by their ability to resist injustice.

CHAPTER 17

Following shariʿa *in the West*

Tariq Ramadan

This whole discussion has one objective in view: to make it possible for us all in the West to live together, understanding each other in a peaceful – and not only peaceful, but *positive* – coexistence, all of us contributing to our shared future here. And not only in the West. We have no right to concentrate just on our own welfare and to forget about injustices elsewhere. We have a long way to go, in order to understand each other and to build what we have to build together.

All such discussions are based on particular definitions and interpretations of the central terms. (And when it comes to religious teachings, neither Abdullahi An-Naʿim nor I would ever claim to represent all Muslims.) Our terms are coloured by the context from within which we are using them. An-Naʿim and I are using the same terms, but he and I would not agree on their definition. Take 'secularism', for example. An-Naʿim suggests that the British system is not secular enough; but in Paris you will hear people say that the British system is not secular *at all*. And in the US there is, as An-Naʿim has pointed out, yet another type of secularism. We too easily confuse the definition of secularism with the particular historical models of secularism under which we live and which we have in mind. We need to clarify the definitions of such terms and the circumstances that affect their interpretation. Some of the differences in definition are indeed normative, but others grow from very specific conditions: some of these conditions are (as we have just seen) historical, and some are psychological.

These psychological conditions are important. I speak frequently with people about secularism. Secularism has a clear meaning for them: a principled neutrality towards religion and between religions. But when they are in dialogue, they abandon that meaning and speak instead of secularism as in *opposition* to religion. A conflict is already being constructed here between religion and secularism, a conflict that is not based either in Islam's teachings or in the way we actually understand and apply the secular law. This conflict, once constructed in our mind, then shapes everything we think. Secularism and religion are imagined as two systems in opposition to each other. But this is not the way I understand things to be.

I need to know, then, in any dialogue, my interlocutors' definitions and the prejudgments and fears that have informed them. Rowan Williams, then Archbishop of Canterbury, knew exactly what he was talking about when he discussed *shari'a*. The reaction he stirred was not a reaction to his normative use of the word, it was a *psychological* reaction to *shari'a* in the minds of many people. *Shari'a*, as some of the media knew well, is a very *scary* word. The reaction was to the connotations that '*shari'a*' has in Britain not to the normative understanding of *shari'a* itself.

We must distinguish what is normative, what is conditioned by particular histories and what is stirred by current fears. If we do not distinguish the principles from the features of a particular historical model or current situation, then our dialogue will collapse in misunderstanding. The discussion we need will not be easy; but our whole future will be still more difficult if we do not all undertake this complex discussion together as responsible and reasonable citizens.

Let me now go to the principal question. I come from within the Muslim universe of reference, and I need to talk about the understanding of *shari'a* that I have as both a Muslim and a European citizen. People often think that that my obedience to *shari'a* will stand in opposition to my obedience to the secular laws. Here again the definition of *shari'a* is very important. (Readers must continue to bear in mind that I do not represent all the current trends in Islam, even though I think that I speak for the mainstream trend in the West and now in many Muslim-majority countries too.) For some of the scholars specialising in law and jurisprudence, *shari'a* is a set of laws that constitute 'Islamic Law'. This *shari'a* emerges from a very specialised consideration of the scriptural sources among scholars who are concerned specifically with laws and jurisprudence. In the West, *shari'a* is often spoken of even more narrowly as simply the penal code of the Muslims. *Shari'a*, we hear, is about cutting off hands, and that is all. But this is quite wrong. First, the penal code is a small part of that juridical part of *shari'a* as a whole at which we have glanced above; and, second, the code itself is being viewed, in such a summary, in a very literalist way.[1] I agree with An-Na'im that we need to see the question from a new angle (even though I would not deploy exactly his definition of *shari'a*). I am not modernising when I argue that we need an overall view of *shari'a* as *the way towards faithfulness*. In this *shari'a*, I

---

[1] Here again the Archbishop of Canterbury showed himself very knowledgeable about the whole subject, supra pp 20–1.

try in a specific time and place and within a culture that has grown from a specific history to be faithful to the principles and the objectives of my religion; it is here and now, in the Europe of the twenty-first century, that I am following my *shariʿa*. The observance of laws is only the means to this end: to be faithful to *shariʿa*'s objectives. So, what are the objectives of this *shariʿa*?

Shariʿa is a question of values: of justice, equality, freedom. And it is a question of principles: of the ways in which I am going to translate these values into something concrete in my society. So it is a question also of daily life within my society: how to realise those values by faithfulness to the objectives of *shariʿa*. So *shariʿa* is not a set of laws or a system which is set over against the other. It is quite wrong to have this binary vision – '*Here* is *shariʿa* and *there* is the secular law' – and then to imagine a conflict between them.

I am then asserting that I am *at home* in Great Britain. (Here some Muslims may have a problem with my argument.) Here there is equal citizenship for all. I am free; I have freedom of conscience and freedom of worship. These are secured by law in this country, so these are my *shariʿa* here, the conditions and aims of my way towards faithfulness. These are the freedoms of citizens who as citizens are *equal*. Equality of citizenship in Britain is my *shariʿa* here, which I must promote and seek to realise. And in attaining this objective I am being faithful to my religion.

Why is this so important? Because in myself I become stronger as result of this. If I am always being told that *shariʿa* is something distinct from my life here, that *here* I am to abide by the secular system and that *shariʿa* is *there*, then I am being prevented from flourishing in an integrated, personal self-consistency.

I am asking my non-Muslim readers to decentre themselves from the binary vision of 'us versus them'. Each of us has his or her own universe of reference. I have my own: I am a Muslim. And among my readers there will be many, I am sure, who are Christian or Jewish or Buddhist as I am not. But we are not here to put different religions in opposition to each other. We can and should be finding in them the values and principles that they share. Our obsession with religious systems is undermining our understanding of the universal values that we have in common. We may even have to oppose the systems in our attempt to realise the objectives of the systems' rules. There are many different routes, through a social space we share, to a place in which we can genuinely be together.

This is why I avoid the distinction – which is not drawn from the Qur'an nor from the prophetic traditions – between *dar al-Islam* and *dar al-harb*, the space or abode of Islam and the abode of war. This distinction has come from scholars and from their own settings in their attempts to define the geography of faith. I myself am among millions of Muslims now here in the West, and in this setting I in turn want to define the geography of faith. In our globalised world I must say what I have to say before all the people around me; I must be a *witness* to my teachings. In the present geography of faith I am in the space or the abode of *testimony*, *dar al-shahada*. This is true not just within Britain, but throughout our present world. I am in the abode of testimony in Saudi Arabia too, for wherever I am I must be faithful to my principles and must be a witness to my teachings.

This brings us to a very important question which – openly or by implication – confronts every Muslim in the West: 'To what are you loyal? Are you first a Muslim, or are you first a British citizen? Are you going to be loyal to the secular laws or are you going to be loyal to Islamic teachings?' Once again we have to be clear what is at issue. I might well be asked in the same spirit: 'Could you do something by the light of your religion which is against the secular law?' In reply I will ask to be shown something – something real and practical, not something hypothetical – that is promoted under the secular law but which will be against my religious teachings. Such conflicts are not so easy to find. There is latitude within both the secular law and within Islam. When both are so supple, we can find our way without conflict; and the wider public can be weaned off the obsession with conflicting systems.

We have heard the debate about *shari'a* in England. There is a widespread belief that Muslims want to be treated by law in a specific, distinctive way. I asked at the time of the Archbishop's lecture: 'Who are the Muslims making such demands?' The law sometimes gives rights to other religious minorities. When the Muslims then ask for the same rights, they are believed to be asking for something specific to themselves. If provision is already made for Jewish courts and for the Jewish tradition, and then the Muslims ask for similar allowances, there is an angry response: 'Oh, what do *they* want?' But the discussion is then no longer about the law. It is psychological. People are scared of the Muslim presence, and imagine Muslims asking for exclusive privileges. I have sometimes advised Muslims not to seek rights comparable to those granted to other religious minorities. It may legally be proper to seek such rights, but nonetheless be inappropriate in our present setting. And we do not need *shari'a*-specific spaces. We can do what we should within the law of the land, and have no reason to send the wrong message to our fellow-citizens.

We do well to stand back for a moment to look more broadly at the apparent demands of Muslims for special treatment. When we are dealing in Britain with unemployment, with marginalisation or with discrimination we should not 'Islamise' socio-economic problems. We need a policy towards full employment, social mixing and good schools. It is disingenuous to point the finger at the Muslims who are creating their own schools and segregating themselves. There is indeed such self-segregation, and it is not the solution. But if we continue to have a second-class school system in the UK, Muslims will set up schools of their own. We have to be honest: to recognise that there are socio-economic problems here that have nothing to do with religion.

So I return to the definition and nature of a secular state. A secular system is properly defined without reference to an imagined opposition with all religions or to an imagined conflict between particular religions. All religions in a secular system are going to be treated equally, and in conformity to a double principle: that freedom of conscience and freedom of worship shall be protected. If a society does not protect these two principles, it is, by the very meaning of the word, not a 'secular' society. These principles are protected everywhere in Western societies; and so long as these two principles are respected, we Muslims will continue to be living in conformity with the law of the land. One can of course be obsessed with small groups and marginal trends, but the mainstream Muslim organisations in Britain, the US, France and elsewhere are all making clear to all Muslims that we Muslims abide by the law of the country. We are *citizens*; and we in turn are protected in our freedom of conscience and freedom of worship.

But this, I know, does not yet address the principal claim or aspiration addressed by An-Na'im. Here, at the heart of the question, he and I may well be heading towards the same destination, but we are taking different routes. An-Na'im insists that there has never been an Islamic state. But I would reply that there have been Muslim societies sustained by Muslim political authorities, and it would be difficult to convince Muslims that in such conditions there has been no connection between society and state. Faced with such a denial, a vast majority of Muslims will stop listening. Even in this brief chapter, my own preferred methodology will have become clear: to return to the scriptural sources and be clear on definitions; to distinguish between principles and historically particular models; to bring the sources and the history into dialectical relation to each other; and so finally to bring the sources and our current reality into such a dialectical inter-relation.

What is to be said to those Western Muslims who are willing to defy laws imposed by the secular state? Either of two approaches is possible. One approach, which I understand and respect, is simply to demand that Muslims differentiate between their religious references on the one hand and on the other a collective rationality to which they as citizens must subscribe. But this, I believe, will never be understood by Muslims. It will not change their mentality or convince them.

Let us take two examples which all of us will condemn. When faced with honour killings or forced marriages, we can say in the name of British law simply that nothing like honour killing or forced marriage is permissible; whatever a person's take on religion may be, at the end of the day there are *laws*, and they must be obeyed. But is this reference to the law going to change the behaviour or the mentality of people likely to commit such crimes? No. It can send a message to be careful, for a perpetrator, if caught, will be jailed. But it is not going to change any mentality. Simply to invoke the law is to build a new framework within which the old mentalities remain unchanged. If we are to prevent such crimes, we must look at them not only from our own viewpoint but from the viewpoint as well of Muslims at large. We must try to understand mentalities from within, and so to change them.

Let us then explore a second approach. We will still insist that the laws in this country are to be obeyed; and we will also work from within the Muslim community by showing that honour killing, forced marriages and domestic violence are *not Islamic*. I want a discourse *from within*, helping Muslims to understand that such acts are a betrayal of their own teachings. This is a far more powerful tool for change. We will have, then, a twofold approach. From within, Muslims will understand that such actions are not Islamic. From the outside, they will understand the common ground of the law.

The same applies to the penal codes. Many Westerners did not understand my position on this when I said we need to impose a moratorium on *hudud* and to open a debate on it within the Muslim-majority countries.[2] Non-Muslims may condemn the penal codes; but Muslims will see in this the West condemning Islam and patronising Islam in an imperialist way and claiming that Western values are higher than Islam's. If you want to change something in the Islamic world, it is not by imposing something from the West. It is by undertaking a process *from within*, with Islamic teachings based on Islamic principles and Islamic tradition. I myself am

---

[2] T Ramadan, 'An international call for moratorium on corporal punishment, stoning and the death penalty in the Islamic world', accessible at <http://tariqramadan.com/spip.php?article264>.

trying to say and to show to Muslims that honour killings and the like are not Islamic, they are a betrayal of Islamic dignity and Islamic teachings.

In such work, we are targeting those with few resources of their own. The conditions for teaching from outside are not in place; and even to attempt it is to disrespect the spirit and objectives of Islamic teachings and their scriptural sources. The West claims to be serious about pluralism. But the West must recognise (difficult though the truth may be to hear) that to be pluralist is not to think that the only values to be respected are one's own, it is to understand and respect the difference of the other and to understand the other's own world of reference. The true pluralist will understand that change is going to be deep when Muslims understand from within what practices are not Islamic. We can help Muslims to move, from within, towards a better understanding of their religion, to engage with the common values that we all share and to join the discussion. We should, then, be making two points at once: honour killing and forced marriages are not Islamic; and the law of the land prohibits them.

This leaves unanswered the important question about centres of authority in Islam. In my book *Radical Reform: Islamic ethics and liberation*,[3] I speak about the crisis of Islam's scattered authority. We have no unique or exclusive centre of authority; so who speaks for us? Muslims do have this problem to face; but it is possible nonetheless to address the question: 'What is Islamic?' At the grass-roots level and within the Muslim-majority countries there are already mainstream trends on which we can and must rely. And we must as well build further understanding through education, open platforms and dialogue. The diversity of Islam needs pluralistic platforms where Muslims can talk to each other. The problem of authority, then, will not be solved by imposing outsiders' views on what Islam should be. The problem has to be solved from within, by critical discussion within the Islamic communities. It is a positive sign, that such discussion is taking place, and mainly in societies where Muslims are most free. What is now emerging among Muslims in Western countries will have a tremendous impact on Muslim-majority countries. We are free here, and can have the critical discussion through which we can try to improve understanding and our management of disputes. So there is indeed real difficulty, even a crisis in Islam; and progress through and out of it can be made only by critical and pluralistic discussion from within.

We have seen, then, that there is an important discussion to be had about loyalties within the Muslim community. Spiritually we belong to the

---

[3] T Ramadan, *Radical Reform: Islamic ethics and liberation* (Oxford, 2008).

umma; but still, when one is in a country, one abides by the law. We can have a spiritual community – as the Christians, Jews and Buddhists have a spiritual community – but on the subject of law, our country and the laws of our country come first. This axiom gives rise to two final questions.

First, do I, on the basis of what I have said, blindly support everything that emerges from my government and from the laws of my country? No. To abide by the law of the country, to be a citizen, and to ask to be treated as a citizen: all this is to be loyal to principles, and not blindly loyal to systems and governments. Any citizen, therefore, if the government is doing something wrong, has a duty of *critical loyalty*. The best citizens are those who are able to speak up against the government's actions if they think that the government is doing wrong. Muslims today are the objects of such great distrust that when a Muslim criticises government policy he or she can seem disloyal to the country. But the truth is exactly the opposite. If Muslim citizens say to the government, 'I think that what you have been doing in Iraq or in Afghanistan is wrong', do not just impugn their loyalty. Listen to their *critical* loyalty. They are being good citizens. If citizens ever lose this readiness and power to be critical, then democracy will end. But we need *trust*, to be able to listen to such criticism from any citizens, whoever they are, whatever their religion.

The same principle applies to Muslims and to the criticism of actions undertaken in the name of Islam. Westerners – all Westerners, Muslim and non-Muslim – are rightly asking that Muslims condemn violent terrorism and the killing of innocent people. And yes, we must. But must we do it to please non-Muslims in the West? Or must we do it because such violence and killing are against our principles? Once again we need *critical loyalty*. I am critically loyal to teachings put out in the name of Islam when in the name of my religion I condemn those teachings of my fellow-Muslims which are promulgated in the name of that religion but contravene it. I am not here to please my fellow citizens in the West. I am here to be consistent with Islam and with myself. This is a far more powerful and trustworthy position. If I set out to please others, then one day, when those others turn their back, I will do whatever I really want. But if I am here to be consistent? I cannot turn my back on myself. I have to be consistent, for the sake of my own dignity and conscience. So I urge non-Muslims: ask Muslims to be consistent with their own values, not to please you. Sometimes non-Muslims look out for a Muslim who will say what non-Muslims want to hear; but they are unsure that such a Muslim is consistent in what he says. Non-Muslims need to decentre themselves from their own point of reference and to adopt the viewpoint and understanding of their Muslim interlocutors.

And so, in conclusion, to my second point: a question about *jihad*. Some people say that to undertake *jihad* – as we must – is to spread Islam. This is not my understanding of *jihad*. Once again, we need a definition: the first principle of *jihad* has nothing to do with war; it has to do with peace. According to the Qur'an the natural state for human beings is not peace; with our own self and with the other, the natural state is a state of tension. We are sometimes aggressive or angry, and are trying to be peaceful and calm. Tension is first, peace is second. We are not peaceful by birth. We have to learn to be peaceful. This struggle, as we resist the temptations within ourselves, is the *jihad*. *Jihad* is this spiritual education.

Jihad plays the same role in societies and collectivities. There are tensions; and we need, through education, to reach peaceful coexistence and mutual respect. We resist temptations in our own self and oppression by the other. And so we move towards the highest level, which is peace. The objective of *jihad* is to progress from tensions to peace. This is exactly the opposite of what is generally understood by *jihad*.

Resistance, then, is the very meaning of *jihad*. Resistance to what? We have just heard about the personal and societal levels. And on the international level or between societies? We will all agree on an ideal: we want non-violence. But then we must move from the ideal to reality: to our own reality in Europe and beyond, and to the connection between reality and our teachings.

Jihad resists oppression. When I am told by the oppressed that the oppressor has killed their family and will return to kill again, and that the oppressed are now planning to resist the oppression, I could, theoretically speaking, urge non-violent resistance; for such non-violence is the ideal. But within Islam it is legitimate, for those who are going to be killed, to resist. At issue is the dignity of the oppressed themselves. At issue too, if oppression is allowed to carry on unresisted, is a widening corruption and the end of human progress.

An-Na'im is completely right to say that some interpretations of Islam have promoted violence in an unacceptable way. But the classical Islamic tradition confirms that one can resist armed oppression, and that one can sometimes be forced to go to war. This is then a violent resistance to a violent oppression. The conditions that justify such resistance are rightly subject to close scrutiny; but we have no right simply to say that we dislike the idea of it. Non-violence is the ideal. But when people in the name of their dignity are resisting oppression and the danger of death, we have as human beings to look at our own history and at our principles and reluctantly to accept that sometimes, in the name of this dignity, armed resistance should be a solution.

We have to be human beings and not – sitting safely and at ease in the UK – to confuse parameters. We have to understand those who speak about resistance and violence; and we must differentiate between understanding what they are saying and justifying what they are doing. We are in the first instance to understand, not to justify. Sometimes, in the light of our understanding, we have to condemn. But sometimes we have to be careful not to go too far (as occasionally we do) in condemning without understanding. These distinctions are prerequisites for reasonable discussion among us.

Let me make an appeal to readers proud of Britain's history. Listen for a moment, here in Britain, to your own British and European history. All the people that you now celebrate from the past are people who resisted oppression and injustice. Who were the people who saved us from Nazism? It was those who would not accept the Nazis' aggression, who urged the nation to resist it and who fought against it. So do not tell the people in the global South to remain non-violent against oppression, when the dignity that you celebrate in your own past is the dignity of those who stood up against oppression and gave their lives for justice. The global South deserves to have at the very least this dignity too.

Hitler's tyranny is an extreme case, but any dictatorship could be chosen as an example. If your own country were subject to dictatorship and oppression, of course you could hope that people would adopt non-violent resistance. I myself would like the people just to oppose the government in accordance with that government's own – ever more restrictive – laws. But is it really possible, when people are being killed, to undertake only such 'lawful' resistance? Non-violence, in an idealistic way, is fine; but it does not always match up to the reality on the ground.

I myself came to the West in political exile. I went to one jail in Egypt, my own country, and the guards were unable to touch me because I had a Swiss passport. So they started to beat someone in front of me to show me how they treat the Egyptians. This is something I have *seen*. Writing and speaking in attractive settings in England, I do not want just to speak up for non-violence and to forget that people are treated in that way. I am sorry to remind my readers, but I must: it has not been good, in recent years, to be an Iraqi in Iraq, facing what the US and the British soldiers have been doing to Iraqis in the name of the US and British governments. Should these military actions have been resisted? We may not like such resistance, but it was legitimate. The *means* must be right, but in principle the resistance was legitimate. This is the starting point also of our dignity, to be able to say this, and not – to please the sophisticated readership of legal essays – just to say I am a philosopher of non-violence. I *am* such a philosopher, but I am also someone who is working for justice. I would be the first to speak up when my country is wrong, and to try, when people are resisting what is wrong, to understand what they are trying to say and do in the name of their dignity.

There are ethical principles to constrain this: never accept or justify the killing of innocent people, of women or of children; never justify the destruction of nature. At the same time I am a European citizen, and I want all of us in Europe to understand and share one principle in the name of our shared beliefs, whatever our religion or our secular world view. I would state this principle as an imperative, binding on all of us who wish to send the message of non-violence to others. We must make clear to our own government and to our own people that as a nation we have no dignity if we ask others to be non-violent but are ourselves unjust to those others and deny them their own dignity.

I am sorry to say that in the Muslim mindset today, the life of an Iranian, a Palestinian or an Iraqi seems to be less valuable to the West than the life of a Westerner. And *equality* is the starting point of justice. Muslims far from Europe and America will listen to our demands for non-violence if we can show at the same time that we value the life of all people at exactly the same level: that we value Arabs and Westerners, Muslims and non-Muslims, Palestinians and Israelis exactly the same. Let us engage our values in our statements – and in our *actions*.

CHAPTER 18

Violence, personal commitment and democracy

Khaled Abou El Fadl

To engage in *jihad* means to strive or exert oneself in a struggle to achieve a morally laudable or just aim. For all the sensationalism stirred by the term *jihad*, this is its indisputable definition in Islamic theology and law. The meaning of *jihad* is both this straightforward and simple and also this complex and indeterminate. *Jihad* could be in the form of armed struggle, but (as explained below) the use of violence could also be considered as a most serious and grave moral crime, that of causing corruption or ruin on earth (*fasad fi al-ard*).

Although the term *jihad* has been appropriated and co-opted in very diverse contextual and historical circumstances, in Islamic theology there is an inherent and integral relationship between the concept of *jihad* and the Qur'anically mandated normative obligation to pursue what is good and to avoid what is bad (*al-amr bi'l ma'ruf wa al-nahy 'ann al-munkar*). By definition, moral worthiness and the justness of the cause are categorical preconditions for the existence and recognition of *jihad* or for a Muslim to be in a state of *jihad* (n. *mujahid*). In the classical philosophical and theological discourses, and especially in the apologetics of *kalam*,[1] there is a vast and complex Islamic scholastic tradition investigating the definition and nature of moral goodness and what constitutes a just cause. In books of classical Islamic legal theory or jurisprudence (*usul al-fiqh*), as opposed to books on Islamic positive law (*ahkam*), there is a much more abridged and narrower discourse on what constitutes a legally recognisable just cause, or what may be considered a valid normative obligation as a matter of law. (We will distinguish further, below, between books on *usul al-fiqh* and books on Islamic positive law, *ahkam*.) This discourse in most classical Islamic sources falls under the general rubric of *husn* (what is good, praiseworthy and beautiful) as opposed to *qubh* (ugliness). While theological and philosophical sources focus on questions of ultimate goodness and the nature of the obligation (*taklif*) to

---

[1] *'Ilm al-kalam* can be broadly understood as theological dialectics, or as scholastic theology. Participants in the field of *kalam* often employed arguments based on text or reason to defend specific dogmas or theological truths.

do good, jurisprudential sources focus for the most part on what may be considered valid or binding as a matter of law.

CONSCIENCE AND INDETERMINACY IN THE ISLAMIC TRADITION

It might be surprising to many non-Muslims, and also to numerous contemporary Muslims, that the classical Islamic tradition often distinguishes moral and theological responsibility from questions of legal liability, and that moral and theological obligations could at times exist in tension with legal responsibility. However inconsistent with the dogmatic and simplistic perceptions of the Islamic tradition that abound in today's world, this differentiation is essential to understanding the historical, as well as the contemporary, role of *shari'a* in Muslim life. Furthermore, an appreciation of this tension between moral and legal imperatives is critical to comprehending the nature of indeterminacy in *shari'a* law and the essential role of conscientious choices and personal commitments in the Islamic tradition. It may indeed be that most contemporary Muslims are not trained or well-read in the Islamic classical tradition, but I would dare claim that most conscientious Muslims would have a theologically founded intuitive and basic awareness of this tension and its consequences.

A clear illustrative example of this tension and its consequences arises in the case of all armed conflict, regardless of whether or not it is declared by a legitimate Muslim authority. Even assuming the existence of a legitimate authority with the legal right to declare war, this does not vitiate an individual Muslim's responsibility to refrain from joining an unjust war and to act conscientiously. Therefore, if a Muslim kills someone in a war that he/she conscientiously knows or should have known to be unjust, this Muslim will be held accountable in the Hereafter by God. Conversely, for disobeying a command that a Muslim conscientiously believes or reasonably should have believed to be unjust, such a Muslim can expect to be rewarded by God in the Hereafter. The subtle discursive role played by conscience and personal commitment in Islamic theology, and the indeterminacy that inevitably resulted, helped spur numerous sectarian movements and rebellions in Islamic history. As a result, there is a truly prodigious amount of discourses in the Islamic classical tradition struggling to balance between, on the one hand, moral and conscientious imperatives binding upon individual Muslims and, on the other, the demands of the rule of law.

The relevance of these classical debates to numerous contemporary situations is obvious. Most recently, unsophisticated versions of the classical arguments were reproduced in debates on the moral and theological responsibility of officers and soldiers who carried out orders to injure or kill demonstrators or rebels in Egypt, Tunisia, Syria, Libya, Bahrain and Yemen. The same discourses arose in the same countries in the context of competing claims as to whether those who died supporting the state or opposing it are martyrs (pl. *shuhada*, sing. *shahid*). Significantly, whether in the classical tradition or in the contemporary Muslim world, the revered status of martyrdom (*shahada*) is not limited to Muslims. In many cases, a non-Muslim killed supporting a just cause is considered a martyr, and so, for instance, it is very common to refer to Christians killed resisting the regimes of Mubarak in Egypt or Assad in Syria as martyrs. In Muslim discourses, Palestinian Christians killed resisting the Israeli occupation, such as those killed in the *intifada*, are regularly referred to as martyrs. However, as a function of the indeterminacy of *shari'a*, no single institution in the Muslim world has the power to grant or revoke the status of martyrdom to any Muslim or non-Muslim. It is readily recognised in both the classical tradition and in modern Muslim theology that only God has the ultimate and absolute right to grant the status of martyrdom. No human claim binds God, and no human institution has the absolute power to speak for God. Any determination based on *shari'a* attempts to make a well-informed approximation of the Divine will but it does not, and cannot, embody it. The issue of martyrdom, perhaps, is inherently controversial and highly politicised, and so indeterminacy is inevitable.

It would be inaccurate, however, to assume that *shari'a* is indeterminate in every case. And I am not making the simplistic argument, often employed by Muslim liberal secularists, that since the role of personal commitment and conscience is central in Islamic theology then, as a necessary consequence, there is no such thing as Islamic law. This type of argument is commonly deployed by Muslim intellectuals who think that it is an effective discursive and polemical strategy in denying *shari'a* any role in public life, but this argument lacks analytic integrity and is persuasive only to people who see little value in the perpetuation of the Islamic legal tradition into the modern age. I will return to this issue later; for now, my point is to underscore the ever present role of conscientious convictions and beliefs in *shari'a* discourses. Muslim jurists consistently tried to negotiate a balance between moral convictions on the one hand and the normative role of positive law (or the *ahkam*) on the other. This negotiative balancing act was not always resolved in favour of indeterminacy, but it led to something that is very familiar to the Western legal tradition: the differentiation between procedural, legalistic or temporal justice on the one hand, and theological, moral and celestial justice on the other.

Although it is not possible to do full justice to this issue in the present short chapter, for demonstrative purposes I will give a few examples of how the balance was struck in different scenarios debated in the classical Islamic tradition. One scenario involved the hypothetical case of a person whose grim job was to execute people sentenced to death by the state. What is the moral or religious obligation of such a person if he/she is ordered to execute a person whom he/she sincerely believes to be unjustly sentenced? If such an executioner carries out his/her lawful job and enforces the legal sentence, is the executioner accountable before God for doing something that he/she believes to be unjust? Most jurists agreed that the state has the right to dismiss or otherwise punish the executioner for failing to perform his/her job; but at the same time most jurists agreed that obeying orders against his/her conscience means that the executioner has committed a sin for which he/she will be held accountable in the Hereafter.

By way of contrast, Muslim jurists found the hypothetical case of a judge who is torn or conflicted about the evidence in a legal case and the demands of his/her conscience to be much harder. There is no dispute that judges must rule pursuant to the evidence before them in a case. But what if the personal conscience of a judge is at odds with the weight of the legal evidence? If the judge sets his/her personal conscience aside, and renders judgment solely on the basis of the legal evidence before him/her, has such a judge committed a sin for which he/she will be held accountable in the Hereafter? It is not possible to summarise accurately the responses of Muslim jurists. But one can say that the responses varied depending on the school of thought to which a jurist belonged. At one end of the range were those who argued that the legal process itself is the ultimate justice; a judge cannot commit a sin by ruling in favour of the evidence since a judge is bound by the rule of law. At the other end were those who argued that the rules of legal procedure cannot shield a judge from moral responsibility for acting against his/her conscience.

A further example demonstrating the tension between the rule of law and moral liability involves the moral status of a person who dies trying to defend his/her property. In classical Islamic jurisprudence, most jurists agreed that if a person dies defending his/her property against criminal assailants, or is killed as a result of refusing to pay unjust or exploitative taxes (*mukus*), such a person dies a martyr. However, Muslim theologians disagreed as to the moral status of a person who dies while defending the seizure of his/her property by the state pursuant to a lawful order or command. Assume for instance that pursuant to a binding legal judgment, a person's property is subject to seizure for a debt. The defendant, however, sincerely and honestly believes the judgment to be unfair and wrongful, and in the process of trying non-violently to prevent the seizure of his property, the defendant is killed. Most classical scholars argued that even if the state actions are legitimate and lawful, this would not deny the status of martyrdom to the deceased as long as he/she honestly and sincerely believed in the wrongfulness of the state's decision, and his/her belief was reasonable (*bi ta'wil muhtamal al-siha*). Significantly, in cases involving what were considered by the classical scholars to be categorical moral imperatives, few concessions were made to personal beliefs or commitments. So, for instance, no concessions were made to those committing the crime of *hiraba* (banditry, brigandage or highway robbery) even if they were acting pursuant to a sincerely held belief in the justness of their cause. Therefore, according to most classical scholars, those killed while terrorising and attacking innocent people indiscriminately cannot be considered martyrs regardless of their beliefs or cause.

Another scenario frequently cited by classical scholars involves the hypothetical case of a Muslim who travels or lives in non-Muslim lands in accordance with an agreement of safe conduct (*aqd aman*). According to scholars of the classical tradition, betrayal of the terms of the safe conduct is always sinful regardless of the personal motivations or justifications for such a violation, and regardless as well of whether a Muslim court has the jurisdiction to punish the culprit. Hence, if a Muslim usurps the property of or otherwise harms non-Muslims because of a sincerely held belief that he/she does so only as retaliation against an injustice suffered, the betrayal of trust is never justified and is sinful. The same obligation not to betray applies whether the agreement of safe conduct was pursuant to an individual agreement or pursuant to a treaty between states. Whether the Muslim state has the power to punish the act of betrayal depends (i) on whether a treaty obligates the Muslim state to do so and (ii) on whether the Muslim state subscribes to a theory of territorial jurisdiction or to a theory of universal jurisdiction over certain types of offences, such as the crimes of banditry (*hiraba*) or of treachery (*khiyanat al-ahd*).

Let us try to find a key to understanding this negotiative interplay, and how Muslim scholars went about striking the appropriate balance between legality and morality. When it came to setting out temporal obligations and determinations, Muslim jurists focused closely on the instrumentalities and mechanics of the law. Moral responsibility and its consequences were analysed by evaluating and applying specific normative guiding principles such as the maxims: do no harm (*la darar wa la dirar*); actions are evaluated per their intentions (*al-a'mal bi'l niyyat*); one wrong does not justify another (*la taziru wazira wizra ukhra*); humans cannot be obeyed if it means disobeying God (*la ta'ata li makhluqin fi ma'siyat al khaliq*); God is sovereign over God's rights but the state is the agent for people's rights (*Allahu awla bi huquqihi wa al-dawla wakilu huquq al-'ibad*); and so on. While the *ahkam* (positive law) is primarily concerned with instrumentalities of law and the deduction of positive commands, the *shari'a*, as a much broader concept, incorporates the axioms and principles of justice and morality, and engages positive law-making in a never ending dialectical negotiation. The interpretive dialectical process that negotiates the space between the *shari'a* and the *ahkam* is known as *fiqh* (understanding and comprehension). While the *ahkam* are determinative and positivistic, the *fiqh* is a broader and deeper undertaking that is often explorative and non-deterministic. The *fiqh* involves a process of appraising normative Divine-based imperatives in the light of numerous contingencies including customs, equity and public interest. It is critical to appreciate that the contingencies evaluated and weighed by the classical Muslim jurists were embedded in specific historical contexts. Even the moral and juridical hypothetical cases deployed by the classical jurists, such as those discussed above, were drawn with the context of particular historical contingencies in mind. Failing to appreciate the role of context and contingency in the Islamic jurisprudential tradition has led to persistent misunderstandings of Islamic law in the modern age.

As explained below, after colonialism Muslims experienced a vacuum of religious authority, and also a profound loss of collective historical memory and a near total sense of alienation from their own inherited intellectual tradition. In practical terms, not just lay Muslims but many graduates of contemporary Muslim seminaries can no longer appreciate the difference between pre-modern primers (or hornbooks) of positive law (*kutub al-ahkam*) and books of evaluative jurisprudence (*kutub al-fiqh*). Most have no way of evaluating the functions of determinacy and indeterminacy, or the roles of moral imperatives, legal commands and personal commitments in Islamic law. The loss of authoritativeness and the resulting chaotic condition is nowhere more evident than in contemporary Muslim discourses on *jihad* and the state.

JIHAD AND VIOLENCE IN ISLAMIC THEOLOGY AND LAW

Salam (peace and tranquility) is a central tenet of Islamic theology; it is considered a profound divine blessing to be cherished and vigilantly pursued. The absence of peace is identified in the Qur'an as a negative condition; it is variously described as a trial and tribulation, as a curse or punishment, or sometimes as a necessary evil. But the absence of peace is never in and of itself a positive or desirable condition. The Qur'an asserts that, if it had not been for divine benevolence, many mosques, churches, synagogues and homes would have been destroyed through violence, but God mercifully intervenes to put out the fires of war and to save human beings from their follies. In the Qur'anic discourse, unjustified and indiscriminate violence is described as *fasad fi al-ard* (spreading ruin and corruption on earth), and it is considered one of the gravest sins possible. Those who corrupt the earth by indiscriminately destroying lives, property and nature are designated as *mufsidun* (corruptors and evil-doers) who in effect wage war against God by dismantling the fabric of creation. Moreover, the Qur'an proclaims: 'God has made you into many nations and tribes so that you will come to know one another (*ta'arafu*). Those most honoured in the eyes of God are those who are most pious'. Most classical Muslim scholars reached the reasonable conclusion that war is not the means most conducive to getting 'to know one another (*ta'aruf*)'. *Ta'aruf* was considered a moral virtue, and also a form of *jihad*, but, like most forms of *jihad*, it was extensively treated in theological and not in legal sources.

In the Islamic classical tradition, most forms of *jihad* involve levels of moral struggle that are proper subjects for discourses on ethics and moral imperatives, and not for legal discourses. The best way to understand the imperative of *jihad* is on a scale ranging from the greatest moral worth to the least. Thus, according to traditions attributed to the Prophet Muhammad, the highest form of *jihad* (*al-jihad al-akbar*) is to struggle to know oneself and cleanse oneself of moral faults. According to the same traditions, armed struggle or warfare is the lower *jihad* (*al-jihad al-asghar*). The Prophet is reported to have said: 'the highest form of *jihad* is to speak a word of truth against [or, in some versions, before] a tyrant'. In the theological tradition, the pursuit of knowledge (*talab al-ilm*), supporting one's parents, speaking against social injustices, striving to end people's suffering or oppression, and supporting the poor are given as examples, among others, of *jihad*. However, the various forms of *jihad* were treated in books of Islamic *law* only if positivist or actual worldly rights or duties followed from them. Forms of *jihad* that involved rewards or liabilities only in the Hereafter would be dealt with in books on ethics and virtue (*akhlaq* or *kutub al-mawa'iz*), but would be omitted from legal primers.

THE QUR'ANIC DISCOURSE ON *JIHAD*

In Qur'anic usage, the word *jihad*, as such, is rarely utilised. The phrase consistently used in the Qur'an is 'strive for the sake of your Lord with your moncy and selves' (*jahidu fi sabili'llahi bi amwalikum wa anfusikum*). The Qur'an also refers to the *mujahidun* (those who strive for the sake of God). Qur'anic references to those who 'strive in the path of God' do not necessarily concern armed struggles. Instead, the Qur'an's references to warfare are more specific; the Qur'an uses the word *qital* to refer specifically to warfare. This is important. Qur'anic references to those who engage in *jihad* are broad and general exhortations; but references to *qital* or warfare are always qualified and made subject to particular restrictions and limitations. Therefore, early Muslims were not allowed to engage in warfare (*qital*) until God gave them specific permission to do so. 'Permission is now given to those who have been attacked to take up arms because they have suffered aggression (*dhulimu*), and God has the power to aid them' (Qur'an 22.39). In various passages the Qur'an instructs Muslims to fight those who fight them but not to transgress, for God does not approve of aggression. The Qur'an instructs Muslims to fight against persecutors; but if the enemy ceases hostilities and seeks peace, Muslims should seek peace as well (2.191–3). The Qur'an also sombrely reminds Muslims not to reject peace, and not to insist on fighting those who do not wish to fight them. If God had willed, God would have empowered their foes, and then they would have fought Muslims. God has the power to inspire in the hearts of non-Muslims a desire for peace, and Muslims must treat such a blessing with gratitude and appreciation, not with defiance and arrogance (4.90–1). In an important passage, the Qur'an in addressing the community of early believers explains that God does not forbid Muslims from socialising with and being kind to non-Muslims. Rather, God commands that Muslims fight against those who have persecuted them and have aggressively driven Muslims from their lands and homes (60.7–9). In one passage that has received considerable attention in the contemporary world, the Qur'an exhorts the believers to fight against the unbelievers until they pay the poll tax (*jizya*) and have been completely subdued (9.29); I return to this passage below.

One of the most overlooked aspects of the Qur'anic discourse on the subject of war is that it places itself within a larger Biblical context. The Qur'an emphasises that God has repeatedly ordained that believers should fight in the support of Abrahamic prophets. Just as Israelites were instructed to fight in support of Moses, David and other prophets, Muslims are now commanded to fight alongside Muhammad (another Abrahamic prophet).[2] The importance of this Qur'anic link to Biblical battles and wars is obvious

---

[2] See Qur'an 2.246–51, 3.146, 5.24, 9.111.

but critical. The Qur'anic discourse on waging war is normative but thoroughly historicised and contextual. This Qur'anic discourse, like the rest of *shari'a*, is highly contingent and non-deterministic. As such, it invites inquiry into its normative principles and into the positive rules that follow from these principles.

JUST CAUSE AND WARFARE

In light of the Qur'anic discourse, classical Muslim jurists posed the question: why did the prophets fight? Did the Abrahamic prophets, including Muhammad, wage war because unbelief is morally culpable and unbelievers in all circumstances must be fought, or did God authorise warfare only as a last measure against oppression and aggression? Depending on the school of thought and the historical period, pre-modern jurists gave a number of responses. After the fourth/tenth century, the clear majority of jurists maintained that fighting non-Muslims must be in direct proportion to the actual threat and risk they pose to Muslims. According to most, belief or unbelief is a matter between a person and God, but Muslims may fight only to repel or avert harm or aggression (*li daf' sharrihim* or *daf' al-sa'il*). Interestingly, regardless of their position on the justification for war, there is a near consensus among classical Muslim jurists that non-combatants – such as children, women, people of advanced age, monks, hermits, priests or anyone else who does not seek to or cannot fight Muslims – are inviolable and may not be targeted even during ongoing hostilities.

Indisputably, pre-modern jurists understood that there are competing moral imperatives setting aggression against non-aggression, oppression against lack of oppression, and justice against injustice. But how they interpreted the implications of these moral imperatives was very much contingent and contextual. In other words, it was a by-product of the historical moment in which they lived and of the prevailing norms of the age. Nowhere is this more evident than in the legal and jurisdictional, but not necessarily moral, territorial divisions invented by the classical jurists. According to the classical tradition, the world was divided into three possible categories: the abode of Islam (*dar al-Islam*), abode of hostilities (*dar al-harb* or *dar al-kufr*) and the abode of non-belligerence (*dar al-'ahd*, *dar al-sulh* or *dar muwada'a*). These abodes were not necessarily substantive moral categories, but pragmatic divisions that reflected the way Muslim jurists read the geo-political divisions of their age. Moral and theological discussions on the appropriate categories reflected a far more complex and dynamic reality; the abodes multiplied in response to sectarian divisions within the Muslim world as well as in response to ethical assessments of the injustices suffered in particular Muslim kingdoms. Therefore, Muslim ethicists and theologians debated categories such as the abode of justice (*dar al-'adl*), the abode of true belief (*dar al-iman*), the abode of truth (*dar al-haqq*), and many others. When positive legal regulations came into tension with moral imperatives, many classical jurists resolved the tension by inventing a legal fiction. This arose with the question of the legal status of Muslims residing in non-Muslim lands. Some classical jurists argued that non-Muslim countries that permitted Muslim minorities freely and openly to practise their faith should be afforded the treatment due to countries of the abode of Islam.

I mentioned above the payment of *jizya* (poll tax) by non-Muslims. Contrary to the understanding of many non-Muslims and some Muslims, in the Islamic tradition such payment was not raised to the level of a moral imperative. The collection of levies in lieu of warfare is a practice that predates Islam; poll taxes were common practice among the Byzantines, Assyrians and pre-Islamic Arabs. The Prophet and first generation of Muslims did not always collect poll taxes, exempting particular Arabian tribes or nations (such as Nubians and Abyssinians) and all non-combatants, including clergy, churches and at times also serfs and peasants, from the *jizya*. Especially after the fourth/tenth century, various groups of Muslims living under non-Muslim tutelage and Muslim kingdoms bordering powerful Christian states paid levies in order to avoid hostilities. Understanding that the issue of poll taxes is an issue of negotiated political interests and exigencies (referred to as *siyasa shar'iyya*), most Muslim jurists deferred to rulers on the question of whether it should be collected. The focus of legal sources was on the obligations and entitlements that followed from the existence of the *jizya*. However, most of the juristic discourses concentrated on technical conflict of laws issues, such as when *dhimmis* (non-Muslims living in Muslim kingdoms) are entitled to self-governance, and what types of cases and litigation would have to be brought in Muslim courts.

THE ISLAMIC TRADITION AND MODERN NATION STATE

The real challenge that confronts contemporary Muslims is how to negotiate and reconstruct their inherited living tradition (*turath*). Until the age of colonialism, Islamic law was the law of the land; it was the platform upon which Muslims not only resolved conflicts but also negotiated issues of identity, normative obligations and the space between public interests and personal commitments. It is true that theocratic systems of governance were alien to the Islamic tradition and that theocracies, such as Saudi Arabia and Iran, are post-colonial inventions. But the legal institutions of Islamic law and Muslim jurists – as a class that commanded a great deal of deference and influence – played a critical role in negotiating the power dynamics between the rulers and the ruled. Muslim jurists in the pre-modern age served the state by acting as a medium for legitimacy and stability, but at the same time the institutions of Islamic law functioned as the instruments for the rule of law. Muslim jurists restrained the excesses of the state and limited its ability to speak for the divine, while playing a mediating role in political and social conflicts. The Islamic legal system worked through locally based guilds of law that functioned very much like a common law system. With the advent of colonialism came the age of legal codifications and the importation of Western legal systems. Eventually, Islamic law guilds were abolished or lost their autonomy from the state and their mediating roles as well. Having lost the ability to negotiate the powers of the state, Islamic law guilds also lost their relevance and legitimacy. But contemporary autocratic states not only abolished the law guilds, they also controlled and dominated all of the influential religious institutions in their respective nations. In doing so, these modern Muslim states induced a serious vacuum and crisis in religious authority.

At the risk of over-simplification, I think one can say that since the advent of modernity, the Muslim world has been locked into a dichotomous cycle. On the one hand, there are those who attempt to challenge the post-colonial condition by searching for a medium through which they can embrace contemporaneous realities, but who at the same time anchor this reality in an indigenously authentic rootedness. In the case of the Muslim world, being rooted in an indigenous culture and history has most often meant an attempt to find ways of reclaiming the role of *shar'a*, in whatever way this *shari'a* is understood or interpreted. On the other hand, there are those who see themselves as pragmatists (or progressives) and therefore embrace the modern condition with all its consequences, bitter and sweet, and who consider attempts at re-inventing some indigenously rooted culture as unrealistic and reactionary. The latter group, in one form or another, has ruled Muslim countries since colonialism, and the results have been abysmal. However, Islamically inspired regimes in countries such as Pakistan, Sudan, Iran, Saudi Arabia and others have not done much better.

In the past decade a critical development has led to an important shift in this dichotomy. There has been the promise of a growing consensus in the Muslim world over the necessary merits of democracy and basic human rights. Democracy and basic human rights are seen as part of the universal and necessary heritage of humanity, and the means for realising an adequate sense of autonomy and dignity. This does not mean that puritanical religious groups have vanished from the Muslim world, but there is a growing distrust of all holistic and totalistic ideologies demanding that individuals dilute themselves into some larger cause that serves a theoretical public good. Without a doubt, there is marked distrust of any group that claims to know and selflessly to represent the Divine will.[3] Nevertheless, I fear that this democratic awakening will be short-lived if, in the name of basic civic rights and equal citizenship, Muslims are once again forced to choose between a presumed enlightened modernity and their own native sense of indigenous identity and culture.

Many among the Western-educated Muslim intellectuals have transplanted liberal democratic secularism into their own discourses with little if any modification. The argument typically proposed by such intellectuals is that democratic citizenship requires that all religious arguments or reasoning be kept out of the public sphere. Religion is purely a matter of private conscience and commitment; only so-called rational arguments can be made the basis of public law in modern democracies. Although many of these intellectuals realise that there are many forms of secularism, and that a strict separation between state and religion is a reality only in very few Western democracies, they quickly resort to the simplistic logic of excluding all religiously-based normative values unless such values are couched in the supposedly neutral logic of rational reasoning and public interest. The implications of this position are monumental, and fraught with risk. According to this argument, there would be no place for references to God in public discourses, including for instance the recitation of the Qur'an on a publicly owned television station or the teaching of religion in public schools. Everything from banking and finance laws to the prohibition of illicit drugs, of pornography or of prostitution could only be articulated and defended through non-religious terms and reasoning. It is worth noting that this position is different from the Rawlsian argument for overlapping consensus. In the above position – as is not the case in the Rawlsian consensus – consensus should never include allowing religion a role in the public sphere.

The notion of self-restraint, within a democratic system of governance, in asserting any argument, religious or not, that is inaccessible to those others

---

[3] MS Fish, *Are Muslims Distinctive? A look at the evidence* (Oxford, 2011), pp 45–68, 229–49; JL Esposito and D Mogahed, *Who speaks for Islam? What a billion Muslims really think* (New York, 2007), pp 46–57.

who do not share its premises seems to me to make a lot of sense.[4] But such self-restraint in the construction of public arguments in order to maintain accessibility and be as inclusive as possible is a far cry from the principled exclusion of religious discourses from the public sphere that is espoused by Abdullahi An-Naʿim and others. Intellectuals espousing this strict secularist position usually assure Muslims that they would be free to follow *shariʿa* as a matter of personal commitment, as long as *shariʿa* stays purely within the private sphere. So, for instance, *shariʿa* maxims such as, 'Do no harm (*la darar*)' or 'Harm must be removed (*al-darar yuzal*)' could not be asserted in the public sphere as *shariʿa* principles but only in neutral or non-religious terms. Furthermore, the rules applicable to marriage, divorce and even to burial and other funeral arrangements could not be based on religious reasons but must be based on rational public grounds.

I have numerous philosophical as well as practical objections to this school of thought, but this is not the place to set them out. I think that different cultural and national contexts call for different negotiated relationships between *shariʿa* and the public sphere. What could be an appropriate solution for a relatively small Muslim minority living in Western liberal democracies cannot be generalised to Muslims living in societies where for centuries Islam and *shariʿa* have been interwoven in the inherited public consciousness. It is analytically inadequate to generalise our discourse on the public sphere without differentiating between, on the one hand, those cultures that autonomously entered modernity (let alone those that created modernity) on the basis of normative values at odds with religion, and, on the other, those cultures that experienced religion in a very different way. We must differentiate between cultures that underwent secularisation as part of a process artificially imposed by hegemonic colonial powers that acted to exclude the institutions of *shariʿa* from the public sphere, and cultures that developed secularism as a home-grown solution. The point is this: between the opposite poles of (i) religion dominating the public sphere and (ii) the exclusion of religion from the public sphere, there are numerous possible negotiated accommodations. If in the public sphere the ethos of human rights and democracy are starkly contrasted with the ethos of *shariʿa*, and Muslim cultures are told that the public sphere can be occupied only by one ethos and not the other, I fear that the results will be disastrous.

Perhaps realising the dangers of this contrast, many Muslim secularists go to great lengths to attempt to anchor the principles of human rights and

---

[4] See K Abou El Fadl, 'Muslim minorities and self-restraint in liberal democracies', (1996) 29 Loy LA Int'l & Comp L Rev 1525.

democracy in the Islamic tradition. But it strikes me as self-defeating to use the Islamic tradition to justify a universal humanistic ethos, only to turn around and exclude the Islamic tradition itself from the public sphere. It is rather disingenuous to use Islam to justify the exclusion of Islam or to contend that in order to truly respect *shari'a*, *shari'a* should be kept out of the public sphere. It seems particularly problematic, in justifying the exclusion of religion from the public sphere, to rely on the fact that the state until the modern age had never successfully monopolised the authority to speak for the Divine or on the fact that a church representing the Divine will has never materialised in Islam, or to cite the indeterminism of *shari'a* law and the existence of multiple jurisprudential schools of thought. Just because all people have an equal right to speak for God, it does not logically follow that all voices claiming to speak in God's name must be excluded from the public sphere. A more fundamental objection, however, is that not all claims to represent the Divine will are equal. In fact, if one were to summarise the history of jurisprudential thought in the Islamic tradition, it could be described as a consistently evolving effort to set systematic, objective standards for making and evaluating claims to know the Divine will, not least in the realisation of people's welfare and justice. Not all claims to be speaking for God's will are equal; some are more legitimate and authoritative than others.[5]

Part of the systematic problem that has plagued post-colonial Muslim cultures is that reformers who have sought to establish an uncompromising form of secularism in Muslim societies have rarely been well versed in the tradition they seek to exclude. While they invest a great deal of intellectual effort in mastering the thought and heritage of Western liberal secularism, they are rarely competent in the Islamic intellectual tradition. Instead of dealing with the normative imperatives and intellectual subtleties of the Islamic moral tradition with the analytic and critical rigour that this tradition rightly deserves, in what has become a persistent pattern of discourse they propose a highly essentialised and superficial narrative of the Islamic tradition and *shari'a*, but only to exclude the inherited Islamic heritage from public life. Not surprisingly, this essentialised and exclusionary discourse only invites an equally essentialised and exclusionary counter-discourse. Despite good intentions, the exclusionary discourse of what can be called vulgar or puritanical secularism, instead of helping Muslims to negotiate an authentically rooted democratic and humanitarian

---

[5] See K Abou El Fadl, *Speaking in God's Name: Islamic law, authority and women* (Oxford, 2001), pp 9–69.

cultural solution, only locks Muslims in a polarised and reactive social dynamic.

Exclusionary vulgar or puritanical secularism is confronted by equally uncompromising forms of Islamism. Well-intentioned secularists who have sought to keep religion out of the public sphere have only succeeded in spurring puritanical reactive religious movements that construct an equally essentialized and artificial view of Islamic history and law. Both puritanical secularists and religious puritans ignore the complex interplay in the *shariʿa* tradition between moral imperatives and positive laws. Both ignore the fact that *shariʿa*, which embodies sacred moral imperatives, engages the private and the public spheres without dominating either of them. As discussed above, *shariʿa* does not function simply as a sacred law nor is it simply a set of temporal positive commands. However, in the same way that puritanical secularists ignore the role of *shariʿa* in the public sphere, religious puritans ignore the role of *shariʿa* in the private sphere. Religious puritans pretend that personal commitments and private consciences are immaterial to *shariʿa* obligations. At the same time, puritanical secularists pretend that *shariʿa* can be limited to the realm of personal commitments and private consciences without regard to *shariʿa*'s role in defining public norms and public moral imperatives. Religious puritans assume that since private commitments are subject to countless contingencies (what they would call *hawa* or whims), then the voices of individuals must be ignored, and the state should be empowered to speak for God. Yet puritanical secularists assume that the innumerable contingencies mediating personal commitments mean that no one should be allowed to speak for God in the public arena; indeed, there should be an absence of God, altogether, from such an arena.

It is encouraging that the secularists and Islamists of the past decade are all a part of the growing consensus in favour of democracy and human rights. Few secularists today are Marxists or Communists, and Islamists have grown weary of the centralised powers of the modern states. Nevertheless, I fear that one exclusion only begets another. If so, the threat is that this emerging recent consensus will be aborted as Muslims are once again locked between two exclusionary and uncompromising orientations.

In the summer of 2011, I had an opportunity to observe this dynamic first hand. Relying on the logic propounded by liberal secularists, Egyptian election laws banned the use of any religious symbolism or rhetoric. The impact of these laws was polarising and divisive, and constituted one further step towards aborting the Egyptian revolution. It is rather typical of Egyptian culture that the public met these laws with a stream of mocking jokes: some wondered whether it is lawful for candidates to greet audiences with 'Peace be upon you' (*al-salamu alaykum*) or to commence speeches 'In the name of God the most Merciful and Compassionate' (*bismi'llahi al-rahman al-rahim*). The reality is that Islamic normative values, which are a part of the living tradition of *shariʿa*, already exist in the collective consciousness of Muslims. As such, religious values already occupy a prominent public space in Muslim cultures. Any theoretical or legal framework that fails to tailor itself to the complex reality of these cultures, and carefully to negotiate between the inherited tradition and the normative commitments necessary for democracy and human rights, will do more harm than good. Democracy and human rights cannot be achieved without normative commitments at the individual and societal levels. It is the duty of Muslim intellectuals to do the cumbersome and toilsome task of persuading their co-religionists that a private and public commitment to democracy and human rights is also a commitment to *shariʿa*, and also that in the contemporary world a commitment in favour of *shariʿa* is best realised through a commitment to democracy and human rights.

PART IV

Prospect: equality before God and before the law

I want to press the distinction between 'programmatic secularism' and what some have called 'procedural secularism'. It is the distinction between the empty public square of a merely instrumental liberalism, which allows maximal private licence, and a crowded and argumentative public square which acknowledges the authority of a legal mediator or broker whose job it is to balance and manage real difference. The empty public square of programmatic secularism implies in effect that the almost value-free atmosphere of public neutrality and the public invisibility of specific commitments is enough to provide sustainable moral energy for a properly self-critical society. But it is not at all self-evident that people can so readily detach their perspectives and policies in social or political discussion from fundamental convictions that are not allowed to be mentioned or manifested in public.

– From the Archbishop of Canterbury's Lecture, 'Secularism, Faith and Freedom', in Rome, 23 November 2006.

The rule of law is thus not the enshrining of priority for the universal/abstract dimension of social existence but the establishing of a space accessible to everyone in which it is possible to affirm and defend a commitment to human dignity as such, independent of membership in any specific human community or tradition, so that when specific communities or traditions are in danger of claiming finality for their own boundaries of practice and understanding, they are reminded that they have to come to terms with the actuality of human diversity – and that the only way of doing this is to acknowledge the category of 'human dignity as such', a non-negotiable assumption that each agent (with his or her historical and social affiliations) could be expected to have a voice in the shaping of some common project for the well-being and order of a human group . . . If the paradoxical idea which I have sketched is true – that universal law and universal right are a way of recognising what is least fathomable and controllable in the human subject – theology still waits for us around the corner of these debates, however hard our culture may try to keep it out. And, as you can imagine, I am not going to complain about that.

– From the Archbishop of Canterbury's Lecture, 'Civil and religious law in England', in the Royal Courts of Justice, 7 February 2008.

CHAPTER 19

Equal before God

David F Ford

Reading through the chapters in this volume with a view to responding to it and looking to the future, I have been immediately struck by two things.

The first is the debt of gratitude owed to Rowan Williams, then Archbishop of Canterbury, for opening up the question of *shariʿa* in Britain in the way he did. It was courageous to face the issue so squarely in his 2008 lecture; in the media storm that followed, the basis for which is so helpfully described by Robin Griffith-Jones, even greater courage was required to hold his ground and respond so patiently and thoroughly to many critics. In retrospect, it seems the sort of statesmanlike contribution to public debate that few others could have made and that exemplifies a healthy way of addressing issues surrounding religion in the life of the nation. It is not that his way of handling the question of *shariʿa* in Britain can now, after the misrepresentations have been identified, be seen as uncontroversial; rather, he has placed the question firmly on the table in a way that, if one returns to his original lecture, helps to ensure that it can be debated with appropriate categories and concepts, and without the sorts of misunderstandings (not least about the nature of *shariʿa*) that are widespread (even in pronouncements of the European Court of Human Rights (ECtHR)). Not least among the benefits of his lecture has been the impetus for drawing together the distinguished contributors to this volume, producing an expert, multi-faceted approach to the topic that should make it required reading far beyond Britain.

The second striking feature is the vital significance of long-term institutions. The Archbishop's lecture was part of the Inner and Middle Temple's festival celebrating the four hundredth anniversary of the Temple Church being entrusted to the Inns of Court by King James I. There is such a thing as institutional courage (perhaps even rarer than individual courage[1]) and

---

[1] It is, of course, often due largely to an individual that an institution will dare to take an initiative – in this case it is important to note that neither the Archbishop's lecture nor this volume would have happened without the vision and perseverance of Robin Griffith-Jones.

the Inns displayed it by bringing to prominence an issue they knew to be controversial. Moreover, as with the Archbishop, the ensuing storm did not deter them from persisting with the debate, of which the present volume is the fruit. It is hard to think of another institution that could fulfil this role on this topic so effectively, and it underlines the importance for our society of robust, independent institutions that have the public good at heart and can take the long view. At their best, both the Church of England and the Inns of Court do this, and both are all too easily criticised, stereotyped or even ridiculed by those with very different interests and perspectives. It is good to see them come together in relation to a matter of considerable importance for many societies in the twenty-first century.

BEFORE GOD, IN A CONFLICTUAL HISTORY

It is such courage and concern for the long-term common good that can be encouraged by being conscious of living before a God who is good, just and eternal. Yet over the centuries God has also been invoked to justify some of the deepest, most violent and longest-lasting conflicts. Religions (and the quasi-religious ideologies such as nationalism, imperialism, fascism and communism that have been such a feature of the past century) have often been involved in clashes whose severity has been exacerbated to the point of violence by the absoluteness of their claims. Europe in the early modern period after the Protestant Reformation was torn apart by religious wars, especially the Thirty Years' War (1618–48), and England suffered its own religion-related violence during its Civil War (1642–51). Debates in England about religion in relation to law are part of this history. It cannot be discussed at length now, but it is worth trying to sum up the situation, shaped by that history, into which questions relating to *shari'a* are now being introduced.

One way of telling the story is of a public sphere becoming increasingly secularised as the power and influence of religion decline and religion is effectively relegated to the private sphere. The result is a secular society (with public vestiges of religion) in which any talk of *shari'a* is bound to seem retrograde and inappropriate. I would argue[2] that the situation is more complex and less linear. There is, as several contributors to this volume contend, no simple opposition between the secular and the religious; nor is there a simple succession from one to the other; many religious voices have supported developments that have led to the present position. There have

[2] See DF Ford, *Shaping Theology: engagements in a religious and secular world* (Oxford, 2007).

been centuries of changes, conflicts and negotiations in order to arrive at the particular settlement we see today. This might be characterised as *a minimalist religious and secular settlement for a complexly religious and secular society*. By minimalist I mean the opposite of a settlement that, like France or China, strongly prescribes a secular (in the sense of non-religious) framework, or, like Iran, strongly prescribes a religious framework. Williams' distinction between 'procedural' and 'programmatic' secularism is helpful here: Britain has a procedurally secular settlement that regulates the public sphere so that it can be genuinely pluralist, with no religious or secular group being paramount; France is programmatically secular, Iran programmatically religious. Given the absolutist claims often made by both religious and secular groups there is a need for procedures – the evolution of customs, the negotiation of rules, the enactment of laws – that protect all from the absolutist bids of any.

In my opinion, there is more pressure towards secular than towards religious absolutism and intolerance in Britain today. This is one reason why it is important to make the sorts of points proposed by many in this volume about *shari'a*, countering misunderstandings and stereotypes, and denying that either the Archbishop of Canterbury or the vast majority of the Muslim community want, for example, anything like Saudi Arabian criminal law to be implemented in this country. Such points help to resist extreme secularist rhetoric which thrives on the type of media frenzy that followed the Archbishop's lecture, using misrepresentations and fears to promote programmatic secularism as the best way to avoid the pathologies allegedly being programmatically promoted by religions.

Yet the dispute about *shari'a* is one of many indications that the historic religious and secular settlement worked out in this country is facing serious challenges. Aspects of the settlement in other spheres of society, from the composition of the House of Lords or the implications of human rights legislation to the existence of faith schools or the code of practice for adoption agencies, are also being problematised or renegotiated, often accompanied by bitter disagreement. A good deal of comment relevant to these challenges is offered by contributors to this volume; I want to make two further points.

The first is that the global context within which our debates are being conducted is that of a resurgence of religion in the public sphere. One of the earliest accounts of this by the sociologist José Casanova is still instructive.[3] He describes how in the 1980s, after such events as the Iranian Revolution

---

[3] J Casanova, *Public Religions in the Modern World* (Chicago and London, 1994).

and the rise of Solidarity in Poland, the very secular public sphere (think of fascism, communism and most forms of capitalism) of the earlier twentieth century was changed. It did not mean that every aspect of the dominant secularisation theories were rendered implausible, but significant parts of them were – such as the inevitable decline in modern societies in the numbers of people practising religions, or the shift of religion almost wholly into the private sphere. Nor did it mean that some societies or parts of them were not, by a range of measurements, becoming more secular. Rather, it offered a more nuanced picture of multiple modernities, some more secularist, some more religiously inflected, and most with complex mixtures, thus undermining the dominant conception of linear, one-way secularisation in the face of the changes of modernity. These developments have been a stimulus to extremists on both sides. Religious extremists have been encouraged to bid for dominance for their own brand of religion. Secular extremists, alarmed at the blow to their confidence in the escalator of modernity carrying all of us automatically into a state of secular dominance, saw that they would have to be more aggressive if this dominance were to be realised. The practical implication of this is that those (among whom I am included) who want a flourishing pluralist society, programmatically neither religious nor secular, should make appropriate alliances (among and between religious and secular groups) in order to achieve it.

The second point is that wiser responses to the current challenges to our settlement are only likely if there is a better quality of wisdom-seeking. Many initial responses to the Archbishop's 2008 lecture might be embraced by the biblical category of 'foolishness' (which the Book of Proverbs often associates with unwise verbal communication). The long-term health of our society requires settings where there can be co-operative wisdom-seeking both about the specific issue of the role of *shariʿa* in relation to English law and about the broader matters that this raises. Wisdom is always needed, but finding it is especially demanding in the midst of complex changes such as we are experiencing. The difficulty is compounded when those who are seeking wisdom owe allegiances to very different traditions.

Mashood Baderin deploys in this volume his typology for categorising the role of religion in relation to law: the separationist, the accommodationist and the double-edged. This is strikingly parallel to the options facing religions in responding to the changes brought by modernity, including various forms of secularisation: they may try to reject the changes, taking an anti-modern position; they may accommodate themselves to them, and risk losing their traditional identity in assimilation to the rest of society; or they may be 'double-edged', rejecting some aspects and welcoming others, maintaining an identity that is in continual critical and constructive engagement with the changes and challenges. This third way is, I suggest, the one preferred by most members of religious traditions in this country. The balance between rejection and welcome on specific issues may vary enormously between groups and among individuals within groups, but these are continually involved in the task of discernment, seeking ways both to be true to their traditions and to respond wisely to new events, situations and ideas. The Archbishop's adoption of Ayelet Shachar's concept of 'transformative accommodation' is in line with this mainstream wisdom.

A key practical question for the future is where the thinking, discussion and deliberation needed by our society to arrive at wisdom in this area might take place. I see four main sites: within each religious community; through inter-religious engagement between faith communities; within the institutions, organisations and settings where people from many faiths and none learn and work together; and throughout society in debates that require increasing religious literacy. The next section will deal with these in turn.

SETTINGS FOR WISDOM-SEEKING

Within each religious community

I have already suggested the basic task of wisdom-seeking within particular communities that are faced with the issues discussed in this volume: trying to discern what to reject and what to welcome, and on that basis in new situations to generate fresh transformations of what they have inherited. This has to be specific to each tradition, and most of the centres for education, scholarship and thought leadership with regard to any particular tradition are, and are likely to remain, those affiliated to that tradition. The world's billion or so Roman Catholics, for example, are mainly served by Catholic institutions even though Catholic scholars and thinkers are also present in many others. In their terms they face the triple task of deep engagement with the past (what the Second Vatican Council called *ressourcement*), deep understanding of contemporary thought, developments and events (what the Second Vatican Council called *aggiornamento*) and wise discernment of the lessons of both for the present and future.[4] Other traditions face analogous tasks and fulfil them in various educational and other settings.

---

[4] For my reading of the challenges facing Christian churches, see DF Ford, *The Future of Christian Theology* (Oxford, 2011).

Given the radical nature of the challenges it is not surprising that no tradition has reason to be complacent. Building up healthy settings for seeking and passing on the learning and wisdom of particular traditions ought to be a top priority for each. In this regard, perhaps the most important set of institutional initiatives in this country today is seen in the development of Muslim educational institutions that are trying to combine classical Muslim learning with engagement in the British context and the academic disciplines of the modern university.[5]

Through inter-faith engagement

There has been a welcome blossoming of inter-faith activity in recent years. At the very least, given the involvement of religions in many of the world's conflict zones, this must be one of the most necessary fields to cultivate if the twenty-first century is to avoid catastrophe. At best, the prospect of the religions drawing together on their resources for peace-building, and for making other contributions to the flourishing of our world, is not only attractive but already exemplified in some places. Yet the challenge of inter-faith wisdom-seeking is enormous. A good deal of rhetoric (including some in this volume) is about 'common ground'. It is, of course, welcome when common ground can be found, but in many important matters profound differences remain, not only in understandings and beliefs but also in practices, attitudes, sensibilities, power-relations and institutions.

Shariʿa seems clearly to be one area where comprehensive agreement is highly unlikely. Yet this should by no means discourage inter-faith engagement around it. On the contrary, in my experience, the best inter-faith conversation faces stubborn differences squarely and tries to improve the quality of disagreements. In many situations, from family life to international relations, disagreements are bound to persist, but their quality matters greatly: each side may yet be committed to deepening their understanding of the other and seeking out non-violent and non-alienating ways of living with them – even friendship can flourish across radical disagreements.

The aim of inter-faith engagement, therefore, is not primarily consensus (welcome though that is if possible) but to enable the parties, through the encounter, to go deeper into their own faith, deeper into the faiths of others,

---

[5] The one I know best is the recently founded Cambridge Muslim College, most of whose students have completed up to six years of study in traditional Muslim institutions before they take a course which combines that with studies aimed at thinking through their faith and practice in dialogue with Western modernity and today's British society.

deeper into joint commitment to the common good beyond their own communities, and, ideally, deeper into the community of those who are committed to those three deepenings.[6] This could be seen as a recipe that might produce the inter-faith conditions for the sort of wise faith required for 'transformative accommodation'; but it is also possible to imagine it (for example, in circumstances where the secular response to *shari'a* takes the line adopted by the ECtHR) leading to better inter-faith understanding and collaboration without further legal pluralism.

Within institutions, organisations and other shared settings

If that third deepening in commitment to the common good is to happen, it needs to be worked out in the many settings where people of faith and others, who do not identify themselves in that way, come together in the common life of society. Here multiple affiliations and loyalties are normal, and inter-faith relations are complicated further by relations with those who are non-religious or vaguely religious in various ways. These are the settings where the complexly religious and secular (or multi-religious and multi-secular) character of our society is most evident. This volume has been about one dimension of society, that of law, which relates to most settings in society but has its own distinct institutions, such as the Inns of Court, where the relevant wisdom-seeking is especially focused.

In this regard, one vital point to note about the Inns is that they are, among other things, educational institutions where those entering the legal profession are taught and apprenticed. It is, inevitably, on the educational institutions of society that a special burden of wisdom-seeking falls, and in the case of English law and *shari'a* this includes not only the universities with their law schools and departments of theology and religious studies but also the Muslim legal and educational institutions where law is discussed, deliberated upon and taught.[7] A challenge for the future is how best to bring such settings into fruitful engagement with each other for the sake of the common good.

It is worth taking encouragement from the fact that, in some of its universities, this country leads the world in having developed the field generally called 'theology and religious studies'. Here our complexly

---

[6] See the discussion of inter-faith engagement in Ford, *The Future of Christian Theology*, supra n 4.
[7] I have noted, supra n 5, a new type of Muslim institution exemplified by the Cambridge Muslim College, where the engagement between classical Muslim learning and modernity is internalised; these need to be complemented by settings inhabited by both Muslims and others.

religious and secular society has generated a setting where those of many faiths and none, together with those who are undecided or searching, can study and discuss the questions raised by, between and about the religions. This happens through a range of academic disciplines, including theology, which can pursue questions of meaning, truth and practice relevant to the religions and the rest of society. In other words, those who believe themselves to be living before God can pursue the truth and implications of that in dialogue with those with whom they may deeply disagree. At their best, such settings enable qualities of wise faith and wise understanding of faiths that are, I consider, most valuable to the flourishing of a pluralist society such as ours.[8]

Through religious literacy for a democratic society

For different groups in our pluralist, democratic society to live in peace and have the debates needed on many matters of common concern, it is a great advantage for them to understand each other better. One aspect of that is religious literacy, well exemplified by the Religious Literacy Leadership Programme.[9] This is funded by the Higher Education Funding Council for England and works with an increasing number of universities (at present sixty) to work out what religious literacy might mean for them in many areas besides teaching, learning and research – for example, in admissions, student support, campus relations, food and catering, accommodation, health, discipline, timetabling, counselling, student societies, issues of equality, diversity and discrimination, chaplaincies, and faith and worship spaces. On the idea of religious literacy the programme says:

> We suggest that religious literacy lies ... in having the knowledge and skills to recognise faith as a legitimate and important area for public attention, a degree of general knowledge about at least some religious traditions and an awareness of and ability to find out about others. Its purpose is to avoid stereotypes, respect and learn from others, and build good relations across difference. In this it is a civic endeavour rather than a theological or religious one, and seeks to support a strong cohesive multi-faith society, which is inclusive of people from all faith traditions and none in a context which is largely suspicious and anxious about religion and belief. The overall aim may be summarised as seeking to inform intelligent,

---

[8] Cf Ford, *The Future of Christian Theology*, supra n 4, chapter 8.
[9] The programme is led by Adam Dinham at the Faiths and Civil Society Unit in Goldsmiths, University of London, and ten Vice-Chancellors together with many other leaders and managers are collaborating in it. See A Dinham and SH Jones, 'An Analysis of Challenges of Religious Faith, and Resources for Meeting them, for University Leaders' (2010) and 'Programme Evaluation Phase I: September 2010-February 2011' (2010), both accessible at <http://religiousliteracyhe.org/leadership-resources/publications>.

thoughtful and rooted approaches to religious faith which countervail unhelpful knee-jerk reactions based on fear and stereotype.[10]

That might seem tailor-made for dealing with many of the responses to the Archbishop's lecture.

I would suggest that if religious literacy is good for universities it is also good for society as a whole. There is widespread ignorance, misinformation, prejudice, discrimination and hostility in relation to religions in our societies, but there is also great potential for interesting learning, fascinating experiences, better community relations, cultural and spiritual enrichment and long term relationships across the differences of religion. Good public education can help reverse the negative and enhance the positive. If this were to be taken sufficiently seriously there would be more possibility of building the sorts of partnerships of difference, based on particular integrities and mutual understanding, that can enhance a modern pluralist society. The task of communicating more widely the understandings of *shari'a* offered in the contributions to this volume has hardly begun.

EQUAL BEFORE GOD

In a pluralist society 'equality before God' is regarded in many very different ways. Some reject the reality of God; those who accept God's reality identify God very diversely; and there is a wide variety of ideas about equality. The sort of pluralist society I have been imagining is one in which all these can be brought into public discourse – where there is, for example, no exclusion of theological or religious discourse from public debate. It is a vision of public discussion being enriched by many traditions and by attempts to translate and understand across traditions. The ideal is of that fourfold deepening described above, in the context of intensive engagements aimed at working out how to live, converse and work together in particular settings and spheres (such as the law and its institutions, schools and universities, businesses, local communities and so on) and a broad attempt across society to raise the level of religious literacy (and, of course, other forms of literacy too).

I would hope that many might share this ideal and that others who do not might be persuaded of it. I would also hope that each tradition might take seriously the invitation that it involves: to articulate its own distinctive understanding of law, justice and the shaping of society, and its contribution to the public debate about *shari'a* and legal pluralism. It is vital to the

---

[10] See Dinham and Jones, 'An Analysis of Challenges', supra n 9.

cohesion of a pluralist society that there may be many different reasons for sharing in any agreed practical settlement – the Jewish reasons for agreeing need not be the same as the Christian, Muslim, secular or other. But, if the settlement is to evoke the commitment it requires to work over the long term, the parties to it each need to have good reasons for their participation.

For example, a mainstream Christian position on equality before God requires answering three interrelated questions: Who is God? What does it mean to live before God? What is equality before this God? The first question is classically answered through the doctrine of the Trinity, which through Christian history has been continually rethought, one of the contexts in which this is happening today being that of inter-faith engagement.[11] The second question requires an account of what it means to be human, made in the image of this God.[12] By the time one reaches the third question, it is clear that the 'equality' of human beings is not so much an essence, a quantity or a sameness shared by all people, as it is their fundamental relationship to God. All are equal in being created by God, loved by God in the person of Jesus Christ and invited to share the life of God's Spirit. The implications of this equality before God embrace every aspect of human existence, including a radical concept of the worth of each person who is born; it also means that in many respects there may be enormous variations, and very different practical conclusions may be drawn.[13]

Here is the challenge with regard to the question of a Christian 'line' on *shariʿa* in relation to English law. On this, as on many other topics, there are no short cuts. Not only must one draw both on the basic testimony of the Bible to living before God and on the wisdom learned over the centuries through trying to do this in different settings; one must also know about *shariʿa* and English law; and then one must make a judgment concerning what is appropriate in the current English religious, political and legal situation. In other words, there is no obvious, clear-cut Christian answer, and one has to take responsibility with others for working out a settlement that rings true to living before God now. And that, as already discussed, includes coming to terms with modernity and engaging deeply in wisdom-seeking with other parties. The Christian rationale for this is fundamentally

---

[11] For a lucid account of the Trinity addressed to Muslims by Archbishop Rowan Williams, see his letter, 'A common word for the common good', in response to the Muslim letter, 'A common word between us and you'. Both letters are online at <http://acommonword.com>. For my account of God as Trinity in the context of a book that also explores inter-faith wisdom, see DF Ford, *Christian Wisdom: desiring God and learning in love* (Cambridge, 2007), chapter 7.

[12] The most thorough recent Christian account of humanity before God is that of DH Kelsey, *Eccentric Existence: a theological anthropology*, 2 vols (Louisville, KY, 2009).

[13] See Kelsey, *Eccentric Existence*, supra n 12, throughout, but especially Part One, Volume 1.

to do with the radical involvement of Jesus Christ in human life, taking responsibility for affirming it, judging it and transforming it; but it can also appeal to the way Jesus, according to the Gospels, dealt with some dilemmas that were put to him.

One relevant story is about his response to being asked whether or not Roman taxes should be paid. The questioners affirm Jesus' commitment to equality before God: 'Teacher, we know that you are sincere, and teach the way of God in accordance with truth, and show deference to no one; for you do not regard people with partiality.' Then they ask whether it is lawful to pay taxes to the emperor. Jesus' answer is to ask for a coin, point to the emperor's head on it, and say: 'Give therefore to the emperor the things that are the emperor's, and to God the things that are God's.' (Matthew 22.15–22) It is a saying that can be taken many ways, but at the least it leaves his hearers with responsibility for working out just how it is to be understood and implemented.

The Archbishop took on that sort of responsibility when he lectured on *shari'a*. Others have undertaken it in responding to him, and the debate has just begun. I myself am still undecided on whether the Archbishop's modest form of legal pluralism, with some competition between systems for the allegiance of citizens, is the best solution. But whatever settlement emerges there will be the continuing need for wisdom in applying it. In this regard, one of the most encouraging chapters in this volume has for me been that of Albie Sachs, 'In Praise of "Fuzzy Law"'. His account of contextual reasoning about *The Satanic Verses*, the Danish cartoons, Holocaust-denial by a South African radio station and eviction of squatters in Port Elizabeth makes the case that 'negotiation and dialogue are absolutely vital in an area such as this. Much current estrangement comes precisely from attempts (even benevolent attempts) by government to find solutions and impose them on people for their own good.'[14] Beyond the good sense that he writes, there is what he represents: the irreducible necessity of wise judges in order to make any legal system work well. However they end up relating to each other, *shari'a* and English law will only flourish if they are served by such people. And perhaps it is not irrelevant that his is a Jewish contribution to a debate about Islamic law begun by a Christian thinker.

---

[14] Supra p 232.

CHAPTER 20

Equal before the law

Nicholas Phillips

I had the honour of chairing the lecture given by Rowan Williams, then Archbishop of Canterbury that is published as chapter 2 in this volume. Given in the Royal Courts of Justice and on the topic of civil and religious law in England, it was a profound lecture and one not readily understood on a single listening. It was, I believe, not clearly understood by all, and certainly not by sections of the media which represented the Archbishop as suggesting the possibility that Muslims in this country might be governed by their own system of *shari'a* law.

That is certainly not what he was suggesting. On the contrary he made it plain that there could not be some subsidiary *shari'a* jurisdiction which, I quote, 'could have the power to deny access to rights granted to other citizens or to punish its members for claiming those rights'. Speaking more specifically of apostasy he said: 'in a society where freedom of religion is secured by law, it is obviously impossible for any group to claim that conversion to another faith is simply disallowed or to claim the right to inflict punishment on a convert.'

A point that the Archbishop was making was that it was possible for individuals voluntarily to conduct their lives in accordance with *shari'a* principles without this being in conflict with the rights guaranteed by our law. To quote him again, 'the refusal of a religious believer to act upon the legal recognition of a right is not, given the plural character of society, a denial to anyone inside or outside the community of access to that right'.

The Archbishop went on to suggest that it might be possible to contemplate, and again I quote, 'a scheme in which individuals retain the liberty to choose the jurisdiction under which they will seek to resolve certain carefully specified matters'. He suggested by way of example, 'aspects of marital law, the regulation of financial transactions and authorised structures of mediation and conflict resolution'.[1]

The text draws on my lecture of the same title given at the London Muslim Centre, 3 July 2008 (2008) L & J 75.
[1] Supra pp 26, 27, 32.

It was not very radical to advocate embracing *shari'a* law in the context of family disputes, for example, and our system already goes a long way towards accommodating the Archbishop's suggestion. Two chapters in this book – one by Elizabeth Butler-Sloss and Mark Hill, the other by Ian Edge – have described in detail the present clearly defined (and thereby clearly delimited) scope for the application of *shari'a* law in family disputes. So far as aspects of matrimonial law are concerned, there is a limited precedent for English law to recognise aspects of religious laws, although when it comes to divorce this can only be effected in accordance with the civil law of this country.

Edge describes as well the permissible role of *shari'a* in commercial disputes and arbitration. It is possible in this country for those who are entering into a contract to agree that the settlement shall be governed by a law other than English law. Those who, in this country, are in dispute as to their respective rights are free to subject that dispute to the mediation of a chosen person, or to agree that the dispute shall be resolved by a chosen arbitrator or arbitrators. There is no reason why principles of *shari'a* law, or any other religious code should not be the basis for mediation or other forms of alternative dispute resolution. It must be recognised, however, that any sanctions for a failure to comply with the agreed terms of the mediation would be drawn from the laws of England and Wales.

Those who provide financial services in this country are subject to regulation in order to protect their customers and that regulation accommodates financial institutions or products that comply with *shari'a* principles. There are Islamic banks authorised by the Financial Services Authority to carry on business in the UK. A number of *sukuk* issues have been listed on the London Stock Exchange. In May 2008 Europe's first Islamic insurance company or *takaful* provider was authorised by the Financial Services Authority. Speaking in 2008, the year of the Archbishop's lecture, Kitty Ussher, the then Economics Secretary said:

> We want to make sure that no-one has their choice of financial services limited by their religion, and to help ensure that Muslims have the same access to financial services as anyone else in Britain.

It has been a privilege to visit Oman and to discuss with lawyers there the manner of the application of *shari'a* law in that country, and to take part in Qatar's first global 'Forum on the Rule of Law' in 2009, which included some discussion of the issues with which we are concerned here.

It has become clear to me that there is widespread misunderstanding in this country as to the nature of *shari'a* law. *Shari'a* consists of a set of principles governing the way that one should live one's life in accordance with the will of God. These principles are based on the Qur'an, as revealed to the Prophet Muhammad and interpreted by Islamic scholars. The principles have much in common with those of other religions. They do not include forced marriage or the repression of women. Compliance with them requires a high level of personal conduct, including abstinence from alcohol. I understand that it is not the case that for a Muslim to lead his or her life in accordance with these principles will be in conflict with the requirements of the law in this country.

What would be in conflict with the law would be to impose certain sanctions for failure to comply with *shari'a* principles. Part of the misconception about *shari'a* law is the belief that *shari'a* is only about mandating sanctions such as flogging, stoning, the cutting off of hands or death for those who fail to comply with the law. And the view of many of *shari'a* law is coloured by violent extremists who invoke it, perversely, to justify terrorist atrocities such as suicide bombing, which I understand to be in conflict with Islamic principles. There can be no question of such sanctions being applied to or by any Muslim who lives within this jurisdiction. Nor, when I was in Oman, did I find that such penalties formed any part of the law applied there. It is true that they have the death penalty for intentional murder, but they do not apply any of the other forms of corporal punishment I have just listed.

It remains the fact that in Muslim countries where the law is founded on *shari'a* principles, the law includes sanctions for failure to observe those principles and there are courts to try those who are alleged to have breached those laws. The definition of the law and the sanctions to be applied for breach of it differ from one Muslim country to another. In some countries the courts interpret *shari'a* law as calling for severe physical punishment. There can be no question of such courts sitting in this country, or such sanctions being applied here. So far as the law is concerned, those who live in this country are governed by English law and subject to the jurisdiction of the English courts.

I add this. The presence of different interpretations of *shari'a* principles reveals the presence of challenges common to other systems; the challenges of reaching correct interpretation and achieving true understanding. Wherever these challenges are present there is room for change over time both in the definition of the law and in the sanctions to be applied for breach of it.

In the lecture I delivered at the Qatar Law Forum in 2009 I advanced six propositions that I suggested were key to a rule of law strong enough for the globalised world in which we live. The sixth proposition concentrated on the importance of dialogue, understanding and mutual respect. The search, I suggested, is not for identical laws or legal procedures, but for common principles and values that we recognise must also be common goals. These go hand in hand with a recognition of different traditions and procedures as we gain a greater understanding of our respective ways of applying the rule of law. There is a need for regular conversations between the judges of different nations, between those who practise law in the Islamic world and those who practise law elsewhere, and between lawyers and academics.

In relation to the rule of law, the third of eight fundamental principles offered by the late Lord Bingham was 'Equality before the Law'.[2] It is quite rightly on this note of equality before the law that the present book ends. It was later in the same year as the Archbishop's lecture that I gave a lecture at the London Muslim Centre with that title. It was one of my last engagements as Lord Chief Justice before being appointed President of the UK Supreme Court. In that lecture I made many of the particular points in relation to *shariʿa* law that I have set out above. More broadly, I also sought to explain that the law in this country has, comparatively recently, reached a stage of development in which a high premium is placed on equality of all who live in this country.

The law to which I referred is the set of rules that govern how we live in society. They are rules made by those with authority to make them and rules that are enforced by those with authority to enforce them.

The judges of this country are independently appointed. We are fiercely proud of our independence. When we are appointed we take an oath or affirmation that we will administer justice 'to do right to all manner of people after the laws and usages of this realm'. We act in accordance with that oath. We treat equally all who come before us, regardless of whether they are men or women, regardless of their race or religion and whether they are rich or poor. We are not influenced by the wishes of the government, and no government minister would dare to attempt to influence a judge to decide a case in a particular way. Any man or woman who appears before a judge in this country will receive equal treatment in the administration of the law. The judge will treat each litigant in the same way.

[2] T Bingham, *The Rule of Law* (London, 2010), pp 55–9.

But the judge's duty is to apply the law, whether he agrees with the law or not. So the important question is not, 'Does the judge treat everyone equally?' but, 'Does the law treat everyone equally?'

In any society, the answer to that question depends upon the motives, the beliefs, the attitudes, the prejudices or lack of prejudices of those who make the law. Our history has a negative side, areas where our laws have in the past certainly discriminated on grounds of race, religion or gender. In general, however, the approach of our law has been that of liberty. Sir John Donaldson, one of my distinguished judicial predecessors, put it in this way:

> The starting point of our domestic law is that every citizen has a right to do what he likes, unless restrained by the common law or by statute.[3]

That statement today is true not merely of British citizens but of anyone who is lawfully within this country. Personal liberty is a right to which the courts of this country have long attached the highest importance. But freedom of individuals from State interference can itself lead to unequal treatment in the way that those individuals behave towards each other. Life in a modern society involves the interdependence of those who live and work together. There is scope for discrimination in many areas if the law does not place restraints on the way people may behave.

It is only in my lifetime that Parliament has legislated to stamp out discrimination in all areas and aspects of society. The catalyst for change was perhaps the horrifying racism of the Nazi regime in Germany before and during the Second World War. This led in 1948 to the Universal Declaration of Human Rights, which included the following statement:

> Recognition of the inherent dignity and the equal and inalienable rights of all members of the human family is the foundation of freedom, justice and peace in the world.

More significantly, the UK helped to draft and, in 1951, signed the European Convention on Human Rights (ECHR). This required all the signatories to ensure that there was no unlawful interference with the fundamental human rights set out in the treaty. Furthermore Article 14 of the ECHR provided:

> The enjoyment of the rights and freedoms set forth in the Convention shall be secured without discrimination on any ground such as sex, race, colour, language, religion, political or other opinion, national or social origin, association with a national minority, property, birth or other status.

---

[3] *Attorney General v Observer Ltd* [1990] 1 AC 109.

The requirement to ensure equal treatment applies in respect of the fundamental human rights protected by the ECHR. In 1998 the Human Rights Act was passed which requires all public authorities to comply with the ECHR, so that individuals now have a legal right to compensation if they are subject to discrimination by agents of the government in relation to their fundamental human rights.

In 1976 the UK ratified a Convention that imposes a general obligation to prohibit civil and political discrimination. Article 26 of the International Covenant on Civil and Political Rights[4] provides:

> All persons are equal before the law and are entitled without any discrimination to the equal protection of the law. In this respect, the law shall prohibit any discrimination and guarantee to all persons equal and effective protection against discrimination on any ground such as race, colour, sex, language, religion, political or other opinion, national or social origin, property, birth or other status.

Parliament has passed laws to ensure that people in this country receive equality of treatment. In 2000 it was calculated that there were no less than thirty acts of Parliament, not to mention statutory regulations and codes of practice, dealing with discrimination.

The law to which I have referred is secular. It does not attempt to enforce the standards of behaviour that the Christian religion or any other religion expects. It is perhaps founded on one ethical principle that the Christian religion shares with most, if not all, other religions: that one should love one's neighbour. And so the law sets out to prevent behaviour that harms others. Behaviour that is contrary to religious principles, but which is detrimental only to those who commit it, is not, in general, contrary to our law. A sin is not necessarily a crime.

Those who come to live in this country must take its laws as they find them. British diversity is valued and the principles of freedom and equality that the law protects should be welcomed by all. Laws in this country are based on the common values of tolerance, openness, equality and respect for the rule of law. Whilst breaches of the requirements of any religion in the UK may not be punished by the law, people are free to practise their religion. That is something to be valued. The different Christian denominations can build their own churches, Jews can build synagogues, Hindus can build temples and Muslims can build mosques, and each of these is free to practise his own faith in his own way. Freedom of speech, long prized and

---

[4] United Nations, Treaty Series, vol 999, p 171, accessible at <http://www.unhcr.org/refward/docid/3ae6b3aa0.html>.

protected in this country, includes freedom to preach the merits of one's own religion and freedom of religion includes the right to change one's faith or to apostatise.

Of course in a modern society there are many ways in which the behaviour of some can harm others, and there have been passed thousands of laws and regulations that are designed to try to prevent such behaviour. These laws and regulations can run into conflict with freedoms. The law can sometimes, quite unintentionally, have an adverse impact on a particular minority. Where this happens we will sometimes be able to make exceptions, to alleviate the impact.

Some may think: 'This equality in law is all very well, but some of those in authority with whom we come into contact do not treat us as equals; and, anyway, how can we be expected to know our legal rights when we are not lawyers?' As to the first point I am well aware that Muslims sometimes feel that they are being unfairly singled out simply because a small minority, who purport to share their religion, have ignored its teachings by turning to a violent extremism that is a threat to society. To those whose job it is to enforce the law I would say this: it is not enough that all in this country are entitled by law to equal treatment; it is up to you to make sure that you, and those for whom you are responsible, treat every man and woman on equal footing, entitled to the same personal dignity and respect.

There are now about 2.4 million Muslims living in this country. They form a vital and valued element of British society. They are well represented by a variety of groups and individuals, who seek to foster better community relations and to work for the good of society as a whole.[5]

As to the problem of knowing what your rights are, that is a problem shared by most citizens who are not in a position to pay for legal advice or who are not in receipt of publicly funded advice. The provision of '*pro bono*' legal advice, that is, the provision without charge by volunteers of legal advice and representation has my strong commendation.[6] More widely, just as David Ford highlights the importance and value of developing religious

---

[5] That aim is undoubtedly promoted by the impressive London Muslim Centre, where I gave my lecture in 2008. Its buildings appropriately embrace one of the East End's oldest synagogues, fostering Jewish–Muslim relations which have been described as the best in the country. I know that the Centre does much to encourage inter-faith relations and community cohesion; this is one of its stated aims. It has every claim to be one of those 'institutions, organisations and settings where people from many faiths ... learn and work together' or 'come together in the common life of society', referred to by DF Ford 'Equal before God', supra p 281.

[6] In my lecture at the London Muslim Centre, I highlighted the '*pro bono*' legal advice service supported by the Centre and through which volunteers provide legal advice and representation without charge to Muslim and non-Muslim alike.

literacy,[7] so too I would highlight the importance and value of developing *legal* literacy. The recent work on public legal education is very timely.[8] To the 'civic endeavour'[9] of 'increasing general knowledge about at least some religious traditions and an awareness of and ability to find out about others'[10] might be added the like endeavour of increasing general knowledge about the law. Legal literacy like religious literacy is 'good for society as a whole',[11] and good public education in both areas 'can help reverse the negative and enhance the positive'.[12]

In this book, Ford concludes his chapter on 'Equality before God' with the opinion that it is clear that 'the "equality" of human beings is not so much an essence, a quantity or a sameness shared by all people as it is their fundamental relationship to God'. Today it can fairly be said that the 'equality' of human beings is also their fundamental relationship before the law.

---

[7] Supra p 282.
[8] See in particular 'Developing capable citizens: the role of public legal education' (2007), a report of the Public Legal Education and Support Task Force chaired by Professor Dame Hazel Genn DBE.
[9] Supra p 282.
[10] A Dinham and SH Jones, 'An Analysis of Challenges of Religious Faith, and Resources for Meeting them, for University Leaders' (2010), cited by Ford, supra n 5 and p 282.
[11] Supra p 283.   [12] Supra p 283.

Select bibliography

Abou El Fadl, K, *Islam and the Challenge of Democracy* (Princeton, 2004).
  'Islamic law and Muslim minorities: the juristic discourse on Muslim minorities from the second/eighth to the eleventh/seventeenth centuries', (1994) 1 *Islamic Law and Societies* 141.
  'Muslim minorities and self-restraint in liberal democracies', (1996) 29 *Loyola Law Review* 1525.
  Rebellion and Violence in Islamic Law (Cambridge, 2001).
  Speaking in God's Name: Islamic law, authority and women (Oxford, 2001).
  The Great Theft: wrestling Islam from the extremists (New York, 2005).
Adil, M, 'The Malaysian state and freedom of religion: a conceptual analysis with particular reference to apostasy' (doctoral thesis, London, 2005).
Ahdar, R, 'Religious group autonomy, gay ordination and human rights law' in R O'Dair and A Lewis (eds), *Law and Religion* (fourth edition, Oxford, 2001).
Ahdar, R and Aroney, N (eds), *Shari'a in the West* (Oxford, 2010).
Ahdar, R and Leigh, I, *Religious Freedom in the Liberal State* (Oxford, 2005).
Ahmed, M, Reetz, D and Johnston, T H, *Who Speaks for Islam? Muslim grassroots leaders and popular preachers in South Asia* (Washington, DC, 2010).
Ali, S S, 'Religious pluralism, human rights and Muslim citizenship in Europe: some preliminary reflections on an evolving methodology for consensus' in MLP Leonon and JE Goldschmidt (eds), *Religious Pluralism and Human Rights in Europe* (Antwerp, 2007).
  'The concept of *jihad* in Islamic international law', (2005) 10 *Journal of Conflict and Security Law* 321.
AlSayyad, N and Castells, M, 'Introduction: Islam and the changing identity of Europe' in N AlSayyad and M Castells (eds), *Muslim Europe or Euro-Islam* (Lanham, MD, 2002).
Al-Umari, A D, *Madinan Society at the Time of the Prophet*, trans H Khattab (Memdon, UA, 1995).
Amghar, S, Boubekeur, A and Emerson M, *European Islam: challenges for public policy and society* (Brussels, 2007).
An-Na'im, A A, *Islam and the Secular State: negotiating the future of Sharia* (Cambridge, MA, 2008).

'The compatibility dialectic: mediating the legitimate coexistence of Islamic law and state law', (2010) 73 *Modern Law Review* 1.

Asad, T, *Formations of the Secular: Christianity, Islam, modernity* (Stanford, CA, 2003).

Attia, G E, *Towards Realization of the Higher Intents of Islamic Law: maqāsid al-Shari'ah: a functional approach* (London, 2007).

Auda, J, *Maqasid al-Shariah as Philosophy of Islamic Law: a systems approach* (London, 2008).

Badawi, Z, 'New *fiqh* for minorities' in I Yilmaz (ed), *Muslim Laws, Politics and Society in Modern Nation States: dynamic legal pluralism in England, Turkey and Pakistan* (Aldershot, 2005).

Baderin, M A, 'Human rights and Islamic law: the myth of discord', (2005) 2 *European Human Rights Law Review* 165.

International Human Rights and Islamic Law (Oxford, 2003).

'Islam and the realization of human rights in the Muslim world: a reflection on two essential approaches and two divergent perspectives', (2007) 4 *Muslim World Journal of Human Rights*.

'Religion and international law: friends or foes?', (2009) 5 *European Human Rights Law Review* 637.

'The role of Islam in human rights and development in Muslim states' in J Rehman and S C Breau (eds), *Religion, Human Rights and International Law* (Leiden, 2007).

Badr, G M, 'A survey of Islamic international law', (1982) 76 *Proceedings of the American Society of International Law* 56.

Bainbridge, S, 'War and peace: negotiating meaning in Islam', (2008) 1 *Critical Studies in Terrorism* 263.

Bakircioglu, O, 'A socio-legal analysis of the concept of jihad', (2010) 59 *International and Comparative Law Quarterly* 413.

Balagangadhara, S N, *The Heathen in his Blindness: Asia, the West, and the dynamic of religion* (New Delhi, 2005).

Ballard, R, *Desh Pardesh: the South Asian presence in Britain* (London, 1994).

'Human rights in the context of ethnic plurality: always a vehicle for liberation?' in R Grillo, R Ballard, A Ferrari, A J Hoekema, M Maussen and P Shah (eds), *Legal Practice and Cultural Diversity* (Farnham, 2009).

'Inside and outside: contrasting perspectives on the dynamics of kinship and marriage in contemporary South Asian transnational networks' in R Grillo (ed), *The Family in Question: immigrant and ethnic minorities in multicultural Europe* (Amsterdam, 2008).

Bano, S, *Complexity, Difference and Muslim Personal Law: rethinking relationships between shariah councils and South Asian Muslim women in Britain* (doctoral thesis, Warwick, 2004).

'In pursuit of religious and legal diversity: a response to the Archbishop of Canterbury and the *"sharia* debate" in Britain', (2008) 10 *Ecclesiastical Law Journal* 282.

'Muslim family justice and human rights: the experience of British Muslim women', (2007) 1 *Journal of Comparative Law* 1.

'Shariah councils and the resolution of matrimonial disputes: gender and justice in the "shadow" of the law' in R T Thiara and A I Gill (eds), *Violence against Women in South Asian Communities* (London, 2009).

Barak, A, *Proportionality: constitutional rights and their limitations* (Cambridge, 2012), p 184.

Barras, A, 'A rights-based discourse to contest the boundaries of state secularism? The case of the headscarf bans in France and Turkey', (2009) 16 *Democratization* 1237.

Bayat, A, 'Islam and democracy: what is the real question?' (ISIM Papers, Amsterdam, 2009).

Making Islam democratic: social movements and the post-Islamist turn (Stanford, 2007).

Berger, M, 'Conflicts law and public policy in Egyptian family law: Islamic law by the backdoor', (2002) 50 *American Journal of Criminal Law* 555.

Berkovits, B, 'Transnational divorces: the Fatima decision', (1988) 104 *Law Quarterly Review* 60.

Bielefeld, H, 'Muslim voices in the human rights debate', (1995) 17 *Human Rights Quarterly* 587.

Bingham, T, *The Rule of Law* (London, 2010).

Bleich, E, 'Muslims and the state in the post-9/11 West', (2009) 35 *Journal of Ethnic and Migration Studies* 353.

Bowen, J, 'How could English courts recognize shariah?', (2010) 7.3 *University of St Thomas Law Journal* 411.

Boyd, M, 'Dispute resolution in family law: protecting choice, Promoting inclusion', <http://www.attorneygeneral.jus.gov.on.ca/english/about/pubs/boyd/>.

Boyle, K, 'Human rights, religion and democracy: the Refah Partisi case', (2004) 1 *Essex Human Rights Review* 1.

Bracke, S and Fadil, N, 'Islam and secular modernity under Western eyes: a genealogy of a constitutive relationship', RSCAS Policy Paper 2008/05 (European University Institute, 2008), <http://cadmus.iue.it/dspace/bitstream/1814/8102/1/RSCAS_2008_05.pdf>.

Bradney, A, 'Faced by faith' in P Oliver, S Douglas Scott, and V Tadros (eds), *Faith in Law: essays in legal theory* (Oxford, 2000).

'How not to marry people', (1989) 19 *Family Law* 408.

Law and Faith in a Sceptical Age (Abingdon, 2008).

Bratza, N, 'The "precious asset": freedom of religion under the European Convention of Human Rights' in M Hill (ed), *Religion and Discrimination Law in the European Union* (Trier, 2012), pp 9–26.

Bribosia, E, Ringelheim, J, and Rorive, I, 'Reasonable accommodation for religious minorities: a promising concept for European antidiscrimination law?', (2010) 17 *Maastricht Journal of European and Comparative Law* 137.

Brice, M A K, 'A minority within a minority: a report on converts to Islam within the United Kingdom' (Swansea, 2010), <http://faith-matters.org/images/stories/fm-reports/a-minority-within-a-minority-a-report-on-converts-to-islam-in-the-uk.pdf>.

Bukay, D, 'Can there be an Islamic democracy?', (2007) 14 *Middle East Quarterly* 71.
Bulac, A, 'The Medina document' in C Kurzaman (ed), *Liberal Islam: a sourcebook* (Oxford, 1998).
Busuttil, J, 'Humanitarian law in Islam', (1991) 30 *The Military Law and Law of War Review* 113.
Cannie, H and Voorhoof, D, 'The abuse clause and freedom of expression in the European Human Rights Convention: an added value for democracy and human rights protection?', (2011) 29 *Netherlands Quarterly of Human Rights* 54.
Casanova, J, *Public Religions in the Modern World* (Chicago and London, 1994).
  'Public religions revisited', in H de Vries (ed), *Religion: beyond a concept* (New York, 2008).
Centre for Social Cohesion, *Beth Din: Jewish law in the UK* (London, 2009).
Chaplin, J, 'Law, religion and public reasoning', (2012) 1 *Oxford Journal of Law and Religion* 1.
Charity Commission for England and Wales, *Catholic Care (Diocese of Leeds) Decision of 21 July 2010, on Application for Consent to a Change of Objects under s. 64 of the Charities Act 1993*, <http://www.charity-commission.gov.uk/library/about_us/catholic_care.pdf>.
Chiba, M, *Asian Indigenous Law: in interaction with received law* (London, 1986).
  Legal Pluralism: towards a general theory through Japanese legal culture (Tokyo, 1989).
Cotran, E and Sherif, A O, *Democracy, the Rule of Law and Islam* (London, 1999).
Cumper, P, 'Europe, Islam and democracy: balancing religious and secular values under the ECHR', (2003–2004) 3 *European Yearbook of Minority Issues* 163.
Cumper, P and Lewis, T, '"Taking religion seriously"? Human rights and hijab in Europe: some problems of adjudication', (2009) 24 *Journal of Law and Religion* 101.
Deveaux, M, 'Political morality and culture: what difference do differences make?', (July 2002) 28 *Social Theory and Practice* 503.
Dinham, A and Jones, S H, 'An Analysis of Challenges of Religious Faith, and Resources for Meeting them, for University Leaders', (2010), <http://religiousliteracyhe.org/leadership-resources/publications>.
  'Programme Evaluation Phase I: September 2010–February 2011', (2010), <http://religiousliteracyhe.org/leadership-resources/publications>.
Douglas, D, Doe, N, Gilliat-Ray, S, Sandberg, R and Khan, A, 'Social cohesion and civil law: marriage, divorce and religious courts' (Cardiff, 2011), <http://www.law.cf.ac.uk/clr/Social%20Cohesion%20and%20Civil%20Law%20Full%20Report.pdf>.
Ercanbrack, J G, 'The regulation of Islamic finance in the United Kingdom', (2011) 13 *Ecclesiastical Law Journal* 69.
Esposito, J L, *Islam and Democracy* (New York, 1996).
Esposito, J L and Mogahed, D (eds), *Who Speaks for Islam? What a billion Muslims really think* (New York, 2008).
Esposito J L and Piscatori, J P, 'Democratization and Islam', (1991) 55 *Middle East Journal* 427.

Esposito, J L and Voll, J O, 'Islam and democracy', (2001) 22 *Humanities*, <http://www.neh.gov/news/humanities/2001-11/islam.html>.
Equality and Human Rights Commission, 'Commission proposes "reasonable accommodation" for religion or belief is needed' (11 July 2011), <http://www.equalityhumanrights.com/news/2011/july/commission-proposes-reasonable-accommodation-for-religion-or-belief-is-needed/>.
Evans, C, 'The "Islamic scarf" in the European Court of Human Rights', (2006) 7 *Melbourne Journal of International Law* 52.
Evans, M D, *Religious Liberty and International Law in Europe* (Cambridge, 2008).
Evans, M and Petkoff, P, 'Secularism, religious rights and international law in the ECHR Jurisprudence', <http://www.ku.dk/satsning/religion/sekularism_and_beyond/pdf/Paper_Petkoff.pdf>.
Feldman, N, *The Fall and Rise of the Islamic State* (Princeton, 2009).
Fernandez, S, 'The crusade over the bodies of women', (2009) 43 *Patterns of Prejudice* 269.
Ferrari, S and Cristofori, R (eds), *Law and Religion in the 21st Century* (Farnham, 2010).
Ferretti, M P and Strnadová, L (eds), 'Rules and exemptions: the politics and difference within liberalism', (2009) 15 *Res Publica* 213.
Fetzer, S and Soper, J C, *Muslims and the State in Britain, France and Germany* (Cambridge, 2005).
Fish, M S, *Are Muslims distinctive? A look at the evidence* (Oxford, 2011).
Ford, D F, *Christian Wisdom: desiring God and learning in love* (Cambridge, 2007).
Shaping Theology: engagements in a religious and secular world (Oxford, 2007).
The Future of Christian Theology (Oxford, 2011).
Fournier, P, 'In the (Canadian) shadow of Islamic law: translating mahr as a bargaining endowment' in R Moon (ed), *Law and Religious Pluralism in Canada* (Vancouver, 2008).
Freedland, M R and Vickers, L, 'Religious expression in the workplace in the United Kingdom', (2009) 30 *Comparative Labor Law & Policy Journal* 597.
Gadirov, J, 'Freedom of religion and legal pluralism' in M L P Loenen and J E Goldschmidt (eds), *Religious Pluralism and Human Rights in Europe: where to draw the line?* (Antwerp, 2007).
Gardet, L, 'Un préalable aux questions soulevées par les droits de l'homme: l'actualisation de la loi religieuse musulmane aujourd'hui', (1983) 9 *Islamochristiana* 1.
Gilliat-Ray, S, *Muslims in Britain: an introduction* (Cambridge, 2010).
Griffiths, J, 'What is legal pluralism?', (1986) 24 *Journal of Legal Pluralism* 1.
Grillo, R, 'Cultural diversity and the law: challenge and accommodation', Working paper 09/14 (Max Planck Institute for the Study of Religious and Ethnic Diversity, 2009).
Gunn, T J, 'Adjudicating rights of conscience under the European Convention on Human Rights' in J van der Vyver and J Witte (eds), *Religious Human Rights in Global Perspective: legal perspectives* (Leiden, 1996).
Hallaq, B, *The Origins and Evolution of Islamic Law* (Cambridge, 2005).
Hallaq, W, 'Was the gate of *ijtihad* closed?', (1984) 16 *International Journal of Middle East Studies* 3.

Hambler, A, 'A no-win situation for public officials with faith convictions', (2010) *Ecclesiastical Law Journal* 3.
Hamidullah, M, *Muslim Conduct of State: being a treatise on siyar* ... (Lahore, 1977).
The First Written Constitution in the World (Lahore, 1981).
Haneef, S S, 'Debate on methodology of renewing Muslim law: a search for a synthetic approach', (2010) 10 *Global Jurist*.
Harris, D, O'Boyle, M and Warbrick, C, *Law of the European Convention on Human Rights* (second edition, Oxford, 2009).
Harris, N, *Education, Law, Diversity* (Oxford, 2007).
Hasan, K, 'The medical and social costs of consanguineous marriages among British Mirpuris', (2009) 29 *South Asia Research* 275.
Held, D, *Democracy and the Global Order* (third edition, Cambridge, 1996).
Models of Democracy (third edition, Cambridge, 2006).
Hellyer, H A, *Muslims of Europe: the 'other' Europeans* (Edinburgh, 2009).
Hill, M and Sandberg, R, 'Is nothing sacred? Clashing symbols in a secular world', (2007) *Public Law* 488.
Hirschl, R and Shachar, A, 'The new wall of separation: permitting diversity, restricting competition', (2008–9) 30 *Cardozo Law Review* 2535.
Holland, T, *In the Shadow of the Sword: the battle for global empire and the end of the ancient world* (London, 2012).
Home Affairs Committee, 'The work of the UK Border Agency', ninth report (November 2010–March 2011).
Hooker, M B, *Legal Pluralism: an introduction to colonial and neo-colonial laws* (Oxford, 1975).
Hopkins, R and Yeginsu, C V, 'Religious liberty in British courts: a critique and some guidance', (2008) 49 *Harvard International Law Journal* 28.
Housby, E, *Islamic Financial Services in the UK* (Edinburgh, 2011).
Hurd, E S, 'The political authority of secularism in international relations', (2004) 10 *European Journal of International Relations* 235.
Ishaque, S, 'Islamic principles on adoption', (2008) 22 *International Journal of Law, Policy and Family* 39.
Jackson, B, '"Transformative accommodation" and religious law', (2009) 11 *Ecclesiastical Law Journal* 131.
Jones, R, 'Planning law and mosque development: the politics of religion and residence in Birmingham' in P Shah (ed), *Law and Ethnic Plurality* (Leiden, 2007).
Joppke, C, 'Liberalism and Muslim integration: through the prism of headscarf restrictions in Europe', <http://131.130.1.78/veil/Home3/index.php?id¼436,79,0,0,1,0>.
'Limits of integration policy: Britain and her muslims', (2009) 35 *Journal of Ethnic and Migration Studies* 453.
Veil: mirror of identity (London, 2009).
Kamali, M H, *Freedom of Expression in Islam* (Cambridge, 1997).
'Law and society: the interplay of revelation and reason in the Shariah' in J L Esposito (ed), *The Oxford History of Islam* (Oxford, 1999).
Principles of Islamic Jurisprudence (Cambridge, 2003).

Kamaruddin, Z, 'Current legal route to division of matrimonial property upon conversion' (2010), <http://ikim.gov.my/v5/index.php/imagesweb/file/index.php?lg=1&opt=com_article&grp=2&sec=&key=2109&cmd=resetall>.

'Insights into the inter-relationship and the associated tension between Shariah and civil family law in Malaysia', (2008) 6 *Malaysian Law Journal* 76.

Kelsey, D H, *Eccentric Existence: a theological anthropology*, 2 vols (Louisville, KY, 2009).

Keshavjee, M, *Dispute Resolution among Muslims in the Diaspora* (doctoral thesis, London, 2009).

Khadduri, M, 'Islam and the Modern law of nations', (1956) 50 *AJIL* 358.

War and Peace in the Law of Islam (Baltimore, MD, 1955).

Klausen, J, *The Islamic Challenge* (New York, 2005).

Laws, J, 'The constitution: morals and rights', (1996) *Public Law* 622.

Lawson, A, *Disability and Equality Law in Britain: the role of reasonable adjustment* (Oxford, 2008).

Leader, S, 'Freedom of futures: personal priorities, institutional demands and freedom of religion', (2007) 70 *Modern Law Review* 713.

Levey, G B and Modood, T, 'Liberal democracy, multicultural citizenship, and the Danish cartoon affair' in G B Levey and T Modood (eds) *Secularism, Religion and Multicultural Citizenship* (Cambridge, 2009).

'The Danish cartoon affair: free speech, racism, Islamism, and integration', (2006) 44 *International Migration* 3.

Lewis, B, 'Legal and historical reflections on the position of Muslim populations under non-Muslim rule', (1992) 13 *Journal of the Institute of Muslim Minority Affairs* 1.

Lewis, P, *The function, education and influence of the 'Ulama in Bradford's Muslim Communities* (Leeds, 1996).

Lewis, T, 'What not to wear: religious rights, the European Court, and the margin of appreciation', (2007) 56 *International and Comparative Law Quarterly* 395.

Loenen, M L P and Goldschmidt, J E (eds), *Religious Pluralism and Human Rights in Europe: where to draw the line?* (Antwerp, 2007).

Lowe, N and Douglas, G, *Bromley's Family Law* (tenth edition, Oxford, 2007).

Macklem, P, 'Militant democracy, legal pluralism, and the paradox of self-determination', (2006) 4 *Journal of International Constitutional Law* 488.

Madera, A, 'Juridical bonds of marriage for Jewish and Islamic women', (2009) 11 *Ecclesiastical Law Journal* 51.

Mahmassani, S, 'International law in the light of Islamic doctrine', (1966) 117 *Recueil de Cours* 201.

Malik, M, 'Faith and the state of jurisprudence', in P Oliver, S Douglas Scott, and V Tadros (eds), *Faith in Law: essays in legal theory* (Oxford, 2000).

'Muslim legal norms and the integration of European Muslims', RSCAS Policy Paper 2009/29 (European University Institute, 2009), <http://cadmus.eui.eu/handle/1814/11653>.

Mayer, A E, *Islam and Human Rights: tradition and politics* (fourth edition, Boulder, CO, 2007).

McColgan, A, 'Class wars? Religion and (in)equality in the workplace', (2009) 38 *Industrial Law Journal* 1.

McCrea, R, 'Limitations on religion in a liberal democratic polity: Christianity and Islam in the public order of the European Union', Law, Society and Economy Working Papers (London, 2007).

McCrudden, C, 'Human dignity and judicial interpretation of human rights', (2008) 19 *European Journal of International Law* 655.

'Multiculturalism, freedom of religion, equality, and the British constitution: the JFS case considered', (2011) 9 *International Journal of Constitutional Law* 200, <http://ssrn.com/abstract=1701289>.

'Religion, human rights, equality and the public sphere', (2011) 13 *Ecclesiastical Law Journal* 26.

McFarlane, A E, '"Am I bothered?" The relevance of religious courts to a civil judge', (2011) 41 *Family Law* 946.

McGoldrick, D, 'Accommodating Muslims in Europe: from adopting *sharia* law to religiously based opt outs from generally applicable laws', (2009) 9 *Human Rights Law Review* 603.

Human Rights and Religion: the Islamic headscarf debate in Europe (Oxford, 2006).

'Muslim veiling controversies in Europe', (2009) 1 *Yearbook of Muslims in Europe* 427.

'Religion in the European public square and in European public life: crucifixes in the classroom?', (2011) 11 *Human Rights Law Review* 451.

Mehdi, R and Nielsen, J (eds), *Embedding Mahr in the European Legal System* (Copenhagen, 2011).

Menski, W, 'Angrezi Shari'at: plural arrangements in family law by Muslims in Britain' (unpublished paper, London, 1993).

Mernissi, F, *The Veil and the Male Elite: a feminist interpretation of women's rights in Islam* (Reading, MA, 1991).

Michelman, F I, 'Constitutional Theocracy', (2012) *Public Law* 173

Mill, J S, 'On liberty', in *On Liberty and other Essays* (Indianapolis, IN, 1956).

Mirza, M, Senthilkumaran, A and Ja'far, Z, 'Living apart together: British Muslims and the paradox of Multiculturalism', <http://www.policyexchange.org.uk/assets/Living_Apart_Together_text.pdf>.

Mitnick, E J, 'Individual vulnerability and cultural transformation', (2002–3) 101 *Michigan Law Review* 1635.

Modood, T, *Multicultural Politics: racism, ethnicity and Muslims in Britain* (Edinburgh, 2005).

'Muslims, incitement to hatred and the law' in J Horton (ed), *Liberalism, Multiculturalism and Toleration* (Basingstoke, 1993).

Moe, C, 'Refah revisited: Strasbourg's construction of Islam' (2005), <http://folk.uio.no/chrismoe/research/hr-isl/refah.en.htm>.

Mogahed, D and Nyriki, Z, 'Reinventing integration', (2007) 29 *Harvard International Review*, <http://hir.harvard.edu/courting-africa/reinventing-integration>.

Mookherjee, M, 'Feminism and multiculturalism: putting Okin and Shachar in question', (2005) 2 *Journal of Moral Philosophy* 237.
Moon, G, 'From equal treatment to appropriate treatment: what lessons can Canadian equality law on dignity and on reasonable accommodation teach the United Kingdom?', (2006) 6 *European Human Rights Law Review* 695.
Moon, R, 'Introduction', in R Moon (ed), *Law and Religious Pluralism in Canada* (Vancouver, 2008).
Moore, K, *The Unfamiliar Abode: Islamic law in the United States and Britain* (Oxford, 2011).
Moore, S F, *Law as Process: an anthropological approach* (London, 1978).
Motha, S, 'Veiled women and the *affect* of religion in democracy', (2007) 34 *Journal of Law and Society* 139.
Mowbray, A, 'The role of the European Court of Human Rights in the promotion of democracy', (1999) *Public Law* 703.
Mullally, S, 'Civic integration, migrant women and the veil: at the limits of rights?', (2011) 74 *Modern Law Review* 27.
Mushkat, R, 'Is war ever justifiable? A comparative survey', (1987) 9 *Loyola of Los Angeles International and Comparative Law Review* 227.
Nasir, J J, *The Status of Women under Islamic law and Modern Islamic Legislation* (third edition, Boston, 2009).
Nehushtan, Y, 'Religious conscientious exemptions', (2011) 30 *Law and Philosophy* 143.
Nielsen, J S and Christoffersen, L (eds), *Shari'a as Discourse: legal traditions and the encounter with Europe* (Farnham, 2010).
O'Connell, R, 'Cinderella comes to the ball: Article 14 and the right to non-discrimination in the ECHR', (2009) 29 *Legal Studies* 211.
Okin, S M, 'Feminism and multiculturalism', (1991) 108 *Ethics* 661.
'"Mistresses of their own destiny": group rights, gender and realistic rights of exit', (2002) 112 *Ethics* 205.
Parekh, B, *Europe and the Muslim Question: does intercultural dialogue make sense?* (Amsterdam, 2007).
'Europe, liberalism and the "Muslim question"', in T Modood, A Triandafyllidou, and R Zapata-Barrero (eds), *Multiculturalism, Muslims and Citizenship: a European approach* (London, 2006).
Patel, P and Siddiqi, H, 'Shrinking secular spaces: Asian women at the intersect of race, religion and gender' in R K Thiara and A K Gill (eds), *Violence against Women in South Asian Communities* (London, 2010).
Pearl, D and Menski, W, *Muslim Family Law* (third edition, London, 1998).
Phillips, N A, 'Equality before the law' (address to the East London Muslim Centre, 3 July 2008), (2008) *Law and Justice* 75.
Pierik, R, 'Multicultural Jurisdictions: review', (2004) 32 *Review in Political Theory* 585.
Plant, R, *Politics, Theology and History* (Cambridge, 2001).
Poulter, S, *Ethnicity, Law and Human Rights: the English experience* (Oxford, 1998).
Probert, R, '"When are we married?" Void, non-existent and presumed marriages', (2002) 22 *Legal Studies* 398.

Raday, F, 'Culture, religion, and gender', (2002) 4 *International Journal of Constitutional Law* 663.

Rahim, A, *Muhammadan Jurisprudence* (Lahore, 1995).

Rahimi, B, 'The discourse of democracy in Shi'i Islamic jurisprudence: the two cases of Montazeri and Sistani', RSCAS Policy Paper 2008/09 (European University Institute, 2008), <http://cadmus.iue.it/dspace/bitstream/1814/8223/3/RSCAS_2008_09.pdf>.

Ramadan, M A, 'Notes on the Shari'a: human rights, democracy, and the European Court of Human Rights' (2007) 40 *Israel Law Review* 156.

Ramadan, T, 'An international call for moratorium on corporal punishment, stoning and the death penalty in the Islamic world', (2005), <http://tariqramadan.com/spip.php?article264>.

Radical Reform: Islamic ethics and liberation (New York, 2009).

Western Muslims and the Future of Islam (New York, 2004).

Rawls, J, *The Law of Peoples: with 'the idea of public reason' revisited* (Cambridge, MA, 1999).

Razack, S, *Casting Out: the eviction of Muslims from Western law and politics* (Toronto, 2008).

Rehman, J, *Islamic State Practices, International Law and the Threat from Terrorism* (Oxford, 2005).

'The *Shariah*, Islamic family laws and international human rights law: examining the theory and practice of polygamy and talaq', (2007) 21 *International Journal of Law, Policy and Family* 108.

Rivers, J, 'Law, religion and gender equality', (2007) 9 *Ecclesiastical Law Journal* 24.

The Law of Organized Religions: between establishment and secularism (Oxford, 2010).

Rohe, M, '*Sharia* in Europe: perspectives of segregation, assimilation or integration for European Muslims?', <http://cmes.hmdc.harvard.edu/files/Mathias.Rohe_.lecture.pdf>.

'The formation of a European sharia', in J Malik (ed), *Muslims in Europe* (Münster, 2004).

Rosiers, N D, 'Introduction' in Law Commission of Canada, *New Perspectives on the Public–Private Divide* (Vancouver, 2003).

Sachedina, A, *Islam and the Challenge of Human Rights* (New York, 2009).

The Islamic Roots of Democratic Pluralism (New York, 2001).

Samuel, K, *The Organization of the Islamic Conference, the UN and Counter-Terrorism Law-Making: competing or complementary legal orders?* (doctoral thesis, Sheffield, 2011).

Sandberg, R, 'Islam and English law', (2010) 164 *Law and Justice* 27.

'Laws and religion: unraveling *McFarlane v Relate Avon Limited*', (2010) 12 *Ecclesiastical Law Journal* 361.

Sandberg, R and Doe, N, 'Religious exemptions in discrimination law', (2007) 66 *Cambridge Law Journal* 302.

Schiek, D, Waddington, L and Bell, M (eds), *Cases, Materials and Texts on National, Supranational and International Non-discrimination Law* (Oxford, 2007).

Schmitter P C and Karl, T L, 'What democracy is . . . and is not', (1991) 2 *Journal of Democracy* 75.
Shachar, A, *Multicultural Jurisdictions: cultural differences and women's rights* (Cambridge, 2001).
  'Privatizing diversity: a cautionary tale from religious arbitration in family law', (2008) 9 *Theoretical Inquiries in Law* 573.
  'Religion, state and the problem of gender: new modes of citizenship and governance in diverse societies', (2005) 50 *McGill Law Journal* 49.
Shah, P, *Legal Pluralism in Conflict* (London, 2005).
  'When South Asians marry trans-jurisdictionally' in L Holden (ed), *Cultural Expertise, and Litigation: patterns, conflicts, narratives.* (London, 2011).
Shavit, U, 'Should Muslims integrate into the West?', (2007) 14 *Middle East Quarterly* 13.
Shaw, A, 'Kinship, cultural preference and immigration: consanguineous marriage among British Pakistanis', (2001) 7 *Journal of the Royal Anthropological Institute* 315.
Shortt, R, *Rowan's Rule* (London, 2008).
Smit, V Z, 'Reconciling the irreconcilable? Recent developments in the German law on abortion', (1994) 3 *Medical Law Review* 302.
Smith, P, 'Engaging with the state for the common good: some reflections on the role of the church', (2009) 11 *Ecclesiastical Law Journal* 169.
Soroush, A, *Reason, Freedom, and Democracy in Islam* (New York, 2002).
Stavros, S, 'Freedom of religion and claims for exemption from generally applicable, neutral laws: lessons from across the pond?', (1997) 6 *European Human Rights Law Review* 607.
Stychin, C F, 'Faith in the future: sexuality, religion and the public sphere', (2009) 29 *Oxford Journal of Legal Studies* 729.
Sunder, M, 'Piercing the veil', (2003) 112 *Yale Law Journal* 1399.
Tamanaha, B Z, 'Understanding legal pluralism: past to present, local to global', (2007) 29 *Sydney Law Review* 375.
Tibi, B, 'Islam and Europe in the age of intercivilizational conflict, diversity and challenges' in M-C Foblets (ed), *Islam and Europe: challenges and opportunities* (Leuven, 2008).
Tsitselikis, K, 'The legal status of Islam in Greece', (2004) 44 *Die Welt des Islam (shari'a in Europe)* 402.
Tucker, A, 'The Archbishop's unsatisfactory legal pluralism', (2008) *Public Law* 463.
Tucker, J, *Women, Family and Gender in Islamic Law* (Cambridge, 2008).
Vakulenko, A, 'Islamic dress in human rights jurisprudence: a critique of current trends', (2007) 7 *Human Rights Law Review* 717.
  '"Islamic headscarves" and the European Convention on Human Rights: an intersectional perspective', (2007) 16 *Social and Legal Studies* 183.
Vickers, L, 'Promoting equality or fostering resentment: the public sector equality duty and religion and belief', (2010) 30 *Legal Studies* 135.
  'Religion and belief discrimination in employment: the EU law' (European Commission, 2007).

'Religious discrimination in the workplace: an emerging hierarchy?', (2010) 12 *Ecclesiastical Law Journal* 280.
Religious Freedom, Religious Discrimination and the Workplace (Oxford, 2007).
'Twin approaches to secularism: organized religion and society', (2012) 19 *OJLS* 197
Watt, W M, *Islamic Political Thought* (Edinburgh, 1980).
Weinrib, L E, 'Ontario's Sharia law debate: law and politics under the charter's shadow' in R Moon (ed), *Law and Religious Pluralism in Canada* (Vancouver, 2008).
Westerfield, J M, 'Behind the veil: an American legal perspective on the European headscarf debate', (2006) *American Journal of Comparative Law* 656.
Wheatley, S, 'Minorities under the ECHR and the construction of a "democratic society"', (2007) 4 *Public Law* 770.
Williams, R, *Resurrection* (London, 2002).
Wilson, R, 'Islamic finance in Europe', RSCAS Policy Papers 2007/02 (European University Institute, 2007), <http://www.eui.eu/RSCAS/WP-Texts/07_02p.pdf>.
Yasmeen, S, 'Muslim migrants living in non-Muslim states: building peace and harmony', (2001) 1 *Islamic Millennium Journal* 43.
Yilmaz, I, *Muslim Laws, Politics and Society in Modern Nation States: dynamic legal pluralism in England, Turkey and Pakistan* (Aldershot, 2005).
Zaidan, A B K, *Individual and the State* (Kuwait, 1983).

Index of cases

A (Leave to Remove: Cultural and Religious Considerations) [2006] EWHC 421 (Fam). 113
A [In the Matter of A (A Child) (No 2)] [2011] EWCA Civ 12. 146
A v T (Ancillary Relief: Cultural Factors) [2004] EWHC 471 (Fam). 155
AAA v ASH, The Registrar General for England and Wales, The Secretary of State for Justice, The Advocate to the Court provided by the Attorney General [2009] EWHC 636 (Fam). 129, 130, 149
A-M v A-M (Divorce: Jurisdiction: Validity of Marriage) [2001] 2 FLR 6. 128, 148
Abbassi v Abbassi & Another [2006] EWCA Civ 355. 149
Ahmad v UK (1982) 4 EHRR 126. 64
Akhtar v Rafiq [2006] 1 FLR 27. 154
Aktas, Bayrak, Gamaleddyn, Ghazal, J Singh, R Singh v France App nos 43563/08 etc. 98
Al-Saedy v Musawi [2010] EWHC 3293. 129
Al-Midani v Al-Midani [1999] 1 Lloyds Rep 923. 122
Alberta v Hutterian Brethren of Wilson Colony (2009) SCC 37. 55
Amicus, see *R (On the Application of Amicus MSF and Others)*
Aneeka Sohrab v Sulman Khan (2002) SLT 1255. 131
Arrowsmith v UK (1978) 3 EHRR 218. 16
Attorney General v Observer Ltd [1990] 1 AC 109. 118, 290
Azmi v Kirklees Metropolitan Borough Council [2007] ICR 1154. 58, 70
Begum, see *R (On the Application of Begum (By Her Litigation Friend, Rahman))*
Berkovits v Grinberg [1995] Fam 142. 131
Beximco, see *Shamil Bank of Bahrain v Beximco Pharmaceuticals Ltd*
Bham, see *R v Bham*
Bhatti v Bhatti [2009] EWHC 3506 (Ch). 122
Bruker v Marcovitz (2007) SCC 54. 55
Bull and Bull v Hall and Preddy [2012] EWCA Civ 83. 58, 71

Campbell and Cosans v United Kingdom (1982) 4 EHRR 293.   94, 100
Catholic Care (Diocese of Leeds) v Charity Commission for England and Wales [2010] EWHC 520 (Ch).   60
Cherfi v G4S Securities Services Ltd [2011] EqLR (EAT).   64
Chief Adjudication Officer v Kirpal Kaur Bath [2000] 1 FLR 8.   128, 148
Choudhury, see *R v Chief Metropolitan Stipendiary Magistrate*
Christian Education South Africa v Minister of Education (CCT 4/00) [2000] ZACC 11.   99, 103, 104, 114, 196
Classroom Crucifix Case, German Constitutional Court, 12 May 1987, BverfGE 93, 1; 1 BvR 1087/91, C. II.3a.   103, 104
Copsey v WWB Devon Clays Ltd [2005] EWCA Civ 932.   64
Dogru v France (2009) 49 EHRR 8.   44
Doogan and Wood, see *R (Doogan and Wood)*
El Fadl v El Fadl [2000] 1 FCR 683.   134
El Gamel v Al Maktoum [2011] EWHC B27 (Fam).   149
EM (Lebanon) (FC) v Secretary of State for the Home Department [2008] UKHL 64.   48, 55
Eweida v British Airways Plc [2010] EWCA Civ 80.   11
Eweida and Chaplin v United Kingdom (App nos 48420/10, 59842/10) [2011] ECHR 738.   4, 65
G v M [2011] EWHC 2651 (Fam).   130
Gandhi v Patel [2001] EWHC Ch 473.   129
Garaudy v France, App No 65831/01 (2003).   98
Gatis Kovalkovs v Latvia, App No 35021/05 (2012).   106
Gereis v Yagoub [1997] 1 FLR 854.   128
Glor v Switzerland, App no 12444/04, 30 April 2009.   106
H v H (2005) SLT 1025.   151
Hafid Ouardiri v Switzerland, App no 65840/09 (2011).   71
HJ (Iran) (FC) v Secretary of State for the Home Department; HT (Cameroon) (FC) v Secretary of State for the Home Department [2010] UKSC 31.   54
Hyde v Hyde [1866] LR 1 P & D 130.   132
IC, see *KC*
In the Matter of A (A Child) (No 2) [2011] EWCA Civ 12.
Islamic Investment Company of the Gulf (Bahamas) Ltd v Symphony Gems NV [2002] All ER (D) 171 (Feb).   120
Jabari v Turkey, App no 40035/98 [2000] ECHR 369.   54
Jakobski v Poland (2010) 30 BHRC 417; App no 18429/06 (2010).   69
Jersild v Denmark (Ser A) no 289 (1995).   98
Jewish Free School, see *R (On the Application of E) v Governing Body of JFS*

Jewish Liturgical Association Cha'are Shalom Ve Tsedek v France [2000] 9 BHRC 27.   16, 98
Jivraj v Hashwani [2010] EWCA 712.   123, 123
Jivraj v Hashwani [2011] UKSC 40.   68, 111
Johns, see *R (Eunice Johns and Owen Johns) v Derby City Council*
K v N, see *Re K (A Local Authority) v N*
Kalac v Turkey (1997) 27 EHRR 522.   16, 64
Kandeel v Hands [2010] EWCA Civ 1233.   132
KC, NNC v City of Westminster Social & Community Services Department, IC (a protected party, by his litigation friend the Official Solicitor) [2008] EWCA Civ 198.   195, 202
Klass and Others v Federal Republic of Germany (1979–80) 2 EHRR 214.   80
Ladele v Islington London Borough Council and Liberty (Intervening) [2008] UKEAT.   58, 59, 196
Ladele v Islington London Borough Council and Liberty (Intervening) [2009] EWCA Civ 1357.   58, 59, 101, 102, 196
Ladele and McFarlane v United Kingdom (App nos 51671/10, 36516/10).   4, 64, 65
Latifah bte Mat Zin v Rosmawati bte Sharibun [2007] 5 MLJ.   193
Lautsi v Italy (2012) 54 EHRR 3; (2010) 50 EHRR 42.   197, 215
Leigh v Hudson [2009] EWHC 1306 (Fam); [2009] EWCA Civ 144.   128, 130
Leyla Sahin v Turkey (2007) 44 EHRR 5 (Grand Chamber).   90, 94
Ligue des Musulmans de Suisse and Others v Switzerland, App no 66274/09 (2011).   71
Lina Joy v Majlis Agama Islam Wilayah Persekutuan [2007] 4 MLJ 585.   193
Liversidge v Anderson [1942] AC 206.   195
MA v JA [2012] EWHC 2219.   130, 134
McFarlane v Relate Avon Limited [2010] EWCA Civ 880.   58, 71
Mr A McClintock v Department of Constitutional Affairs [2008] IRLR 29 (EAT).   63
Multani v Marguerite-Bourgeoys (2006) SCC 6.   104
N v N (Jurisdiction: Pre Nuptial Agreement) (also known as: *N v N (Divorce: Judaism)*) [1999] 2 FLR 745.   155
Nadia Eweida and Shirley Chaplin v United Kingdom, App no 48420/10 [2011] ECHR 738.   65
Norwood v United Kingdom, App No 23131/03 (2004).   98
O v O (Jurisdiction: Jewish Divorce) [2000] 2 FLR 147.   155
O'Donoghue and Others v United Kingdom [2011] All ER (D) 46 (Jan).   150
Otto-Preminger-Institut v Austria (1995) 19 EHRR 34.   215

Parochial Church Council of Aston Cantlow v Wallbank [2004] 1 AC 546.   108

Pichon and Sajous v France, App no 49853/99, 2 October 2001.   63

Port Elizabeth Municipality v Various Occupiers (CCT 53/03) [2004] ZACC 7.   228, 229, 230

R v Chief Metropolitan Stipendiary Magistrate ex porte Choudhury [1990] 3 WLR 98; [1991] 1 QB 429.   211

R v Bham [1966] 1 QB 159.   129

R v Iftikhar Ahmed and Farzana Ahmed (2012).   54

R v Kiranjit Ahluwalia [1992] EWCA Crim 1.   202

R v Secretary of State for Education and Employment and Others [2005] UKHL 15.   114

R v Zoora Ghulam Shah [1998] EWCA Crim 1441.   202

R (Doogan and Wood) v Greates Glasgow and Clyde Health Board [2012] scots CSOH32.   56

R (Eunice Johns and Owen Johns) v Derby City Council [2011] EWHC 375 (Admin).   58, 71, 195

R (Imran Bashir) v The Independent Adjudicator and Anor [2011] EWHC 1108 (Admin).   69

R (On the Application of Amicus MSF and Others) v Secretary of State for Trade and Industry and Others [2004] EWHC 860 (Admin).   61, 62

R (On the Application of Begum (By Her Litigation Friend, Rahman)) v Headteacher, Governors of Denbigh High School [2006] UKHL 15.   17, 64, 69, 70, 98, 99

R (On the Application of E) v Governing Body of JFS and the Admissions Appeal Panel of JFS and Others [2009] UKSC 15.   17, 61

R (On the Application of X (By Her Father and Litigation Friend)) v The Headteachers of Y School, The Governors of Y School [2007] EWHC 298 (Admin).   70

R (Williamson and Others) v The Secretary of State for Education and Employment [2002] EWCA Civ 1926.   16, 100

R (Williamson and Others) v The Secretary of State for Education and Employment [2005] 2 AC 246.

Radmacher (formerly Granatino) v Granatino [2010] UKSC 42.   152

Re K (A Local Authority) v N [2005] EWHC 2956 (Fam).   146

Re S (Children) (Specific Issue Order: Religion: Circumcision) [2004] EWHC 1282 (Fam).   113

Reaney v Hereford Diocesan Board of Finance (2008) 10 Ecc LJ 130.   194

Refah Partisi (Welfare Party) and Others v Turkey (No 1) (2002) 35 EHRR 3.   3, 35, 38, 39, 45–51, 68, 69, 74, 77, 78, 105

Refah Partisi (Welfare Party) and Others v Turkey (No 2) (2003) 37 EHRR 1 (Grand Chamber). 38–41, 45–51, 68, 69, 74, 77, 78, 81, 84, 86, 94, 105, 146, 147
S, see *Re S (Children)*
S v Mamabolo (CCT 44/00) [2001] ZACC 17. 227
Serif v Greece (1999) 31 EHRR 561. 53
Serife Yigit v Turkey, App no 3976/05 (2010). 54, 69, 147
Sessa v Italy, App no 28790/08 (2012). 106
Shamala Sathiyaseelan v Dr Jeyaganesh C Mogarajah [2004] 1 CLJ 505; 2 CLJ 416. 193
Shamil Bank of Bahrain v Beximco Pharmaceuticals Ltd [2004] EWCA Civ 19. 120
Socialist Party v Turkey (1998) 27 EHRR 51 (GC). 49
Soleimany v Soleimany [1999] QB 785. 122
South African National Defence Union v Minister of Defence and Another [1999] ZACC 7. 227
Stedman v United Kingdom (1997) 23 EHRR CD 168. 64, 98
Subashini Rajasingam v Saravanan Thangathoray [2008] 2 MLJ 147. 193
Sulaiman v Juffali [2002] 1 FLR 479. 195
Syndicat Northcrest v Amselem [2004] 2 SCR 551; [2004] SCC 47. 10, 105
Tang Sung Mooi v Too Miew Kim [1994] 3 MLJ 117. 193
The Islamic Unity Convention v The Independent Broadcasting Authority and Others [2002] ZACC 3. 226, 227
The Official Solicitor to the Senior Courts v Yemoh & Others [2010] EWHC 3727 (Ch). 42
Thlimmenos v Greece (2001) 31 EHRR 15 (GC). 57, 105, 106
Uddin v Choudhury [2009] EWCA Civ 1205. 203, 204
United Communist Party of Turkey and Others v Turkey (1998) 26 EHRR 121 (GC). 49, 80
Vejdeland and Others v Sweden, App no 1813/07 (2012). 98
Williamson, see *R (Williamson and Others)*
WP and Others v Poland, App No 42264/98 (2004). 98
X v United Kingdom (1984) 6 EHRR 558. 16
XCC v AA, BB, CC and DD [2012] EWHC 2183. 203

Index

This index records mention of cases in the chapters' principal text. See further, Index of Cases, 306–10.

Abortion Act 1967 56, 61
abortions, opt-outs from undertaking 10, 31, 229
accommodation 43, 52, 91, 117, 118, 119, 139
   co-operative 198–204
   competitive 188, 204
   reasonable 64n111, 64, 65n114, 65, 105–6, 106n39
   transformative, *see* transformative accommodation
   see also harmonistic/accommodationist perspectives
adoption agencies (Roman Catholic), opt-outs for 10, 21, 59–60
adoption (Islamic) *see* 'special guardianship' 55n69, 55
adversarial/separationist perspectives 77–8
agunah ('chained' woman in Jewish marriage) 131
ahkam (positive law) 75, 256, 261, *see also* shari'a law
Ali, Lord, 11, 12n12
Ali, Shaheen Sardar 3, 192, 202
Ali, Syed Mumtaz 178, 190–1
Allawi, Ali 1
aman (state protection for minorities) 159, 162
An-Naʿim, Abdullahi 245, 249
angrezi shariʿat (English *shariʿa*) 140–1, 195
animal slaughter 16n26, 139n85, 139, 166n18
apostasy (in Islam) 27, 54
aqd aman (safe conduct), betrayal of 260
'Arab Spring' (2010–) 85–6
arbitration 3, 62, 111n10, 121–3, 287
   and arbitrability 123
   in Canada 176–7, 184
   enforcement 121–2, 122n28
   faith-based 178, 184, 185, 186
   Islamic 68, 119, 121, 136–7, 288, *see also* Muslim Arbitration Tribunal
   in Ontario 68, 176–86, 190–1
   and power imbalance between parties 179, 181
Arbitration Act 1996 68, 121, 122, 123

Arbitration and Mediation Services (Equality) Bill (2011) 67n121, 124
arbitrators
   faith based 122–3
   training and qualifications 177, 179, 180
Arjoman, Homa 181
as-siyar (Islamic international law) 164, 165, 167
Asad, Talal 90

Bach, Lord 124
Badawi, Zaki 166
Baderin, Mashood 3, 278
Badr, Gamal 164
Balls, Ed 119–20
Banerjee, Milinda 1
Bangladesh, administration of law in 195, 202–3
Bano, Samia 191
Bayat, Asef 84
Benedict XVI 11
Beth Din, pl Battei Din (Jewish tribunal(s)) 109, 122, 131, 139, 201n38, 248
Bhatti, GK, *Behzti* (*Dishonour*) play controversy (2004) 213n9
blasphemous libel 9n2, 9, 211, 214–15, 216, 232
Boyd, Marion 3, 190
Boyle, Kevin 77–8
Bradney, Anthony 23–4, 25
Bratza, Nicolas 3
burqa, prohibition of wearing 70n134, 70n135, 70
Butler-Sloss, Elizabeth 3, 287

Cairo Declaration on Human Rights in Islam (CDHRI) 83
Cambridge Muslim College 280n5, 281n7
Campbell and Cosans case 100, *see also* Index of Cases
Canadian Council of Muslim Women 181
Canadian Society of Muslims 190
Carey, Lord 195–7

311

Index

cartoons, controversial 214n12, 222, *see also* Danish newspaper cartoons controversy
Casanova, José 277
censure vs censorship 221, 222, 223, 224
Chaplin case 64, 65, *see also* Index of Cases
child custody 48, 55, 113n17–113n18, 113n18, 113, 137
child welfare 112–14
Children, Schools and Families Bill 2009-10, amendment to 11n11, 11
Christ, character of 14
Christian Education South Africa case 99n14, 104–5, *see also* Index of Cases
churches, and rights of members with multiple affiliations 193–4
citizenship 23, 26, 29, 185, 231, 240, 242, 267
 and (critical) loyalty 32, 248, 251–2
 and engagement with state in country of origin 160
 links with migration 174
 Muslims as British citizens 157, 247
 Muslims as European citizens 163, 169, 174, 175
 treatment according to, vs treatment according to religion 240, 242
 and *umma* membership 22, 27, 251
civic reason 240
civil partnerships and registrar's conscience 56, *see also Ladele* case
civility 3, 29, 173
clash of civilisations 91, 158
Coalition of Jewish Women for the *Get* (Canada) 183–4
common good 7, 12, 22, 194, 276, 281
communal/religious identity and duties (legal regard to)
 and appeals to religious scruple 25
 and legal monopoly/ universalism 28, 29–30, 31, 32
 and recognition of supplementary jurisdictions 25–8, 32, *see also* transformative accommodation
community membership, 23, *see also umma* membership and citizenship
conscience
 executioner's refusal to act against 259
 freedom of 10n7, 10, 16n26, 19, 249, 257
 judge's refusal to act against 259
 protection for religious 24, 56, *see also* opt-outs
constitutionalism 83
contraceptives, opt-outs from supplying 63n101, 63
Contracts (Applicable Law) Act 1990 120–1
corporal punishment 113, *see also Williamson* case
Coulson, Noel 76
Council of Europe, Parliamentary Assembly Resolution 800 (1983) 81
Cox, Baroness 124

criminal law, Islamic 86, 92, *see also hudud* (penal sanctions)
cross wearing at work, forbidden (UK) *see Eweida* case
crucifixes, allowable in state schools (Italy) *see Lautsi* case
culture
 reactive culturalism 190, 193, 199
 and religion 16, 161
 secularised Christian 17
 selective/partial exit from 189

Danchin, Peter 74
Danish newspaper cartoons controversy (2005) 208, 209, 214–15, 218–19, 222–3, 224, 225, 231
 publisher's defence 214
dar al-'adl (abode of justice) 265
dar al-haqq (abode of truth) 265
dar al-harb / dar al-kufr (abode of hostilities) 163, 164, 165, 166, 247, 264
dar al-iman (abode of true belief) 265
dar al-Islam (abode of Islam), 164n9, 164, 165–6, 168, 247, 264
dar al-shada (abode of testimony) 248
dar al-sulh / dar al-'ahd / dar muwada'a (abode of peace) 162, 164, 165, 166, 167–73, 174, 264
democracy 50, 77–8, 79, 89
 and European Convention on Human Rights 80, 91
 and freedom of speech 227–8
 in Islam 266–7, 270, 271
 militant democracy 46n22, 46, 97, 99
 and *shari'a* law 40, 48, 49, 72, 81–2, 84
Der Stürmer cartoons 222n6, 222
dietary laws 16
dignity 30, 31, 102–3
 and British courts 94, 99–101
 and European Convention on Human Rights 94
 and European Court of Human Rights 94, 100, 101–2, 105
 human dignity threshold test 99–105
 and Islam 102
discrimination 47, 57–60, 61–2, 105–6, 290–1, *see also* European Convention on Human Rights, Article 14 (freedom from discrimination)
divorce 111, 131–2
 and conversion to/from Islam 192–3
 Coptic 141–2
 foreign 134n75, 134, 149–50
 Islamic 54n65, 54, 135–6, 152–5, 154n25, 155, 159–60, 192, 201n38
 faskh 153, 201n38
 khula (wife's initiative) 76, 153, 173
 mubaraat (agreed) 153, 154

Index

talaq (husband's initiative) 134, 142, 153, 155, 173n44, 173
Jewish 131–2, 139, 155, 183, 201n37, *see also* Beth Din
religious (Canada) 183
Divorce (Religious Marriages Act) 2002 111n12, 132, 139, 155, 201n38
domestic violence 109n5, 109, 201n40, 250, *see also* women, protection of rights
Donaldson, Sir John 290

Edge, Ian 3, 287
Employment Equality (Religion or Belief) Regulations (2003) 64, 123
Enlightenment 28, 31
equality 11, 48, 255
  before God 283–5, 293
  before the law 117–18, 289, 290–2
  equality rights vs freedom of speech/expression 220
  hierarchy of rights 57
Equality Act 2010 61
Equality Bill (2010), amendments to 11, 12n12
Equality and Human Rights Commission (UK) 65
Europe
  Islamic classification of 163–6, 174, *see also dar al-harb / dar al-kufr* (abode of hostilities); *dar al-Islam* (abode of Islam); *dar al-sulh / dar al-'ahd / dar muwada'a* (abode of peace)
  Muslim institutions in 169–73, *see also* imams/mullahs; *shari'a* councils/tribunals
European Convention on Human Rights (ECHR) 78, 80, 122
  Article 2 100
  Article 3 100–1
  Article 9 (freedom of religion) 15–16, 55n68, 69, 73, 78, 95, 99, 102, 106
  Article 10 98
  Article 11 (freedom of assembly and association) 35, 39n1–41n2, 39
  Article 14 (freedom from discrimination) 47, 105–6, 290
  Article 16 96
  Article 17 97, 98, 99
  and compatibility with *shari'a* 2–3, 39–40, 53–4, 72, 86–7
  and democracy 79–80, 91
  and dignity 94
  and freedom of expression 208
  and freedom of religion 73, 91, 208, *see also* Article 9 (freedom of religion)
  value for Muslims 68–70
European Court of Human Rights (ECtHR)
  and democracy 80, 101

and dignity 94, 100, 101–2, 105
and *shari'a* 2–3
see also Chaplin case; *Eweida* case; *Ladele* case; *Lautsi* case; *McFarlane* case; *Refah* case
Evans, Malcolm 73
Eweida case 11n10, 11, 64, 65, *see also* Index of Cases
exemptions *see* opt-outs

faith
  geography of 248
  value of 71n141
Family Law Act (1996) 136
family law dispute resolution
  in England 3, 108–15, 123, 125–31
  in Ontario 177–86
  see also divorce; marriage
Family Law Protocol (2006) 136
financial services (Islamic) 62, 92, 119–21, 287
Ford, David 4, 292, 293
freedom of conscience *see* conscience
freedom of religion *see* religion, freedom of
freedom of worship *see* worship, freedom of
fuzziness, principles of 233, 234–5

gender relations (Muslim), stereotyping of 145–6
get (Jewish marriage release) 131–2, 155
al-Ghanoushi, Rashid 84
globalisation 144, 156
Glor case, 106, *see also* Index of Cases
Griffith-Jones, Robin 2, 3, 4
Griffiths, John 140

Hale, Baroness 113–14
Hamidullah, M 164, 167, 168
harmonistic/accommodationist perspectives 77, 78–9
hate speech 97–8, 209
hatred
  incitement to 218
    racial hatred 216, 222
    religious hatred 24, 209, 216, 219
headscarf wearing 69–70, 103, *see also Sahin* case
Held, David 79–82
Hill, Mark 3, 24, 287
hiraba (banditry) 260
Holocaust-denial 97, 216, 217 n3, 217, 226
honour killings, 54n63, 54, 250, 251
hudud (penal sanctions) 240–1, 246, 250, 288
human, meaning of being 284
human rights 77, 90–78, 91, *see also* European Convention on Human Rights (ECHR); European Court of Human Rights (ECtHR)

human rights (cont.)
  in Islam 266–7, 268, 270, 271, see also under shari'a law, compatibility
Human Rights Act 1998 10n7, 122, 291

IC case 202–4, see also Index of Cases: KC NNC v City of Westminster Social & Community Services Dept IC
ijma' (consensus) 85
ijtihad (legal reasoning) 21, 75, 85
  'closed' 75n7, 75
  neo-ijtihad 76
ikhtilaf (doctrine of difference) 140n91
imams/mullahs, home country vs European status 169–70, 173
India, treatment of non-registered marriages 150–1
inheritance law 54, 134–5
  and intestacy rules 135n78
  in Ontario 176
  rights of widows (Islamic) 26
institutions, value of long term 275–6
inter-faith engagement 280
International Covenant on Civil and Political Rights, Article 26 291
Islam
  five pillars of 166
  historical development 164–5
  and politics 241
  twentieth-century resurgence 1
Islamic Institute of Civil Justice 177, 178
Islamic law
  basis for dialogue 159
  and colonialism 266, 268
  and context and contingency 261, 264
  definition 116n1
  denial of existence, rejected 258
  and modernity 266
  and Ontario see Ontario Arbitration Act
  and post-colonialism 238–9, 261, 266
  and pre-colonialism 265–6
  rulings, categories 88
  schools of 88
  and Western scholarship 161
  see also shari'a (Islamic legal principles and tradition); shari'a law (Islamic applied law)
Islamic Shari'a Council 25, 56, 199, 203–4
Islamic state
  existence asserted 249
  existence not required or possible 238, 239–41
Islamic tradition 269
Islamophobia 52
Ismaili Conciliation and Arbitration Boards 136–7

Jackson, Bernard 19, 55
Jesus, portrayal of in West 215

Jewish Free School case 17, see also Index of Cases: R (On the Application of E) . . .
jihad 164, 238, 262
  as pursuit of the good 256
  in Qur'an 262–3
  as resistance to oppression 253
  as seeking peace 253
  as spreading Islam 253
  as striving for Islamic society vs Islamic state 243
  violent 8, 243
jizya (poll tax), payment of 263, 265
Judaism, conversion to 17
judges, role of 154–6, 195, 289–90, 292
jurisdictions
  multiple 192–3, see also legal pluralism
  relations between 112, 202–3
  supplementary 25–8, 32, 112
  trans-jurisdictional reality of Muslim communities 149
Jyllands-Posten see Danish newspaper cartoons controversy (2005)

kalam (theological dialectics) 256n1, 256
Kamali, Hashim 15, 76
Kearney, Martha 12[end of table]
Khaddouri, Majid 164
Khursid Bibi v Muhammad Amin case 76
Kovler, Anatoly 146, 147
kutub al-ahkham (primers of positive law) 261
kutub al-fiqh (books of evaluative jurisprudence) 261

Ladele case 58–9, 59n86, 59n87, 64, 65, 101, see also Index of Cases
laicism (France) 126n49
Landau, Christopher 12, 13
Langa, Pius 227–8
Lautsi case 197–8, see also Index of Cases
law
  nature of 33
  role in Islam 15, 16
  role in Judaism 16
  rule of 29–30, 273–4
  and dialogue 289
  and equality before the law 117–18, 289, 290–2
  theology of 30–1
law guilds (Islamic) 266
legal education, public (Canada) 179, 184–5
legal fiction 265
legal literacy 292–3
legal maxims 260–1
legal pluralism 40, 46, 48, 49, 53n54, 70n131, 137–42, 144–5, 147, 156, 285
  non-state/unofficial 139
  prerequisites for dialogue on 158–9

producing uncertainty/inefficiency 141–2
state/official 138–9
'strong' 140
unacceptable 119, 142
undesired 142
legal universalism 29–30, 31, 32, 33
liberalism, totalising, 11n7
'Liberation from forced marriages' (Muslim Arbitration Tribunal, 2008) 199–200
liberty, personal 290
Lister, Sir Jim 136
'Living Apart Together' report (2007) 52
London Muslim Centre, 292n5
loyalty
  critical loyalty 252
  as Muslim or citizen 32, 248, 251–2

McCrudden, Christopher 3
McFarlane case, 64, 65, 196, 197, *see also* Index of Cases
McFarlane, Sir Andrew 112–13, 115
McGoldrick, Dominic xi, 3, 201
MacIntyre, Alasdair 23
mahr (dowry) payment/repayment 136n81, 137, 173n45, 173, 174n46, 178, 204
Malaysia, multiple jurisdictions in 192–3
Malicious Communications Act 1988 209
Malik, Maleiha 23
marriage 152
  buildings-based registration 125, 126–7, 148, 151n15, 172
  cases, 128n54–130n60, 128–30
  celebrant-based registration 125, 126, 130, 135, 201
  Church of England 126
  forced marriage 20, 25, 26, 199–200, 250, 251
  foreign, recognition of 133, 151
  Islamic 127, 148–52, 198–9, *see also below* unregistered marriage
  Jewish 126, 131, 135n79
  limping marriage 111, 172
  non-marriage 128n54, 129–30, 130n60
  permission to marry, and immigration law 150n13, 150
  presumption of marriage 129–30, 148–9
  Roman Catholic 126–7
  and Scottish law 148–9, 151
  Society of Friends (Quaker) 126
  unregistered marriage 111, 127, 129–30, 150–1, 172
  void marriage 128, 129, 133
Marriage Act (1949) 125–7, 131
Marriage Act (1994), 151n15
Marriage (Registration of Buildings) Act (1990), 151n15
martyrdom *see shahada* (martyrdom)
Mazrui, Ali 213n8, 213

mediation 110, 111n10, 123, 287
  in Canada 177
  Islamic 67, 136–7, 287
  in marital disputes 136–7
Medina, constitution of 83
Menski, Werner 140, 194, 195
migration (Islamic) 162, 163n6
Mill, John Stuart 216, 220
minarets, prohibition of building (Switzerland), 71n138
Modood, Tariq 3, 208, 209, 210
Moe, Christian 77
moral deficiency, presumption of 144
moral vs legal imperatives 257, 258–60
mortgages (Islamic) 120
Multani case 104, *see also* Index of Cases
multi-dimensionality 185
multiculturalism 57, 67, 91, 177, 184, 188
Muslim Arbitration Tribunal 122, 201n40, *see also* 'Liberation from forced marriages'
Muslim converts in West 91
Muslim Court of Arbitration (Ontario) 190
Muslim identity, European and Islamic 70
Muslim Institute, London *see* 'Muslim marriage contract'
'Muslim marriage contract' (Muslim Institute, London, 2008) 198–9
Muslims living in non-Muslim territories
  obligations 162–3, 167–8
  seeking distinctive treatment inappropriate 248

nation-state, modern, and Islamic tradition 265–71
National Association of Women in Law (Canada) 181
National Immigrant Women's Coalition (Canada) 181
National Socialist Party (Germany) 46n22
nikah (Muslim marriage contract), registration 148–52
niqab, prohibition of wearing 70n135, 70
non-interference principle 64, 68
non-Muslims living in Muslim territories, rights and obligations 162, 167, *see also dar al-sulh / dar al-'ahd / dar muwada'a* (abode of peace)

Obscene Publications Act 1960 233n11
Ontario Arbitration Act 1991 177
  amendments 190–1
  review (2004) 'Boyd Report' recommendations 178–80, 185
  and confusion over civil and criminal law 182
  opposition 180–1
  partial implementation 183, 184
  support 182
Ontario Children's Law Reform Act 1990 176

Ontario Family Law Act 1990 176, 179n1
Ontario Family Law Amendment Act 2006 184
Ontario Succession Reform Act 1990 176
opt-outs 10, 31, 43, 61 n95
　already existing 61–2
　case against 57–60
　case for 55–6
　for Muslims specifically 55–61, 62–3

patriarchy 11n7, 159
Pearl, David 194
personal law (Islamic) 73, 74, 92
Phillips, Nicolas 4
　'Equality before the law' lecture (2008) 52, 62, 110, 117–18
Phillips, Trevor 66
Plant, Raymond 30
pluralism 251
　interactive 33
　liberal 24
　normative 50n40
　political 23, 40
　respectful 71n140
　social 29, 144–5
　see also legal pluralism
political party, dissolution of (Turkey) see *Refah* case
politics and the state, distinction between 241
polygamy 54n62, 54, 132n69, 132–4, 159–60
　actually polygamous marriage 133–4
　potentially polygamous marriage 133
Port Elizabeth case 228–9, 230, see also Index of Cases
Prentice, Bridget 110–11, 118, 124
property rights vs homeless rights 228–9, 230
proportionality 71n140, 95–6, 98, 99n13, 99, 102, 103–4, 228, 230–1, 233
　and evidence 103
　and practical concordance 103–4
Public Order Act 1986 209
Public–private divide 89, 90, see also under religion, and public sphere
puritans
　religious (Islamists) 267, 270
　secular (puritanical secularists) 269–70

qanum (state-promulgated legislation) 159, 167, 174
al-Qaradawi, Yusuf 76, 83, 85
qital (warfare) 263

race 228
Racial and Religious Hatred Act 2006 209
Ramadan, Moussa Abou 78
Ramadan, Tariq 20, 21

Refah case 39–41, 46–51, 77–8, 81, 84, 94, 105, 146–7, see also Index of Cases
Refah Party (Turkey), dissolution of 38–9, 46, see also *Refah* case
registrar, conscience of, and civil partnerships 56, see also *Ladele* case
religion
　and culture 16, 161
　definition 10n3
　and law 278
　and modernity 278–9
　and morality 74
　and public sphere xiii, 73, 267, 268, 269, 277–8
　requirements of 15–16, 16n24
　value of, 11n7
religion, freedom of 73, 208, 292, see also European Convention on Human Rights, Article 9
　and compatibility with human dignity, see also dignity
　freedom to change see apostasy (in Islam)
　interference in (legal interpretation) 98–9
　and offence to Christians 215
religious courts 138–9
　Church of England 119n16
　and citizenship rights 26
　delegation of legal functions to 25
　Islamic see *shari'a* councils/tribunals
religious dress
　restrictions on wearing 101, 102, 104, 139n85, 139
　see also *burqa*, prohibition of wearing; headscarf wearing; *niqab*, prohibition of wearing; *Sahin* case
religious literacy 282–3, 293
Religious Literacy Leadership Programme 282n9, 282–3
religious symbolism and rhetoric, ban in elections (Egypt) 270
religious traditions, respect for multiple 175
resistance
　armed/violent 253–5, see also *jihad*
　non-violent 244, 253, 254, 255
　understanding vs justification of 254
Rida, Muhammad Rashid 76
rights
　absolute 94, 95
　commitment to individual 185–6
　exceptions to 96
　human see human rights
　qualified 95, 96
　relevance of claimant's motives 97
Roman Catholic Church 279
　and marriage 126–7
　see also adoption agencies (Roman Catholic), opt-outs for

Rose, Flemming 214
Rosiers, Nathalie 90
Rushdie, Salman
  Satanic Verses (1988) controversy 208, 209, 211–13, 218–19, 221, 223, 224, 225, 231
  author's defence, 213n7, 213

Sachs, Albie 3, 99, 208, 209, 210, 285
Sacks, Lord 17
Sahin case 90, 94, 101, 103, 105, *see also* Index of Cases: *Leyla Sahin . . .*
salam (peace and tranquillity) 261
schools
  faith schools 33, 61n94, 66
  Muslim schools 249
  treatment of Muslims in state schools 66
secular and religious domains, interdependence 241–2
secular state 249
  and freedom of conscience and freedom of worship 249
  Muslim attitudes to law in 250, *see also dar al-sulh / dar al-ʿahd / dar muwadaʾa* (abode of peace)
  neutrality/impartiality on religion 47, 241–2
secularisation 268, 278, *see also* secularism
secularism 10–11, 89–90, 161–2, 181, 245–6, 267, 268, 269, 276–7
  Christian 198
  procedural 277
  programmatic 277
segregation
  educational 66
  self-segregation 249
self-restraint 221, 222, 267–8
Serife Yigit case 147, *see also* Index of Cases
Shachar, Ayelet 7, 12, 27–8, 32, 141, 185, 186, 188–91, 279
Shah, Prakash 3, 202
shahada (martyrdom) 258, 259–60
Shaltut, Mahmud 76
shariʿa councils/tribunals 92, 109, 136, 170, 191–2
  in countries of origin 172
  and criminal proceedings 202n41
  regulation of 192
  and women's rights 67n121, 67, 172–3, 178
  see also divorce, Islamic; Islamic Shariʿa Council; Muslim Arbitration Tribunal
shariʿa (Islamic legal principles and tradition) 21, 22, 33, 74–5, 116n11, 145, 158, 166
shariʿa law (Islamic applied law) 40, 43–4, 75–6, 82, 246, 288
  compatibility
    with British law, 24, 35, 72, 116n2, 118–19, 142n96, 142
    with democracy 40, 48, 49, 79, 81, 84, 93
    with European Convention on Human Rights 39–40, 47–8, 54–5, 72
    with human rights 45, 49, 79
  degree of recognition 42n1
  and family disputes 62, 287
  fears about 20–1, 246
  flexibility 82–3
  general vs particular adoption 51–2
  indeterminacy in 44, 48, 53, 257, 258, 269
  interpretation 44, 241, 288
    evolutionary 75–6, 86–7
    historical 75n7, 75, 86, 87
  modified 53
  as Muslim penal code 246, *see also hudud* (penal sanctions)
  objectives 87
  as personal commitment 239, 268, *see also* personal law (Islamic)
  as promotion of equality of citizenship in Britain 247
  and public sphere 268
  and temporal (*muʿāmalāt*) governance 82–3
  as way towards faithfulness 246
shūrā (consultation) 84, 85
Siddiqi, Shaikh 204
Siddiqui, Mona 22
siyasa sharʾiyya (law-making) 84 n41, 84, 167, 172, 174
'special guardianship' 55n69, 55
speech
  freedom of 208–10, 291, 292
    and casual offence 233–4
    and context/proportionality 228, 230–1, 233
    and democracy 227–8
    and emotions of victims 217–18, 220
    in India 231
    in Indonesia 230–1
    in South Africa 225–8, 233–4, *see also* Index of Cases: *The Islamic Unity Convention*
    and threat of immediate violence 216–17
    vs freedom of enquiry 220, 224
    vs respect and equality rights 220
  stereotyping 145–6, 160
Straw, Jack 118–19
sukuk (Islamic bonds) 287

taʾaruf (knowing one another) 262
takaful (insurance) 287
terrorism 102
testimony, value of men's and women's 114n21, 114
Thlimmenos case 105, 106, *see also* Index of Cases
Tibi, Bassam 158
transformative accommodation 7, 12, 32, 62, 186, 188, 191, 193, 279

tribunals
  religious 112–14, 143
    subservience to English law 108–12
    see also shariʻa councils/tribunals
Trinity 284n11, 284

umma membership and citizenship 22, 27, 251
Union of Muslim Organisations of the UK (UMO) 142n96
United Kingdom
  Islamic population 116n4
  pre-immigration vs contemporary perceptions of 157–8
Universal Declaration of Human Rights (1948) 290
Universal Islamic Declaration on Human Rights (UIDHR) 82
usul al-fiqh (evaluative jurisprudence) 15, 75, 159, 256, 261

Vickers, Lucy 104
violence
  as *fasad fi al-ard* (spreading corruption/ruin on earth) 262, 271
  as free speech against Islam 3–4
  state monopoly of legitimate violence 29
  see also resistance

warfare 263–4, see also *qital* (warfare)
  and non-combatants 264
Williams, Rowan
  'Civil and religious law in England' lecture (2008) viii, 2, 7, 9, 12, 19, 51, 56, 73, 116, 188, 214, 273–4, 275, 286
  media reaction 12–13, 14n17, 14
  text 20–33
  Opening Address to General Synod (2008) 10
  'Religious Hatred and Religious Offence' lecture (2008) 9, 24n8, 24
  'Sovereignty, Democracy, Justice' Magna Carta lecture (2012)
Williamson case 16, 100–1, see also Index of Cases: *R (Williamson and Others)*
wisdom-seeking 278, 279, 283
  and inter-faith engagement 280
  and legal and educational institutions 280, 281–2
  and religious communities 279–80
  and religious literacy 282–3
women
  protection of rights 178, 189, 190–1, 201–2
  unaccompanied air travel permitted 76
  value of testimony 114n21, 114
worship, freedom of 15, 73, 95, 249